North to Aztlán

A HISTORY OF MEXICAN AMERICANS IN THE UNITED STATES

Twayne's Immigrant Heritage of America Series

Thomas J. Archdeacon, General Editor

North to Aztlán

A HISTORY OF MEXICAN AMERICANS IN THE UNITED STATES

Richard Griswold del Castillo
and
Arnoldo De León

TWAYNE PUBLISHERS
An Imprint of Simon & Schuster Macmillan
New York
PRENTICE HALL INTERNATIONAL
London Mexico City New Delhi Singapore Sydney Toronto

North to Aztlán: A History of Mexican Americans in the United States
Richard Griswold del Castillo and Arnoldo De León

Twayne's Immigrant Heritage of America Series

Copyright © 1996, 1997 Twayne Publishers

Twayne Publishers
An Imprint of Simon & Schuster Macmillan
1633 Broadway
New York, NY 10019

Library of Congress Cataloging-in-Publication Data

Griswold del Castillo, Richard.
     North to Aztlán : a history of Mexican Americans in the United States /
Richard Griswold del Castillo, Arnoldo de León.
        p.   cm. — (Twayne's immigrant heritage of America series)
     Includes bibliographical references and index.
     ISBN 0-8057-4586-6; ISBN 0-8057-4587-4 (pbk.)
     1. Mexican Americans—History.   I. De León, Arnoldo, 1945–
II. Title.   III. Series.
E184.M5G74   1996
973'.046872—dc20   96-11777
                                                                     CIP

The paper used in this publication meets the minimum requirements of American National Standard for Information Sciences—Permanence of Paper for Printed Library Materials, ANSI Z39.48-1992 (Permanence of Paper).

Printing Number
10 9 8 7 6 5 4

Printed in the United States of America.

Contents

List of Illustrations

List of Tables

Preface

Since 1848 the Mexican people have been engaged in the slow-going process of repossessing lands that they lost to the United States as a result of war. This reoccupation of former territories (and Mexicans' entrance into some new ones) has been brought about by the twin forces of Mexican immigration and a population boom among Spanish-speaking within the United States. This demographic shift has been accompanied by a cultural resurgence in Mexican-American and Chicano literary and artistic production as well as the maturation of a generation of Mexican-American scholars who have sought to uncover the historical roots of the Mexican people in the United States. This book is a contribution to a growing body of English-language literature that provides a means of understanding this growing ethnic group.

Many contemporary observers have declared that the American Southwest is fast becoming "Mexicanized" owing to the magnitude of newest waves of immigration from Mexico. While appealing to nativists and activists alike, this view ignores the history of this region as well as contemporary social reality. What today is called the American Southwest was once part of Mexico and before that was claimed by Spain. The Mexican people and their culture have been continuously present in this territory for the past 400 years. While a majority of present-day Mexican Americans are descended from Mexican immigrants in the twentieth century, a significant number can trace their roots back to the time before an international border existed between the United States and Mexico.

The term *Mexicanization* is also an inaccurate description of contemporary reality. Since 1848 a heterogeneous ethnic group that incorporates long-term Mexican immigrants has been steadily growing, and since 1930 it has been dominated by U.S.-born Mexican Americans. This subtle historical process of social and political change and adaptation, north and south of the international boundary, has created a people with diverse backgrounds and cultures. Certain sectors of Mexican American society have been shaped by the challenge of new ecological and social environments. In the three centuries before the Mexican North became part of the United States, modifications regarding culture, language, food, and customs were nurtured by their geographic distance from the metropolitan civilization in the valley of Mexico. Other elements of present-day Chicano culture can be conceptualized as variants of Mexican *norteño* life, itself a diverse variation of central Mexican themes. Mexican immigrants who have come to El Norte since 1848, moreover, eventually joined the larger native-born Spanish-speaking population. Though most did not intend to stay long, they did; they married, had children, and inevitably changed to accommodate the "American way of life."

Different segments of Chicano society have responded to population cluster-ings of Mexican colonias in the United States, to a kinship with La Raza, to xenophobia and nativism, to conflict and violent confrontations between them-selves and Anglos, to their status as a proletarian group and to other aspects of political, educational, and social power of "Anglo-America." Still other cohorts within the Mexican-American community have been influenced by the urban, postindustrial, English-speaking (Anglo-American) society. Thus, rather the than a one-way Mexicanization of the U.S. Southwest, since 1848 there has been a complex process of cultural and economic exchange between Mexican immigrants, Mexican Americans, and a racially and ethnically diverse North American society.

Still, the tremendous growth of Mexican American barrios and colonias in the United States owes much to Mexican immigration. For a set of reasons, among them lack of opportunity in their native country and news of an open society in the United States, people since the mid-nineteenth century have waded the Rio Grande in Texas, crossed over the international boundary from El Paso to San Diego, and dispersed to almost every corner of the United States. Migration has varied according to era. Prior to the Mexican Revolution in 1910 there was only a modest trickle of Mexicans who came north. But during the first two decades of the Revolution more than a million immigrants joined their compatriots. After a period of massive repatriation and labor strife during the 1930s, Mexicans began once again to enter the United States in large num-bers—this time at the U.S. government's request. During the period 1945 to 1990 probably more than six million documented and undocumented immi-grants from Mexico entered the United States, more than in any comparable period. This immigration acted to bond Mexico and the United States, sustain-ing Spanish-speaking communities with traditional group values and beliefs, nationalist sentiments, language, religion, and various accoutrements.

Historically, Mexican immigrants have usually had their first experiences in the United States mediated by Mexican Americans, living side by side with them in the barrios and colonias. Like the immigrants, Mexican Americans are, for the most part, Mestizos—of mixed Indian, European, and African heritage— who can share or at least relate to and appreciate Mexican culture. Though membership in the Mexican-American community varies in region of birth, degree of acculturation, generational mind-set, social standing, and ideology, most function biculturally within an English-speaking urban environnment and usually assume the role of spokepersons for what it means to be a Mexican in the United States. In this capacity, they have advanced proposals ranging from bilingual education to political separation. Thus they have been the brokers for millions of nameless immigrants who have come north.

Over the years the newly arrived immigrants presented Mexican Americans with a series of economic, cultural, and political dilemmas. Sometimes conflict and competititon erupted beween the two groups, especially during labor strikes and times of recession. But being Mestizos and often sharing the same experi-ence of racism and poverty as many Mexican Americans, the immigrants silently have challenged the older generations and the middle class not to forget their roots. Ultimately the Mexican immigrants reminded the Mexican Americans, Chicanos, Latinos, and Hispanics that as a people, La Raza, they share a common destiny linked to the constantly occurring processes of racial and cultural mixing in Latin America.

Mexican Americans, therefore, are a people who have survived within the United States while retaining a sense of ethnicity or peoplehood—at times a mythic and idealistic construction born of remembrance of times past and a desire to gain recognition for themselves within American society. The diversity and complexity of this ethnic group, including the disparate characteristics of the immigrants, has only just recently been appreciated by social science researchers.

This study traces the development of Chicano/Latino/Mexican-American culture and society from the earliest recorded history to the present. It is an attempt to discern the most important events in the history of these peoples. Because this volume was written to be part of Twayne's Immigrant Heritage of America Series, special attention has been given to the importance of immigration and the influence of Mexico, as a culture and a people, on the evolving identity of Mexican Americans. Obviously this is a very complex story to tell. A complete analysis of this process would demand many volumes and resources than are currently available. We have sought to shape a basic survey useful to students of Mexican Americans, recognizing from the outset that there has never been a monolithic Mexican culture just as there has not been a homogeneous Mexican-American community.

The role of gender in shaping the cultural and political history of Mexican Americans needs to be analyzed in much more depth than is possible in this volume. As of this writing much more primary research on Chicana history needs to be done in order for us to provide a balanced and fair assessment. It is minimally possible to reference some of the outstanding Mexicana and Chicana political and cultural leaders. What is really needed is the examination of gender within the context of social and economic change.

We have also tried to give a fuller assessment than have other surveys of the cultural contributions made by Mexicans within the United States. To that end we have attempted to integrate some of the most important intellectual contributions of hundreds of Mexican and Mexican-American politicians, academics, writers and journalists, and labor leaders. We also give space to the works of artists, poets, playwrights, and composers, and to musicians and performers. Our introduction to Mexican-American cultural history in the United States is, of course, incomplete and worthy of a much larger study, but that will have to await later scholarship.

Several excellent surveys that give very detailed histories of the political and economic trends were consulted in writing this book. For both the Spanish and Mexican periods, the texts written by David J. Weber are the most comprehensive. Scores of other scholars, in both Mexico and the United States, have devoted their lives to the study of the Spanish and Mexican periods. Rodolfo Acuña has written perhaps the most complete history of the Chicano for the nineteenth and twentieth centuries, and his research and interpretation have contributed immensely to the development of Chicano history. There are other good surveys authored by Matt Meier and Feliciano Rivera and Julian Samora and Patricia Vandel. There is also a growing number of monographic histories of Mexican Americans, most of which we have consulted for this work. Our hope is that this text, by discussing five centuries of Chicano history with attention to immigration, gender, and culture, will complement these works and give a more holistic vision of the development of Mexican-American society.

Discussions of the evolution of the Mexican-origin communities within the United States generally call for definitions of labels. Often people are confused by the plethora of terms used to describe this population. This confusion of terminology arises from the very social, economic, and political heterogeneity of the Spanish-speaking population. We have used many terms, depending on the historical and social context of the discussion. The term *Mexican,* or its Spanish equivalent *Mexicano,* sometimes used interchangeably with *Mexican American,* applies to the Mestizo population on both sides of the border. Usually the term *Mexican* or *Mexicano* refer to a cultural orientation rather than a political status. The terms *Hispanic* and *Latino* are of fairly recent coinage and describe a larger population than just those of Mexican descent. The term *Chicano,* in popular Spanish-speaking usage since at least 1900 is used in context to denote either a particular generational experience or as another way of saying *Mexican American.* Ultimately the meanings of terms used to describe the Spanish-speaking populations of Mexican descent in the United States are variable depending on the perspective of the reader. In recent years a convention has arisen regarding the desire to include gender, especially when using the noun as an adjective, such as *Chicana/o,* or *Latina/o.* This usuage, too, illustrates the evolving nature of the Mexican-origin society within the United States.

This study has been made possible by the generosity and support of many institutions, starting with our home universities, Angelo State University and San Diego State University. SDSU provided grant-in-aid support to pay for author consultations and research trips. The Centro de Investigaciones Sobre Los Estados Unidos de America (CISEUA), a center within the National Autonomous University of Mexico (UNAM), and the U.S. Fulbright Hayes Commission funded a five-month period of research and writing.

A portion of this text first appeared as the essay "Latinos and the New Immigration: Mainstreaming and Polarization," by Richard Griswold del Castillo, in *The Renato Rosaldo Lecture Series Monograph* 10 (1994), published by the Mexican American Studies and Research Center at the University of Arizona.

We also would like to acknowledge the scores of librarians and staff members in Mexico and the United States who assisted us in small and great ways throughout the project.

Finally, we owe a very serious debt of gratitude to the scores of Chicano scholars who have published articles and monographs on the subjects treated in this study. Without their work we would not have been able to produce this interpretation. It is to them that we would like to dedicate this book.

one

Native American and Spanish Settlements

The vast territory north of the Tropic of Cancer and west of the Mississippi River is a land of many contrasts. It contains expansive deserts, snow-capped mountain ranges, semi-tropical wetlands, and Mediterranean shores. Geographers aptly describe this area of the world with adjectives such as *highest* or *lowest, wettest* or *driest, hottest* or *coldest.* For more than 500 centuries people have sought to endure the environment and eke out a living. If they persevered the harsh tests of nature, their next task was to survive in a social environment as the various groups moved into the greater Southwest competing for living space, food, and political dominance.

From the beginning myth has been an important part of the history of this region. From the perspectives of the first people to enter this area, the Native Americans, powerful forces in the spirit world connected the land and its living creatures. For them, this space was intimately sacred. The Aztecs believed that their ancestral homeland was located in the North. They called it Aztlán, the land of the Huron, an island surrounded by water. Other urbanized Indian peoples from central Mexico, such as the Toltecs, reflected their disdain for the less "civilized" tribes of the northern wastelands and called this region the land of the "Chichimeca"—meaning a region where the "sons of dogs" (barbarians) lived. The Spanish-speaking explorers saw the land with their myths. They believed that they would find there the fabulously wealthy Indian cities of Gran Quivira and Cíbola, rich pearl fisheries, and an island kingdom inhabited entirely by women.

The Europeans soon divided the seemingly limitless territory of their northern frontier into political and economic areas to promote its colonization and exploitation. The region became part of their viceroyalty of New Spain. In the first decades of the nineteenth century, the Mexican people, mostly Mestizos (mixed races), emerged to assert their independence from Europe. They adopted the name *Mexico* from the indigenous name for the Aztecs, the Meshica. For the Mexicans, this region continued to be a *frontera* bordering a powerful northern neighbor. In the middle of the nineteenth century Mexico went to war to defend its frontiers and lost. The United States then occupied Mexico's northern territories, and this region became part of the American West. Anglo-Americans began to use the term *Southwest* to describe this arid place inhabited by Indians and Mexicans.

The historical diversity of the Mexican northern frontier and the American Southwest has shaped the Mexican-American people. Native American, Spanish, African, Anglo-American, Asian, and European migrants and immigrants have all been part of the saga of the Spanish-speaking people who have lived in this region.

The Native Heritage

People of Mexican descent in the United States assert that they are an indigenous people, an understanding based on the fact that most Mexican Americans are in part descended from the tribes and groups that populated America before Christopher Columbus's voyage. Along with most Mexicans, Chicanos are also Mestizos, a biological as well as cultural mixture of Indian and Spanish with some traces of African and Asian peoples. Because this mixing process occurred many centuries ago, Mexicans and Chicanos may not know the exact Indian tribe or group from which they descend. Hence, many identify their lineage with the most impressive and powerful of the Indian civilizations of Mesoamerica: the Toltecs, Mayan, and Aztecs. It is probably true that some twentieth-century Mexican immigrants descend from these civilizations. For at least 300 years most of the settlers in the Spanish frontier issued from the mixture of the Indian groups from northern Mexico with ethnically mixed settlers from central Mexico. The Mexican-American heritage became tied by blood to the less romanticized historical cultures of the Seri, Tauhumara, Navajo, Pueblo, Ute, Pima, Papago, Yang-na, and hundreds of other Indian groups throughout the American Southwest and northern Mexico.

A conservative estimate is that in 1492 perhaps as many as 700,000 people lived in the present-day U.S. Southwest and 200,000 in the northern Mexican frontier (see Table 1.1). The most densely settled regions were in Alta California, northern New Mexico and Arizona, and the west coast of Sonora and Sinaloa.

Table 1.1. *Estimated Population of Native Americans in the American Southwest, California, and Northern Mexico in 1500*

Region	Estimated Population
California	221,000[1]
Southwest (New Mexico, Arizona)	454,000[1]
Texas	32,300[2]
Great Basin	37,000[1]
Northern Mexican Frontier	200,000[3]
Total	944,300

[1]Douglas H. Ubelaker, "North American Indian Population Size, A.D. 1500 to 1985," *American Journal of Physical Anthropology* 77 (1988): 289–94.

[2]A. L. Kroeber, "The Demography of American Indians," in *The North American Indians: A Sourcebook*, ed. Roger C. Owen, James J. F. Deetz, and Anthony D. Fisher (New York and London: Macmillan, 1967), 43–44.

[3]A. L. Kroeber, *Cultural and Natural Areas of Native North America*, Publications in American Archaeology and Ethnology, Vol. 38 (Berkeley: University of California Press, 1939), 166.

Ecological and geographical factors were paramount in determining where the native peoples would live. Northern New Mexico was the most populated area, particularly those lands bordering the Rio Grande and its tributaries. Perhaps the most urbanized group of native people in the northern frontier were those called *los pueblos* by the Spanish. The Pueblo Indians, as they came to be called, were a collection of many different language and cultural groups. Most anthropologists believe that the Pueblos are descended from more ancient peoples— the Anasazi, Mogollan, Sinagua, and Hohokam (200 B.C. to A.D. 1000). These peoples had built impressive villages and apartment complexes out of stone and adobe throughout large areas of New Mexico and Arizona.

The more than 200,000 Indians in Alta California were divided into more than 100 language and dialect groups that were related to languages spoken elsewhere in North America (suggesting that they had migrated to California). The native people of California lived in small *rancherías* of about 200 people. They gathered edible plants, hunted and fished, and seasonally traded shell money for additional food and luxury items with peoples elsewhere in California. The people of the California coastal plains supplemented their diet with acorns that they harvested in the foothills, but they did not practice traditional agriculture, except to grow small amounts of tobacco for use in religious ceremonies. The Chumash Indians in central California built large canoes to fish and hunt small whales and seals. California native arts included clay pottery, baskets of intricate design and water-tight weave, and sea-shell jewelry that was highly prized by natives as far inland as Arizona. While most of the indigenous groups appear to have been peaceful, in northern California tribes engaged in frequent warfare.[1]

The coastal region of California sustained a large native population owing to the temporal climate and the abundance of edible plants, small game, and fish. Settlement patterns followed the availability of water and plentitude of game. The relative scarcity of rivers made it more necessary for dense settlement near water sources. These were semi-permanent villages, abandoned during the summer and fall during the acorn harvest.

The balance of the native peoples in the Southwest—the Navajos in Arizona and New Mexico, the Utes in southern Colorado and northern New Mexico, and the Comanches in Texas—were nomadic. Game, seasonal harvest, and water shaped their living patterns. Although practicing some agriculture and remaining within a defined geographical area, they lived primarily by raiding and hunting. The Navajo and Apache bands were native to Alaska. They had migrated from their homelands and had been forced from the Great Plains by other tribes about 1300 B.C., but they did not arrive in the Southwest until the 1400s. The Navajos lived in a symbiotic relationship with the eastern Pueblos, the Zuñi and Hopi, intermarrying with them and occasionally raiding their villages for food.

The Apaches, who descended from the same group as the Navajos, were also newcomers to the region. At the time of the first European contacts, they lived scattered throughout southern Arizona and New Mexico in several bands. They were migratory people who often crossed into present day Sonora and Chihuahaua and had temporary villages in the Mexican Sierras. The Europeans gave the Apache bands Spanish names: the Jicarilla, Mescalero, Chiricahua, San Carlos, Tonto, Mimbreño, Lipán, Gila, and Arivaipa. Even before the introduction of the horse by the Spanish, the more settled Indians feared the Apache's consummate war and raiding skills.

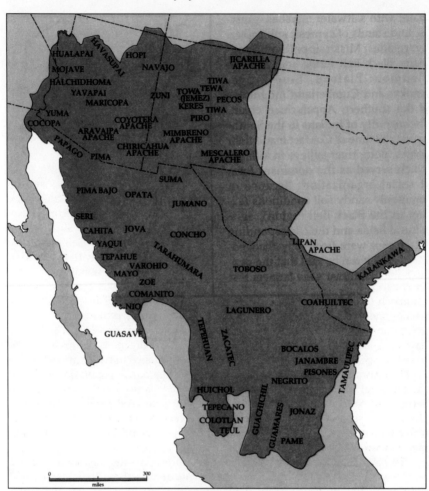

The California culture area, showing approximate tribal locations (with modern boundaries). From *Atlas of the North American Indian*, by Carl Waldman. Copyright © 1985 by Carl Waldman. Reprinted by permission of Facts on File, Inc., New York.

Another group of semi-nomadic raiders were the Utes and Comanches who were Plains Indians living at the northern and eastern fringes of the Spanish frontier. They hunted buffalo on foot until they acquired horses from the Europeans. For all the nomadic bands, the horse increased their range and success as hunters and raiders.

The Spanish in the Northern Frontier

One consequence of what turned out to be perhaps the most momentous event in the history of the secular world—Christopher Columbus's "discovery" of the New World in 1492—was what Alfred Crosby has called a "Columbian Exchange": the transposition of microbes, animals, and plants. The biological

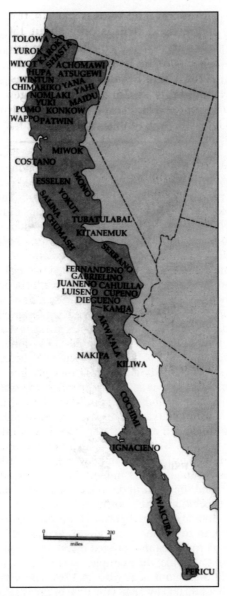

The Southwest culture area, showing approximate tribal locations (with modern boundaries).
From *Atlas of the North American Indian,* by Carl Waldman. Copyright © 1985 by Carl Waldman.
Reprinted by permission of Facts on File, Inc., New York.

stuff brought by the Europeans and that which they transported back to the
Old World, either intentionally or unintentionally, set in motion ecological
transformations that permanently changed the demographic history of the
world.[2] After Columbus, the export of newly discovered foods—mainly corn,
potatoes, and beans—stimulated a worldwide population explosion that is still

taking place. The importation of new animals and plants to the Americas radically changed the ecology that had sustained millions of native American peoples and ultimately led to the starvation and death of millions of them.

Another unforseen and unintended consequence of the conquest of the New World was the creation of new societies and ethnic groups. For the next 500 years the biological mixing of peoples from Africa, Europe, and Asia with the native Indians in the New World created dynamic new ethnic societies. The conquest also created a heritage of slavery, exploitation, and racism that conditioned the subsequent history of this new land.

The dramatic conquest of Mexico-Tenochtitlán (Mexico City) in 1521 by Hernán Cortés served as a prototype for later expansion into the frontier regions north and south. With a small Spanish army, Cortés succeeded in defeating the powerful Aztecs, primarily because of the lack of unity among the 20 million Indians in the valley of Mexico. Hundreds of thousands of Indians allies eagerly joined the Spanish to destroy their hated enemy. After military victory, the Spanish destroyed or coopted the native ruling classes, of both their former enemies and their allies, and used them as intermediaries to exploit, Christianize, and Hispanicize the native masses. Having pacified strategic Indian populations, the Spanish began to exploit the land and its wealth by introducing livestock and new crops. The Spanish needed workers for their new *estancias* (large farms) and especially for the mines. The royal officials allowed the Spaniards to demand forced labor from the Indian peoples (*encomienda*). Thus the natives inevitably came into contact with new diseases—among them smallpox, influenza, and the common cold—that proved fatal because of their lack of immunological resistance. In the absence of their traditional religious leaders, the Indians became easy converts, especially when the priests pointed out the retribution that the Spanish God visited on those who resisted His faith. No one knows how many died of starvation, disease, exposure, suicide, or brutal treatment. Estimates of the death among the Indians in central Mexico range from 15 million to 20 million. The total population in central Mexico probably declined from 25 million in 1519 to about one million by 1630.[3]

As the Spanish conquistadors moved north and south from Mexico-Tenochtitlán, they used the political divisions among the Indian peoples to their advantage. Every expedition to the northern frontier depended on Indian allies for its success and Indians suffered gravely from the European encroachments. Population thus began to decline. The rate of demographic decrease varied by region, depending on the resistance offered by the Indian group and intensity of Spanish contact. In California, for example, where the Spanish began an intensive mission-building program beginning in 1769, the native peoples declined from 200,000 to about 80,000 by 1848 (the date of the Anglo-American takeover of California). The death rate was higher in New Mexico and Arizona where the Indians were more established in permanent settlements and where the Spanish contacts were more prolonged. In 1500 more than 454,000 Indians lived in this Southwestern area. By 1800 the native population was reduced to 215,000 and by 1848 to approximately 176,000, a decline of more than half.[4]

Most of the *pobladores* (settlers) and soldiers came to the frontier from adjacent Mexican provinces that were themselves frontier areas. Royal policy called for planned settlement expeditions, so that most of those migrating north came in family units or as entire communities, generally led by an authorized colonist well-connected to the crown. Thus the government recruited most of the settlers in New Mexico from the province of Nueva Vizcaya. Those who migrated to Texas came from Mexico's northeast: Coahuila, Nuevo Santander, and Nuevo León. The settlers in Alta California came from Sonora, Sinaloa, Pimería Alta (Arizona), and Baja California. They brought with them their experience in living in a remote arid region beset by threats of annihilation by hostile natives. Many of them had strong biological and cultural ties to the native peoples of the Mexican north. They were independent of spirit but attuned to the necessity of banding together as families and communities for survival. After the initial settlement, there was very little voluntary migration from central Mexico. Some individuals did make for the north, wanting to flee dire conditions in haciendas or wanting to make new lives on the frontier, but they were the exception instead of the rule.[5]

The question of why Mexicans were not more enthusiastic in migrating to their frontier, in contradistinction to the Anglo-Americans, is open to conjecture and debate. In general, the Mexican culture, in both its pre-Hispanic and colonial periods, was more metropolitan and centralized. Ambitious persons who wanted to seek a fortune or consolidate a dynasty did not move to the frontier; they moved toward the center, Mexico City. The Spanish colonial system was much more able to control its subjects than was the English colonial administration. The Spanish crown discouraged private initiatives that were not under royal supervision. Group movement into the frontier areas had to have prior approval of the crown. Given the apparent lack of mineral wealth in the Far North, economic incentives were not very strong in attracting settlers. Finally, many Mexicanos were not economically able to leave their pueblos and haciendas.

Whatever the answer regarding the factors for immigration north, once in the frontier the *pobladores* faced adjustments, whether to the immediate historical moment, to a hostile terrain, or to the indigenous populations. The newcomers at times sought to coexist with the natives. The Series, Yaquis, Mayos, Tarahumaras, and other tribespeople living south of the present-day U.S.-Mexican border, for example, became the guides and porters for the first Spanish explorers. They were also among the earliest Christianized Native Americans who assisted the friars in the Spanish policy of conversion. The offspring of unions of various northern Christianized Indians became the Mestizo *poblabdores* who founded the ranches and towns in the northern limits of New Spain.

More often than not, however, encroachments only incited the tribes. The nomadic Indians living along the northern frontier reacted violently to the slow advance and consolidation of the European settlements. The Spanish policy of encouraging large-scale slave trade among Indians to gather workers for domestic and mining purposes only upset a delicate balance of power among native groups and stimulated new warfare and strife.[6] Then, at various times, the Europeans sought the Indians' annihilation through all-out war. They never succeeded, and Indian resistance ensured that the northern frontier would remain underpopulated until the last part of the nineteenth century.[7] Edward Spicer, who studied the history of the Spanish and Anglo-American programs for subjugating and controlling the Indians of the Southwest, believes that Native Americans endured because the conquerers—whether Spaniard, Mexican, or

Anglo-American—failed to incorporate the natives economically: "Because Indian land, labor and resources were of so little importance for the economies of the dominant peoples, the Indians were not brought into these economies and hence the programs for cultural change did not affect them in consistent or progressive fashion."[8] The Indians adopted the Spanish weapons and domesticated animals including the horse in order to better fight for their survival. Indians became bi- and trilingual to negotiate with the various foreigners who impinged on their fate. They learned quickly that the heart of their identity as a people was their religion and language, and they fought valiantly to preserve them. Ultimately, the strength of the Indian peoples' family bonds and community organizations contributed to their remarkable endurance.

Frontier Settlements and Institutions

Migration north into the frontier regions produced varied population expriences. New Mexico, first settled by an expedition led by Juan de Oñate in 1598, evolved into a civilian frontier of small farmers and ranchers. At first the large Pueblo Indian population appeared to offer possibilities for missionization and exploitation, but the native people proved uncooperative. The most dramatic uprising was the Pueblo Revolt in 1680, when an alliance of Pueblo villages killed 380 settlers and forced the remaining Spanish to flee New Mexico. The natives of New Mexico and Arizona were free from Spanish domination for 13 years. When the Spanish reconquered the province in 1693, a core of migrants from Coahuila, Mexico, went north and slowly reclaimed old

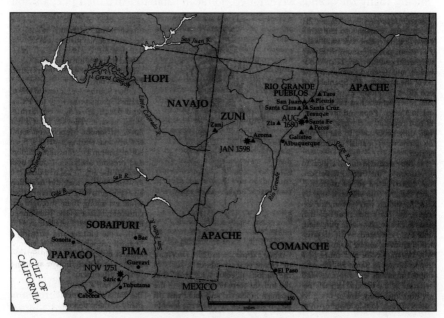

Indian rebellions against the Spanish north of Mexico, showing selected pueblos and missions (with modern boundaries). From *Atlas of the North American Indian*, by Carl Waldman. Copyright © 1985 by Carl Waldman. Reprinted by permission of Facts on File, Inc., New York.

settlements or founded new ones. These settlements formed the backbone of New Mexican society well into the twentieth century. Through natural increase, intermarriage with local natives, and the Hispanicization of captured Indians, the New Mexican population increased to about 24,000 by 1800. Almost all of this increase was due to the excess of births to deaths. Because there was no mineral wealth to be found, there was little attraction for new settlers.[9]

Texas developed as a military and missionary frontier, and it did so much slower than New Mexico. The initial policy to found missions, presidios, pueblos, and *ranchos* had been made by the king to head off a possible French takeover of the Spanish Empire's northern territories. The king authorized the establishment of scores of presidios and missions from 1690 to 1716, but the soldiers, families, and priests abandoned most of them after a short time because of the migratory habits of the natives and their attacks on the mission settlements. Settlements that endured were Nacogdoches (1779), La Bahía (1749), and Laredo (1755). For the next 50 years the population of Texas remained small but reached about 5,000 at the height of the Spanish period.[10]

Arizona was called Pimería Alta by the Spanish crown. It was the land of the Pima Indians in the upper region of the present-day state of Sonora. Arizona was a sparsely settled missionary frontier founded largely by the efforts of Eusebio Kino, an Austrian Jesuit who organized the construction of scores of missions extending from northern Sonora to southern Arizona. By 1678 there were 28 missions serving more than 40,000 Indians and 72 villages.[11] The most important mission in present-day Arizona was San Xavier de Bac (1783), near Tucson. Most of the civilian settlements were farther south in Sonora, where pioneers founded the towns of Guymas (1617), Arizpe (1644), Magdalena (1689), Caborca (1692), and Altar (1694). To protect these pueblos and the Jesuit missions, the military established several presidios whose garrisons became the nucleus for later towns. In present-day Arizona they built San Ignacio de Tubac (1752) and San Augustín de Tucson (1776). During the Spanish era the settlers in Pimería Alta lived a precarious existence surrounded by thousands of unconquered Apache and Yaqui bands. Historians estimate the province's population during the late eighteenth century at somewhere below 1,000.[12]

Like Pimería Alta, the Spanish settled Alta California as a missionary frontier, but a favorable climate and a large, peaceful Indian population created the conditions for the growth of a prosperous colony. The Spanish government, fearing Russian and English encroachment on their claims, subsidized the first expeditions to California. The government gave Junípero Serra, a Franciscan priest, the formidable task of organizing a chain of missions to pacify the native population and bring them the Gospel. The first mission was at San Diego de Alcalá in 1769, and Father Serra went on to establish 12 more along the California coast. After his death in 1784 his successor, Father Fermín Lasuén, continued the effort, and eventually 23 missions extended from San Diego to Sonoma. These missions grew to include about 10,000 neophytes (mission Indians) at their peak.

The Spanish Catholic Church dominated in Alta California, more than any other frontier territory except Pimería Alta. The Franciscan missions had the best lands and most of the available labor, and they prospered. There are many indications that the mission Indians suffered under the friars. The mission annals recorded 62,600 deaths but only 29,100 births from 1769 to 1834.[13] There were periodic neophyte rebellions, and thousands of Indians ran away to escape the harsh treatment and near starvation rations given them by the priests. At first the civilian settlements were dependent on the missions for their sustenance. Gradually small populations grew around the three official pueblos that the crown established—San José (1777), Los Angeles (1781), and Branciforte (1797). The king provided the *pobladores* parcels of land and a daily ration for three years to get started. The civilian population grew because of occasional overland migration from mainland Mexico but mostly because of natural increase. During this period the Spanish government also distributed land grants to retired soldiers as reward for their services. At the end of the eighteenth century the Hispanic population of Alta California was about 1,000.[14]

To implement a frontier policy of expansion, conversion, and defensive settlement, the Spanish crown used four frontier institutions: the *mission*, the *presidio*, the *villa/pueblo*, and the *rancho*. Each of these had a different purpose and constituency, but ultimately they all worked to create a dynamic social, demographic, and economic growth of the hinterlands.

Missions functioned on the frontier as settings for converting native population. Subsidized by both the church and the state, the missionaries (usually Franciscans or Jesuits) were to establish a mission compound, transform the neophytes into Christian Spanish subjects, then turn them over to secular clergymen who would then minister to the Hispanicized Indians along with other *pobladores*. Missions were of primary importance in California and Pimería Alta, where they also served as the basis for a flourishing local economy based on stock-raising and primary agriculture. The cultivation of European foods— wheat, apples, oranges, tangerines, pears, and olives—first took place on the missions and became the foundation for modern agricultural developments in the nineteenth century.

The presidios (frontier military posts) had as their primary purpose the protection of the mission friars and settlers as well as the disciplining of the neo-

Table 1.2. Estimated Spanish-Speaking Populations of the
Provincias Internas, 1815–1821

Nuevo Santander	38,000
Nuevo León	26,000
Coahuila	50,600
Nueva Vizcaya	190,504
Sonora and Sinaloa	123,854
Baja California	800
Alta California	3,270
New Mexico	36,579
Texas	4,015
Total	473,718

Source: Thomas D. Hall, *Social Change in the Southwest, 1350–1880*
(Lawrence: University of Kansas Press, 1989), 46, table 7.2.
Reprinted by permission of University of Kansas Press.

phytes. The soldiers often married native women, and their children became the future *pobladores* of new towns or were given land grants and founded the *ranchos*. These garrisons also stimulated economic activity as local businessmen and *rancheros* met the presidio's needs for mercantile goods and food.

Urban settlements that the Spanish founded on the frontier ultimately were their most long-lasting and influential contributions. Villas and pueblos served as centers for socialization, economic activity, religious work, and governance. They acted to transmit Spanish concepts of law and local government and ultimately facilitated the expansion of Hispanic culture in the Far North. In particular, the town governments, the *cabildo,* helped maintain a secure frontier society that had a democratic character.

The *rancho* in the frontier could be owned both communally or privately. During Spain's initial thrust into the Far North, the crown followed a general policy of distributing lands to communities, the church, or worthy individuals: *pobladores* then clustered in small farmsteads or ranches. In northern New Mexico life revolved around land grants, many of which went to groups instead of individuals. In rural villages that emerged from such grants, families had their own houses and agricultural plots, but equal access to the grants' grazing lands and water. In Texas and to a lesser degree in Pimería Alta, *ranchos* provided beef, hides, and tallow needed on the frontier, as well as mules, horses, and oxen. In California private *ranchos* developed relatively late in the colonial era. There the missions were much more important economically. Those who had received individual grants of land and various opportunists did try to exploit the land for personal gain. Texas *rancheros,* for example, engaged in a flourishing contraband trade with Louisiana in what amounted to a barter economy. Farming did not succeed to any magnitude in the Far North.[15]

Life on the Frontier

After the mid-eighteenth century numerous forces worked to stimulate the frontier economy. They partly emanated from the Spanish crown's concerns about international competition with a growing British economic and military power. Beginning in the 1760s Spain's Bourbon kings initated a series of reforms designed to build a stronger centralized state, a key component of which was to make the colonial administration of the Spanish colonies more efficient. In the northern frontier of New Spain the Bourbons wanted to protect its valuable silver mines from attack by Indians or foreigners.

First they were concerned with making peace with the *indios bárbaros*. To these ends frontier defenses were reorganized and strengthened. Royal officials sent new people and resources to the North to attempt to subdue or bribe the most warlike native groups into accepting peace. The political structure of the frontier was reorganized into an administrative body called the Provincias Internas and governed by a *comandante general* who reported directly to the king.[16] Second, crown officials took steps to revitalize commerce and industry and generate more income for the state. For this purpose, they lifted longstanding trade restrictions with other provinces. Also the crown encouraged hundreds of artisans and farmers from the Mexican heartland to migrate north to increase New Mexico's economic vitality.

The Bourbon reforms affected the Far North in a number of ways.

Economically, they catalyzed a surge toward capitalist formation during the waning decades of the eighteenth century. With friendly pacts negotatited between Indians and *pobladores* and mutually beneficial trade for both peoples developed, peace permitted ambitious entrepreneurs—merchants, stock raisers, and miners—to expand their investments into territories previously exposed to attacks. New opportunities created by the Bourbon policies offered these entreprenuerial elements fresh incentives. *Rancheros* from Texas drove their livestock to Coahuila and Nuevo León and then brought back finished products needed on the frontier. In Pimería Alta ranchers traded with Sonora, while those in New Mexico carried small amounts of wheat, corn, and beans as well as sheep and wollen products to Chihuahua and even to California. In New Mexico the Bourbon reforms resulted in an increased amount of specie that found its way into business negotiations. Throughout the Far North, however, the economy never fully developed into market capitalism during this time.

The economic transition also had its side effects. It led to the increase of land concentration and elite formation. In New Mexico, particularly, the need for more grazing and farming lands forced landholders to encroach on neighboring real estate. The poor increasingly found themselves landless and becoming wage laborers. They entered the ranks of a discernible laboring class, struggling as unskilled workers, ranch hands, freighters, servants, and the like. Peonage became more a feature of economic survival, as displaced rural villages committed themselves to working for some member of the rising socioeconomic elite.[17]

The majority of the *pobladores* and soldiers who went north were Spanish only in a political or cultural sense: most were the products of racial mixture known as *mestizaje*—the racial and cultural mixture of Spaniards, Indians, Africans, mulattos, and a variety of other ethnicities. On the frontier this cross-cultural amalgamation of races and cultures continued, varying according to ecological conditions and the types of native populations. For most of the Spanish period the settlers in present day Texas and Arizona lived in fear of extermination by warlike tribes and were unable to attract many immigrants from central Mexico. For this reason neither Texas nor Pimería Alta developed a robust population base, and there was comparatively less intermixture with the surrounding native populations. Conversely, the more pacific natives in California and New Mexico allowed the settlers to develop more populous farming and ranching districts. Concurrently through slave trade, rape, concubinage, and marriage there was more racial mixture in both New Mexico and California.[18]

Caste distinctions were reinforced by socioeconomic and political ones. Most of the top administrators, comandantes, missionaries, and officials were Spanish Europeans or had the status of *criollo*—European-stock settlers born in the Americas. They received the best political appointments and the choicest lands. Often, however, the category *español* (Spanish) was imprecise on the frontier: it could mean anyone living a "civilized" life—that is, being Spanish-speaking and Catholic. Many of those who were considered *españoles* had mixed-blood linkages like the rest of the lower classes. Beneath this upper stratum were the mass of mixed-blood *castas* and Native Americans. The Texas census of 1777 listed 957 Spaniards, 871 Indians, 111 Mestizos, and 669 as *colores quebrados* (literally "broken colors," other mixtures). In New Mexico, the oldest and most populous of the northern frontier provinces, Oakah Jones estimated that even though the settlers there retained their identification as *españoles*, as much as 80 percent or 90 percent of them were of mixed blood. Others have given estimates of about 60 percent being Mestizo.[19]

Also in New Mexico, *nuevomexicano* culture developed as a synthesis of Indian and Spanish influences, as would be seen in the development of the *genízaro* caste—Hispanicized, detribalized Indians who adopted Spanish culture. Alta California's first settlers reflected the ethnicity of African and Indian mixtures prevailing on the northwestern frontier. The first census of the settlement of San Diego, taken in 1790, counted 190 persons. Of the 96 adults, 49 were *españoles*, but only three had been born in Europe. The rest had probably been "whitened" (on the frontier people could "pass" depending on their wealth and occupation) to meet Mexico City's requirements that most of the soldiers be *español*. The census listed the balance of the soldiers as mulattos, *colores quebrados* (some African ancestry), Mestizos, *coyotes* (Indian-Spanish mixture), and *indios*.[20] Of the 46 persons who founded Los Angeles in 1781, the census listed only two as Spanish. The rest were from the lower castes.

In New Spain Iberian dialects changed, influenced by native languages, the new conditions, and distance from the cultural core. In the valley of Mexico, Mexican Spanish evolved rapidly under the influence of Nahuatl, the language spoken by the Aztecs. On the frontier a wide variety of local Indian words became part of the Spanish vocabulary as well. The Catholic faith also underwent a transformation. The *pobladores* came to venerate special saints that were identified with their home, villa, or province. They celebrated feast days and rituals that were influenced by local native traditions. Culturally the Spanish values of family and personal honor, patriarchy, and *limpieza de sangre* continued in the official ideology but in practice were modified by harsh frontier realities. The regulation and control of women's roles, a foundation of Iberian family life, was less rigorous in communities where every adult's labor was so important.[21] The settlers sought as much as possible to recapitulate Hispanic culture on the frontier, but inevitably the result was to create a number of regional variations. The mutations, however, were more Hispanic than native.

two

The Spanish/Mexican Northern Frontier

For 300 years after the conquest of Mexico, the Far North remained a colony of the Spanish Empire. In 1810, however, patriots in Mexico raised the banner of independence, and after 11 years of struggle, overthrew the imperial yoke. Throughout the old kingdom, Spanish subjects immediately became citizens of Mexico; for the *pobladores* of the northern frontier, Mexican rule would last only until about mid-century. In 1848 the United States defeated Mexico in a two-year war, and as their booty the *americanos* gained what became the states of Texas, New Mexico, Arizona, California, Colorado, and other parts of the old frontier. Mexicans residing in this new American region now became citizens of the United States.

New Spain's Revolt

Discontented *criollos* (the New World offspring of Spaniards) throughout New Spain increasingly questioned their subservient status to Spain. After 300 years of colonialism many considered themselves distinct from the people of the mother country and the equals of the Europeans.[1] The examples of the American Revolution of 1776 and the French Revolution later in 1789 only whetted the *criollos'* desire to put into practice the Enlightenment ideals of freedom, equality, and other natural rights of man. Contributing further to an independence spirit were the Bourbon reforms, some of which alienated the colonials. Many in New Spain took umbrage at the new peninsular appointees who arrived in the colony to man the streamlined royal administration and even toward the Spanish priests who displaced the native clergy from the more prestigious and influential ecclesiastical posts. The encouragement given to trade, ranching, and farming had been welcomed aspects of the reforms, but landowners throughout New Spain resented the increased regulation of local economies. Aristocrats protested the abolishment of the *repartimiento,* which had required the forced labor of natives for the benefit of regional strongmen. Merchants saw their financial future in contraband—be it with foreign powers or with neighboring provinces.[2]

European wars in the 1790s and in the early 1800s strained colonial budgets to unprecedented levels and undermined military commitments to frontiers. Indian attacks from the more fierce tribes persisted—in places sporadically, in others viciously—despite newer policies extending the *indios bárbaros* a velvet glove. The pioneers protested their neglect, though at the same time resisted crown policies to curtail local autonomy. Tejanos, for instance, did not like the crown's administration of the ranch and cattle industry, imposition of new taxes, and intrusions into the prerogatives of the local *cabildos*.[3]

In Mexico a priest from the village of Dolores, Guanajuato, raised the cry of revolt against Spanish rule on 16 September 1810 (this date became the national Mexican holiday of Diez y Seis de Septiembre). To his side flocked the oppressed lower classes, bent on venting hatreds on the Spaniards, whether foreign- or native-born. The death and destruction that followed only galvanized opposition to Miguel Hidalgo y Costilla's cry for independence as aristocrats, crown officials, and the clergy all rallied to quiet the mass insurgence. Royalists forces indeed captured and executed Hidalgo in 1811, but others of Hidalgo's ilk kept up the rebellion until Mexico succeeded in acquiring independence in 1821.

In Arizona and California the war passed practically unnoticed as crown representatives prevented seditious ideas from spreading among the masses, and in remote New Mexico the movement hardly caused a ripple.[4] But Hidalgo's *Grito de Dolores* did animate Texas politics. A former military man named Juan Bautista de las Casas led a revolt in San Antonio against royal authority in the province; he had the support of men from the local presidio, some members of the city's lower class, and even a few *rancheros* who sympathized with Hidalgo's cause. But his rebellion proved to be short-lived, as other elements within San Antonio society successfully reinstated royalist rule, only to see that reversed when Bernardo Gutiérrez de Lara marched in from Louisiana at the head of the Republican Army of the North to declare Texas independent in early 1813. In response, Spanish officials ordered commandant general José Joaquín Arredondo to the province, and his forces successfully chased the last of the rebels out of the frontier by late summer. For the remainder of the decade, Texas became a chaotic region. By 1820 its population had declined precipitously, and the eastern part of the province neared depopulation.[5]

Mexico's Rule, 1821–1848

In 1821 Agustín de Iturbide emerged as the leader of newly independent Mexico. He proved autocratic, however, and in 1822 proclaimed himself emperor, an initiative that contradicted the spirit of republicanism that had motivated Mexicans toward their independence. The next year a popular rebellion ousted him from power, and Mexicans banished him from the country under the penalty of death (Iturbide returned and was indeed executed). A philosophical debate ensued between those wanting to establish a government based on the country's traditional Spanish past and those wishing to establish a federal republic. The latter won out in 1824 by writing a democratic constitution.

Based on precepts of the Enlightenment, the Spanish Constitution of 1812, and the U.S. Constitution of 1787, the Constitution of 1824 established the first democratic government in Mexico. Theoretically, it granted increased power to the country's states and provinces to govern themselves, but the rule did not apply to any of the regions of the Far North, as Texas and Pimería Alta (which was part of Sonora) were attached to the states of Coahuila and Sinaloa, respectively, and New Mexico and California were designated as territories under the direct control of the national Congress.[6] In 1835 Antonio López de Santa Anna staged a coup that ended federalism, and for the next decade or so all of Mexico came to be governed by Centralists—those belonging to a conservative party intent on weakening the states and territories and strengthening the Mexico City government. For the north country, it meant rule by officials—usually military men—assigned to the frontier from the interior. While resenting encroachment on their autonomy, the *pobladores* nonetheless complained that these outsiders did not understand local problems and in fact did not care too much for their lot. Economic, military, and religious neglect typified governance under the Centralists.[7]

Dissatisfaction with Centralist rule after 1835 produced a series of revolts in the Far North and in Texas became partly responsible for the Anglo-American war for independence from Mexico in 1836. For years the Spanish crown had considered various options for populating the Texas outpost in an effort to stem the westward push of Anglo-Americans from the United States. In 1820 the Spanish government turned to the desperate policy of using Anglo-American settlers to come to Texas and protect it from other Anglo-Americans. Moses Austin of Missouri negotiated the first colonization contract, and in 1821 his son Stephen began establishing a settlement called San Felipe de Austin in eastern Texas. Other colonizing agents from the United States brought more families into Mexican Texas in subsequent years. All the Anglo-Americans settled in the eastern part of the province away from Mexican ranches and towns in central Texas.

By the late 1820s the settlers had become a problem of concern in Mexico's interior. Despite their promises to abide by national laws, the immigrants insisted on preserving U.S. political traditions, homesteaded the land illegally, engaged in land speculation, carried out contraband trade, and proclaimed a commitment to chattel slavery. Yet they saw Mexico's policies toward Texas as despotic. An urge for establishing a way of life based on republican doctrines, a desire to break away from the economic policies that retarded the development of the region, the need to ensure the preservation of slavery, and racist dislike for Mexicans in general all explain rising discontent within the Anglo-American communities. Santa Anna's 1835 coup, which restricted provincial autonomy, became the immediate catalyst for the rebellion. On 2 March 1836 the people of Texas declared their independence from Mexico. Though defeated at the Alamo on 6 March, the Texans routed the military forces of Santa Anna at the Battle of San Jacinto on 21 April 1836 and thus gained their independence.[8]

In New Mexico the new politics incited a rebellion in 1837 among the lower classes (who grieved to the Centralist governor about their poverty, social inequality, and forced service against the *indios bárbaros*), but the oligarchs and other leading citizens sided with government authorities to squelch the movement. The territory remained more or less deferential to Mexico City's rule after that.[9]

In California *arribeños* (those living north of Los Angeles) removed two Centralist governors in 1836 before declaring themselves independent (the *abajeños*—those residing from Los Angeles to San Diego—sympathized with the *arribeños* but showed reluctance to support their rebellion fearing political subordination in an independent state dominated by northern Californios). Astute diplomacy on the part of the Centralists the next year brought California back to the fold, but an uneasy relationship between the territory and the mother country persisted. Indeed, another insurrection against Centralist intervention broke out in 1844, with the interior government able to do little about it except live with the autonomy the Californios proclaimed.[10]

Several factors may have pushed the frontierspeople toward rebelliousness. In Texas historians have attributed the war for independence to the various causes already discussed. In New Mexico and California the *pobladores* may have been motivated by other forces, among them isolation, rising exposure to foreign trade, federalist ideas, a feeling that they had outgrown their dependent status, or to sentimental attachment to the land of their upbringing. Local power plays among political or regional cliques may also have incited discontent, as may have friction among social classes.[11]

Despite a woeful situation, Mexico made a concerted effort following its own war for independence to get people from the heartland to relocate in the Far North. The region still remained depopulated, and the prospects of a foreign takeover, especially from the United States, seemed more perilous by the early nineteenth century. Finding volunteers to head northward in massive waves proved difficult, however. Mexico's major success turned out to be in Texas— an ironic turn, for, as we have seen, the immigrants sequestered the province by 1836.[12]

In Arizona the Mexican government sought to reinforce the small communities around Tucson and Tubac by making grants of land to soldiers during the 1820s and 1830s. Soon *rancheros* established productive lands along the Santa Cruz and San Pedro rivers, around the San Rafael Valley and near Babocómari Creek.[13]

Those who trekked into California during the Mexican period derived from all walks of life, though most descended from the landless lower class (*cholos*) and included various types of social reprobates, among them *presidarios* (convicts) whom the government dispatched north on a regular basis. In the 1830s the government tried to colonize the territory under a program led by José María Híjar and José María Padrés. It met opposition from the native Californios who believed the two colonizers had orders to distribute secularized mission lands to neophytes and other settlers from Mexico. The initiative collapsed, though some of the pioneers who had come from around Mexico City remained in various parts of the province. During the late 1830s and continuing into the 1840s, governors initiated land-grant programs that appealed to new settlers as well as to Anglo-Americans already in the province.[14]

Comparatively, New Mexico saw very few outsiders enter its borders during the Mexican era. Land grants to attract settlers and develop the region were made judiciously in New Mexico, albeit not until the late 1830s and the first half of the 1840s. Governor Manuel Armijo, for one, disposed of some five to six million acres in modern-day Colorado to Charles Beaubien (Maxwell Grant), Stephen Louis Lee (Sangre de Cristo Grant), Ceran St. Vrain (Las Animas Grant), and Gervais Nolan (San Carlos Grant). All of these grantees, however, were naturalized Mexican citizens who had Mexican families and had contributed to New Mexico society constructively. Despite the land-grant program, the U.S. Census of 1850 counted fewer than 400 people of Mexican descent to have been born outside New Mexico.[15]

The figure of *la muerte*, pictured here with bow in hand, was used in ceremonial processions in New Mexico to remind the *pobladores* of their mortality. Photograph courtesy of the Taylor Museum for Southwestern Studies of the Colorado Springs Fine Arts Center.

The demographic patterns of settlement that took form in the colonial era persisted into the 1840s. Spanish/Mexicans born on the frontier huddled around established communities, and immigrants situated themselves in the same locales. Tejanos remained concentrated in the eighteenth-century communities of San Antonio, Goliad, and Nacogdoches, while below the Nueces River toward the lower Rio Grande, *pobladores* worked ranchlands they had received as far back as the colonization projects of the 1740s and 1750s.

In Arizona pioneers found it safest to hunker down in the southernmost part of the modern-day state. Apache attacks after the 1830s forced them to forsake their other settlements in the province and to leave the great herds that had made up the *ranchos* at Babocómari and San Bernardino. Until the 1840s the region around Tucson remained the only settlement sustaining its position.[16]

The upper Rio Grande, along an area that stretched from Taos in the north to Sabinal in the south, remained the major center of settlement for *nuevomexicanos,* but some expansion east to the Pecos River area and south to the Socorro Valley occurred by the mid-nineteenth century. The largest towns continued to be Albuquerque and Santa Fe (the capital of the province).[17]

In California settlers lived throughout the 500-mile coastal plain around the urban sites of Los Angeles, San Diego, Monterey, and San Francisco. In the early 1830s the province became the scene of a veritable land rush when in 1833

A carving of the archangel San Miguel slaying the devil, probably from the eighteenth century. New Mexican craftsmen—called *santeros*—carved hundreds of images of the saints for homes and churches throughout New Mexico. Photograph courtesy of the Taylor Museum for Southwestern Studies of the Colorado Springs Fine Arts Center.

the government passed a secularization decree that dispossessed the Church of all its mission properties—neophyte Indians, cattle herds, and real estate. Hundreds of petitioners profitted from the new policy of land tenure. Ranch settlements rapidly spread outward toward the countryside around Los Angeles and San José, stretching as far north and east as the Sacramento and San Joaquín rivers.[18]

When the United States conducted the first census of the conquered territories in 1850, the population of Texas had increased from about 4,000 in 1836 to about 14,000, no doubt because the Anglo-American settlement of the republic now acted as a buffer against hostile Native American tribes and because newer opportunities in bucolic tasks enticed immigrants from Mexico. According to the best available figures, California had a population of 7,300 in 1845, owing in part to the successful land-grant policy and the secularization of the mission lands that had enticed people northward. New Mexico had by far the most settlers. Natural reproduction combined with in-migration put the number of *nuevomexicanos* at some 60,000. Arizona had no more than 1,000 *pobladores* as of 1846, mainly in Tucson.[19]

Toward an American Future

Anglo-Americans had visited New Spain's far-northern lands since the 1790s, and in the first decade of the nineteenth century they began wantonly showing up in the borderlands. For various reasons, including trade, exploration, and filibustering, Anglo Americans continued illegally entering the lands of Texas and New Mexico during the decade of Mexico's war for independence.[20] Traders from Missouri led by William Becknell arrived in New Mexico in 1821, and soon after more merchants followed. The Santa Fe trade was on, giving stimulus to the borderlands economy. Anglos imported cloth and other manufactured items from the United States and bartered them for anything available not only in New Mexico but beyond. New Mexico (and Mexico) in turn exported mules, donkeys, rugs made from buffalo hides, blankets, wool, and gold bullion. The amount of specie now increased in New Mexico not only because of commerce with the Mexican interior where currency circulated more freely, but also because of the extraction of bullion from the Placers deposits of the Ortíz Mountains south of Santa Fe.

New Mexicans eagerly bought from the Anglos hoping to sell the foreign merchandise elsewhere. Within a generation, they dominated just about every facet of the trade by journeying to Missouri themselves and acquiring the goods firsthand, and by ensuring that Santa Fe remained the central point of commerce that extended to markets in Chihuahua, Sonora, Zacatecas, and Durango.[21] The early Santa Fe traders took back news of the abundance of fur-bearing animals in New Mexico, and by the 1820s trappers poured into New Mexico and penetrated what became modern-day Colorado. By the mid-1820s, mountain men had migrated west to southern Arizona to trap beaver, primarily along the Gila River. Tucson never did attract Anglo merchants in the manner that did the other provinces of the Far North, however.[22]

Americans and other foreigners began landing in the coastal ports of California during the 1820s; their presence violated the law but the Californios received them warmly. The pobladores awaited the foreign smugglers along the coast and exchanged their hides and tallow as well as otter and seal pelts for various kinds of U.S.-made goods. Anglo mountaineers crossing overland, led by Jedediah Smith, descended on California by the mid-1820s, and soon engaged in trapping operations there. By the late 1830s the Californios had established significant links to North American capitalism, as had the *nuevomexicanos* years earlier.[23]

These earliest intruders into the Far North did not hold particularly favorable attitudes toward the *pobladores*. Many who during the 1820s and 1830s recorded their feelings as part of travel narratives described Mexicans as descended from a mongrel race and prone to indolence, immorality, cowardice, filthiness, debauchery, cruelty, and frivolity. Their impressions derived from deep-seated racial attitudes American society held toward nonwhite peoples, but also from religious impulses and republican nationalism. By the 1830s, indeed, many Americans came to subscribe to the belief that it was their manifest destiny to spread the Anglo-Saxon way of life throughout the vast North American continent occupied by supposedly inferior people.[24]

A range of impulses motivated other Anglos westwardly, among them the need to escape debt in the United States, the urge to start afresh in a frontier land, and the desire to establish some business in a region they saw with unlimited potential. In California, Anglo newcomers gravitated toward the southern half, while in New Mexico they clustered in the Rio Arriba region.[25] Most adjusted to the ways of the natives, learning Spanish, converting to Catholicism, and (often abiding by local rules of courtship) intermarrying with native women. An estimate based on a study of church records notes that as many as 75 percent of Anglo newcomers to New Mexico between the 1820s and 1840s married Mexican women, though the figure could have been higher as many entered into common-law unions.[26]

For the Yankees, allying themselves with the *pobladores* offered opportunities for making profits in mercantile and agricultural pursuits. Marriage brought them specific privileges, among them citizenship, which legally permitted them to trap and trade. More important, Anglos could gain access to real estate, as they did during the 1830s and 1840s, when the Mexican government issued millions of acres in land grants in the Far North. Political ambitions could also have been another reason for intermarriage, and some foreigners in New Mexico and California found their way into political office.[27]

Though the natives disliked the Anglos' crass ambition, they accepted the newcomers into their society just as they had historically integrated some of the Indian peoples or Europeans into their communities. The elites, especially, saw advantages in alliances. In California the aristocracy was attracted to the foreigners' white skin as it differed markedly from that of the Indians with whom the *gente de razón* (which had pretentions of being "European") did not wish to be classified. Persuading a daughter to marry an Anglo merchant meant uplifting the family racially and advancing it socially, as the marriage distanced the elite from the lower-class *peones,* at least psychologically. New Mexico's elite also displayed sensitivity to skin pigmentation, and intermarriage afforded them an opportunity to "whiten" the family and improve its social categorization.[28] More practically, intermarriage served as a move toward establishing or strengthening an aristocrat's financial base in times of economic transition. For wealthy families, it meant connections to the spreading capitalist economy in the region; for poorer families it had even greater social implications. Mestizo women could automatically achieve social upgrading and economic security by marrying Anglo newcomers with an acumen for business success. According to recent research, most of the women in New Mexico that intermarried with Anglos before 1848 descended from the lower stratum.[29]

As the *pobladores* accepted Anglos into their society, the Mexican government began having second thoughts about the Yankees. Foreigners kept pouring into the borderlands, and those arriving there during the 1840s displayed less assimilative tendencies than had their forerunners of the 1820s and 1830s. The new pioneers seemed more a part of the wave of manifest destiny then driving Americans into Mexico's far-northern frontier. The central government had reason for concern. In 1841 Anglo-Texans had undertaken the Texas-Santa Fe Expedition, an excursion into the New Mexico territory designed to annex it.

The New Mexican governor had intercepted the party, but for many in the interior the overture manifested American designs on the borderlands. In California more ominous events transpired. Anglo-Americans, who in the 1840s had preferred settlement in the Sacramento Valley, saw new opportunities in the northern region of the province and petitioned the Mexican government for parcels of recently secularized lands.[30] In 1842 a part of the U.S. Pacific naval squadron sailed into Monterey and captured it in the erroneous belief that the United States had declared war on Mexico. In 1843 John C. Frémont led a surveying expedition into the province, then returned two years later to build fortifications close to Monterey.

For a variety of reasons, including the annexation of Texas, the United States and Mexico went to war in May of 1846. As American military forces marched into Mexico proper, Frémont used the troops under his command to assist what came to be known as the Bear Flag Rebellion, an uprising of Anglos who had drifted into California in recent years. Some of the Californios, among them members of the elite, welcomed the possible annexation of the province into the United States, but other elements resisted the invasion through guerrilla warfare. They won significant battles in Los Angeles and Santa Barbara during the latter half of 1846 but were eventually defeated. Similarly, the governor of New Mexico allowed occupation forces to enter the province (allegedly, he sought to protect his economic interests, developed over the years from the Santa Fe trade), but patriots raised the cry of rebellion in Taos late in 1846. In January 1847 the *insurrectos* killed the new governor, Charles Bent, and for a while resisted the U.S. troops sent into northern New Mexico to suppress them. In the interior of Mexico, American troops occupied Mexico City in the fall of 1847 and forced the motherland to agree to the Treaty of Guadalupe Hidalgo, signed on 2 February 1848. According to the treaty the Far North became a part of the United States, but the rights and property of the residents of said frontier were to be guaranteed. Thus did citizens of Mexico become citizens of the United States.[31]

three

Natives in a Foreign Land

Demographic Profile of the First Mexican Americans

The first census of the United States in the conquered territories took place in 1850. The estimates on the size of the Hispanic population varies. Oscar J. Martínez, who studied the question extensively, reckoned that the population ranged somewhere between 86,000 to 116,000. By 1880 the size of the Mexican-American community had grown considerably; Martínez estimates the figure for that year at varying between 226,000 to 327,000. His adjusted figures by region in 1850 are as follows: New Mexico had some 62,000 to 77,000 residents; California, 9,100 to 14,300; Texas, 13,900 to 23,200; and Arizona, 1,000 to 1,600.[1]

In the 30 or so years after the Treaty of Guadalupe Hidalgo, a number of Mexican immigrants arrived in the United States. Most sought seasonal work; others refuge from peonage and oppression in Mexico, and still others pursued fortunes. During this era Mexican immigration did not act as a major force in the development of Mexican communities in the Southwest. It would become more important after 1880. No one demographer can really determine with any kind of accuracy the number of Mexican immigrants who trekked across the international border between 1850 and 1880. Exact sums come with difficulty since so many transborder migrants shuttled between the United States and Mexico searching for work, visiting kin and acquaintances, or engaging in business transactions (legal or otherwise). The federal census, moreover, consistently undercounted the population in the United States, especially that of ethnic qroups. Despite these handicaps, historians can still draw approximate conclusions regarding immigration to the United States between 1850 and 1880.

The gold rush attracted, according to one estimate, some 25,000 people from Sonora and other northern Mexican states to the California mines between 1848 and 1852. This wave subsided by the mid-1850s owing to violence and anti-Mexican laws in northern California, but prospective ranch hands nonetheless entered the southern regions of California from Chihuahua, Sonora, Durango, and other western states in Mexico; during the 1860s and 1870s many of these immigrants dispersed into Arizona, Colorado, Nevada, and even the Pacific Northwest to seek new opportunities in gold and silver mines there. A similar pattern of migration, primarily from Sonora, occurred into Arizona, where the ranches and the emerging mining industry (copper, silver, and gold) at mid-century beckoned for cheap laborers. Mechanized deep-shaft mining in the 1870s demanded more workers, and those responding included peones fleeing the drudgery of the Sonoran haciendas. As a result, the Arizona immigrant population increased from 4,348 in 1870 to 9,330 in 1880. From Nuevo León, Coahuila, and Tamaulipas streamed workers seeking employment in Texas cattle and sheep ranches and in towns then emerging owing to Anglo-American expansion toward the southern and western sections of the state. Not many immigrants headed toward New Mexico during this period. Those who did originated in such states as Chihuahua, Durango, and Zacatecas, and they tended to settle in the southern parts of the state.[2]

Immigrant culture from Mexico reinforced traditional lifestyles among the native Mexican population, for newcomers from south of the United States introduced newspapers; recent notions of nationalism and patriotism; restrictive attitudes toward women; social rules about conduct, comportment, or etiquette; and a host of other tenets that sometimes transformed pre-1848 settlements into veritable immigrant enclaves. Amalgamation resulted, ensuring the survival of the old and familiar.

Ill treatment at the hands of Anglos also worked to sustain old ways, for it heightened Mexican Americans' awareness of their distinctiveness as an "ethnic group." For the most part, some of the negative feelings expressed before the conquest persisted, fueled anew by the sense of the conquerers' destiny in the West and a feeling of superiority emanating from the defeat they inflicted upon the Mexican nation in 1848. For protection, Mexicans found solace in their own group, identifying themselves now along racial lines and turning to such self-designated labels as *La Raza*. By this they meant the Mexican people; the term connoted individual pride in community and a uniqueness of experience and condition that set them apart from the dominant class. Self-designation occurred in rural villages, in *ranchos,* and in urban enclaves called *barrios.* The latter term derived from both the Iberian and Aztec traditions and applied to city districts inhabited by individuals having common familial ties. In New Spain and its frontier settlements, the term referred to particular urban neighborhoods. After 1848 people used it to denote a discernible section of a town site inhabited by Mexicans.[3]

Still, Mexican life in the period following the conquest was not monolithic. While the American economy proletarianized a good number of Mexicans, some elites withstood the onslaught, and so social differentiation continued to typify Mexican settlements. Furthermore, the better classes still strived to maintain the old social distance between themselves and their inferiors, in numerous cases by seeking acceptance into the world of Anglo-Americans and going to the extent of labeling themselves "Spaniards." White society lumped new arrivals from south of the international border together with the native lower classes into the category of "Mexicans," *"cholos,"* or "greasers."[4]

Even physical environment played a role in diversifying communities. Immigrants hailed from numerous states in Mexico, so that place of origin added distinguishable features to those areas where newcomers settled. Because the geography of the Southwest itself varied, Mexican-American enclaves tended to differ among California, New Mexico, Texas, and Arizona, and even within regional boundaries. The terrain in New Mexico remained ideal for sheep raising, giving its Hispanic inhabitants somewhat of a different cultural orientation than did Texas and California, where life revolved around the cattle ranch. A vibrant Native American heritage in the territory also added flavor to *nuevomexicano* society, where it did not to Hispanic life in Texas, Arizona, or California. Lastly, New Mexico proved an enduring geographical stronghold for Mexicans; Anglos did not gain a numerical advantage there until the twentieth century. Actually, the same disparity applied to Arizona. By comparisons, Mexicans in Texas, California, and Colorado had become minorities within years after the conquest.

Socialization into an Anglo world further diversified Mexican communities everywhere. In the years after the conquest, some Mexicans embraced their American citizenship enthusiastically, just as others rejected the American presence in their homelands. There came to exist variations in degrees of acculturation to American society. Some had spent more time in the United States; as the years went by, they held an edge on recent arrivals, who had little familiarity with American institutions. Then, the elites attempted to learn the ways of the Anglos in their effort to earn a niche in the rapidly developing capitalist order. It might also be probable that gender difference surfaced, with women as a group being less acculturated than men, for the latter interacted with white society on a more regular basis. Within barrios and rural villages, hence, there existed disparate levels of acculturation, some inhabitants remaining "Mexican," others bicultural, and a few completely absorbed into Anglo-American life.

Increasing hetereogeneity typified Mexican-American life after 1848. Ideological clashes within the community, different positions on political issues, conflicting attitudes regarding relationships with the Anglo-American majority, dissimilarities in standard of living, and uneven patterns of land transfers and urban decline according to location in the Southwest, all would characterize life under American rule.

The immigrants arriving from Mexico settled in those general areas already occupied by Mexican Americans, most of which were the same ones where Mexicans had lived before the conquest. The Californios resided in villages and ranchos throughout the state, but their stronghold remained the southern region. In Arizona, the district below the Gila River persisted as the center of Mexican population, with the two most prominent settlements being Tubac and Tucson. Mexicans in Texas continued to localize from San Antonio to the Rio Grande, then along the border to El Paso. Population pressures after 1848 forced New Mexican stockmen, farmers, and other settlers to expand outward from the upper Rio Grande villages into the northeastern and northwestern corners of the territory, the Canadian Valley, and even into Oklahoma, the Texas Panhandle, and southward below Socorro, though the least diffusion occurred there. They also pushed into the fertile valleys of southern Colorado, where they engaged in commerce, trapping, sheep raising, and small-scale farming.[5]

All these regions of the old Mexican frontier featured clearly delineated nodes of Anglo and Mexican settlements. Until the 1870s, most California Anglos lived in the northern reaches of the state (having absorbed much of the ranch lands following the gold rush), while Mexicanos outnumbered Anglos in the southern sections. In New Mexico, Hispanos dominated Anglos numerically in the upper Rio Grande counties, but during the 1870s Anglo cattlemen began overturning the Hispano presence in the eastern sections of the territory and transforming the southern counties into cattle ranges. South and far-west Texas along the Rio Grande contained the major Tejano settlements, though a minority resided in San Antonio and surrounding rural areas. Arizona featured similar demographic patterns, even as Anglos did not immigrate into that territory as they did elsewhere in the Southwest; lack of agricultural appeal and fear of Indian depredations deterred them. Tucson remained Mexican in context, but around it, and in the mining camps and other settlements, including the towns of Phoenix and Prescott, Anglos predominated.[6]

Economic and Social Effects of the Conquest

Relations between Mexican Americans of the conquered provinces and the newcomers were both cordial and rancorous in the decades after the war with Mexico. In some regions of the Southwest—southern California, southern Arizona, northern New Mexico, and south and far-west Texas—Anglos and Mexican leaders negotiated what David Montejano refers to as a "peace structure." In such situations, which lasted until the 1870s, Anglos converted to the Catholic faith, acculturated into the social world of Mexicans, and assumed commitments derived from sponsoring Mexican children or young adults at baptism, confirmation, or weddings. They then entered into alliances with the native gentry, undertaking business partnerships, political office-sharing at the local level, and intermarriage with the women of the landholding class. This latter practice corresponded to prevailing sex ratios in given geographical areas. Where Anglo males constituted a minority, such as in the towns of Los Angeles during the 1850s and Santa Fe and Tucson until much later, interracial unions occurrred more frequently than in places where sexual parity between Anglo men and women existed.

Overall, accommodation proved beneficial to the economic interests of both Anglo and Mexican elites. For Mexicans it permitted them to protect their possessions and to retain social prestige in the midst of change, and for the Anglo newcomers it gave them an opportunity to solidify control of the region's economic base (especially land). Coalitions also made for rewarding partnerships if trade with Mexico presented itself as a possibility or, conversely, if the Mexican elite wished to tap into the new U.S. economy. Cooperation also allowed for defense against Indian threats or outlaw gangs, and it led to political appointments and other kinds of government patronage.[7]

Under such circumstances, therefore, Mexican men of property or others of business acumen found a niche in the new economics. They redirected their energies from such initiatives as the Santa Fe trade to emerging opportunities, went on tending to their land (even acquiring new properties) and selling their stock as opportunities opened up, launched mercantile enterprises in the international trade with Mexico, established entrepreneurial operations in freighting or local retailing, and even intrigued with Anglo Americans to defraud fellow Hispanics of their real estate.[8]

The American domination of the southwestern economy disrupted Mexican life everywhere, and though some of the *rancheros* retained their lands by means explained above—or, as was the case with others, acquired small parcels of real estate—gradually just about every stockman or farmer became obliged to ward off ambitious white men seeking to oust them from their holdings. Some Mexicans succeeded, most did not.

Fraud proved an effective mechanism in dispossessing the old landowners of their properties, including the minerals in those lands. Sheriff sales—wherein county courts sold lands at public auction once owners failed to pay taxes or debts—came to be one of the most common ways of displacing *rancheros* throughout the Southwest. In New Mexico the Santa Fe ring—consisting of some who had carved a niche in the province's economy even before 1846, of men attached to the military, and of merchants and lawyers and common swindlers—used friendships with influential government officials outside the new territory to gain from the natives, both rich and poor, claims to generations-old land titles.[9]

Similar cases of land acquisition occurred in Arizona after 1856 following the arrival of the military. Occupants had moved in and out of the region in the face of Apache attacks during the Mexican period, and speculators now flocked into the frontier seeking out likely heirs and offering them token remuneration for rights to land titles. The government set no specific time limit for settling ownership in the territory, and so contention between Mexican owners and Anglo settlers remained for the rest of the century.[10]

In California federal laws in the 1850s required the *rancheros* to go before a three-man land commission and have their titles screened for authenticity. Many, however, could not afford the appearance or distrusted the commission's intentions; consequently, they lost their holdings when the land reverted to the public domain. Simultaneously, the northern California *rancheros* contended with greedy squatters who moved into the best lands, cleared pastures, took over roving stock, fenced in their claim to the estate, and killed trespassers. Land lawyers coming to the assistance of the rancheros often proved to be nothing less than confidence men who connived with the judicial system to defraud them further. Similar machinations spread to the southern *ranchos* by the late 1850s, and after that the pattern of land usurpation came to be a replication of the earlier fate of the northern Californios.[11]

Intermarriage, once seen by the *rancheros* as a way of uplifting their social status or guarding their estates, now became problematic. White men who had married for opportunity instead of love gave new direction to the *rancho*'s operation, in numerous instances, to the detriment of the landowners. At other times Anglo owners disposed of the ranch (if they had inherited it on the haciendado's death) without taking into account the long-term interests of his Hispanic relatives. After the conquest, also, land-hungry suitors would often court a widow to gain control of her inheritance.[12]

But grantees also lost their lands by their inability to adjust swiftly and adequately to the capitalist orientation of the new economic system. The old haciendas had proven themselves capable of producing beyond subsistence when the need arose (and thus capable of surviving through adaptation in the new market economy), but many *rancheros* still considered their landholdings as they had before 1848: as an institution intended to provide for the family, not a profit-making operation. Most claimed no assets beyond their lands and encountered difficulties in keeping up with modernization, especially after the Civil War. They lacked funds to make essential improvements, including fencing their lands with barbed wire or improving the quality of their herds so that the stock could compete with new breeds introduced by Anglo ranchers. Furthermore, they could not afford to drive their own cattle to markets, or dig wells or construct new tanks for watering their cattle and sheep when fences cut the animals off from rivers and streams. Disadvantaged by their outlooks, by money powers that felt reluctant to extend them credit, by unscrupulous loan sharks that charged them exhorbitant rates for money borrowed to pay legal fees, by an inability to pay taxes, and by a lack of access to mainstream markets, many fell victim to the downturns in the economy, especially when demand for their livestock plummeted.[13]

Calamities of nature also seemed to work their designs on Mexican *rancheros*. In California rainy seasons alternated with dry spells during the 1860s, each taking their toll on the cattle herds—drowning the livestock and starving them, respectively—and loosening the tenuous hold of the *rancheros* on their old properties. Texas Mexican ranchers who had been able to cling to their lands during the 1850s found themselves facing similar bouts with the weather in the 1860s and 1870s. A land lawyer, a merchant, an Anglo rancher, or even a foreign lending agency usually turned out the beneficiary in times of such natural catastrophes.[14]

Doña Mariana Coronel Grinding Corn, painting by Alexander F. Harmer, ca. 1885. The Coronel family was among the Californio elite (Antonio F. Coronel was elected as the first—and last—Mexican-American mayor of Los Angeles in the 1850s) whose fortunes declined after the mid-nineteenth century. Photograph courtesy of the Seaver Center for Western History Research, Natural History Museum of Los Angeles County.

The Lot of the Masses

For all their innovations, the foreigners found labor arrangements from the Mexican era suitable to their needs. They took the old haciendas and transformed them into more modernized, resilient, and productive units, but they adopted the old work structure in which *patrones* presided paternalistically over *peones*. Ranch hands from California to Texas, either cowboys or landless peasants, continued to work the range in time-tested Spanish-Mexican traditions, while owners looked out for their charges by providing them housing, sustenance, and such goods as footwear, clothing, tobacco, spirits in the form of *aguardiente*, and perhaps a little cash. Mexican elites who managed to maintain their lands used the same techniques. In New Mexico, territorial law even recognized peonage, at least until the Civil War destroyed slavery and debt bondage along with it. After that, work situations similar to those in California and Texas formed in the territory's farming areas and to some extent in the newer settlements that sprouted out from frontier expansion. In some autonomous regions of the New Mexico countryside, however, many peasants still lived in community-owned lands and did not come under the labor situations described above.[15]

For a time following the conquest, the lower classes survived as common workers in the *ranchos* and farms, but land loss by the Hispanic elites, Anglo images of treacherous *cholos* and greasers, the need for a servile labor force, the Anglo-American determination to control the marketplace, and initial strides toward commercial farming and newer developments in urban economies following the Civil War "proletarianized" Mexican-American workers. Mexicans now faced general joblessness or underemployment, often lacking the needed skills demanded by a rapidly changing economy.[16]

Tejanos witnessed displacement from freighting, agriculture, and certain craft occupations into the general grouping of "unspecialized" workers. Many sought a new livelihood as day laborers, cooks, servants, and a miscellany of other unskilled tasks. The Californios turned to work in the mercury and gold mines; to seasonal work as *vaqueros* or sheep-shearers throughout surviving California *ranchos;* to the mule-pack train system they introduced into Oregon, the Washington Territory, and even British Columbia; and to whatever menial occupations availed themselves in the new market economy. Arizona workers also took jobs in the fledgling mines, albeit performing dangerous tasks, earning only survival wages and facing continuous debt at the company store.[17] Women, in the meantime, became participants in the work force in increasing numbers, most of them finding employment as laundresses, cleaning women, seamstresses, or domestics at dismal wages, though others did acquire employment in semi-skilled and even skilled capacities. Many assumed the added responsibility of heading families when men took to the migrant trail in search of work.[18]

Proletarization became the lot of most Mexicans, but extenuating circumstances sometimes permitted some to succeed where others failed. Circumstances unique to a geographic area might also be underscored as a factor assisting entire communities to achieve a better standard of living. Tucson, for example, stood out as a case in point. There the Mexican majority successfuly postponed its domination for decades by persuading Anglo leaders to become "Mexicanized" and exhorting them to work cooperatively to ward off Indian attacks. In comparison to Los Angeles and San Antonio between 1850 and 1880, research shows, Tucson had fewer people relegated to unskilled occupations.[19]

Conflict on the Frontier

Violence also served Anglos in ruling over Mexicans. Historians have found Anglo rationalizations for the use of physical force in the sentiments of manifest destiny, a revenge factor, racial distrust, competition for old lands, the need to access water and grazing in the open range, disagreements between cattlemen and sheepmen, and the fluidity of times. Anglos unabashedly expressed contempt toward the Mexican race and the proletariat in particular, which they referred to disparingly as "greasers." Whether it be the California cholos, the Tejano lower classes, the Arizona poor, or New Mexican villagers, Anglos saw in the Mexican physiognomy, in leisure habits and manner of living, the stamps of an inferior people. Anglo Texans passed laws prohibiting the fandango (which they thought lascivious), and Anglo New Mexicans passed similar decrees levying fines to deter such long-standing Hispano customs (which the outsiders deemed immoral or unsanitary) as burying loved ones under the church floor or in the cemetery next to the church (if the building stood inside the city limits), holding fiestas and religious festivities on Sunday, and marriages between close relatives or among minors (girls under 18, boys under 21). Anglos also considered the natives a decadent folk with treacherous and criminal propensities. Gender did not exclude Mexicans from racist attitudes or actions. Women came in for disapproval, scorned for an alleged easy virtue as revealed in attitudes toward sexuality, fashion, or dancing the fandango.[20]

Violence seemed more pervasive in those areas where a crass component of cowboys or a rough and transient element engaged in the "taming" of the frontier, where the economy lacked stability, where white outsiders were in the rugged stages of exploiting a region's natural resources, or where a middle class, owing to its absence, could not mediate against the mistreatment of the laboring poor. Such settings included the gold mines of California, the frontier in northern Arizona and west Texas, or the cattle ranges of south Texas and southern New Mexico, where, after the Civil War Anglos were bent on redeeming the wilderness. But areas where Anglos and Mexican elites cooperated for mutual welfare hardly escaped violence. White men recognized the social differences between the landed class and the cholos, but under tension they tended to categorize the elites alongside the despised "greasers." Ostensibly, whites sought the formation of a racially stratified arrangement where they presided over Mexicans, regardless of the latter's social standing.[21]

Ethnic conflict thus surfaced throughout the Southwest in the wake of the conquest. It broke out in central Texas during the 1850s in the form of the expulsion of Tejano families allegedly involved in enticing slaves to run off to Mexico. The "Cart War," a campaign of destruction leveled against Tejano freighters who underbid the transportation cost of Anglos, followed in 1857. The episode passed from the scene within months, as even Anglos interceded to ensure the continued movement of goods from the interior to the coast. But conflict spread to south Texas, where new troubles, dubbed the "Cortina War," broke out in 1859-60. After the Civil War a "Cattle War" engulfed the untamed ranges of the trans-Nueces as both Anglos and Mexicans clashed over the wild steer then in great demand in northern U.S. markets; together the two groups inflicted severe casualties on the region's innocent Mexican-American population.[22]

In New Mexico violent skirmishes similarly erupted throughout the territory, though the most notorious occurred in Lincoln County during the 1870s. There Hispanos clashed with two other competing Anglo factions (both reinforced by Mexican-hating Texans) desiring control of the water sources and open grasslands. A decade of feuding hardly settled the question of rights to the range, so that the region continued being a setting for animosity between Anglo cattlemen and Hispano sheep herdsmen for years to come. During the last decades of the nineteenth century, however, the advantage tipped toward the Anglo entrepreneurs who had used their ties to capital and political influence outside the region.[23]

In Arizona the mining frontier during the 1850s and 1860s proved as volatile as anywhere. Anglo miners, who saw Mexicans as competition to fair wages or as a people unentitled to exploit American natural resources, murdered or lynched Mexicans without fear of retribution. Cowboys inflicted similar crimes on Mexicans, and Mexicans in turn killed Anglo ranchers or mining officials. The 1872 slaying of Don Francisco Gándara, Jr., near the town of Blackwater, came to rank among the most heinous atrocities in Arizona. Anglo vigilantes, suspecting Gándara of the killing of a white men, burst into his home and killed him in full view of his wife and daughters. Talk of vengeance ensued among Gándara's friends and relatives, but Anglo gangs stiffled it with further killings. Public sentiment later conceded Gándara's innocence.[24]

Numerous acts of vindictiveness accompanied the California gold rush and included whippings, lynchings, mutilations, and hangings, with the most dastardly example being the case of Juanita (or Josefa) who in 1851 in the town of Downieville defended herself from harassment by an Anglo miner only to be lynched for murdering him. Violence moved south after the exhaustion of the gold rush, touching the southern Californios with equal venom. The turmoil produced a "race war in Los Angeles" in 1856 when a deputy constable killed a well-respected Angeleño in an incident involving the repossession of a guitar. The Mexican community in the city then stormed the local jail in an attempt to apprehend the deputy and try him before a popular tribunal, but Anglos rallied and summarily quelled the "Mexican revolution" with vigilante justice. A semblance of order returned by the 1860s, but by then the Anglo newcomers had taken much of the region's best lands, laid claim to its natural resources, and displaced the Californios as the ruling class.[25]

The Politics of Domination

The conquest of 1848 also ushered in a new political order into the Southwest. The rules of government changed, but so did the political types that assumed leadership. Many of them held ties to state and national bureaucracies, and, indeed, the territories of New Mexico and Arizona contained numerous officials—among them the governor, the marshals, and the district judges—who received their appointments from the federal government. But also formed were influential cliques, such as the aforementioned Santa Fe ring (1865–85), which developed similar connections to high-level authorities, then went on to control territorial affairs. Though their counterparts in Texas, Arizona, and California lacked the New Mexicans' organization and notoriety, machines in those areas nonetheless held political force. This could well involve efforts to disenfranchise the Mexican population, suffocate the will of the local electorate, or, conversely, use the Mexican to swing the vote in state and national elections.[26] The native residents pursued diverse political tacts in dealing with these circumstances. Some, generally from the upper class, accepted the circumstances and sought acculturation. More nationalistic elements retreated to the familiar world of the barrios, trekked south to Mexico, or rebelled against the white establishment. Most Mexican Americans probably compromised with white society, wishing to live peaceful and practical lives as ethnic Mexicans.

Several elites responded to the new politics with accommodation—a decision attributable to disillusionment with previous Mexican rule, admiration for the American union, desire to form convenient political and economic partnerships with the newcomers (some of whom adapted themselves to native ways), or callous opportunism. Cooperative alliances allowed the propertied Mexicans to retain a semblance of their former leadership, keep portions of their old lands, or use their Anglo business colleagues as intermediaries for acquiring lucrative government contracts. These relationships also permitted elites to integrate themselves into the realm of political bossism, many times as members of local subrings that answered to the more powerful Anglo nabobs.[27] Bossism in the nineteenth century theoretically carried reciprocal obligations. Voters gained political experience and acquaintance with the political process under the tutelage of the boss, whether Anglo or Mexican. They received employment when available or help in times of emergency, and they could look to the political leader to voice their concerns. Unfortunately, bosses were inclined to be selfish, corrupt, and untrustworthy.

On more than one occasion, however, Mexican elites used their power and influence for the good of the community. Altruism, common decency, or the pain of disparaging Anglo attitudes often motivated them to take action. Pablo de la Guerra of California and Estévan Ochoa of Arizona stand out as influential men who spoke out prominently in behalf of Mexicans. The latter used his friendship with influential legislators to have discrimination in the territory addressed, to get language restrictions from jury service abolished, and even to have the state consider court proceedings and important state business conducted in a bilingual format.[28] Accommodationist politics served the Mexican community to some advantage. Politicos from the Mexican community served as aldermen, county commissioners, justices of the peace, county clerks, constables, and other elective posts in southern California, southern Texas, the El Paso Valley, southern Arizona, northern New Mexico, and southern Colorado. Prominent political figures in these four regions included José Antonio Navarro and Santos Benavides of Texas, Pablo de la Guerra of California, Casimiro Barela of Colorado, and Estévan Ochoa of Arizona.[29]

It was in New Mexico, however, that the Hispano population claimed more political clout, even as so many offices fell outside their selection. During the long colonial and Mexican periods, the *nuevomexicanos* had honed their political skills as a matter of survival in an isolated expanse. Outnumbering the Anglo population, they now attuned their political instincts and capitalized on the oportunity to occupy newly created positions throughout the land. They elected, for instance, a Mexican-American delegate-in-congress consistently during the territorial era, Hispano officials on a regular basis to both houses of the territorial legislature, and other native New Mexicans to local office almost routinely. The names of Miguel A. Otero and Donaciano Vigil became well associated with New Mexican politics of the era before 1880. This pattern of incumbency allowed the *nuevomexicanos* to thwart the kind of political domination that befell Mexicanos in other parts of the Southwest.[30]

Throughout the Southwest, Mexican-American politicos worked through the two established parties. Consequently, Mexican communities tended to be as ideologically diverse as those of Anglo-Americans, a fact highlighted by the stands they took on a variety of issues pertinent not only to their own welfare but to the entire country. Issues of national magnitude that concerned them included the status of slaves and freed African Americans, the role of the military in protecting the frontier from Indian attacks, and, for those in Arizona and New Mexico, the federal government's position regarding territorial status. The most divisive of these national concerns during the decades following the conquest was, however, the Civil War. When the Civil War erupted some Mexicans considered it an Anglo affair and took a position of neutrality, though many fought for either the Confederate gray or Union blue. Some 9,900 Mexican Americans served between 1861 and 1865. Almost half of these came from New Mexico, but Texas contributed a good share, while natives from California fought in a battalion named the Native California Cavalry, and, toward the end of the war, Arizonenses joined a regiment called the First Battalion of Arizona Infantry.

The most prominent examples of Mexican participation in the Southwest took place in New Mexico and Texas. In the New Mexican territory, Hispanos participated in the repulsion of a Confederate invasion from El Paso and up the Rio Grande in 1862. At Glorietta Pass (close to Santa Fe), New Mexico's Lt. Col. Manuel Chávez on 28 March 1862 led a contingent of Colorado men that destroyed the enemy's supply train and sent them reeling in retreat toward Texas. This triumph effectively liberated New Mexico from the Confederacy. In the trans-Nueces region of Texas, Santos Benavides distinguished himself as a colonel for the Confederacy, while Juan N. Cortina and Cecilio and Juan Valerio carried out guerrilla attacks on behalf of the Union forces. Their activity diverted southern attention from the eastern strategy.[31]

Resistance and Revolt

While some native residents accepted American rule, other segments of the population spurned it. Mexican landholders defended their property with weapons; settlers resisted attempted removal from old communal lands; ordinary people lashed out at racists, white supremacists, and outlaw gangs; sheep-raisers in New Mexico fought cattlemen; Spanish-language journalists editorialized against *gringo* injustice; and whole communities at times raised arms against greedy capitalists. In 1859, for instance, much of the Mexican population of south Texas made common cause with Juan Nepomuceno Cortina. A descendant of an old grantee family in the lower Rio Grande Valley, Cortina had personally witnessed the fradulent transfer of lands from Mexican to Anglo hands during the 1850s. A fateful confrontation between himself and the Anglo city marshal at a Brownsville café in July 1859 eventually swelled into a movement with the objective of ousting the gringos from the area. From his headquarters at his mother's ranch near Brownsville, he issued proclamations denouncing the Anglo intruders and called on the Mexican population to rally to his cause. Hundreds responded, seeing him as the hero who would bring redress to their grievances. Historians have disagreed on Cortina's role in history, but all concede his appeal. Before being defeated by federal troops in the early part of 1860, his bold leadership had made him a folk personage, one admired and respected for facing the hated enemy, for attempting to uphold his name, and for defending the integrity of the downtrodden.[32]

Other cases of rebellion involved only a single figure, though communities extended surreptitious support to these rebels in the form of intelligence, sustenance, and refuge, as in the Joaquín Murieta and Tiburcio Vásquez episodes in California. The former was vaulted into the public imagination in 1851 when, allegedly, he launched a war of terror against the gringos in northern California. Actually, the historical Murieta remains a mystery; contemporaries believed him to go by several aliases and he appeared to be in different places simultaneously. Until his capture and execution in the summer of 1853, however, he evolved into a hero and a legend among the Spanish-speaking, even though there may have been no one Californio named Murieta but possibly several bandits acting throughout the region who became "Joaquín" in the public mind. Whatever the case, Mexicanos approved of the mysterious Joaquín's escapades; like other such rebels, he audaciously avenged injustices perpetrated on the Spanish-speaking with selective strikes on Anglo ranches, settlements, and other symbols of white domination. Poor folks vicariously identified with his war of reprisal.[33]

Tiburcio Vásquez similarly emerged a hero in California communities during the latter 1850s and 1860s. Supposedly, gringo injustice had pushed him into a life of crime, and until 1870 he spent much of his time alternating between prison and outlawry. Between 1870 and 1874 he attracted unprecedented attention for his cattle rustling and holdups, all the while receiving shelter, help, and approval from decent and principled people who knew him only by reputation. Because he victimized mostly Anglos, the peasantry offered him sanctuary, as they had for Murieta. Though captured in 1874 and executed the next year, his reputation lived on as an underdog who defied gringo insults and abuses, albeit through a life of crime.[34]

A third form of rebellion might involve an aggregate of characters—either dishonest or law-abiding—coming together for the expressed purpose of avenging some perceived wrong. In California in 1857 numerous outlaws led by Juan Flores, a fugitive from the penitentiary, waged a brief war of revenge and retaliation against white businessmen in San Juan Capistrano and then threatened the white community of Los Angeles. Historians have explained that the compulsion to avenge Anglo cruelties bonded Flores and his desperadoes. Whites responded to the "Flores War" with ruthlessness. They rounded up suspects and summarily hanged many of them, including Flores.[35]

A classic episode involving people amassing to avenge an outrage took place in far-west Texas in 1877. For generations the people of the El Paso Valley and those across the river in Mexico had turned for their economic survival to the salt deposits located some 100 miles down river from El Paso. These natural resources belonged to the entire community, but following the Civil War Anglo entrepreneurs arrived in this isolated region with ambitions of laying claim to the salt beds for personal profit. Years of bitterness between the Mexicans and Anglos culiminated in the killing in October 1877 of an Anglo who sympathized with the Mexicans. The natives demanded vengeance from the white minority in the valley but saw only the release on bail of the perpetrator, who then proceeded to restrain Mexicans from going to the salt beds. In December 1877 people from both sides of the border raised arms against him and his supporters, and several days of violence at the town of San Elizario resulted in the deaths of several Anglos. Texas Rangers and other Anglo volunteer groups who descended on the region wanting to even scores finally restored peace and order. This so-called El Paso Salt War faded, but the people of the valley never recaptured their claim to the common ownership of the salt lakes.[36]

Family, Religion, Education

In the decades after the conquest the Mexican family remained anchored in patriarchal traditions and customs. Men remained committed to the notion that women belonged in the home; these constraints bore down most heavily on middle-class women whom society expected to accept the patriarchal structure. Upper-class women were to be chaste at first marriage, for instance; men, meanwhile, could court mistresses or outwardly display their masculinity.[37] The concept of *compadrazgo* also endured with little modification: the kin network carried with it specific duties and obligations, with godparents still bound to care for their godchildren in times of distress and the latter owing their sponsors deference and respect. Fathers and mothers had the role of instilling in their children dignity and respect, the esteemed custom of addressing older folks in the formal *usted* (as opposed to the informal *tú*), and the tradition of honoring parents by avoiding smoking in their presence or of requesting consent to attend formal occasions. Mothers and grandmothers assumed the responsibility for ensuring the chaperoning of young girls at public affairs and preparing young women for marriage, generally by the time girls reached their mid-teens. Betrothing one's children involved a formal custom in which the groom dispatched an upstanding citizen to petition the bride's parents for her hand in marriage. In turn, the bride's father and mother responded to the groom's overtures through another intermediary, usually the girl's godmother.[38]

Mexican-American society also continued tolerant of interracial marriages, and women from the both lower and upper classes entered into such bonds, especially in those areas where sexual imbalances existed, such as the New Mexico territory into which Anglos generally immigrated as single men (the federal census schedules for 1870 and 1880 show a preponderance of them married to native New Mexican women). As in the Mexican era, such cross-cultural unions offered women an improvement in social standing, for Anglos tended to be literate and better positioned for acquiring jobs in skilled capacities. Mexican men and Anglo women rarely married, though such unions existed.[39] Mexican-American norms also countenanced extramarital cohabitation. Tradition on the frontier (such as in the Arizona mines in the 1860s), especially, permitted this kind of sexual freedom among lower-class women. Women in such partnerships received companionship and intimacy in a forbidding frontier, but, equally important, an improvement in life standard for their mates often earned a better livelihood than Mexican counterparts.[40]

The family ideal did experience reassessment over time, however. Patriarchy underwent alteration in view of modern trends that extolled romantic love, in light of women's ability to contribute to the household when compelled to join the work force and because young men left the family in search of work.[41] In some cases perceptions of woman's role within the family became more tolerant. More "modern" attitudes led to new freedoms and privileges for spouses or common-law wives. But such tolerant sentiments that had helped women overcome the confining rules of Hispanic society also contained a judgmental strain. Other Anglos stigmatized cohabitation (which, incidentally, declined as Anglo women and families moved into frontier regions after the 1870s), frowned on the old festive fandango that women had performed without inhibition, weakened the freedoms recognized under colonial and Mexican rule, and ridiculed women's religious and folk expressions.[42]

After the conquest Mexicans adhered to their religious beliefs of the pre-1848 era—in most cases Catholicism—but they tended to slight such things as regular church observances, the sacrament of marriage, and the custom of showing deference to priests. The conquest brought new Church appointees to the Southwest, many of them Europeans appointed by the Roman Catholic Church of the United States, who then railed against the beliefs and morality of the lower class, criticized the merriment that accompanied religious festivals, disparaged folk healers (*curanderos*), refused to recognize the Penitentes as a religious society, and resisted the movement for women's suffrage.[43] Discontent with the Church intensified and came to the fore in the refusal to pay fees for the administration of rites, in mediocre support for the Church as an institution, and in the running fight that developed between the famous Padre Antonio José Martínez of New Mexico and the new bishop in the territory in 1850, John B. Lamy.[44]

Dissatisfaction with the priesthood also opened up possibilities for missionary work by the Protestant denominations, though apparently such efforts did not gain too many followers during this period. Presbyterian missionaries carried out evangelizing programs in New Mexico during the 1870s by subordinating pastoral work to teaching and the establishment of schools for prospective converts. Comparatively, their work in Texas, southern Colorado, Arizona, and California until the 1880s was less intense, though by no means absent.[45]

Mexican citizens of the new regions saw little in the form of educational uplifting. All states and territories in the Southwest did mandate the establishment of public school systems, but in the years following the conquest few legislatures made serious efforts to implement such provisions. Consequently, Mexican Americans from the elite class tried to expedite public schooling. In Arizona, Don Estévan Ochoa and other prominent Mexicans led such a drive in the early 1870s, though they had in mind the education of young men. In New Mexico, Catholics opposed Anglo-American-sponsored public school legislation;

led by the Church, upper-class *nuevomexicanos* fended off every initiative to establish a nonsectarian, state-funded public school system until 1872. Allowed to occupy a number of school boards and teaching positions, Church officials thereafter softened their stern opposition. *Nuevomexicanos* and clergymen now reconciled themselves to having the schools act as the agent through which the young would be instructed in both Catholic and democratic ideals.

Between 1848 until 1880 parents encourged their children to attend school, and youngsters thus enrolled not only in the few fledgling public schoolhouses but also in Catholic and Protestant institutions in rural and urban areas, or in urban, privately established community schools. Though it is almost impossible to determine what percentage of children attended schools on any regular basis, it appears that somewhere between 25 percent and 40 percent of all school-age children found the opportunity to attend some sort of educational facility every year, with the number of those in the urban areas even higher after the 1870s.[46]

Summary

Multiple cultures converged in Mexico's old northern frontier from 1850 to 1880. From the U.S. interior came people from the North and the South—pioneer settlers, miners, cowhands, ranchers, entrepreneurs, and professionals. Immigrants from Europe and Latin America (primarily from Mexico) joined them in the newly acquired lands, all looking for new beginnings. They joined the native folks—Mexicans and Indians—in unremitting competition for survival.

Contact was at times fierce and merciless. Anglos and European defined Indians as "savage" and in many cases regarded Mexicans as not much better. White men may have made exceptions of the Hispanic elite, but overall they considered Mexicans a people to be subordinated instead of integrated into the mainstream. Conflict thus characterized relationships, Americans at times waging the same wars of extermination on Mexicans as they did on the Native Americans, and Mexicans in turn retaliating with their own brand of violence. Discreet efforts at racial control involved limiting job opportunites and relegating Mexicans to menial tasks. Controlling Mexicans also meant restricting their choice of settlement in cities and ranches: by the 1860s what historians call *barrioization,* or the pattern of restricting Mexicans to specific sections of town, emerged as a cornerstone of racial understandings.

Mexicans, who save in New Mexico and Arizona quickly became a minority population, persevered. Institutional life remained stable, though changes occurred where inevitable. The size of the population, for one thing, ensured the preservation of the old culture; people believed in traditional ways and made conscious efforts to keep them. Seclusion from white settlements insulated people from the customs of the intruders, and the knowledge that Anglos rejected association with Mexicans further heightened the sense of in-group uniqueness, of being La Raza. Persistent immigration from Mexico led to syncretism, a blending of borderlands and Mexico's traditions.

The American presence produced new accords, nonetheless. Most Mexicans faced a grim future, but a few found fortuitous opportunities in the economy and joined Anglo-Americans as *rancheros* or businessmen and even launched political and professional careers. These and others came to accept the many tenets of American life so that varying degrees of Americanization within communities evolved. Numerous other things changed, albeit moderately—family structure, religious instruction, fashions and dress, and even ways of working the range. The direction Anglos came to give specific regions, the demographic ratios prevailing between Anglos and Mexicans, and the intensity of racism in a particular environment all determined the newer life for Mexicans.

four

The Borderlands in Transition

The period from 1880 to the early 1900s was as much a watershed in Mexican-American history as the period following the conquest. A far-reaching transformation swept across the Southwest during this time, taking the region into an age of modernity. This chapter describes the forces bearing on Mexican urban enclaves and rural settlements during the transition, the manner by which Mexicans dealt with the adversity brought on by the changing times, and the dispersal of native-born Mexicans and immigrant communities beyond the old population clusters in south and far-west Texas, southern Arizona, southern California, and northern New Mexico.

Structural change had as its catalyst an expanding economic system that penetrated the Indian and Mexican Southwest with great energy around the 1870s and 1880s. The taming of the frontier and the prospects of the new business ventures attracted eastern railroad lines to the West. The iron rail now facilitated the conveyance of a variety of raw products from Texas to California (minerals, vegetables, and cotton) to major commercial centers in the East and other world markets.[1]

Large-scale commercial farming matured after the 1880s. Small farmers still provided sustenance for their families and surrounding areas, but the drive into modernity moved land cultivation toward concentrated agricultural production. Capitalists purchased old ranchlands throughout the Southwest and in the Midwest (in western Nebraska, Colorado, Ohio, and Michigan) and converted them into massive farms with crops such as beets, which met the tremendous demand for sugar. Irrigation projects developed with federal subsidies assisted in the rise of new farming enterprises, as did reclamation projects that permitted agribusiness entities to turn desert lands into productive estates. Railroad lines played their own part in promoting the harvest of citrus and cotton from south Texas to the West Coast. California farms, particularly, came to typify the nascent commercialization of the Southwest. Run as corporations, these bucolic California factories specialized in producing huge amounts of wheat and grains, a variety of fruits (grapes, lemons, and oranges), nuts, and an assortment of perishable vegetables such as lettuce.[2]

Mining during the 1880s moved away from extracting silver and gold only and concentrated on the development of copper and coal at a time when railroads and steel plants in the eastern United States demanded the latter minerals. Mining companies now imported modern technology to find and exploit natural deposits in New Mexico, Colorado, Arizona, and Oklahoma, as well as Idaho and Montana. Mining as a significant investment in the Southwest thus joined the current toward modernization.[3]

Comparatively, the entire range industry faced difficulty throughout the West, owing in part to a slumping demand for beef, weather calamaties that affected the size of herds, and laws passed by eastern states to prevent cattle diseases from infecting their stock. Ranching endured as a feature of the west, of course, supplying beef to the miners, soldiers, and Indians in New Mexico or Arizona who lived in reservations, as well as the burgeoning towns. Sheep ranching also remained profitable, primarily in New Mexico, parts of Texas, and California, but the day of ranching as a big-time industry was over.[4]

Actually, the transformation of the new era did not extend to every location, so that some Mexican Americans continued living in the countryside in circumstances not much unlike those before the 1880s. Rural villages in southern Texas and northern New Mexico stand out as examples. Class, racial, labor, and political relations of the old frontier persisted in these places, although such localities began feeling the changing tide by the early 1900s.

Mexicans in the New Southwest

Simultaneous with the above process, convulsive events unfolded in Mexico that would affect the destinies of people on both sides of the U.S.–Mexican border. During his presidency (1876–1911) Porfirio Díaz sought the modernization of Mexico, but his policies only exacerbated the living conditions of the downtrodden masses. He sought to create an efficient agricultural sector capable of raising surplus farm products for export outside Mexico, but the policies resulted in the destruction of *ejidos* (the communal lands from which villagers derived their livelihood) as a landed elite encroached into peasant properties, casting villagers into a life of unemployment, forced labor in the expanding haciendas, or seasonal work throughout the country. The Porfiristas also promoted plans for colonizing Mexico with settlers from other parts of the country and Europe, but such colonizing projects further displaced the peasantry from their *ejidos* (which Díaz perceived as unproductive units anyway).[5]

On the haciendas, poor folks experienced dire conditions. Their living standards plummeted owing to unexpected circumstances during the Porfiriato. Incredibly, population increased, partly because of the peace and stability created by Don Porfirio, but also because of advances in health care. Unforseen survival rates added more people to a predominantly rural economy whose inability to produce enough crops for the excess population led to higher food prices. Urban workers lived as poorly, putting in 12 or more hours daily at local factories, receiving minuscule wages, and toiling under hazardous conditions.[6]

In its further attempts to modernize the country, the Díaz government during the 1880s launched a railroad-building plan. The attractive wages offered by railroad construction projects lured poor and unemployed migrants from their villages toward the north of Mexico, where aggressive track-laying was under way. This trek north would prove to be the initial steps that immigrants, predominantly from the rural areas of Mexico, would make to the "promised land" of the United States.[7]

Table 4.1. Legal Immigration from Mexico to the United States, 1869–1973

Year	Total Immigrants	Year	Total Immigrants	Year	Total Immigrants
1869	320	1905	2,637	1941	2,068
1870	463	1906	1,997	1942	2,182
1871	402	1907	1,406	1943	3,985
1872	569	1908	6,067	1944	6,399
1873	606	1909	16,251	1945	6,455
1874	386	1910	17,760	1946	6,805
1875	610	1911	18,784	1947	7,775
1876	631	1912	22,001	1948	8,730
1877	445	1913	10,954	1949	7,977
1878	465	1914	13,089	1950	6,841
1879	556	1915	10,993	1951	6,372
1880	492	1916	17,198	1952	9,600
1881	325	1917	16,438	1953	18,454
1882	366	1918	17,602	1954	37,456
1883	469	1919	28,844	1955	50,772
1884	430	1920	51,042	1956	65,047
1885	323	1921	29,603	1957	49,154
1886	n.a.	1922	18,246	1958	26,712
1887	n.a.	1923	62,709	1959	23,061
1888	n.a.	1924	87,648	1960	32,084
1889	n.a.	1925	32,378	1961	41,632
1890	n.a.	1926	42,638	1962	55,291
1891	n.a.	1927	66,766	1963	55,253
1892	n.a.	1928	57,765	1964	32,967
1893	n.a.	1929	38,980	1965	37,969
1894	109	1930	11,915	1966	45,163
1895	116	1931	2,627	1967	42,371
1896	150	1932	1,674	1968	43,563
1897	91	1933	1,514	1969	44,623
1898	107	1934	1,470	1970	44,469
1899	163	1935	1,232	1971	50,103
1900	237	1936	1,306	1972	64,040
1901	347	1937	1,918	1973	70,141
1902	700	1938	2,014	Total	1,736,576
1903	528	1939	2,265		
1904	1,009	1940	1,914		

Note: n.a. = data not available.

Sources: For 1869–1969, Julian Samora, "Mexican Immigration," in Gus Taylor, ed., *Mexican-Americans Tomorrow: Educational and Economic Perspectives* (Albuquerque: University of New Mexico Press, 1975), 78. For 1970–73, *Annual Reports of U.S. Immigration and Naturalization Service,* cited in *View across the Border,* Stanley Ross, ed. (Albuquerque: University of New Mexico Press, 1978), 166. Reprinted by permission.

The migration that commenced gradually in the latter decades of the nineteenth century accelerated in the early years of the twentieth as economic forces simultaneously propelled people from their homeland and pulled them into the United States. During this period unskilled Mexican laborers found their way into farms in Texas, Oklahoma, and Colorado, while more skilled hands joined a migratory wave that made its way toward the southern Arizona mines or toward Southwest communities along railroad lines. Many lived as members of track crews in these areas at improved wages unimaginable in the land of their birth.[8]

Not all who moved north belonged to the peon class, for a few members of the well-to-do also entered the United States. Some pursued better opportunities, while others left embittered with certain aspects of the Díaz dictatorship. Doctors, pharmacists, lawyers, businessmen, journalists, and even intellectuals, authors, and artists generally gravitated toward the larger towns, among them El Paso, San Antonio, Los Angeles, and Tucson. Many retained a conservative bent, even agreeing with Díaz on some issues, and in the United States encouraged the community to use Mexico as a cultural model, to retain a patriotic commitment to the homeland, and to reject assimilative pressures in the United States.[9] Others moved north, however, with a broader agenda. Ricardo Flores Magón, certainly the most prominent figure from this latter element, fled to Laredo, Texas, in 1904 to escape political persecution. From San Antonio, and various other parts of the United States thereafter, he campaigned for the overthrow of Díaz and a complete restructuring of Mexican society that would improve the lot of the country's working masses.[10]

No one knows exactly how many people moved into the United States during this era. According to one estimate, residents in the United States who were Mexico-born in 1900 and 1910 numbered 103,393 and 221,915, respectively. According to these figures, in 1900 some 71,000 Mexico-born people resided in Texas; 14,000 in Arizona; 8,000 in California; 6,600 in New Mexico; 274 in Colorado; and 3,150 in others parts of the United States. As of 1910, about 125,000 foreign-born Mexicans now made their home in Texas; 30,000 in Arizona; 34,000 in California; 12,000 in New Mexico; 2,600 in Colorado; and 19,000 in other regions of the country. No reliable figures exist for the overall 1900 and 1910 Mexican-American population.[11]

Culture in a Modernizing Society

While regions underwent rapid change, Mexican life therein remained grounded in generations-old customs. For one thing, immigration buttressed familiar standards. Wherever the immigrants settled, they nourished old cultural norms. Whether rich or poor, they carried on nationalist sentiments and native customs and moved to the forefront of preserving that way of life by efforts such as organizing fiestas patrias commemorations, founding fraternal and literary societies, and staging theatrical performances in Spanish.

Variables such as isolation from mainstream life also contributed to cultural retention, for most Mexican Americans lived in remote *ranchos* or segregated barrios where they had infrequent contact with Anglos. The niche that most *obreros* (workers) held at the bottom of the occupational ladder further distanced them from white people who refused doing "Mexican work." Government indifference also insulated Mexican *colonias* (Mexican urban communities made up of one or more barrios), for officials took only lukewarm initiatives such as those seen in northern cities to Americanize immigrant populations. Political officials looked on the Mexican-American community as a stepchild of society.

Racism similarly strengthened in-group behavior. People responded to ill-treatment and inclined to shun what they perceived to be crassness in Anglo life. Anglo-enforced patterns of racial segregation further minimized the contact working-class Mexicans had with Anglos, and Mexicans themselves might have preferred restricting contact to the workplace.

Ironically, such forces that heightened the preference for Mexican things at the same time led to problems of identity. During the last decades of the nineteenth century, Anglo boosters sought to promote tourism and immigration to California, and statehood for New Mexico and Arizona, by glorifying the region's Spanish legacy. Repeated emphasis on a Spanish past comprised of cultured and civilized "Spaniards" influenced many Mexican Americans to deny their "Mexican" roots.[12]

Whatever allegiance Mexicans had toward their heritage, modification inevitably occurred. The Southwest became increasingly Americanized after the 1880s. Anglos consolidated their political and economic clout and introduced new accoutrements: consumer products, foods, fashions, and recreational forms, for example. Mexican Americans entered Anglo situations more frequently, among them fledgling mining towns, modern farms, growing urban centers where Anglos enjoyed a significant majority, and new environments in states outside the old borderlands.

Also, teachers introduced Mexican-American children to the American dream in the public schools. Catholic Church instructors, many of them nuns, made it their commitment to replace Mexican customs with American ones. Protestant sects increased their initiatives during this epoch, establishing day and boarding schools where instructors taught Mexican-American children different modes of conduct and American attitudes toward gender roles, family life, comportment, and morality.[13]

Cultural transformation resulted, as indeed had been the case since the 1820s. In the towns some people absorbed English words into the Spanish vocabulary and even Anglicized their names. Northern New Mexican migrant workers accepted from former German soldiers living in Colorado their methods for making beer or potato pancakes. Mexican Americans sought upgrading their homes with modern windows and siding and pitched roofs, as well as factory-made furniture and domestic appliances. Farmers acquired new machinery to substitute for agricultural implements of an earlier generation. Common folks borrowed from American material culture such items as Victorian dresses and denim working attire.[14]

Modification also showed in the diverse views people took concerning their residence in the United States. By the latter years of the nineteenth century, several degrees of adapation existed. Some folks were "Mexican" on every count. These voices looked to Mexico as the dear motherland. They took an interest in the politics of the old country and gave support to proto-revolutionist Ricardo Flores Magón or Catarino Garza. The latter activist in 1891–92 invaded Mexican soil from south Texas in a failed effort to remove Díaz. Mexico's admirers argued against Americanization, fearing the formation of a community that amounted to neither Mexican nor American but a corruption of both heritages. Bicultural individuals claimed the United States to be their only country and worked for the right to reap of its fruits. They emphasized the learning of English for its practicality and stressed the immediate need to lobby Anglo-Americans so that they would recognize the validity of such programs as bilingual education in New Mexico. *México-Texano* and *la Colonia Hispano-Americana* were their self-designated terms.[15] Then there were those who were completely Americanized, as was the case with Miguel A. Otero, Jr., the New Mexican territorial governor from 1897 to 1906.

Intra- and Interstate Migration

During this time period Mexican Americans began fanning out from the old centers of population. The migratory and seasonal patterns of the Gilded Age and the early twentieth century involved new frontier movements that took Texas Mexicans toward central and east Texas farms, California Mexicans toward new agricultural estates in the San Joaquin Valley, and *nuevomexicanos* into railroads, mines, farms, sheep ranches, and cities of southern Colorado, and even into newer areas such as Utah.[16]

Simultaneously, immigrants from Mexico began working in Texas by the late nineteenth century. They cleared brush and performed stoop labor there, picking cotton and perishable goods. Thousands of workers from Sinaloa and Sonora flooded Arizona yearly, answering the call for copper miners and farmworkers around the Phoenix area, though many searched out better opportunities in the frontier regions of the territory. By the early twentieth century, hundreds of other immigrants were being lured into the fields of the midwestern United States, though in small numbers. By 1910 the lower midwestern United States had witnessed a sizable increase in the number of Mexicans; some 8,500 residents of Mexican origin lived in Kansas that year. Primarily, however, immigrants headed into the beet, cotton, citrus, and vegetable farms of southern California as well as the beet and vegetable fields of the South Platte Valley of Colorado. They also made their way into the coal-mining industry, heading toward the mines around Pueblo and Trinidad in Colorado; Gallup, New Mexico; Oklahoma; southern Texas; and southern Arizona.[17] Such diaspora invigorated the motherland's culture or spread it into new settings. The migrants repeated the cycle regularly and seldom severed ties with families and old friends or contacts with the original point of departure. Newly arrived immigrants generally integrated themselves into old and new Mexican-American communities.

As Mexicans pushed outwardly from their old strongholds in the Southwest, Anglos arrived there in increased numbers. South Texas became a magnet for new Anglo farmers, many of them from the Midwest, who within a few years in the early 1900s converted ranchland into farm acreage and diluted the overall population advantage that Mexicans previously held.[18] The same pattern of demographic change unfolded in New Mexico: Anglo-American life became more visible in old towns such as Albuquerque and to a lesser exent Santa Fe. By the early years of the twentieth century, the entire territory seemed destined for Americanization.[19] In southern California, where some of the Californios still influenced culture and managed a modicum of land ownership, a real estate boom in the 1880s that ushered in railroad building and new economic ventures undermined what remained of the old order. Los Angeles, for one, became an Anglo entreprenuerial city even as immigrants from Mexico entered it during the same period.[20] Arizona experienced the same transformation, as railroad expansion and new mines attracted easterners. By the late 1880s more Anglo-Americans lived in the territory than did Mexicans, and southern Arizona had been metamorphosed from a Mexican to an American region.[21]

In the Workplace

The developments of the Gilded Age restructured previous relations between Anglos and the Hispanic elite. Forces that had held the alliance together in the old ranching society—such as sexual disparities, the need to keep the lands productive, and the struggle against frontier obstacles—lost their cohesive power. There followed a realignment between the two groups; Anglos now increasingly dropped labels of "Spanish" and "Castilian" toward the hapless elite and lumped them into the general category of "Mexicans." Inter-cultural marriages declined.[22] Lost prestige, less opportunities to develop economic coalitions with Anglos, and fading political power to protect what remained from olden days became the fate of the old upper class in the time of transition.

Despite the oppressive forces of the era, Mexican Americans did gain from the new circumstances. Whether in Texas, New Mexico, Arizona, or California, the story of successful entrepreneurs could be duplicated many times over. Middle-class ranchers from the 1880s to the first decade of the twentieth century existed in the counties of south Texas, parts of southern California and southern Arizona, as well as in New Mexico's plains, where sheep men still owned land outright.[23] Other Mexicans with business acumen ferreted out attractive opportunities in the transformation. Some found their livelihood in a market based on an expanding Hispanic population. There further emerged old or newfound enclaves and agrarian settlements deriving from population dispersals or immigration from Mexico where a clientele demanded specific goods and services. Mexican districts in the larger cities (such as San Antonio, El Paso, Albuquerque, Los Angeles, and Santa Barbara) featured general mom and pop stores, funeral parlors, meat markets, bakeries, restaurants and bars, real estate agencies, newspaper offices, tailors, jewelry stores, apothecaries, lending agencies, labor-contracting firms, and numerous other kinds of small-scale operations.[24] The most successful of these merchants lived in Tucson.[25]

As a cohort, however, ranchers, businessmen, and professionals everywhere fought a battle for survival. The railroad rendered freighting obsolete, severely injuring merchants such as Tucson's Estévan Ochoa and Carlos Tully, who had monopolized commerce in the territory for years. Huge mining operations in southern Arizona with close connections to eastern capital easily outmuscled small mining outfits. The same things could be said about cattle and farming corporations with proper financial resources needed to improve breeds, feed stock in enclosed areas, experiment with new crops, and irrigate massive acreage. In New Mexico and Arizona government regulations designed to protect the public lands disabled Hispanic stockmen, who could no longer graze their sheep in ranges they had relied on for generations. Speculators, squatters, farmers, irrigation enterprises, land companies, real estate developers, and others wishing to turn a profit all moved in to harass whomever had survived the dispossession that followed the conquest.[26]

Concentration in lower-level occupations remained the fate for the greater bulk of the Mexican-American community. Many still lived on ranches working cattle, though now as seasonal wage workers—an arrangement strikingly different from that which prevailed before the decline of the range industry. Only in scattered ranches of south Texas and southern Arizona and in the rural society of southern Colorado and northern New Mexico did vestiges of the old paternalism persist. In northern New Mexico *patrones* in rural communities still honored the mutual obligation to care for the work force, though the practice, which existed in various structural arrangements, began dissipating by the early 1900s, when modernizing forces linked to the railroad, timber, and mining industries displaced the leadership role of the old *patrón* and altered traditional community life. *Partidarios* who had previously worked sheep on shares with the hope of amassing their own herds now faced a life of debt, beholden as wage workers to Anglo sheep owners.[27]

The majority of agricultural hands worked in large farms or agribusiness estates. Others eked out a living as migratory sheep-herders and sheep-shearers, traveling for wages in crews of families and friends throughout the Southwest, but also as far as Nevada, Wyoming, and Utah. Others jumped from region to region or across states to clear lands, or plant, thin, and harvest vegetables at picking times. The migratory cycle could well take a California family to pick lettuce in the north from March to December and force them down to southern California for a new lettuce crop the same year. Other agricultural hands found employment in the related industries of packing and canning.[28]

The market-driven economy created a variety of new jobs that required vast numbers of workers, and Mexicans filled the need. Mexicans helped in building the infrastructure in the Midwest and Southwest, working in track and section maintenance as well as the railroad yards. In the coal mines Mexicans cut wood, performed general tasks, or extracted the minerals with crude tools. Mexican workers also moved into lumber towns and camps to work the saw mills.[29]

In the cities Mexican workers took jobs as day laborers, cooks and waiters, porters, gardeners, janitors, butchers, cigar-makers, brick-layers, plasterers, construction and pick and shovel workers, smelter workers, and pecan-shellers. Those who had made their way into Kansas and Nebraska by 1910 worked in railroad shops and meat-packing plants. More skilled workers took jobs as clerks and pressmen.[30]

Urbanization

Urbanization became a byproduct of the age of transition. Towns emerged as centers of railroad, mining, timbering, and ranching activity, and they underwent architectural, technological, and social and culture changes. City officials redrew old boundaries; one marked alteration involved the relegation of old historic city sections to secondary significance. Los Angeles and Santa Barbara, for example, saw the old pueblos either engulfed by the new cityscape or partly destroyed by expansion. Urbanization had similar impacts on cities such as Tucson and Albuquerque, as new Anglo neighborhoods adjoined the old plazas, and San Antonio and El Paso.[31]

With such change, barrios become more visible. New immigrants arrived in San Antonio, El Paso, Los Angeles, Santa Barbara, Kansas City, Kansas, and numerous towns throughout the Southwest, searching for work in the railroads and budding urban industries. With the decline of the *rancho* (and its traditions of providing year-around support for its hands), furthermore, people became citybound, also hoping for employment, or at the very least a residence from which they might undertake seasonal excursions to the farmlands. Because Anglo-American officials and urban folks preferred racial segregation (and enforced it de facto), the patterns of barrioization that surfaced after the conquest accelerated. City governments neglected the needs of the barrios' underemployed or poorly paid inhabitants, and mean conditions resulted: squalor, poverty, dismal housing, overcrowding, disease, flooding, crime, and vice. The poorest housing consisted of *jacales*, though in New Mexico and parts of Texas huts built of adobe adjoined these makeshift structures. Ordinarily, such crude dwellings lacked sanitary facilities, so that residents used outside privies and improvised at cooking and acquiring water for daily consumption. Most endured the unpredictability of weather conditions, braving extreme cold or heat and heavy rains and snow.[32]

Despite these problems, however, barrios acted as space for the distillation and continuation of ethnic culture, territories wherein Mexicans could be among their own kind and interact in solidarity, using familiar language and customs. The enclaves provided informal mechanisms required for survival. Within their confines lived fellow Mexicans who were acquainted with Anglos known to be friendly toward the hiring of Mexicans, with house lots where tents might be pitched or *jacales* might be erected, or with the doctors or midwives needed in emergencies.[33]

Mexican workers laying track during the construction of Los Angeles's inter-urban railway system, ca. 1903. Photograph reprinted by permission of the Huntington Library, San Marino, California.

Jim Crow in the Southwest

Anglo-American attitudes redolent of those pervasive in the decades following the conquest remained in place even as the age of the frontier passed. Anchored in racist sentiments, anthropological beliefs, class conflicts, and pressing laboring needs, prejudice expressed itself in remarks regarding skin color and physiognomy and a wide range of stereotypical notions about Mexicans. American officials, for instance, still considered Mexicans the embodiment of backwardness, an alien people unwilling to accept the American system of government and education. Whites looked on Mexicans as carriers of a decadent streak, displayed first hand in the indolence, crime, gambling, prostitution, and other vices plaguing urban neighborhoods or villages in the countryside. Mexicans were still considered a contemptible lot, and at least two legislators, J. T. Canales of Texas and another from Colorado (presumably Casimiro Barela), were considered no less than "greasers" by Anglo detractors.[34] In California attitudes toward Mexicans produced sentiments negating the mixed-bloods' role in the state's history. In novels, short stories, new histories, and even reminiscences, Anglos and nostalgic Californios in the 1880s and 1890s created a "Spanish fantasy heritage," the myth of an arcadian California of Catholic missions, genteel dons, lavish fiestas, and everything else associated with "Spanish" civilization.[35] Literary romanticizers also formed a similar image of New Mexico during this era. According to recent researchers, statehood advocates joined them in fostering the myth, publicizing a territory inhabited almost exclusively by cultured descendants of Iberian colonizers.[36]

Prejudice could also be found in violent encounters and in the subtleties of the legal system. Small riots that pitted Mexicans against Anglos erupted in Texas during the 1880s and 1890s, and lynchings with racial motives occurred throughout the Southwest: lynch mobs hung Francisco Torres in southern California in 1892, and as late as 1910 and 1911 white mobs killed two Mexicans in Texas. In each of these cases, the victims were accused of having killed white folks.[37] Less conspicuously, Mexicans dealt with police brutality, exclusion from juries, disproportionate rates of conviction for criminal violations, skepticism about their loyalty, suppression of political activity, and infringement on their rights of free speech. Nativism flared up periodically: bad economic times in the 1890s produced drives to prevent Catholics and immigrants in Arizona from holding office or from being hired in specific types of jobs thought to displace Anglo workers. In the early 1900s American officials responding to requests from Mexican government representatives hounded Ricardo Flores Magón in Texas, Missouri, and California until the Los Angeles police department in 1907 jailed him for violating the neutrality laws.[38]

Political Losses and Gains

Reinforced by population increases, capital, the power of corporations, law-enforcement agencies, and the backing of state and territorial officials, Anglos tightened their control on political institutions, almost to the extent of the Mexicans' total exclusion.[39] In areas where Mexican people predominated, such as the counties of south Texas, northern New Mexico, and southern Colorado, Anglos formed coalitions with Mexican-American elites that handicapped the masses from organizing effectively. Additionally, Anglo power brokers launched organized efforts to prevent any one Mexican leader or bloc from becoming too powerful. Bossism and the manipulation of the Mexican vote continued until Progressive reforms and newcomer farmers, merchants, Protestants, railroad corporations, and timber companies attempted the overthrow of the old Anglo order. But the new arrivals also employed their own devices for controlling the Mexican electorate, including the poll tax and white-only primaries in Texas.[40]

Whether Mexicans lived in majority or minority surroundings, working within mainstream politics remained the most reasonable option for achieving goals and pursuing interests. As before, the most active politicos derived from the ranks of the more privileged. By the last years of the nineteenth century, Mexican-American communities contained leaders quite familiar with American politics, having been prepared for participation by fledgling schools, churches, and other enculturating agencies. White society may actually have conceded these leadership roles to Mexicans as a way of controlling separated communities.[41]

Mexican-American community activists recognized the need for political involvement to ensure self-preservation. Periodically, they organized factions or "tickets" that offered constituents some ethnic representation. Spokesmen implored Mexican Americans to rally behind Mexican slates and rid themselves of bossism and the corruption of unprincipled officials, lawyers, and the new monopolies. In 1892 newspapermen in New Mexico came together in Las Vegas to found *La Prensa Asociada Hispano-Americana*. The founders sought the establishment of a collective group devoted to protecting the interests of Mexican Americans and preserving Hispanic culture. That same year an El Paso newspaper urged Mexican Americans in every state of the Southwest to organize as one unit and press for rights owed them under the constitution.[42]

People belonged to both major national parties, and political clubs such as Club Mexicano Republicano and Club Demócrato Mexicano surfaced in many areas where Mexicans lived, although the Hispanos of New Mexico were inclined toward the Republican party since Republican presidents presided over the Gilded and Progressive eras and controlled patronage in the territory.[43] It was not irregular for political conflict involving Mexicans on opposing sides to break out. Such intra-ethnic episodes included the Laredo City Election Riot of 1886 and a string of political assassinations in New Mexico between the 1880s and the early twentieth century. Some of the conflicts were sparked by conservative leaders' opposition to the radicalism of Ricardo Flores Magón.[44]

Sentiments were also divided when the United States initiated the Spanish-American War in 1898. Some Spanish-language newspaper editors in the Southwest supported Spain, and others warned Cubans of American domination, but most Mexican Americans rallied behind the American intervention once Congress proclaimed war against Spain. Leading politicians like Miguel A. Otero, Jr., and Casimiro Barela called on their compatriots to rally behind the flag, and hundreds of Mexican Americans responded. Some of them served as part of Teddy Roosevelt's Rough Riders, including Maximiliano Luna of New Mexico who fought valiantly at San Juan Hill.[45]

Political gains accrued despite internal division and the clout of Anglo-American opponents. Advances were confined primarily to local levels, however. Mexicans served as city councilmen, county judges, or commissioners and policemen, sheriffs, and chiefs of police.[46] Others received federal appointments to custom houses and postal departments. Still, exceptions to the rule of local incumbency were numerous. In New Mexico several Hispanos retained seats in the territorial House and Council. There also, Amado Chávez became the first superintendent of public instruction in 1892, followed later in the early twentieth century by J. Francisco Chávez. Hispanic politicians such as Salomón Luna participated in New Mexico's constitutional convention of 1910 (Hispanics constituted approximately one-third of the 100 delegates), and, as mentioned earlier, Miguel A. Otero, Jr., held the position of territorial governor from 1897 to 1906. Though generally regarded as an Americanized politico of Mexican descent (born of an Anglo mother and educated in the East), Otero maintained a respectable following among Mexican Americans; he curried this support by concerning himself with problems common people encountered at the local level and by intervening on behalf of Mexicans who periodically brushed with the law. Colorado had legislators such as Casimiro Barela; California had state senator Reginaldo del Valle; and Texas had J. T. Canales, as mentioned earlier. In Arizona, Mariano Samaniego served as a territorial legislator from 1880 until Arizona became a state in 1912.[47] Politicians of national prominence included Félix Martínez, a former county official, territorial legislator, and newspaper man from New Mexico who, after moving to El Paso in 1899, earned a reputation during the William Howard Taft presidency (1909–13) and later as a respected negotiator in international affairs with Latin America and Spain.[48]

By no means did these examples of successful politicians signify empowerment for the rank-and-file, however. Even in New Mexico where so many Hispanos served in the territorial legislature, the more powerful posts in the executive and judicial branches went to Anglo appointees, beholden thereafter to Washington, D.C., and not to the people they represented.[49]

Popular Uprisings

As had been the case following the conquest, Mexican Americans did not accept their condition of subordination but engaged in individual and mass resistance. Gone were the likes of the old western figures such as Juan Cortina, Joaquín Murieta, and Tiburcio Vásquez, but newer "heroes" emerged. Among them were Gregorio Cortez in Texas and Juan José Herrera and Elfego Baca in New Mexico. Baca achieved prominence in western annals following a shoot-out with Anglos in San Francisco (modern-day Reserve) in 1884, though in his subsequent career as a mainstream politician and lawyer he balanced conservative causes with commitments to the Hispano community. Denunciation of mistreatment and racism also emanated from the professional and intellectual segments of the Mexican-American community. In newspaper columns and in creative literature, this element decried discriminatory treatment.[50]

Mexicans also expressed discontent through mass uprisings. Community upheaval occurred primarily in New Mexico, for in contrast to other regions in the Southwest, Mexican Americans continued living in isolated but self-supporting communities and small farmlands. One major confrontation between Anglo intruders and villagers erupted on soil belonging to the Maxwell Land Grant and Railway Company of England. When the company acquired the property in 1870, it inherited problems with both Mexican and American settlers who claimed the right to live within the original grant by virtue of their residence since the days when the grant's claim had been in dispute.

Disagreement and drawn-out sniping and violence among the various residents followed, with Mexican villagers who saw encroachment as disruptive to their lives and property caught in the middle. No real political agenda coalesced the Mexican villagers in their long skirmish with the outsiders: resistance revolved around their desire to retain their self-sufficent way of life. When efforts began in earnest during the late 1880s to evict them from their lands, *pobladores* resisted law-enforcement officials by using force, by intimidating company agents, and by rustling the company's livestock and destroying its crops and property. By the early 1890s, however, the physical struggle and court litigation had taxed many of the Mexican resisters and they found the company's offer of leases an attractive option. By 1900 the Maxwell Company had gained the upper hand.[51]

Equally significant were the troubles in San Miguel County, where poor people sought to retain the rights to their common lands from new claimants, the Las Vegas Land Cattle Company. In 1889 masked riders calling themselves Las Gorras Blancas (White Caps, in reference to their masks) attacked railroad lines, cut down ranch fences, and sabotaged the farm machinery of large ranchers. Ordinary folks and local leaders from villages that grazed stock or raised crops on the common lands, members of the national labor union the Knights of Labor (which saw the Las Vegas Company as a speculative venture wanting to deprive common folks of their communal lands), and even adventurers constituted the ranks of Las Gorras. Their stated objective was "to protect the rights of the people in general and especially those of the helpless classes."[52]

In 1890 the Gorras converted themselves into a political party under the name El Partido del Pueblo Unido (People's party). Its rank-and-file remained the poor people, but leadership fell to an alliance of middle-class Hispanos such as Juan José Herrera, a well-educated man and former labor organizer in Colorado, and to members of the Knights of Labor to which Herrera belonged. For a time the Partido saw electoral successes, but it fell to disagreement between the middle-class spokespersons and the constituency. It also began losing the support of more idealistic Knight members reluctant to be associated with a party inclined to condone violence as a means of redress. Soon the Partido faced strong denunciation from conservative Hispano elements in the region. Furthermore, it failed to bring a change of heart among the Las Vegas Company or the railroads, and the territorial legislature in 1903 passed a a law depriving the Hispano settlers from the right to use the communal lands.[53]

Early Labor Struggles

The economic transformation and the concomitant proletarization of laborers produced incipient labor struggles in protest of discriminatory wages and miserable conditions in the workplace. By the 1880s Mexicans from Texas to California had developed a penchant for joining labor organizations (including the Knights of Labor and the American Federation of Labor), though Anglo-dominated locals tended to discourage their membership. Strikes became part of the rising consciousness. In Texas they broke out sporadically but throughout the state: in the Panhandle, the Galveston area, Thurber, Laredo, and El Paso.[54]

In Los Angeles, Mexican trackmen, many of them immigrants belonging to the Unión Federal Mexicana, in 1903 struck for higher wages against the streetcar lines of the Pacific Electric railroad. Though showing tenacity, the strikers ultimately failed when management hired strike breakers and intimidated sympathetic Anglo workers who contemplated joining the strike.[55] In the rural regions Mexican farmworkers staged strikes around Fresno, San Francisco, and Redlands between 1901 and 1903. In Oxnard, also, Mexicans allied themselves with Japanese workers in the beet fields and in 1903 won a slight victory in wages, recruitment practices, and policies at the company store. Packers and sheep-shearers in Santa Barbara also struck against their respective industries for higher wages and shorter hours during the first decade of the twentieth century, albeit with mixed successes.[56]

In the Southwest mines Mexicans participated in a number of work stoppages to protest subsistence wages and dangerous conditions. Strikes broke out in Colorado between 1901 and 1904 and in Arizona in 1886 and later in the summer of 1903. The cause for the latter incident revolved around actions by the Arizona legislature (prompted by Anglo union workers) prohibiting mining companies from employing laborers for more than eight hours. Management complied with the law but reduced wages (miners had assumed they would receive the same salary for the shorter hours as they had for the 10-hour day). Mexican workers walked out in protest on 2 June, and conducted armed demonstrations in Morenci, but torrential rains and the arrival of Arizona Rangers, U.S. soldiers, and the National Guard effectively suppresed the strike, and leading Mexican participants were imprisoned.[57]

In later years miners found particular inspiration from the work of the previously mentioned Mexican exile, Ricardo Flores Magón, founder of the Partido Liberal Mexicano (PLM) and editor of the newspaper *Regeneración*, which published from different parts of the United States after 1904. In addition to urging Porfirio Díaz's removal, Flores Magón's PLM advocated a labor platform that emphasized maximum hours and minimum wages, an end to child labor, and improvement of conditions in the workplace. Appropriate to Mexican Americans, the PLM railed against their second-class status, racist practices, and the inequality of the justice system.[58]

The Family in Transition

Most Mexican Americans remained faithful to traditional familial understandings, even as the family unit experienced change. They mostly lived in nuclear households, shunned divorce, and maintained old kinship ties with extended family members. Deep regard for *compadres* and *padrinos* remained, and godparents dutifully performed their roles of caring for their godchildren during troubled times. Families expected to rely on *compadres* in times of desperation, as when young mothers required extra assistance with small children if husbands left for migratory work, when the family needed to be separated because contagious diseases threatened the household, or when temporary unemployment proved burdensome on the family budget.[59] Also, many Mexican Americans supported the values of patriarchy and other ideals that proved restrictive to women. Women were to be chaste and, upon marriage, faithful to their role of caring wives and mothers and subservient to the male head of the household. Still, recorded instances exist of women challenging the subordinated role prescribed for them,[60] and by this time arranged marriages became an anachronism.

As the frontier declined and the Southwest made the transition toward modernity, Mexicanos attuned familial arrangements to immediate sociological circumstances. Tejanos, as an example, reduced the number of dependents previously supported by the household.[61] But family life during this era moved away from previous expectations for other reasons. Partly, although this is difficult to measure, change resulted from the impact of American institutions. Children learned new ideas at school, and Mexican girls, especially the few who came under the care of Protestant missionaries, received instructions on Anglo notions of child-rearing and domesticity and survival in a changing world.[62]

To maintain the tradition of staying at home, some women rented out space to guests in their household. Others did embroidering, quilting, or ironing for pay. But modern economic life increasingly forced women to supplement the income of main wage earners who faced underemployment or migrant work. Many of the newer occupations of the late nineteenth century also proved to be dangerous, especially work in the mines and railroad construction, and they left increasing numbers of widows and orphans. For these and other reasons the number of female-headed households rose during the period.[63]

Women joined the proletariat as domestics, laundresses, or seamstresses; as field migrants shuttling from farm to farm picking cotton, beets, vegetables, nuts, or fruits; or, in the case of California, as packing-house and cannery workers in the local towns. In the villages of northern New Mexico and southern Colorado wives also accepted roles as washerwomen, cooks, and domestics. But they likewise assumed jobs that required relocation to new railroad towns, mining camps, or lumber companies. Such new occupations summarily uprooted them from traditional reliance on communal lands.[64]

Politically, women still lived with notions that they ought not to infringe on what was deemed a man's domain. Male society did not tolerate women taking activist roles; nonetheless, women had memberships in mutual aid societies (frequently parallel women's clubs) or participated in the social affairs of such organizations. Women activists included Tejanas such as Sara Estela Ramírez, a poet and essayist from Laredo, who played an organizing role in south Texas on behalf of Ricardo Flores Magón's PLM in the early 1900s. Only a fraction of the Mexican-American community fully supported the suffragist movement during the Gilded Age, though some men did campaign on behalf of the women's franchise. When Mexicanas gained the vote in Colorado in 1893, they assumed roles as officeholders and political candidates.[65]

Little is known about the lives of women belonging to middle-class families. Wives and daughters of successful businessmen, professionals, and *rancheros* enjoyed certain perquisites only vaguely imaginable to the rest of the population. They crossed into Mexico for apparel and luxuries and in some cases conducted long-distance mail ordering from such New York City department stores as Bloomingdale's. They could afford to have stylish dresses made for special occasions and purchase expensive jewelry and perfumes. Daughters attended prestigious schools, either in Mexico or the United States, or vacationed or traveled in both countries.[66] Numerous cases exist of single women or widows owning property or managing and working their own land with the help of children or hired hands.[67]

Religion

While Mexican Americans who lived across the Southwest during this era differed from one another in broader terms, the great majority belonged to an ethnic community loyal to fully defined customs, traditions, and cultural forms. Suspicious of an unfriendly Anglo-American society, clustered in segregated enclaves, and preferring the ways of their community to those outside it, they sought to carry on the shared experience rooted in Mexican life, yet altered or adjusted for survival in the mainstream American culture.

The preponderance of Mexicanos remained loyal to the Catholic Church. Whether adherents of orthodox Catholicism or folk variants, they generally observed specific religious holidays. They joined religious organizations like the Sociedad de María and prayer groups at the local parish. Women participated in this activism to an equal degree as men.

The majority of Mexican Americans still believed in the ritual of a church wedding, but the Southwest remained isolated, and only irregularly did itinerant priests tour rural areas and the barrios to officiate blessings of common-law arrangements, baptize children, and hear confessions. Mexicans still resented having to pay high marriage fees to the clergy, while urban residents by the 1880s came to accept a more secular view on the marital state and tended to be more tolerant of marrying before a justice of the peace.[68]

Mexicanos also gave credence to the intercession of certain saints and even the healing powers of *curanderos*. Indeed, it was in the 1890s and early twentieth century when two of the most famous *curanderos* practiced their calling as healers—Don Pedrito Jaramillo in Texas and Santa Teresa in Arizona, both of whom immigrated from Mexico. Reportedly, each produced miraculous cures, and their reputation spread far beyond the immediate area of their activity.[69]

Meanwhile, Protestant sects intensified their efforts to convert Mexicans. Methodists and Presbyterians seemed to have been especially animated, though they were not very successful in Arizona, Colorado, and California. In Texas, however, devoted Protestant proselytizers rode horseback over hundreds of miles, holding outdoor preaching sessions and training evangelists. In northern New Mexico, Presbyterian educators erected a number of such missionary posts. By the turn of the century Protestant chapels of every denomination could be found throughout the Southwest.[70]

Education

Though state governments neglected the educational needs of Mexican-American youngsters, the historical record indicates that Mexican-American parents desired the educational uplifting of their children. Public school systems languished in the early stages of development during this period (New Mexico did not establish an effective public school system until 1891), but Anglo communities took local initiatives to establish schools, though the ones designated for Mexicans tended to be dilapidated and segregated. Curricula varied, but programs in Mexican schools emphasized learning English and fundamental arithmetic, as well as virtues like thriftiness, honesty, and hygiene. A few children attended private academies.[71]

The Catholic Church also attempted the education of Mexican children through parochial schools in larger cities. There the Church sought to propagate the faith, ward off the influence of Protestant missionary schools or the public school system, and teach basic courses in grammar, civics, and arithmetic.[72] Meanwhile, the Protestants pushed their own mission schools, using innovative methods and devising plans of instruction specifically for the Spanish-speaking, or for training Mexican-American teachers who could then go on to spread the Protestant word within barrios. In New Mexico (and southern Colorado) the Protestants appeared to have had a special zeal for instruction; by the mid-1880s they had established some 33 missionary schools in New Mexico that tended to more than 1,000 children. Mission women seemed especially determined to train Mexican-American children, primarily girls, and transform them into productive members of society.[73]

Well-to-do Mexicans pursued advanced education by finding appropriate academies or state institutions (such as Texas University) in the larger cities or schools in the eastern United States or in Mexico. J. T. Canales of Brownsville, Texas, for instance, received his law degree from Michigan in 1899, while Maximiliano Luna and Amado Chávez of New Mexico went to Georgetown University in the 1880s. Others attended the University of Notre Dame.[74]

Mutual Aid Societies

Mutual aid societies, which first surfaced across the Southwest during the 1870s, now became a fixture of many communities. Their ubiquity resulted, in part, from the increase of migration from Mexico, as the foreign-born now improvised in the new setting (especially towns) at finding ways to replace established family networks or the paternalistic system found in the *ranchos* or haciendas in the old country. These fraternal lodges offered assistance to poor people in the form of insurance, health, and funeral benefits. They acted as a type of support group for a people sharing a common background and condition in the United States. Deliberations were conducted in the language of their membership, and often organizations chose the names of Mexican heroes after which to title their societies.[75]

The largest of these organizations became the Alianza Hispano-Americana, founded in Arizona in 1894 by a cadre of prominent men in Tucson. It endeavored to advance the condition of Mexicanos and protect the Mexican-American community from hostile Anglo society. Its appeal spread first throughout Arizona and then California by the early 1900s, primarily among middle-class leaders who desired to see sickness and unemployment insurance benefits applied to the Mexican community. Politically, it steered a centrist course emphasizing fraternity, brotherhood, and cultural pride.[76]

In addition to benefit societies, nonpolitical clubs including patriotic, recreative, literary, and labor associations gained headway in Mexican-American communities. In the 1890s Los Angeles featured organizations with names like El Club Filarmónico Mexicano, El Club Musical Hispano-Americano, and El Club Estudiantil Hispano-Americano.[77]

Literature

As in the pre-1880 era, literature found its major manifestation in the oral tradition. For the common man, *corridos* remained popular as a vehicle for orally narrating historical events and other matters of significance to the community. Through *corridos,* singers told of magnificent weddings, of lovers befallen by tragedy, of historic events, and of courageous figures. In Texas *corridos* took on unique themes related to life along the border, specifically ethnic friction. "El corrido de Gregorio Cortez," for instance, narrated the tribulations of a tenant farmer named Gregorio Cortez who in 1901 faced the threat of lynch law after killing a peace officer in a misunderstanding. *Corridos* also acted as mechanisms for survival, a medium for releasing emotional frustration, or a way through which Mexican Americans demonstrated a longing for the old and the familiar.[78]

The proliferation of Spanish-language newspapers in the latter decades of the century provided a new forum for group expression. The number of newspapers publishing for a Spanish-speaking audience increased during the era as the sizes of settlements expanded, as educated men from Mexico set up journals for the good of local enclaves, and as small community learning centers and religious schools instructed their students in the Spanish language.[79] Newspapers ordinarily limited themselves to publishing local-interest stories (meetings of benefit societies, news about social activities, the *fiestas patrias*), disseminating information from government sources or fellow newspapers, and issuing advice to readers concerning comportment, education, patriotism, and the like.

Many newspapers, however, took bold political stands. *La voz de la mujer* in El Paso (1907) and *El Obrero* in San Antonio (1909), both founded by Mexican women, campaigned for the downfall of Don Porfirio. Other newspapers focused on community discontent with Anglo discrimination. Carlos I. Velasco of Tucson's *El Fronterizo* (1878–1914), for instance, regularly editorialized against injustice, and he used his newspaper as a vehicle for campaigning on behalf of the rights of the Spanish-speaking. Editors denounced disparaging portrayals of Mexicans in the United States and sought to paint a more positive image of Mexicanos.[80] Newspapers also took partisan positions on political issues, as did *La Voz del Pueblo* in Las Vegas, New Mexico, a staunch defender of Las Gorras Blancas and of the Partido del Pueblo Unido.[81] Other points heatedly debated by editors of the Spanish-language press included disenfranchisement, exclusion from jury duty, segregated or second-class education, secular versus religious schooling, racism, disloyalty, and the merits of statehood in Arizona and New Mexico. Topics about women also came in for discussion, as women activists wrote editorials or columns on feminist issues.[82]

Those writing for the Spanish-language *prensas* reflected on the circumstances of their times, often recording in verse and short stories their feelings about land theft, discriminatory politics, banditry, culture, nationalism, and

Americanization. Other pieces of literature, however, targeted only the public's reading pleasure, and elaborated on prosaic topics that touched on chivalry, bravery, love, or abstract themes such as liberty.[83]

Some authors brought out fiction in serial form through newspapers, while others published theirs privately (some works never saw print). Manuel M. Salazar of New Mexico is recognized as the first to have a Mexican-American novel published; it went by the title of *La historia de un caminante, o sea Gervacio y Aurora* (*A Traveler's History; or, Gervacio and Aurora* [1881]), which chronicled the amorous life of the protagonist Gervacio.[84] Among the best know of the era's novelists was Eusebio Chacón, an extremely literate (he held a law degree from Notre Dame), multitalented *nuevomexicano* with a gift for oratory and a passion for his Hispanic culture. His novels *El hijo de la tempestad* (*Son of the Storm*) and *Tras la tormenta la calma* (*The Calm after the Storm*), both published in 1892, discussed the outlawry of the era and the theme of honor, respectively.[85] Chacón's contemporary Manuel C. de Baca wrote *Historia de Vicente Silva y sus cuarenta bandidos, sus crimenes y retribuciones* (*The Story of Vicente Silva and His Forty Bandits, Their Crimes and Retributions*), which was published in 1896; it indicted a callous bandit leader named Vicente Silva who, for personal gain (along with his 40 thieves), preyed on his own people during the 1890s.[86] Additionally, there exists a rather weak novel by María Amparo Ruíz Burton under the pen name of C. Loyal titled *The Squatter and the Don: A Novel Description of Contemporary Occurrences in California* (1885).[87] The *nuevomexicanos* produced a more recognizable harvest of literature than did their counterparts in other parts of the Southwest, owing in part to the greater size of the Hispanic population, the cultural influence that Hispanos wielded in the territory, and the sizable number of Spanish-language newspapers there. More literary societies were to be found in New Mexico than any other part of the Southwest.[88]

Nonfiction during this period did not match the quality of the creative works. Only a handful of individuals wrote autobiographies, and even fewer published them. Exceptions include José Policarpo Rodríguez whose "The Old Guide": His Life in His Own Words recapped his story as a man of many trades, including Protestant missionary work, and Rafael Chacón who in *Memories* (1906–12) reminisced about the tribulations Hispanos encountered after U.S. rule, about life as a soldier in the Civil War, and the struggles he faced on the frontier to keep his family alive following his move to Colorado in the late 1860s. Juan de Toro, a newspaper man, in 1882 issued his *Brief Sketch of the Colonization of California and the Foundation of the Pueblo of Our Lady of Los Angeles* to commemorate the centennary of Los Angeles's founding. Additionally, there existed a plethora of literary works in the form of newspaper editorials or essays. Primarily the fruits of the more literate middle and upper classes, their subjects ranged from proper citizenship to the need to preserve the Spanish language and Mexican customs, but they also included the necessity to learn the English language and to participate in mainstream affairs. Biculturalism, in short, became a matter for discourse by the late nineteenth and early twentieth centuries.[89]

As the Southwest drove toward modernity, communities still held traditional *pastorelas* (Christmas plays), especially *Los Pastores*, and sponsored other kinds of folk performances, usually under the aegis of a local family or group. But the traveling theatrical groups that made their way from northern Mexico into the

Southwest during the 1870s began performing with increased frequency (usually on Sunday evenings) in Laredo and San Antonio in Texas, in southern New Mexico, and around the Tucson region, as well as in southern California. The Carlos Villalongín Company stands out as one of the most prominent of these traveling companies. The high point of theatrical groups' contribution to the Hispanic theater, however, would not come until after the Mexican Revolution of 1910.[90]

Toward the Twentieth Century

A new economic order led by industrialists and farming corporations replaced the old frontier economy that westering merchants, army personnel, land lawyers, and Mexican-American elites had ushered in at mid-century. Emerging economic concerns—railroads, mining, sheep-raising, and farming—appealed for multitudes of laborers, and those heeding the cry included both native-born Mexicans and others crossing the international border into El Norte. Capitalists preferred a tractable labor pool willing to accept low wages under trying conditions and, equally desirable, one that could be hectored into rebuffing political or union-organizing drives. At the most basic level, both natives and immigrants devised appropriate responses to the rapidly changing order. For example, men took up migratory work as a means of sustaining their families the year around. Women adjusted spousal roles commensurately, either filling in as heads of the household or assuming new kinds of work. Talk of accepting the ways of the Anglos began to be voiced publicly. Americanization would enhance not only individual goals but ultimately the full integration of Mexicans into the American mainstream. At the group stratum, Mexicanos organized lobbying rings, joined mutual aid societies, or even supported Las Gorras Blancas, Ricardo Flores Magón, or Gregorio Cortez.

The forces being unleashed by the new age, therefore, hardly threw communities into disarray. Unique situations such as those in Tucson and northern New Mexico provided auspicious circumstances for a distinguished cadre of entrepreneurs and politicians (respectively) to make good. Just about every community, however impoverished, had mechanisms in place to maintain that enclave's viability—stores, patriotic associations, entertainment forms, access to Spanish-language newspapers, schooling facilities, churches, and certainly an informal network for assisting friends and neighbors to find work or emergency care. Such internally devised structures would sustain Mexicans into the rest of the twentieth century when the travail that beset most people intensified.

five

The New Colonias: Development, Dispersal, and Diversification

By the 1910s a fully matured market economy existed throughout the old Mexican settlements in the Southwest, as it did across the United States. So did the new inventions: electricity, telephones, automobiles, movies, trolley cars, paved roads, and other modern accoutrements that accompanied the new urbanization. Politics, meanwhile, still emphasized white supremacy and control. Though reformers, the Progressives of the early twentieth century were too much driven by the moral principles of Anglo-Americans, while Republican party supremacy in the 1920s thrived on a conservative political mood. Society became increasingly nativist, racist, and intolerant. During this epoch the country experienced race riots and the "Red Scare," and saw the rising influence of eugenicists, the Ku Klux Klan, and anti-union ideas.

At the same time, people from Mexico in unprecedented numbers trekked across the international boundary, giving old ethnic communities in the United States fresh injections of immigrant culture. Simultaneously, industrial and agricultural firms in the Midwest, as well as almost all states in the trans-Mississippi, solicited Mexican workers (both foreign- and native-born). Permanent and stable settlements far north of the borderlands resulted.

The repercussions of the new immigration meant far more than increased numbers. The new arrivals suspended, at least momentarily, the direction of ethnic adjustment and evolution that had been under way since 1848. Americanization persisted, naturally, but only within a lean segment of the population, for the newcomers outnumbered native-born Mexican Americans and rejected the legitimacy of American institutions (many of them waited for trouble to subside in Mexico so they could return). Ideological cleavages between the native- and foreign-born thus arose over such issues as politics, patriotism, and citizenship. Ethnic and nationalist differences became a standard characteristic of Hispanic communities. An understanding of their "Mexican" identity, a faith in certain tenets of Mexico's culture, and a common group experience with Anglo discrimination, however, welded the community in solidarity.

The New Industries

Historical processes unfurled in the nation's economy during the early twentieth century. The switch to dry-farming techniques and the federal subsidiza-
tion of new reclamation projects during the era turned previously unproductive lands into fertile fields. Throughout the country by the 1920s, the farms of
the modern age became agribusiness estates resembling rural factories that
required huge numbers of mobile, cheap, and not necessarily skilled workers
to pick an assortment of crops, including cotton, beets, and a variety of vegetables.[1] Railroads expanded also, reaching their apogee into the trans-
Mississippi during the late 1910s. The growing popularity of the motor vehicle
caused a decline of railroad construction by the 1920s, but the automobile
industry created newer types of work in the country's infrastructure.[2] The
exploitation of minerals also saw intensification, though this was localized to
regions such as southeastern Arizona and the Central Plains states.[3] The most
dramatic transformation in the U.S. economy during the era occurred in
industry, with states in the Great Lakes region, among others in the North,
seeing expansion in firms manufacturing steel, rubber, automobiles, and elec-
trical products.[4]

Mexicans Answer the Call

The immigration trends of the late nineteenth century peaked during the first
three decades of the 1900s, owing in part to revolutionary troubles in Mexico,
labor shortages created by World War I, and continued demand for Mexican
workers by a flourishing U.S. economy. In the case of pushing factors, the
movement to oust the dictator Porfirio Díaz in 1910 initiated bloody strife that
destabilized the political order in Mexico until the 1920s. As people of Mexico
endured revolution and reconstruction, the United States economy issued
enticing offers for an improved life. Since the late nineteenth century, immigration statutes had attempted to keep out foreigners. During the 1880s a
series of laws imposed a head tax on people wanting to come to America, prohibited the immigration of anyone who might become a burden on society,
and barred the contracting of foreign laborers. Another piece of legislation
passed in 1917 restricted illiterates from entering the United States. Starting
in 1918 and continuing until the late 1920s, however, federal agencies cooperated with businessmen and agribusiness interests to make special exemption
of laborers from Mexico. In 1918 the commissioner general of immigration
lifted almost all restrictions imposed since 1882, including the prohibition
placed on contract labor. The 1924 National Origins Act, which established
quota for European countries, excluded Mexico.[5]

Between 1900 and 1930, some historians estimate, about 10 percent of
Mexico's population moved into the United States, a fraction that adds up to
some 1.5 million people (see Table 4.1).[6] For the most part, the large percentage
of immigrants who came north during the early twentieth century descended
from the ranks of the lower class. Some 80 percent to 90 percent of them had
experience in nothing other than agricultural work or unskilled occupations.
The rest were clerks, craftsmen, and other types of skilled laborers.[7] The latter
groups encompassed elites escaping the wrath of *campesinos* or revolutionary

Table 5.1. Mexican-Born Population in the United States: 1910, 1920, and 1930

	1910	1920	1930
California	33,694	88,771	191,346
Arizona	29,987	61,580	47,855
New Mexico	11,918	20,272	15,983
Colorado	2,602	11,037	12,816
Texas	125,016	251,827	262,672
Illinois	672	4,032	29,069
Kansas	8.429	13,770	11,012
Other States	9,597	35,129	77,264
Total	221,915	486,418	639,017

Source: Arthur F. Corwin, ed., *Immigrants—and Immigrants: Perspectives on Mexican Labor Migration to the United States* (Westport, Conn.: Greenwood Press, 1978), 110, 116. Reprinted by permission of Greenwood Publishing Group, Inc., Westport, Conn. © 1978 by Greenwood Publishing Group, Inc.

armies bent on retaliation for past injustices and oppression. Their ranks included political refugees with ties to the Díaz regime, as well as a middle class of *hacendados*, businessmen, and professionals such as lawyers, physicians, journalists, and educators.[8]

The immigrants' destination within the United States, regardless of social standing, varied. Those from northern Mexico streamed into the border states owing to their proximity and the abundance of available jobs therein. Residents from Tamaulipas, Nuevo León, and Coahuila ordinarily qravitated toward Texas. Those from Guanajuato, Michoacán, Jalisco, and San Luis Potosí headed for California, though the same states fed laborers to the U.S. Midwest (immigrants from the Central Plateau of Mexico bypassed the U.S. Southwest because the earlier immigrants from northern states had already claimed jobs throughout the borderlands).[9] Table 5.1 shows the dispersal of immigrant settlements between 1910 and 1930.

A Temporary Stay

A small element within the immigrant community brought a political agenda with it. Even in the Midwest, for instance, diverse elements could be found wanting to support the old regime (Díaz) while in exile or to oppose the Revolution itself.[10] At another level were immigrants who worked toward relieving the misery of the lower classes in Mexico. The PLM led by the aforementioned Ricardo Flores Magón sought such an end. After being released from prison in 1910 following his conviction for violating the neutrality laws in 1907, Magón regrouped and reinstated *Regeneración* in Los Angeles. Through the pages of this newspaper, Magón and the PLM advocated revolution against Díaz and argued for labor reforms and other radical measures. When the Revolution broke out, the PLM even launched an armed invasion of Baja California. But the campaign went awry and it led to Magón's temporary imprisonment in 1912 on charges of conspiracy to invade a friendly country from U.S. soil. When released in 1914, Magón (in Los Angeles) resumed the cause for Mexico's liberation, but his PLM now lacked effectiveness. Nonetheless, it inspired the Plan de San Diego in 1915, carried on propaganda activities against Mexico's governments, and condemned U.S. exploitation of Mexicans and Mexican Americans. In 1918 the U.S. government charged Flores Magón with espionage and sent him to prison, where he died in 1922.[11]

The majority of the immigrants had little interest in such kinds of politics; they sought to flee conditions in the homeland and find opportunity in the United States. In the new land poor folks tried reconstructing their lives, joining the swelling numbers of refugees in transplanted communities. Elites, for their part, assisted in sustaining Mexico in the United States by their efforts to resurrect a semblance of their former aristocratic lives: they formed societies, social clubs, and theaters and promoted their *mexicanidad* by publishing or selling Mexican books, Spanish music, and newspapers. Both groups relied on the Mexican consul when problems with discrimination, unemployment, repatriation, or trouble with the law came up.[12]

The course of events during this age touched the new arrivals and modified their sentiments. These developments involved aspects of material culture such as clothing, new durable goods being invented during the age, and modern housing techniques. Other influences included sports (basketball and baseball) and moving pictures in Mexican American–owned theaters that featured the most prominent stars of the day such as Charlie Chaplin and Mary Pickford. The fashions of the 1920s, including bobbed hair and short skirts converted many young women to new lifestyles. The "sheik" look (well-groomed pomaded hair, pointed sideburns, and expensive-looking attire) made fashionable by Rudolph Valentino similarly affected impressionable adolescent males. American values had their own impact, often to the dismay of the older folks who identified American life with independence, defiance of parental authority, and violation of the customs of the motherland. The English language also produced slang expression such as *sitijol* (city hall), *troque* (truck), *tichar* (teach), *esplear* (spell), or *tochar* (touch).[13]

Of major significance in Americanizing communities was World War I. In an effort to integrate all groups into war-mobilization efforts, the government sought at every level the help of the Mexican-descent community, both at the civilian and military front. Anglo-Americans appealed to Mexican Americans and the immigrants to buy liberty bonds, organized "Loyalty Leaguers" in the colonias, and sponsored mass meetings in Mexican communities to explain the war effort. The stridency of these undertakings gave Mexican-descent people a feeling of belonging to the country of residence—the United States—as for the first time the government treated them as citizens instead of stepchildren of the nation. For soldiers, many of whom distinguished themselves in the battlefield, it produced a certain esprit de corps and satisfaction in having contributed to the defeat of the Germans.[14]

Simultaneously, as part of the Americanization drive that developed in the early twentieth century, Anglo-American reformers, charity and religious groups, social workers, and educators launched a crusade to convert the Mexicans, both native- and foreign-born. In California some of the Americanizing programs directed themselves at immigrant women, on the premise that Mexican mothers assumed primary responsibility for instructing the children on cultural values; Americanized mothers would raise American children.[15] In the end such Americanizing efforts yielded only minimal success. None of the reform movements advocated full equality even after acculturation. Consequently, many Mexicans remained distrustful of white society and unwilling to surrender their cultural identity. Until the depression decade, therefore, the Mexican-descent population in the United States lacked command of the English language and still harbored doubts about accepting the credibility of the American way of life.[16]

But the preceding developments planted the seeds of what historians refer to as the "Mexican-American Generation," a cohort that between 1930 and 1960 gave direction to Mexican-American communities as "Americans." During the early period of the twentieth century, however, Mexican enclaves embraced diverse ideological strains; some native- and foreign-born Mexicans still adhered to the traditions of Old Mexico, while others practiced bilingualism and biculturalism. Dilemmas over identity thus surfaced frequently, for there existed among these disparate elements differences in patriotic passion for the United States and Mexico. Problems were posed whenever the American press attacked Mexico, or when during the years of the Revolution the United States invaded Mexican territory and Pancho Villa attacked New Mexico in 1916, or when Anglo-Americans associated, stereotyped, and classified all Mexicans as one regardless of nativity. The latter situation, especially, placed great stress on those

A float of the mutual aid society La Alianza Hispano Americana during the celebration in San Diego of Mexican Independence Day, 1924. Photograph reprinted by permission of the San Diego Historical Society.

who considered themselves Americans and different from the foreign-born; they inclined to disassociate themselves from the newcomers. As had been the case in the nineteenth century, old citizens in New Mexico and California used such terms as *Spanish Americans* and *Hispanos* as self-referents to distinguish themselves from the newcomers (the immigrants reciprocated with the word *"pocho,"* meaning that the Mexican-American personality had become a corruption of Mexican and American cultures). In New Mexico, one sociologist has recently proposed, the label also acted as a valid term invoked regularly by Hispano leaders to rally *nuevomexicanos* behind ethnic platforms.[17]

Despite all this, a common Mexicanist identity solidified communities. Notwithstanding social divergence, variation in degree of acculturation, and philosophical disagreements, most people abided by certain nationalistic principles, emphasized by a common experience of poverty, discrimination, and exploitation that unified them as La Raza or as Mexicanos.[18]

The New Colonias

As of the early twentieth century, the entire Mexican-descent population (immigrants and native-born Mexican Americans together) remained heavily clustered in the states along the U.S.–Mexican border as the figures for 1930 in Table 5.2 show (see also Table 5.1). During the era, however, new demographic trends unfolded. First, unprecedented migration occurred within a state: from south Texas to the Panhandle, for example. Second, a new wave of immigrants, joined by fellow Mexican Americans, headed for areas beyond the borderlands. Lastly, intraregional (Texas to California, or New Mexico to Colorado; Michigan to Wisconsin, or to Indiana; and Kansas to other Great Plains states) and interregional movements (from the Southwest to the Midwest, from the Great Plains states to the Midwest, and from the Southwest to the Pacific Northwest) became common.[19]

As noted in the previous chapter, Mexicans had begun entering the midwestern states of Ohio, Indiana, Illinois, Michigan, Wisconsin, and Minnesota since the early 1900s, but in small numbers. Now migration and settlement to the Great Lakes area escalated simultaneous with the region's surge toward

Table 5.2. Mexican-Descent Population in the United States, 1930

Texas	673,681
California	368,013
Arizona	114,173
New Mexico	59,340
Colorado	57,676
Other States	166,412
Total	1,449,295

Source: Arthur F. Corwin, ed., *Immigrants—and Immigrants: Perspectives on Mexican Labor Migration to the United States* (Westport, Conn.: Greenwood Press, 1978), 116. Reprinted by permission of Greenwood Publishing Group, Inc., Westport, Conn. © 1978 by Greenwood Publishing Group, Inc.

manufacturing, meat-packing, railroad construction, and beet growing. The steel mills of Chicago and the automobile plants in Detroit issued calls for Mexican workers, as did beet companies wanting *betabeleros* (beet pickers) able to sustain grueling stoop labor. Farmers actively recruited in south Texas and the Southwest and then undertook concerted campaigns to retain the Mexican workers permanently.[20] (Table 5.3 reports the best estimates on the number of Mexican-descent people residing in these states.) Mexican Americans and immigrants also searched for work in the Central and Northern Plains states such as Oklahoma, Kansas, Nebraska, Missouri, the Dakotas, and Iowa, where they found employment as section hands on railroad lines, in the slaughter houses and meat-packing industry, as well as the beet fields of western Nebraska and the Dakotas.[21]

The Rocky Mountain states similarly attracted prospective employees— among them Mexican nationals, Mexican Americans from other states, and Hispanos from New Mexico. As these groups pushed northward after World War I, they augmented the small Mexican American communities that had taken root there before 1910. Such a scenario unfolded in northeastern Colorado's South Platte Valley, the city of Denver, and Fort Collins, where people went to do seasonal work in the beet industry. Others founded new colonias in the northern parts of Colorado adjacent to Wyoming and Nebraska where they worked in the mines and on the sheep ranches.[22] Mexican-origin people also neared the Canadian border in the Pacific Northwest by the 1920s, enticed there by labor recruiters from Oregon and Washington representing beet companies. Available openings in land clearing, farm irrigation, railroad maintenance, and other tasks attracted others. By 1930 Mexican-descent trackmen constituted about 60 percent of railroad crews in the Pacific Northwest.[23]

By World War I, Mexican nationals and Mexican Americans had reached New England and New York State, working in eating establishments, hotels, packing houses, and the steel industry. In the early 1920s Bethlehem Steel in Pennsylvania imported some 900 Mexicans from Texas to meet demands for cheap laborers.[24]

Table 5.3. Mexican Population in the Midwest, 1850–1970

	1850–1890	1900	1910	1920	1930	1940	1950	1960	1970
Ohio	134	53	85	942	3,099	2,792	5,959	9,960	13,349
Indiana	98	43	47	680	7,589	4,530	8,677	14,041	18,325
Illinois	240	156	672	4,032	20,963	23,545	34,538	63,063	117,268
Michigan	127	56	86	1,333	9,921	9,474	16,540	24,298	31,067
Wisconsin	59	499	39	178	1,853	1,716	3,272	6,705	9,160
Minnesota	308	162	52	248	2,448	2,976	3,305	3,436	4,575
Iowa	75	29	620	2,650	2,760	3,959	3,973	3,374	4,546
Missouri	37	24	1,413	3,411	3,482	4,783	5,862	8,159	8,353
Nebraska	48	27	290	2,611	4,178	5,333	6,023	5,858	5,552
Kansas	126	71	8,429	13,770	12,900	13,742	13,429	12,972	13,728
Total	1,252	1,122	11,733	29,855	69,193	72,476	101,578	151,866	225,923

Source: *Census of Population, 1850–1970*, cited in Gilbert Cárdenas, "Los Desarraigados: Chicanos in the Midwestern Region of the United States," *Aztlán* 7 (Summer 1976): 155. Reprinted by permission of Gilbert Cárdenas.

"Shotgun" houses in the Mexican-American barrio in Dallas, ca. 1920s. Barrios grew up around industrial areas, such as the mill in the background here. Photograph courtesy of the Dallas Public Library, Texas/Dallas History and Archives Division.

By 1930, therefore, Mexican culture and community had been transplanted to newer outposts, where it added to American cultural pluralism, sustained by more arrivals either from Mexico or the borderlands and by the contacts the trailblazers retained with their point of departure. Diversification of Mexican communities resulted, however, owing to myriad variables: the absence of already-settled Hispanic communities that could aid in the resettlement process; the ratio of Anglos (and in some places, European ethnic groups) to the Mexican newcomers; the type of work performed in a region (whether it be rural, the slaughterhouses, factories, or railroads, for instance); and the migrants' place of origin in the motherland.

The Place of Mexicans

Stresses and strains accompanied the modern age, and they sparked bitter emotions toward the immigrants and Mexican Americans. The unprecedented immigration, the appearance of new and unassimilable immigrant communities, conflicts along the Texas and New Mexico border and feared German intrigue therein, revolutionary activity such as that undertaken by the PLM, and agitation by unions with predominant Mexican membership acted to worsen living situations for Mexican communities everywhere.[25]

For a brief moment during the World War I years, Anglo society tolerated Mexican Americans and the arriving immigrants for the good of the war effort, but once the crisis ended white folks reverted to old hatreds. Mexicans faced renewed prejudice and discrimination in the borderlands and outside it. Anglo society labeled Mexican-origin people as ignorant, disease-ridden, criminally inclined, immoral, and unhygienic. Such stereotypes were widely acccepted, even by the new motion-picture industry, which portrayed Mexicans as bandits, robbers, lustful fiends, and murderers. Anglos also callously employed disparaging terms like "Mexes" or "greasers" or just "Mexican" in a pejorative way and refused to distinguish between the native- and foreign-born (to the point, as noted earlier, that Mexican Americans shunned the term "Mexican"). Distinctions once made between old elite "Castilian" Mexicans and Mexican "Indians" passed away. In 1930 the Census Bureau did not list Mexicans as Caucasians but in the category of "other races."[26]

Racial separation, present since the Yankee conquest, continued apace, even in newfound rural and urban settlements outside the Southwest. In the regions north of the borderlands, Mexicans clustered in enclaves near their place of employment, kept there by economic disadvantage and prejudice rather than a fully defined doctrine of segregation. In the borderlands, whites designated segments of the city space as the Mexican quarter and prohibited Mexicans from venturing into the Anglo district. Jim Crow traditions found applicability to Mexicans and Mexican Americans. Anglos kept Mexicans from swimming pools, movie houses, barber shops, and eating places and openly displayed signs that read "No Mexicans Allowed" or "No Mexican Trade Wanted."[27]

Nativism toward Mexicans and Mexican Americans surfaced between 1910 and 1920 in response to American's alarm over unrestricted immigration and the fear that Mexican revolutionaries had designs on U.S. soil. In 1914 California authorities harassed Magonistas and eventually immobilized the PLM movement in the United States. Fears of border invasions led white authorities to increase scrutiny of Mexican communities and to arrest suspected agitators working for revolutionary governments. When Pancho Villa invaded Columbus, New Mexico, in March 1916, Los Angeles's mayor banned selling liquor and firearms to residents of the Mexican community and strengthened security around Mexican neighborhoods. Response to the Plan de San Diego (1915) in Texas placed suspicion on Mexicans in south Texas and in California, where authorities learned that Flores Magón had ties to the insurrection.[28]

By the 1920s nativists throughout the nation insisted on an all-out stop-gap policy toward immigration, including the influx from Mexico. The more racist elements argued that Mexicans had a debilitating effect on society, given their biological inferiority. Urbanites feared the immigrants would create some real social problems because they imported disease, crime, and poverty. Labor unions, Anglo field hands, and other Americans argued that Mexicans depressed wages and displaced "native" American workers. They supported the Box Bill, a piece of legislation sponsored by John C. Box of Texas in 1926 to bar immigration from Latin America. Those who favored continued immigration, on the other hand, pointed to needs of the American economy, especially in the agricultural sector. They noted that the immigrants made reliable and tractable workers who did not require much for existence. Anti-restrictionists conceded the possibility of a "Mexican problem," but that could be managed by containing the immigrants to the fields and keeping them away from mainstream life. In 1929 the restrictionists had their way. Congress that year enacted legislation imposing strict penalties on foreigners attempting to gain entry into the United

States. Also the State Department agreed to be more diligent in administering the restrictive provisions of existing immigration laws, among them collecting the head tax, enforcing literacy requirements, prohibiting contract labor, and preventing the admission of those likely to become wards of society. When the Great Depression hit after 1929, the economic downturn in the United States discouraged further large-scale immigration.[29]

"Little Mexicos"

Massive rural to urban migration occurred during this era: by 1930 about 50 percent of Mexican-descent families resided in the urban centers.[30] New arrivals generally settled in barrios in the process of expansion, such as San Antonio's West Side and Los Angeles's East Side (Los Angeles during the 1920s surpassed the San Antonio Hispanic community in size and emerged with the sobriquet of the "Mexican capital" of the United States). Or they would settle in fledgling ethnic quarters on the outskirts of town. Beyond the borderlands, as in Chicago (by the late 1920s the Windy City consisted of five main colonias), the new enclaves sprouted out close to the inhabitants' place of work—a slaughter house, a processing shop, a railroad yard, an automobile

Table 5.4. Distribution of Chicanos in Urban Areas, 1920 and 1930

	1920	1930
Los Angeles	29,757	97,116
San Antonio, Texas	41,469	82,373
El Paso, Texas	39,571	58,291
Laredo, Texas	n.a.	23,482
Belvedere, California	n.a.	20,125
Chicago	1,265	19,362
Houston	5,002	14,149
Corpus Christi, Texas	n.a.	11,377
San Diego	4,007	9,266
San Francisco	3,908	7,922
San Bernardino, California	n.a.	6,839
Denver	1,722	6,837
Detroit	683	6,515
Dallas	2,838	5,901
East Chicago	n.a.	5,343
Austin, Texas	n.a.	5,014
Fort Worth, Texas	4,426	3,955
Riverside, California	n.a.	3,942
Santa Ana, California	n.a.	3,633
Gary, Indiana	169	3,486

Source:*Fifteenth Census of the United States: 1930,* cited in Ricardo Romo, "The Urbanization of Southwestern Chicanos in the Early Twentieth Century," in *New Directions in Chicano Scholarship,* ed. Ricardo Romo and Raymund A. Paredes (La Jolla: University of California at San Diego, 1978), 185. Reprinted by permission of Ricardo Romo.

plant, or a soap factory.[31] (Estimates of the number of people residing in the several major cities of the United States are presented in Table 5.4.)

Conditions for residents in these barrio communities bordered on the primitive. Often the newcomers huddled in sheds, animal shelters, tents, corrals, boxcars, tumbledown shacks made of scrap wood or other second-hand materials, inhospitable basements, and, in the Midwest, structures abandoned by European immigrant groups. So-called spiktowns, cholo districts, or Little Mexicos lacked paved streets, sanitary facilities, conveniences such as light and water, garbage collection services, and privacy. Often, rats and roaches ran about unchecked. Disease infested these Mexican sections, among them typhoid fever, tuberculosis, pneumonia, rickets, and influenza. Infant mortality plagued families, and high death rates haunted the general population.[32]

Despite such problems, however, the barrio remained the hub of in-group life, whether in northern Colorado, the Midwest, the Great Plains states, or the Northwest, for even these communities had already been stabilized by the mid-1920s as Mexicans arrived in family groups. In these ethnic quarters people found friendly conversation from relatives, acquaintances, and newcomers from the home country, receptive ears for their feelings of nationalism, and support from familial networks, associations, and religious organizations that assisted in finding employment or coming to their rescue in times of despair. The barrios met Hispanic needs through movie houses, pharmacies, restaurants, grocery stores, law firms, labor agencies, *panaderías* (bakeries), barbershops, and a miscellany of mercantile operations.[33]

Fortunate Few, an Unfortunate Many

Amid the circumstances begot by revolution, immigration, and urbanization, the resilient middle class of the pre-1910 era held fast. It consisted of survivors—ranchers, *comerciantes*, and professionals—that had made it through the conquest and the transformation of the late nineteenth century. It embraced ambitious native-born Mexican Americans from the lower stratum, poor folks from Mexico who through dint of labor made something of themselves in foreign soil, and, more discernibly, refugees who transferred their wealth or training to the United States or whose command of the English language permitted them to find jobs with labor agencies, mercantile firms, restaurants, and boarding houses. In many enclaves, therefore, including those beyond the borderlands, there perdured a class of middling status composed of government workers, clerks, managers, teachers, lawyers, doctors, and other trained professionals. In Los Angeles there even thrived an exiled community of playrights, composers, actors, and theater people that enjoyed fruitful relations with the local newspapers, movie industry, and publishing houses.[34]

For the most part, this middle class—which survived primarily by servicing the Hispanic community—lost as many members to the struggle for survival as it won. Landowners still faced problems with creditors, businessmen found it difficult to find markets outside the Mexican quarter, and opportunities for training in the professions did not readily present themselves. As of 1930, less than 10 percent of the Mexican-American community held such middle-class occupations as managers, proprietors, and clerks.[35]

The bulk of Mexican-origin people, therefore, remained stagnated in the lower class, contributing to the American enterprise through grueling, low-paying work. Those in the city turned to manual labor of several sorts, such as house-building, street repair, and construction in the various public projects. Urbanites also found jobs in bakeries, print shops, cleaning establishments, restaurants, freight companies, and candy, pecan, and cigar companies (see Table 5.5). Increasingly, many went to work in local smelters, iron factories, cement companies, and textile firms throughout such southwestern cities as San Antonio, El Paso, and Los Angeles. Those heading for the Midwest and the Great Plains states joined the work force of nascent rubber, steel, leather, automobile, cement, glass, and food-processing plants that appeared there after World War I.[36]

Outside the city Mexicans found work in every sector of the expanding economy, including the railroad lines, where they engaged in blasting, laying track, cleaning engines, or performing different tasks at the roundhouse and railroad shops. By the 1920s they made up between 75 percent to 85 percent of track workers in the southwestern states. In the area around Chicago, Mexicans constituted about 40 percent of all railroad crews during the 1920s and in some cases as much as 80 percent of the maintenance gang of a particular railroad line. In the quarries Mexicans also made up a substantial part of the work force, accounting for approximately 60 percent of all miners in the Southwest (as in Arizona) according to one estimate.[37]

On Rural Estates

Farms begged for armies of migrant hands, but Mexicans worked the fields only seasonally and for subsistence wages, doing the labor-intensive tasks of planting, picking, thinning, and topping, including using the hideous *el cortito*, the truncated hoe that many times disabled workers who had to crouch and bend over to tend the *betabel* (beet plants) and other crops. Some observers during the 1920s estimated that Mexican immigrants and native-born Mexican Americans jointly constituted about one-half of cotton pickers in the Southwest (including Colorado) and between 60 percent to 70 percent of those who picked the region's vegetables and fruits. The same occupational pattern existed in the beet fields of the Midwest and the Great Plains states.[38]

To make ends meet, entire Mexican families followed the migrant trail across the nation, traveling in trucks or cars seeking out employment in the railroad lines, the mines, and the countryside. In the farms, they camped out in the fields for weeks at a time, living under tents or bridges and doing without the most essential sanitary requirements. In the beet fields of the Dakotas, Iowa, and Minnesota, Mexican workers sought shelter in converted barns, vacated farmhouses, tool rooms, or sheds for farm machinery, and brought in their own water for cooking and washing lest local sources be polluted. After finishing the migrant cycle, the family returned to its home base only for a brief period of time.[39]

In farmlands across the United States, agribusiness employed "labor-repressive" methods to manipulate field hands. By the 1920s these mechanisms involved the use of debt peonage, threats, detention within compounds, downright physical punishment, conspiracies by farmers to keep production costs low,

Table 5.5. Occupational Distribution of Chicanos, 1930, by States of the Southwest and Sex (Percentages)

Occupational Level	Texas		New Mexico		Colorado		Arizona		California		Southwest	
	M	F	M	F	M	F	M	F	M	F	M	F
Professional and Technical	0.8	2.9	0.5	3.6	0.3	1.0	0.6	3.4	1.0	3.0	0.9	2.9
Managers, Proprietors, and Officials	3.4	2.6	1.3	2.8	0.4	0.4	2.9	3.3	1.9	1.8	2.8	2.4
Clerical	1.1	4.3	0.5	3.6	0.3	2.1	1.4	8.2	1.0	9.5	1.0	5.8
Sales	2.6	4.4	1.3	2.5	0.6	1.4	2.7	6.6	2.2	4.1	2.4	4.3
Craftsmen and Foremen (Skilled)	7.3	0.4	4.6	0.3	2.2	0.3	7.9	0.5	7.0	1.4	6.8	0.6
Operatives (Semiskilled)	6.1	16.4	19.2	9.0	14.7	6.3	26.1	13.1	8.1	40.8	9.1	21.9
Laborers (Unskilled)	23.6	2.3	20.7	1.6	25.3	3.4	26.5	1.5	37.6	4.7	28.2	2.8
Service	4.2	39.7	3.0	67.2	1.7	41.6	3.0	55.0	4.2	27.5	4.0	38.4
Farm Laborers	35.0	25.9	35.1	5.2	48.8	41.5	26.4	7.9	35.7	7.1	35.1	19.7
Farmers and Farm Managers	15.9	1.2	13.9	4.2	5.7	2.1	2.5	0.6	1.3	0.1	9.8	1.0

Sources: Southwest, males, from Vernon M. Briggs, Jr., Walter Fogel, and Fred Schmidt, *The Chicano Worker* (Austin: University of Texas Press, 1977), 76. ©1977. Reprinted by permission of University of Texas Press. Other data computed from *Fifteenth Census of the United States: 1930. Population. Volume 5: General Report on Occupations*, table 4. Census classification was for "Mexican" gainful workers 10 years old and over. Data have been reclassified under major occupational categories used by the Bureau of the Census after 1930, on the basis of a table in E. P. Hutchinson, *Immigrants and Their Children* (New York: Wiley, 1966), app. D. This table was originally published in Mario Barrera, *Race and Class in the Southwest: A Theory of Racial Inequality* (Notre Dame, Ind.: University of Notre Dame Press, 1979), 113.

and a plethora of other techniques.[40] Additionally, attitudes about "Mexican work" produced occupational stratification for Mexican-descent people. Anglos believed Mexicans good only for certain duties, such as grubbing, cotton-picking, and beet-topping. Similarly, railroads and mining companies confined Mexicans to the more difficult responsibilities and restricted them from supervisory or management positions. In the industrial regions outside the Southwest, employers generally relegated Mexicans to unskilled or semi-skilled jobs, such as in the steel industry.[41]

For the rural villagers in northern New Mexico still trying to eke a living off their traditional lands, life did not differ markedly. Hispanos found themselves under siege owing to population encroachment and large-scale attempts to make available tillable lands for agribusiness. New irrigation projects deprived the villagers of the waters from the Rio Grande or, alternatively, devastated their soil with unanticipated flooding or polluted it with silt.[42]

Political Struggles, Old and New

The institutionalization in Texas of the White Man's Primary Association, the use of the poll tax, and the designs of commercial farmers and Progressives wishing to clean up governmnent by disenfranchising Mexicans who had served to prop up the old bosses all neutralized political gains Mexican Americans made up to 1910. Elsewhere, such forces—in addition to racism and the nativism arising in response to immigration and to international episodes such as Villa's Raid—subdued Mexican-American political participation.[43]

A combination of accommodationist and confrontational strategy nonetheless typified the politics of the Mexican-American and immigrant community. In the first case, activists continued joining or forming political clubs with the objective of generating interest in issues relevant to the Hispanic community. The *nuevomexicanos* once again edged their fellow Mexican-American politicians in officeholding during the 1910s and 1920s. Two served as governors during this time, one of them being Octaviano Larrazolo (1918–20), whose administration embraced support for bilingual public-school instruction and legislation to help small farmers and field laborers. Women also won election to different offices, including the position of secretary of state in 1922.[44]

Resistance as a political option also expressed itself, as in the case when some 400 Texas Mexicans came together in Laredo at El Primer Congreso Mexicanista in 1911 to address the many problems that plagued the Mexican-American and immigrant communities. Delegates discussed numerous issues, among them unequal education, lynchings, poor employment, political impotence, loss of land, and racism. Efforts to implement long-range plans for a league with the charge of protecting Texas Mexicans' rights, however, failed to materialize.[45]

Mexican Americans also joined or gave support to Ricardo Flores Magón's PLM. In southern California, Magón denounced racial oppression, economic exploitation of Mexicanos, segregation, lynchings, and the numerous cases of unjustified arrests and incarceration. His politics ostensibly inspired supporters of the Plan de San Diego (PSD), an ambitious idea issued in 1915 in the south Texas county of Duval. The PSD summoned Tejanos to an insurrection against

Anglo society with the objective of erecting a new republic composed of the states in the U.S. Southwest. The leadership of the PSD had read *Regeneración*, noting the relevance of PLM doctrine to conditions of Texas Mexicans; they found willing recruits among those who had suffered under Anglo control since the nineteenth century. In a manifestation of radical protest regarding long-standing grievances, Mexicans of various backgrounds now joined PSD leaders in attacks on Anglo ranchers, roads, railroad tracks, and other symbols of Anglo supremacy. Texas Rangers, federal troops, and vigilante groups quelled the movement by 1917, but not until both sides had perpetrated numerous deaths and thousands of dollars of destruction on south Texas.[46] In New Mexico lingering resistance against commercial farms encroaching on the northern villages produced attacks by vigilantes such as Las Manos Negras. This secretive group cut fences that prevented the villagers from access to traditional lands.[47]

Aside from resistance struggles, an incipient movement for civil rights and legal equality surfaced during the 1920s. Cases dealing with discriminatory treatment in public places appeared, as World War I veterans took leading roles in demanding constitutional guarantees. In Texas a combination of veterans and civilian activists founded the Orden Hijos de América (Order Sons of America) in 1921. Though led by the more "Americanized" elements within Tejano society, its efforts to desegregate public places and schools and to achieve civic and political equity embraced all of Mexican origin. Though the OSA did not thrive, it became the precursor of the League of Latin American Citizens, founded in 1929.[48]

Ethnicity, Class, and Labor Organizing

Labor unionization proved difficult for any group during this era, and even more so for immigrants and Mexican Americans. Several factors deterred effective organization: the conservativism of the times, especially in the 1920s; bitter anti-labor passions; the deliberate strategy undertaken by management to divide and rule the workers; and the power of employers to use scabs, violence, police authority (the use of Texas Rangers in Texas), and threats of deportation or incarceration.[49] Still, Mexican immigrants and native Mexican Americans undertook efforts to improve conditions in the workplace, increase dismal wages, and reduce the length of the work day. Such impulses derived from different wellsprings, among them the continued acquaintance of native-born Mexican Americans with American life, the expectations that immigrants held about improving their status in the new land, the general political struggles to improve conditions, and, equally significant, the responses to immediate circumstances, be they invitations by mainstream unions to join organized labor or rapidly deteriorating economic conditions. Among Mexican communities, moreover, there prevailed a unifying sentiment of mutuality that transcended diversity and coalesced Mexican immigrants and Mexican Americans in a common struggle against racism and other exploitative forces.[50]

Expressions of discontent toward work conditions sometimes revealed themselves in subtle forms, as in the case of field workers who resisted exploitation by avoiding farms known for their callous indifference toward laborers, by slowing down on the job, by breaking tools or destroying plants, or simply by leaving the premises in protest of low wages or other unacceptable circumstances.[51]

Actually, Mexican immigrants and Mexican Americans used more formal steps to improve their lot; they organized around nationality, around the conservative ideology of the American Federation of Labor (AFL), or around the more ambitious ideas of the Socialist party, which advocated radical social change. In undertaking ethnic struggle, Mexicanos at the community level founded *mutualistas*, Masonic orders, patriotic clubs, and various other associations that constituted part of barrio life, then moved to petition employers for specific concessions. Other workers maintained connections with such groups as the Mexico-oriented PLM. Moreover, recent arrivals from the old land (such as supporters of Flores Magón) plunged into the labor-union struggle in the United States. The constant shuttling between the two countries influenced these immigrant laborites to take approaches used in Mexico and apply them to the United States.[52]

Still other operatives came together along ethnic lines, as did the members of Los Angeles's Federation of Mexican Societies (consisting of several mutual aid societies) who formed the Confederación de Uniones de Obreras Mexicanas (CUOM; Confederation of Mexican Workers Union), which recruited in 1928 between 2,000 and 3,000 *campesinos* to its ranks with talk of AFL affiliation and an end to the exploitation of laborers. (Unfortunately the confederation lasted only until the eve of the depression, however.) Simultaneously, Mexican farmworkers organized La Unión de Trabajadores del Valle Imperial (Workers Union of the Imperial Valley) to petition for better wages and conditions in the fields of the Imperial Valley of southern California, where agribusiness operated huge irrigated melon and vegetable farms.[53]

Strike activity with ethnicity as a cohesive element was evident wherever Mexicans constituted a significant segment of the work force. It occurred throughout cities and farms, along railroads and in mines, and in the construction, canning, and meat-packing industries.[54] In the countryside the more prominent strikes broke out in the California estates during the 1910s, though the most significant one occurred in the Imperial Valley cantaloupe farms in May 1928, led by La Unión de Trabajadores del Valle Imperial.[55] Railroad workers also registered discontent and led at least two railroad strikes in Tucson—one in 1919 and another in 1922.[56]

Mexicans also followed a pattern of joining prominent, nationally established Anglo labor unions, for in them they saw opportunities to support universal working-class solidarity or to profit materially from such an association. Thus they turned to the craft-oriented, albeit moderate, American Federation of Labor, or the more militant Industrial Workers of the World (IWW), which focused on class struggle and even social revolution. AFL affiliates were active in large cities such as El Paso and San Antonio. On the farms Mexicans also found the AFL appealing, despite its ethnocentrism and its disinterest in organizing agricultural hands. In Texas and parts of the Southwest, Tejano Clemente Idar succeeded to some extent in organizing diverse elements within the Mexican-American agricultural and urban work force during the late 1910s and early 1920s. Beet-field workers in Nebraska, Wyoming, and Colorado joined AFL's Beet Workers Association in 1929. Generally, however, Mexicans still felt suspicion toward the AFL and joined it only after having organized their own locals.[57]

Many also trusted the IWW, a labor organization more radical in its attempt to unite and free the working class, and Colorado beet-field workers participated in the union's activities during the late 1920s. Similarly, the Socialist party conducted organizing campaigns among Tejano tenant farmers and farm laborers who turned to its affiliate, the Land League of America (1914–17), fearing displacement by immigration and other forces.[58]

As members of these and other mainstream unions, Mexicans participated in strikes just as they did as members of the ethnic-based associations. Among the most noted of such agricultural work stoppages in the pre-depression era was the Wheatland, California (upper Sacramento Valley), strike of 1913. There farmhands (represented by the IWW) at Durst Ranch abandoned the fields demanding better wages and basic human necessities such as separate toilet facilities for the men and women and water at least twice daily. Violence ensued between the antagonists and ended only with the arrival of the National Guard.[59] Rural strikes led by mainstream unions do not seem prominent during the 1920s.

Tragically, violence also touched Mexican-descent members of the AFL and IWW who participated in strike activity in southwestern mining camps. In 1914, for instance, Mexicans in Colorado were among the victims of the Ludlow Massacre, a tragedy in which the National Guard, dispatched by the governor to quell the strike, torched the tent colonies the miners had erected. The troops killed several of the strikers' families and children and effectively ended the strike.[60]

In the end, labor movements during the 1910–1930 period produced few tangible results for Mexicans. Ethnic-oriented efforts faced almost certain failure. Association with the AFL, the IWW, and other locals proved to be dubious strategies. The AFL tended to be racist and cared little for farmworkers, while the IWW focused too much on ideology to help Mexicans desperate for survival. In any case, the IWW ceased to be a strong organizing force after about 1920.[61]

Women's Roles

Though patriarchy as known in the colonial era no longer prevailed, Mexican men, especially immigrants, still believed their role to be that of supporting their wife and children. In their view, also, women had no business working outside the home. Even Ricardo Flores Magón and his PLM followers, despite their encouragement of women's participation in the PLM, fell victim to old beliefs. They slighted the PLM platform on sexual equality; instead, their inclination was to assign female PLM members duties traditionally associated with the "women's sphere."[62]

But circumstances of the era compelled men, especially of the lower class, to forego their attitudes: they needed women's contribution to the family budget. Women, consequently, entered the labor force in greater numbers during the 1910s and 1920s. In the cities women did "women's work," finding employment as laundresses, servants, seamstresses in the garment industry, waitresses, pecan-shellers, and cannery workers. In the midwestern cities women were hired in some factories as inspectors, sorters, candy dippers and in an assortment of other light functions (see Table 5.5). But the overwhelming number of Mexican women joined men in particular tasks such as agriculture. According to census figures for 1930, some 20 percent of women did field work, but this ranged as high as 50 percent in the labor force of North Dakota. Whether in the urban or rural settings, women encountered the same sort of conditions as men: undesirable jobs at less pay than Anglos.[63]

Still, women at times challenged male attitudes toward prescribed roles. The women who belonged to the PLM, for example, addressed numerous public rallies, helped define strategy, and articulated views (through *Regeneración* and other outlets) on the meaning of the Mexican Revolution, on worker solidarity, and on the constraints of male domination.[64] Younger women workers by the 1920s tended to express a desire for independence from family restrictions rooted in the old country. Many pressed for lifting the common custom of chaperonage, while a few even risked censure by renting their own apartments. But they did not intend the efforts to disrupt family values. Instead, the assertiveness was part of the process of adjusting to changing circumstances, as well as to acculturation that would eventually syncretize the values of the U.S. family with the more conservative ones from Mexico.[65]

Countless women succeeded in rising above expectations. Increasingly, women made their way into clerical and sales occupations, working either for small barrio retail stores or in Anglo businesses wishing to tap into the Spanish-speaking trade, and, along the border, to the clientele from Mexico through bilingual clerks and salespersons. In northern New Mexico, Hispanic women began infiltrating the education profession in the 1910s, and the emergency of World War I made available to them more openings in the teaching field as well as occupations such as stenographers. New Mexico, also, produced Adelina Otero-Warren, a labor activist, educator, lobbyist, politician, and suffragist who successfully worked to see the ratification of the Nineteenth Amendment by the state legislator. Few women in the pre-depression era, however, entered the more skilled and professional occupations.[66]

Modern Schooling

After World War I educators developed a new agenda designed to inculcate American ideals and traditions onto the immigrant child, with the goal of getting the students to forego their native tongue and customs. Still, schooling during the era barely reached Hispanic enclaves or rural settlements, and if it did it bordered on inadequacy. Furthermore, the schools did not pursue a plan of full integration of Mexican pupils into the mainstream; rather, they sought to prepare students for their future roles as manual workers. As such, curricula emphasized vocational training in such things as woodwork, sewing, laundering, homemaking, and various practical trades.[67]

Segregated schools typified the age both in the old borderlands and outside it, although New Mexico's Constitution of 1912 expressly outlawed the segregation of Hispanic children (the document also made provisions that the students be assisted by bilingual instructors). In the more racist states of the Southwest, school boards generally built educational facilities close to the barrios or some distance away from the Anglo schools (or when this appeared impossible, they segregated Hispanic students in rooms). Justification for such separational patterns rested on the Anglo belief that Mexican children smelled because of improper hygiene, or that they descended from a decadent race. Educators also argued for separation because many Mexican children did not speak English (in Texas in the late 1920s, some 90 percent of the children spoke primarily Spanish when they enrolled in school), had different needs from those of Anglo children, or attended school so irregularly as to be unable to keep up with other children.[68]

But parents dispatched youngsters to class (despite the above curriculum and practices), for it meant that at least their children could acquire the skills and means to succeed in American society. Also, the intellectual level of the community might be elevated. Where public schools were unavailable or in dire straits, communities established private educational concerns. Furthermore, youngsters attended Catholic parochial schools or facilities set up by Protestant denominations. Some 38 Protestant learning institutions for Mexicans could be found across the Southwest by 1930, with the Methodists and Episcopalians being the most attentive to Hispanic needs.[69]

Religion

Folk beliefs that had come down through the generations remained into the modern age, reinforced by the new immigration. Some parishioners retained faith in the miraculous powers of *curanderos*, while others remained convinced that saints possessed the power to intervene on behalf of the desperate. Hispanic Catholics made *mandas* (vows, a *promesa*) to favorite saints, promising to fulfill a sacrifice in return for help in a time of crisis—to bring family members safely home, to cure a loved one, or to end a personal problem, for example. In New Mexico and Colorado the Penitentes remained as viable as ever, practicing in their *moradas* (houses of worship) as they had done since the early nineteenth century.[70]

Mexicans displayed their commitment to the Catholic faith by joining an array of church organizations and groups, among them the St. Vincent de Paul Society (men), the women's group the Sociedad Guadalupana, or youth societies such as the Club de Santa Teresita (Tucson). They carried on other Hispanic traditions, such as holding *posadas* or staging *pastorelas* at Christmastime.[71]

In the meantime, Protestant churches continued their unrelenting work among Hispanics, and with increased success. Churches of all Protestant denominations could be found in the many colonias; Protestant missions actively proselytized in remote villages, rural towns, migrant camps such as those in northern Colorado, and the growing communities of the urban Midwest.[72]

Voluntary Organizations

A host of community associations proliferated within old and new colonias beteen 1910 and 1930. Most prominent were the *mutualistas,* the benefit societies that had surfaced in the latter decades of the nineteenth century. Many now became immigrant associations, tending to newcomers with relief, health, and funeral benefits; camaraderie and entertainment; patriotic displays and exhibits; literary programs; and *fiestas patrias* commemorations. Such immigrant *mutualistas* strived to perpetuate the language, culture, and traditions of the motherland and to ensure the survival of the group's ethnic consciousness while in exile. Working with the consul, the societies periodically branched out from their immediate purpose to defend the rights of members and others in the immigrant community.[73]

Other *mutualistas* such as the Liga Protectora Latina encouraged the membership of native-born Mexican Americans, accepting people on the basis of ethnicity instead of place of birth. Started in 1914 in Phoenix, Arizona, the Liga pursued several objectives, among them defending Mexicans from racial discrimination in the workplace. By the latter 1910s the Liga had expanded beyond Arizona and had founded chapters in New Mexico and California. In 1919, in fact, it affiliated itself with the Liga Protectora Mexicana of Los Angeles; the merger made the organization one of the most prominent *mutualistas* in the Southwest. For various reasons, the Liga Protectora Latina experienced decline during the 1920s, and apparently ceased to function during the depression.[74]

Also, there continued the Alianza Hispano Americana, which harkened back to the 1890s. During the 1910s and 1920s it established new branches in the Southwest and even Mexico, thereby augmenting its reputation as one of the most powerful U.S.-based Hispanic organizations. The Alianza enticed members with low insurance rates and its interstate reputation.[75]

Associations that accepted women into their membership, that had strict women membership or had as their purpose working among Hispanic women in the community, also summoned interest. Women's clubs engaged in projects such as organizing social events or coordinating programs for the entertainment of the barrios. Some of these organizations, however, had much more important purposes; among these were the Cruz Azul, a charity group linked to the national organization in Mexico by the same name. Cruz Azul (Mexican Blue Cross) chapters during the 1920s conducted relief work within Hispanic communities, helped the aged with home care, raised money for the infirmed unable to afford professional medical assistance, and intervened in cases of community or family crisis.[76]

Popular Theater

Spanish-language theater rose to popularity during the 1910s and 1920s as the new immigrants clamored for stage presentations. In the influx of the age had come actors and entire theatrical companies that aspired to practice their craft in the United States.[77] In automobiles or trains, touring companies by the 1920s followed itineraries that took them from the West Coast to Texas, to the Great Plains states and the Midwest, and even to the major cities of the northeastern United States. Mexican communities in San Antonio, El Paso, and Laredo in Texas; small ones in southern New Mexico; Tucson in Arizona; Chicago and Detroit in the Midwest; and San Francisco and Los Angeles in California established theaters for the performance of these professional companies or for local groups.[78]

The touring groups sought to meet the diverse tastes of communities, and thus they developed a variety of presentations that ranged from serious drama to comedy to the *revista*. The latter incorporated themes familiar to the local audience—plots that ranged from the Mexican Revolution to the experience of having to deal with difficult situations in the United States—and through the blending of satire and humor they served to permit spectators some emotional release from daily worries. A more working-class theater was the *carpa*, a performance given under a tent by a traveling family. The actors played on folk humor and comic types familiar to local communities. This brand of theater ordinarily visited remote locales often neglected by the larger professional groups.[79]

Singers and Performers

Corridos continued as a means of folkloric expression for the proletarian masses (the more literate within the community turned to poetry, short stories, and novels for conveying their own worldviews). In these folk ballads common people expressed lament over having to leave Mexico or revealed a longing for the homeland. *Corridos* also captured the sagas of Mexicans and Mexican Americans who stood up to gringos, either individually or collectively, especially during the border conflicts of the 1910s. Or they recorded the misfortunes of those entangled in the Anglo-American justice system. *Corridos* related the adventures or travail of migrant workers, as did the "Corrido de la Pensilvania," which narrated the journey of railroad workers heading for Pennsylvania. Or they could extol the patriotism of Mexicans and Mexican Americans who fought in World War I. The *corrido* also expressed the immigrants' disdain for Americanization and contempt for those who rejected *lo mexicano* by adopting the fashions, language, and habits of the Anglos.[80]

At a more sophisticated platform, two Tucsonensas made lofty contributions to the *canción* (the song). Luisa Espinel (née Luisa Ronstadt) gained international renown during the 1920s and after for her Spanish folk musical performances. Julia Rebeil achieved status as an accomplished pianist who gave several concerts throughout the United States and parts of Europe. In 1926 Rebeil became head of the piano department at the University of Arizona.[81]

Bilingual Literature

Most fiction writers of this time composed in Spanish and turned to the Spanish-language newspapers as an outlet for their work. In this medium essayists satirically expounded on a wide range of topics that involved Americanization, the degeneracy of U.S. culture, the insubordination of women, and the frailties of humankind (such as jealousy, gluttony, ambition, suspicion, dishonesty, and pretentiousness). Poets debated the Mexican Revolution, extolled the cultural heritage of Mexicans, lauded the patriotism of soldiers who participated in World War I, and complimented efforts designed to unify Mexican-American communities. Women writers contributed to the literary arena with exemplary compositions of prose and poetry on topics as wide-ranging as those of men. Their works at times belied the stereotypical role of women being traditionally dominated by men. Anarchist newspapers such as *Pluma roja* (Los Angeles, 1913–15), for instance, stridently advocated women's rights and called for their liberation from the manacling influences of government, religion, and materialism. Novelists also used the newspapers for merchandising their material: Mariano Azuela in 1915 turned to the pages of *El Paso del Norte* (El Paso, Texas) to publish his story of the Revolution entitled *Los de abajo* (the paper later published Azuela's classic in book form).[82]

The novelists of this era also wrote in Spanish, among them Daniel Venegas of Los Angeles, who in 1928 authored *Las Aventuras de Don Chipote o Cuando los pericos mamen* (*The Adventures of don Chipote; or, When Parakeets May Suckle Their Young*). Using a format that has been identified as a precursor to the Chicano novels of the 1960s (i.e., using working-class language and exploring themes associated with the life of ordinary folks), Venegas narrates the misadventures of a young and naive Mexican immigrant whose rustic background served him poorly in his quest to find success in the land of opportunity (i.e., the United States).[83]

Other fiction writers turned to a bilingual format. In New Mexico, Vicente J. Bernal penned *Las Primicias* (*First Fruits*) in 1916, using Spanish to write half the text of poems and essays. The other prominent *nuevomexicano* novelist was Felipe Maximiliano Chacón, who in 1924 produced *Obras de Felipe Maximiliano Chacón, "El Cantón Neomexicano": Poesía y Prosa* (*Works of Felipe Maximiliano Chacón, "the New Mexican Bard": Poetry and Prose*). In this collection (most of it is Spanish, part in English) the well-educated businessman and journalist exhorted Hispanos to cherish their heritage, and he reminded readers of the Hispano loyalty to the United States as witnessed in their contribution to numerous wars. Bernal's book and Chacón's poems placed emphasis on New Mexico's "Spanish" heritage, yet each work disclosed the influence made by contemporary writers from Mexico and Europe.[84]

A third group of authors published strictly in English. Mexico-born Josephina Niggli used the short story and novel to write about life in northern Mexico. *Step Down, Elder Brother* (1917) had as its protagonist a young man from an elite Monterrey family involved in two romantic affairs—one with an Anglo woman and the other with the daughter of a sadistic officer in the Revolution.[85] During this period Miguel Antonio Otero penned (though published later) *My Life on the Frontier, 1865–1882: Incidents and Characters of the Period When Kansas, Colorado, and New Mexico Were Passing through the Last of Their Wild and Romantic Years* (1935), *My Nine Years as Governor of the Territory of New Mexico, 1897–1906* (1935), and other pieces, one of which dealt with Billy the Kid.[86] Actually, such writers as Niggli and Otero came from the literate classes, so that their works do not truly reflect the experience of the masses. According to one authority, many of the Spanish-surnamed authors until the time of World War II came from privileged backgrounds whose families owned property or had professional careers.[87]

Brown Journalism

Spanish-language journalism as a profession expanded 1910 and 1930 (during that time, in fact, newspaper owners founded publishing firms that commodified novels or plays by talented writers, many of them refugees). Immigration and the growth of Hispanic communities produced circumstances wherein colonias demanded stories about events in the old homeland or relevant news about their immediate surroundings. Some of the refugees had been journalists in Mexico and now applied their trade to the new settings in the United States.

Newspapers delivered a variety of news, including keeping the exiles abreast of the chaos in the homeland. Reflecting the diversity of Hispanic communities, editors took different stands on the meaning of the Revolution. The PLM's *Regeneración*, as noted, spoke to the needs of the laboring classes. It sought the overthrow of the existing capitalist order in Mexico and its replacement with an anarchist utopia. *La Prensa* of San Antonio, on the other hand, took a harsh stance against the fighting, and under the editorial guidance of Ignacio E. Lozano, who founded the paper in 1913, spoke for those who wished to bring back the order and progress of Don Porfirio.[88]

Many of the immigrant newspapers during the 1910s and 1920s projected a nationalistic tone, including those in the growing colonias north of the borderlands, but they also offered readers information on numerous matters, such as Mexico's policies regarding the status of immigrants, available employment opportunities, or places of business that might help the newcomers communicate with their loved ones back home. Additionally, Spanish-language newspapers designated space for classified ads, features, literary pieces, and reprints from other newspapers outside the immediate locale. Parts of an issue could be devoted to informing readers (the middle-class editors regularly directed themselves at the poorer workers) on the need for unity or on the necessity for proper comportment, citizenship, behavior, and obedience of the law. The immigrant press also directed readers to make avail of their temporary stay in the United States to study in American schools, but it simultanesouly criticized discrimination, inequality in the workplace, and stereotypical portrayals of Mexicanos. *La Opinión* of Los Angeles, also founded by Ignacio E. Lozano (though not until 1926), was typical of these newspapers that directed their writings to *México de afuera*. As of 1930 it had a circulation of some 25,000 throughout California and just about every other area settled by Mexicans during the early decades of the twentieth century.[89]

But the newspapers of the era, especially those owned by Mexican Americans, also addressed the interests of native-born Hispanics, urging organization so that they could enjoy the same privileges as Anglo citizens. Conversely, *Regeneración* asked Mexican Americans to unite with their working compatriots in Mexico and help implement the PLM's ideals. Newspapers in New Mexico targeted a more specific audience, at times refusing to take stands regarding issues of the Mexican Revolution or other episodes occurring in Mexico. They confined themselves to local and state stories of interest to the Hispano population.[90]

A Time of Adjustment

Easy generalizations are difficult to apply to the process of community formation between 1910 and 1930. Outside the borderlands, for example, immigrants and Mexican Americans faced less of the blatant racism, institutionalized segregation, and harsh working environments that existed in the Southwest. In fact, residents of the midwestern states earned better wages.[91] On the other hand, immigrant and Mexican-American enclaves, wherever they existed across the United States, displayed certain similiarites. All owed much to the new immigration; they received from it fresh infusion of old customs, folkloric tales, Spanish-language newspapers, benificence societies, and the like. Within these settlements, most Mexican-origin people encountered some form of racism, segregation, exploitation, and oppression.

But Mexicans of every stripe and in different parts of the country also came in contact with acculturating influences that Americanized them to diverse degrees. All communities became grounds for competing ideological currents and for thoughts expressed by the new arrivals, by young people undergoing Americanization, and by Mexican Americans acquainted with U.S. institutions. Already by this time, in fact, there existed the makings of those who, owing to their birth in the United States, their upbringing in this country, or their World War I experiences, prepared to direct communities away from *lo mexicano* and toward a "Mexican-American" identity. That phase of Chicano history makes up the subject of the next chapter.

six

Communities under Stress: Depression and War

In the era from 1930 until the coming of World War II, the Great Depression played havoc with the lives of rich and poor. The features of the age are well known: a plunge in production capacity in both industry and agriculture, bankruptcies aplenty, a decline in wages, and high unemployment that hovered around 10 million jobless people at the end of the 1930s.[1] For Mexican-descent people the times posed even more severe circumstances: unemployment deeper than ever, a resurgence of nativism that questioned their right to New Deal benefits, competition for scarce employment, and fears of deportation and repatriation to Mexico.

Despite the gravity of the pre–World War II years, Mexican-origin people weathered the crisis and persevered with institutions and community intact. Life struggles went on. Common folks survived by taking whatever jobs availed themselves: in the beet fields they often accepted lower wages than those paid by New Deal programs. The politically minded founded new, more animated organizations, among them the League of United Latin American Citizens (LULAC), the Mexican American Movement (MAM), and the Spanish-Speaking Congress, all of which worked to make possible the American promise for the Spanish-speaking. Workers used labor activism as a political avenue toward self-amelioration, so that labor organization and activity reached unprecedented briskness. Women took new initiatives to define gender roles, using to advantage their experiences in the workplace, their participation in labor organizing, the lessons derived from their wartime employment, and new freedoms gained by other American women during the era. During this time, in fact, the number of newspapers in circulation, of children attending public schools, of people from the middle class who spoke out for the distressed masses, of women activists, and of scholars writing at the university level all increased.

Immigration Stifled

Because of the depression, immigration from Mexico slowed to a trickle. Some historians place the number of entrants to the United States at around 22,000 for 1940, but others who have studied immigration trends during the era note that some 150,000 other immigrants may have crossed the international boundary undetected. Comparatively, the 1940 census indicates that approximately 377,000 that year were born in Mexico.[2]

Despite their dilution in numbers, Mexico-born people still influenced the cadence of life in the segregated barrios and in rural settlements, where clubs, religious societies, *teatro*, Spanish-language newspapers, Mexican music, churches, and *fiestas patrias* observations all invigorated *lo mexicano*. Efforts by consuls—some of whom intervened in barrio affairs to deal with folks in destitution, to assist in labor-organizing drives, and to help upgrade education—also reinforced people's ties with old ways. Among those appreciating such intervention by a consul were residents of the small barrio of Lemon Grove in San Diego, California. In 1930 these residents complained of practices that relegated their children exclusively to a Mexican school. The consul helped move the case into the courts and won a ruling in 1931 stating that segregation violated state law. The court directed school officials to rectify the policy.[3]

Equally important in perpetuating a Mexicanist identity in the United States was the presence of those from the upper ranks of pre-Díaz society who had sought exile in the United States and still found the revolutionary atmosphere in Mexico unfriendly. Congregated in the larger cities such as San Antonio, Los Angeles, El Paso, and Tucson, they steadfastly maintained a "Mexican" outlook and promoted their worldview at bookstores and record stores, in public lectures, and in newspapers such as *La Prensa* and *La Opinión*. Someday, they hoped, Mexicans in exile would return home, as indeed many of them did in the late 1930s and early 1940s, when Mexico's presidents granted them amnesty.[4]

A Dual Identity

Simultaneous with the persistence of Mexico's values and traditions there unfolded a shift toward *lo americano*. Several circumstances, many of them unique to the 1930–45 era, engineered the change. Birth and upbringing acted as significant catalysts. By 1930 some 56 percent of the Mexican-stock population had been born in the United States according to the federal census, so that many of second- or third-generation Mexicans coming of age during this time had known only American institutions (though they heard about Mexico from their parents or sojourned there occasionally). Second, school curricula still pressed to substitute children's Mexican customs with American ways of thinking, speaking, and acting. Also, federal programs such as those enacted by the New Dealers convinced some in the colonias of the beneficence of the U.S. government. Similarly, contact with groups such as the YMCA and settlement houses in the cities of the Midwest exposed Mexicans to sentiments of solid citizenship and democracy. Acceptance of American habits led to increased participation in mainstream affairs (including labor unions and school boards) and the adoption of cultural aspects such as the swing music of Tommy Dorsey, Benny Goodman, and Glenn Miller; American fashions, crazes, and hairstyles; the idolization of Hollywood screen stars such as Clark Gable and Robert Taylor; and American dating norms and traditions.[5]

Such a transformation indicates that despite the hard times of the 1930s and World War II years, community tenacity prevailed. In fact, the lean middle class became slightly more perceptible, not for its economic prominence (it hardly expanded from its former size) but for the political clout it came to brandish. Among these men and women, some of whom made their living as teachers, doctors, lawyers, and businesspeople lay the foundation of what historians call the Mexican-American Generation, a cohort of individuals whose loyalty unequivocally belonged to the United States. Themselves victims of unnerving experiences with white society, they nonetheless endorsed the validity of American institutions and the ideas, values, and notions of U.S. citizenship. They considered themselves "Mexican Americans," though pride in their Mexican culture proved durable.[6]

The preceding discussion makes apparent that within colonias, much possibility existed for philosophical clashes, especially between those who still felt allegiance to the motherland and those who had accepted American outlooks and now mocked the old loyalty (and vice versa, of course). Indeed, friction emerged over such issues as nationality and class, as had ever been the case. Native-born Mexican Americans referred derisively to the immigrants as *cholos* or *chicanos*, while the newcomers responded with old disparaging term of *pochos*. Even those who belonged to the middle class distinguished themselves from the native-born members of the lower stratum. This "difference" over identity seemed to have been more pronounced in New Mexico among the native-born Hispanos. Certainly, many rejected the term *Mexican*, which Anglos associated with dirtiness, laziness, criminality, and backwardness—traits popularly given to the immigrants—and chose the more neutral term *Latin American*, which connoted U.S. origin.[7]

Geographic Diffusion

The 1940 U.S. census put the country's total Mexican-stock population at 1,624,733. Some historians dispute this datum, arguing that a more realistic figure would be 2,125,000 as many families avoided the census takers fearing deportation.[8] Mexican-descent people still lived overwhelmingly in the states of the American Southwest. Only about 10 percent resided outside the region (see Table 6.1).

Dispersal north from the borderlands persisted because of sustained demand for field workers. Mexicans from California and other southwestern states went north to Oregon, Washington, and Idaho to work the sugar, pea, potato, and hop crops, where some stayed as permanent settlers. By the late 1930s Mexican Americans, many of them from Texas, found employment in resuscitating factories (packing houses, foundaries, canneries, and the like) and fruit and vegetable fields in the states of the Midwest. While many of these migrants returned to Texas after the season, others stayed, attracted by the region's tolerance. The coming of World War II created further labor shortages in midwestern cities such as Chicago, attracting more folks from the Southwest. The arrivals of *braceros* during the war years into southwestern farms displaced indigenous Mexican-American workers, further driving people to the Midwest.[9]

In northern New Mexico and southern Colorado, the depression forced a return to the old villages. Folks who had establish settlements in northern Colorado and other Rocky Mountain states during the 1910s and 1920s now drifted back home. To stop interstate migration, in fact, Colorado's governor in 1935 and 1936 used police officers and the National Guard to block Mexican beet-field workers at Colorado's southern border. Though pressure from Spanish Americans from Colorado and New Mexico lifted the quarantine, the number of people using the old migratory network during the 1930s was dwarfed by pre-

Table 6.1. Geographic Distribution of Persons of Mexican Stock, by Region and State, 1910–1960

A. Born in Mexico

	1910	1920	1930	1940	1950	1960
Arizona	13.4	12.6	7.6	6.6	5.5	6.2
California	15.2	18.1	31.2	35.6	36.0	43.2
Colorado	1.2	2.3	2.1	1.7	1.2	0.8
New Mexico	5.4	4.2	2.6	2.4	2.1	1.9
Texas	56.5	52.2	41.6	42.2	43.5	35.3
Southwest	91.7	89.3	85.1	88.4	88.4	87.4
Other	8.3	10.7	14.9	11.6	11.6	12.6

B. Mexican or Mixed Parentage

	1910	1920	1930	1940	1950	1960
Arizona	13.3	12.5	8.9	7.7	6.4	5.9
California	10.8	16.1	27.3	31.5	35.7	38.6
Colorado	0.5	1.5	2.2	2.1	1.7	1.3
New Mexico	6.2	5.7	3.6	3.0	2.4	2.1
Texas	67.0	59.2	49.7	46.5	42.4	39.3
Southwest	97.9	95.0	91.6	90.8	88.7	87.1
Other	2.1	5.0	8.4	9.2	11.3	12.9

C. Mexican Stock (A Plus B)

	1910	1920	1930	1940	1950	1960
Arizona	13.4	12.6	8.2	7.3	6.1	6.0
California	13.4	17.4	29.3	32.9	35.8	40.1
Colorado	0.9	2.0	2.1	2.0	1.5	1.2
New Mexico	5.7	4.7	3.1	2.8	2.3	2.0
Texas	61.0	54.6	45.5	45.0	42.8	37.9
Southwest	94.3	91.3	88.2	90.0	88.6	87.2
Other	5.7	8.7	11.8	10.0	11.4	12.8

Note: Over the decades, the Bureau of the Census has reported only on the percentage of *white* foreign stock, except for some censuses in the early 1900s. In 1930 the Bureau of the Census changed its definition of Mexicans and classified them as nonwhite. As a consequence, the number of persons counted under white foreign stock declined drastically. In 1940 the census again classified Mexicans as white and issued revised 1930 figures for white foreign stock from Mexico as well as for total white foreign stock. However, no corrected figures were published for Arizona or New Mexico. In this table, 1930 figures for these two states are estimates based on relationships in 1920 and 1940.

Source: *U.S. Census of Population,* cited in Leo Grebler, Joan W. Moore, and Ralph Guzmán, *The Mexican-American People: The Nation's Second Largest Minority* (New York: Free Press, 1970), 111. ©1970 by The Free Press, a Division of Simon & Schuster, Inc. Reprinted with permission of the publisher.

depression levels. Then suddenly following the outbreak of World War II, the villages once more poured out their inhabitants: to Colorado to meet the demand for agricultlural hands, to Arizona to supply railroad and mine workers, to other parts of the state to provide laborers for airfield construction, and to other regions of the country (but usually California) to feed the need for operatives in wartime industry. The World War II exodus resulted in the depopulation and even the death knell of these generations-old rural villages.[10]

Handling Mexicans

Traumatic for Mexican immigrants (and Mexican Americans as well) were the deportation drives that occurred throughout the country during the depression. Initially (ca. 1929–31), some 200,000 people from throughout all parts of the United States responded to the economic crisis by returning to Mexico on their own volition. After 1931, however, government agencies undertook well-planned deportation campaigns, feeling it more economical to deport people than have them drain relief sources indefinitely. Coordinators for such initiatives used a variety of approaches. Locally, relief agencies might offer to subsidize the return home for those willing to accept repatriation (or they might threaten others with deportation if they resided in the country illegally); if agreed, officials organized train convoys and escorted the repatriates to the border. Church groups, associations such as the Red Cross, Mexican-American mutual aid societies, and *comités pro-repatriados* (pro-repatriation committees) having as their objective the humane expulsion of Mexican nationals undertook their own campaigns, underwriting the cost of the trek to Mexico. The harshest aspects of repatriation involved Anglo communities rounding up Mexicans and forcefully escorting them to the border.[11]

Conversely, Mexican consuls in the United States, various coordinating agencies in Mexico proper, and even persons from Mexico acting individually participated in the repatriation movements. Consuls worked closely with local authorities to lessen the strain of relocation and sponsored benefit dances and assorted events to raise the needed funds to pay for their compatriots' homecoming. Among those who took an individual initiative in assisting repatriates was the famous muralist Diego Rivera, who in 1932 founded La Liga de Obreros y Campesinos (League of Workers and Peasants) while working at the Detroit Institute of Arts. Between 1932 and 1933 Rivera and the Liga worked strenuously to get people to return to Mexico and settle in new colonies, but his efforts met only nominal success.[12]

After about 1932 the repatriation movement declined, though it persisted at subdued levels. Potential repatriates now laid low, no longer volunteering as before, having heard through word of mouth or having read accounts about even more grim conditions in Mexico. Many turned to agricultural work, where they felt more secure from detection. A small pecentage found refuge in New Deal programs implemented after 1933, though this did not make for a reliable option. All totaled, it seems as if the several deportation and repatriation initiatives produced the return of some 500,000 people.[13]

Psychologically, the depression era inflicted acute stress on Mexican-American communities. Repatriation campaigns instilled fear on families; as self-protection, many individuals refused petitioning for relief and even avoided doctors lest they be identified as potential repatriates or deportees. In addition to deportation or its threat, Mexican Americans faced bitterness from Anglos who looked on Mexican workers as competitors for scarce employment, or ones who benefitted from federal public works projects reserved for "Americans." Many states made extended residency a criterion for relief, a requirement that disqualified many Mexican Americans.[14]

Anxiety within communities continued into the World War II years; in some of the larger cities (Tucson, Houston, and Los Angeles, for example), it heightened as a cultural phenomenon known as *pachuquismo* (zoot-suiterism) and produced a frenzy among Anglos. By the late 1930s and early 1940s, youths within barrios had adopted the faddish zoot suit of the era and turned to a specific slang (an argot called *caló*) that combined the vocabulary of the Spanish gypsies and the Anglicization of Spanish in the barrios. Unfortunately, the *pachucos* (zoot-suiters) also engaged in behavior that included crimes ranging from petty harassment to murder.

In Los Angeles troubles crested in 1942 in what became popularly known as the "Sleepy Lagoon Case," an incident involving adolescent gang members allegedly killing a Mexican-American teenager at a swimming hole dubbed Sleepy Lagoon. In the trial of nine of the gang members, supposed experts attributed gang warfare and bloody killings to the Mexicans' ancestry: the Mexicans' Indian blood, it was argued, ostensibly inclined them to a life of delinquency, crime, and wretchedness. Subsequent to the case, the police kept a close vigil on the Mexican colonia in Los Angeles, as the local newspapers reported constant skirmishes between the pachucos and sailors stationed at local bases. The efforts of citizen committees, legal groups, and concerned labor organizations in 1944 resulted in the exoneration of the nine defendants in the Sleepy Lagoon case.

Finally, on 3 June 1943, the "zoot-suit riots" burst forth following an incident between Mexican boys and sailors. During the disturbance, servicemen in uniforms from the several military bases in Los Angeles infiltrated the east-side barrio and attacked, beat up, "unpantsed," and sheared the heads of the *pachucos* and anyone else in their path. Not until a week following the start of the riots did commanders declare Los Angeles off limits to the troops, and only then did the "riots" end.[15]

Coping in the Cities and the Fields

Near hopeless conditions in barrios before the 1930s persisted during the depression. The 1940 census did not provide information on the occupational distribution of Mexican Americans, but historians generally agree that little change occurred in the material standing of Hispanic communities during the 1930s.

Life in the metropolitan areas reflected the misery of the age. With city budgets strained, barrio streets went unpaved and unlighted, drainage and garbage collection went unheeded, and health problems (including a rise in tuberculosis and digestive illnesses), crime, teenage gang activity, and delinquency were left unattended. The poorest took refuge in makeshift shelters of whatever type: the worst housing consisted of any available item capable of keeping out the elements and insects: wooden scraps, cardboard, tin cans, and rocks. Such dwellings lacked privacy, bathroom facilities, electricity, floors, or kitchens: cooking had to be done outside, often in open pits.[16]

A few fortunate folks profited from some of the New Deal programs, such as the Works Progress Administration and the Civilian Conservation Corps. In the villages of New Mexico and Colorado, especially, the federal government introduced Hispanos to new literacy training courses, crafts lessons, and instruction in such health-related issues as proper dieting and midwifery, but such initiatives seldom "modernized" the villages.[17] For the lot of urban Mexican Americans, the 1930s called for coping by whatever means. Locally, some did find public relief or help from charitable societies. Many ate whatever such agencies provided, in many cases foods on the verge of spoilage, or items unfamiliar to the Mexican diet, such as pumpernickel bread. Some rummaged for old papers, tin cans, bottles, or scrap metal to sell; peddled tamales and other delicacies in the colonias; or hunted game, planted gardens, or killed the family hog. Rural folks in New Mexico and in Colorado moved to the cities, where they survived through similar methods, or by finding assistance in schooling programs, labor unions, barrio societies, and other organizations unavailable in the rural villages or migrant towns. In every colonia across the country, middle-class business-people able to afford it led drives to help poverty-stricken inhabitants, to provide food to school-age children in need, or to make medicine available to those who could not afford it. Consuls also worked unflaggingly to assist the unemployed in their despair.[18]

In the agrarian sector, life fared no better. In New Mexico's rural upper and middle Rio Grande Valley people struggled with some of the most pitiful conditions in the United States. According to one scholar, "New Mexico had, by far, the highest birth and death rates in the nation, with infant mortality amounting to 136 deaths for every thousand births. In the counties with 50 percent or more Hispanos, infants died at the rate of 144.4 per thousand."[19]

For Mexican Americans outside New Mexico, finding field work amounted to a blessing, but only because it helped them survive. Farm hands worked at the whim of the grower: they had no guarantee to a minimum wage, to sanitary facilities, or to the right of organizing. Still, farmwork remained a way of life: in Texas the "Big Swing," the movement of cotton pickers from south Texas into north and west Texas, actually escalated. So did the migration to the beet farms of the Midwest and the Rocky Mountain states: Tejanos made the long, often dangerous treks in groups of 25 to 50 persons crammed in trucks. Drivers stopped only intermittently along the two- to three-day journey, fearing detection by Texas police enforcing laws that levied taxes and other fees upon labor agents, or rebuffs by merchants along the way who did not serve or want Mexicans in their towns.[20]

Once in the migrant camps, people endured horrendous circumstances. Those working in the beet fields of the Midwest took refuge in crude habitations that included chicken houses, farm shanties, or tents. Vegetable and fruit pickers lived in "jungles," the name of the temporary accommodations converted from old abandoned railroad camps of a past age, or in alternate quarters erected near the harvest. Everywhere, migrants lived with dysentry, diphtheria, tuberculosis, and several other communicable diseases.[21] To make matters worse, dust bowl migrants from Arkansas and Oklahoma during the mid-1930s began displacing Mexican laborers, especially in California fields. Incredibly, after 1936 Anglos constituted nearly 90 percent of the migrants in California, where they had comprised no more than 20 percent of the roving work force in that state before the depression.[22]

A quick demographic adjustment occurred within Mexican-American communities when World War II began. Mexican-American farmworkers now headed for the city, as did those Anglo-Americans who had turned to farmwork in desperation. The vacuum created by the shift and the draft calls after 1940 led to agricultural labor shortages that produced what is known as the *bracero* (one who works with the arms) program, a binational agreement between Mexico and the United States (launched through the 1942 Bilateral Agreement and then enacted by Congress in 1943 under Public Law 45) to have laborers from Mexico come work farms in the United States during the war emergency. In implementing the program, the United States once more suspended laws in effect from the 1880s to 1918 and during the depression era and now permitted contract laborers (in the form of braceros) to enter the country without paying a head tax or meeting literacy requirments. As a consequence, some 4.5 million such temporary workers made the trip to the fields and the food-processing plants of the United States between 1942 and 1946. Officials from Mexico and the United States cooperated in screening prospective workers and seeing to their transportation to the United States and eventually their return home. Mexico insisted that employers finance the roundtrip, offer the braceros the same wages as paid to local labor, provide the guest workers with adequate

"Rosita la Remachadora," or Rosie the Riveter, Mexican-American style. Mexican-American women worked in a variety of formerly all-male occupations during World War II. Photograph reprinted by permission of the Arizona Historical Society Library.

accommodations, and permit them to shop anywhere. The Mexican government also sought to shield its nationals from discrimination. Despite all efforts aimed at protecting the braceros, the contracted hands still encountered exploitation, inadequate living conditions, and discrimination—problems long familiar to Mexican Americans.[23]

Then the war created new jobs for Mexican Americans, as Anglos who would have gotten priority went off to the front. Furthermore, the federal government established in 1941 the Fair Employment Practice Committee to ensure against racial discrimination in defense plants, though the agency encountered too many obstacles to be effective. Also, Mexican-American civic groups and leaders pressed government to promote occupational equality. Moreover, Mexico brought pressure to bear on the United States to either end discrimination against Mexican-descent people or face a blacklist of braceros to the United States. Overall, however, wartime opportunities rarely led to promotions or career enhancement. Employers channeled Mexicans into lower-level routines, paid them less for similar work done by Anglos, and segregated them in job assignments.[24]

Politics and the "Mexican-American Generation"

Mexican American communities made little political headway between 1930 and 1945. Old impediments to voting—poll taxes among them—persisted, as did bossism in a more diluted form, primarily in the more rural areas such as in south Texas but also in cities such as San Antonio. Additionally, several factors eliminated many from voting, among them their immigrant status, their age (a significant proportion of Mexican Americans were under the voting age of twenty-one) or lack of schooling. Moreover, people worried about more immediate things, such as providing for their families.[25]

By no means did the times still political involvement, however. All states in the Southwest had elected Hispanics to the legislatures by the late 1930s, though the incumbents of the age generally espoused moderate political views, whether they belonged to the Democratic or Republican parties. As had been the case historically, the Hispanos of New Mexico outmatched Mexican Americans of other states. They used, on occasion, their common identity with "Spanishness"—that is, they fused behind the concept of the aforementioned "Spanish heritage"—to pursue ethnic goals. Between 1930 and 1945 they held visible representation in the state house (in fact, five Hispanas served in the New Mexico legislature during the depression era). In New Mexico, also, Dennis Chávez, a Georgetown University law school graduate, was elected a U.S. senator in 1935 (he had been a House member since 1930) and retained his seat until 1962. The Hispanos managed even better representation at the local level.[26]

During the 1930s, also, Mexican Americans launched a variety of broad-based political initiatives. Wherever Mexican-American colonias existed, Mexican-American leaders—with ties to the aforementioned middle class, with the better jobs, or with labor-union affiliations—tried to coalesce both their cohorts of middling status as well as common folks behind associations, confederations, and leagues for the purpose of fighting discriminatory policies and establishing programs for uplifting Mexican Americans.[27] The factors behind this spurt vary; historians count among them the traditional impulse among

Mexican Americans to strive for life improvement, the response of communities to the immediate circumstances created by the depression, and the continued acculturation of Mexican Americans, especially those who constituted the Mexican-American Generation.

The most prominent and enduring of the several civic organizations to come out of the depression era was the League of United Latin American Citizens (LULAC), a descendent of the OHA discussed in Chapter 5. It pursued several ambitious and unambiguous goals: to erase discrimination, bring about equality, instill good citizenship in all, improve the educational status of Mexican-origin people, and assert the political clout of Mexican-American communities. It concerned itself primarily with the native-born or naturalized Mexican Americans, not the immigrants; the foreign-born had the consul to represent them. LULAC urged acculturation but insisted on a bicultural population faithful to its Mexican upbringing and customs yet American in political sentiment. By the mid-1930s the league had expanded from Texas to most of the states in the Southwest, but the leadership then spread the LULAC word to other regions of the country.[28]

The LULAC style conformed to the times, a hardly tolerant era. Most of them patriotic middle-class liberals, LULAC members sought reform, not a reshaping of society. They extolled the capitalist system, despite its exploitative nature. They opposed strategies that might give impressions of disloyalty, such as strikes and violent demonstrations. Their loyalty belonged to the United States, not to Mexico as in the case with those immigrants still attached to the homeland. As part of their effort to get Mexican Americans to take pride in their status as Americans, they worked toward youth involvement in Boy Scouts, held dances for scholarships, and encouraged adults to attend night classes that would make them better citizens.[29]

Officially nonpolitical, LULAC nevertheless took on political causes, among them campaigns for educational equality. Their first major attempt involved the 1931 case of *Independent School District et al. v. Salvatierra*, wherein LULAC sought the end to school segregation in Del Rio, Texas. Though a court of civil appeals judge ruled that school officials could not segregate Mexican children strictly on ethnicity, the court sided with school board members who maintained that the instruction of students worked better under separate environments. Also, LULAC members individually joined minor clubs that acted as fronts for achieving their political goals. In San Antonio, for instance, they protested discrimination on the part of city government or businesses, took stands in labor strikes unfolding during the 1930s, and campaigned for political candidates as members of the Club Democrativo and the League of Loyal Americans. In Houston clubs such as the Latin Sons of Texas served the same purpose.[30] True to their patriotism, many LULAC members joined the military ranks during World War II. Enlistment resulted in a decline in the LULAC membership and a hiatus from orqanizing during the war. It would rebuild after 1945 and resume its prewar objectives.[31]

In the Midwest, after the worst of the depression passed, Mexican Americans (many of them native-born or naturalized) in East Chicago founded the First Mexican-American Political Club for the intended purpose of arousing people politically and instructing colonia residents to vote intelligently. Though not very successful, it symbolized the initial efforts of the colonias in East Chicago to gain a foothold in local politics. Other societies launched during the late 1930s and 1940s in Chicago took similar assimilative postures.[32]

In Los Angeles middle-class professionals politicized by their participation in YMCA programs in the mid-1930s founded the Mexican American Movement (MAM) during the early 1940s. Throughout the decade, MAM sought to act to ameliorate dismal conditions in colonias, improve the educational status for Mexican Americans in California, eliminate discrimination, inspire youths to think and act like Americans, get young people to reject gangs or delinquency, prepare effective leaders, and generate the rise of a large middle and professional class. MAM did not prove to have staying power, however. It found it difficult to attract members during the war years, and its inability to acquire funds produced its dissolution in 1950.[33]

While the preceding organizations advocated moderate reforms, El Congreso del Pueblo de Habla Español (the Spanish-Speaking Congress) espoused leftist principles. Originally organized by Luisa Moreno, a veteran labor activist (Guatemalan-born but U.S.-educated), the Congreso and its progressive allies— among them members of the Communist party, independent labor organizers, liberals, and various Mexican-American groups—worked toward (according to resolutions adopted at its first meeting in Los Angeles in April 1939) erasing discrimination, educating Mexican Americans about their heritage (though it supported biculturalism), improving the material conditions of the Spanish-speaking, gaining women's rights, unionizing laborers including the unnaturalized, protesting police brutality, and helping youths. Among those who emerged as the major advocate of the Congreso was Josefina Fierro de Bright (born in Mexico but U.S.-educated), herself a former organizer in the Los Angeles community. She led the struggle for carrying out the Congreso's purpose. Unfortunately, the Congreso never found success outside California. By 1942 it had fallen victim to financial woes, an absence of organizing talent, competition from other Mexican-American civic organizations, and its own leftist leanings.[34]

Work and Labor Organizing

Several reasons explain a continuation of worker mobilization and union struggles in the depression and World War II eras. Obviously the travail of workers both in the city and farm motivated many to seek alleviation of their condition through labor organization. The impulse given to industrial unions by the New Deal also emboldened urban laborers, while neglect of agricultural workers by the same New Dealers drove field hands toward renewed campaigns designed to relieve their adversity. Communist unions and the Congress of Industrial Organizations (CIO) intensifed designs to recruit among the unskilled labor forces, and Mexicans accepted the overtures as part of their political agenda for self-improvement. The continued acquaintance of Mexican-American workers with the lofty principles of the Constitution, moreover, impelled some to seek equality through labor unionism. Those in the leadership of the labor movement generally came from the lower working classes, though a handful of organizers—Luisa Moreno, Josefina Fierro de Bright, and Ernesto Galarza among them—did have roots in the middle class.[35]

Because organized labor tended to ignore their needs or openly reject their membership, Mexican-American and immigrant laborers acted on their own to confront the everyday problems of the workplace. In any case, Mexicans appeared more comfortable in collectivities of their own creation, and such workingmen's associations existed as far north as Chicago. In 1935 Chicago laborers established El Frente Popular Mexicano (the Popular Mexican Front), a leftist group with links to organized labor in Mexico. Another labor society, the Sociedad de Obreros Libres Mexicanos de Sud Chicago (Society of Free Mexican Workers of South Chicago), targeted the needs of steel and foundary employees. Similarly, dismal conditions in the rural sector produced a number of indepen-dent ethnic labor groups, among them the Confederación de Uniones de Campesinos y Obreros Mexicanos (CUCOM), a confederation in California that broke away from a Communist party union (the Cannery and Agricultural Workers Industrial Union) in 1933 and for a while during the mid-1930s took the leadership role in representing some 10,000 California farmworkers.[36]

Spontaneously or as rank-and-file members of independent worker organiza-tions, Mexican Americans and Mexican immigrants launched several strikes during the depression, some of them in San Antonio and namely against the city's cigar industry and some of its bakeries. In the rural areas workers seemed even more militant. They appeared especially bold in California, where CUCOM led them in a series of small but effective strikes in the orange orchards of San Bernardino and Riverside (1934), in Orange and San Diego counties (1935), in Compton (1936), in Los Angeles county celery farms (1936), and in Orange County citrus-fruit operations. In 1937 CUCOM joined a CIO affiliate called the United Cannery, Agricultural, Packing, and Allied Workers of America.[37]

Also engaging in independent strike activity during the era were the braceros from Mexico. Many bracero strikes occurred in the northwestern states. There the scarcity of Mexican labor inspectors made if difficult to assist braceros who complained about low wages and higher pay for Anglo workers performing sim-ilar work. Though northwestern farmers experienced a desperate shortage of workers during the war years, they still effectively countered the strike move-ment using violence and threats.[38]

While Mexicans may have preferred their own independent locals, they heeded the advantages of joining national unions. Indeed, the extent of partici-pation in trade union movement seems to have exceeded the degree of involve-ment with ethnic organizations. Frequently, alliances with Anglo unions rested on pragmatism, convenience, or lack of alternatives; ideologically the Mexican community distrusted the more extremist unions such as Communist or Socialist orqanizations that offered them a helping hand during the 1930s.[39]

Nonetheless, urban laborers were affiliated with a wide array of industrial unions. In Detroit, factory hands employed in the automotive industry associ-ated themselves with the United Auto Workers. Elsewhere, Mexican Americans turned to the CIO following its birth in 1938. Some 15,000 had joined it in Los Angeles by the middle of World War II; hundreds belonged to Warehouse Local 1-26, which attracted Mexican Americans working in the warehouses, flour mills, paper factories, hardware stores, and refuse plants around the city.[40] In El Paso, Mexicano members of the CIO's International Union of Mine, Mill, and Smelter Workers strived through the war years to extract needed concessions from the city's smelters and refineries, and by 1945 they had achieved union recognition, fair wages, and hour limitations. A strike in 1946 by Mine Mill members in El Paso produced further benefits.[41] Similarly, the International

Ladies Garment Workers Union (ILGWU) and the United Cannery, Agricultural, Packing, and Allied Workers of America (UCAPAWA) worked energetically in the urban areas to assist the Mexican proletariat. A leftist union founded in Denver in 1937, UCAPAWA moved promptly into Texas and California to organize the walnut, pecan, and cannery industries, as well as seafood canning and processing. In California UCAPAWA claimed successes that same year in its plan to organize packing-shed workers and cannery operatives, but the conservative AFL contested its control and soon won the right to represent some 60,000 workers (the locals ordinarily amounted to company unions) in the cannery industry. In Texas UCAPAWA assumed the organization of pecan-shellers in San Antonio following a 1938 strike.[42]

Comparable mainstream union organizing spread to the agricultural sector, but efforts there achieved mixed results. The AFL found willing recruits among beet- and onion-field workers of the midwestern states, but by 1936 it transferred its energies to urban areas. The CIO demonstrated no more commitment, and, in any event, midwestern growers devised ways to counter unionizing activity—tactics that included importing Mexican-American strikebreakers from Texas. The work of UCAPAWA fell short also, and though it led several strike actions in California farms, by 1940 it suspended its activities among California farmworkers. In Texas UCAPAWA entered the Rio Grande Valley in 1938 but with no more effectiveness.[43]

In urban areas Mexican-American members of organized labor struck periodically. In Chicago they participated in strikes launched in 1937 by the Steel Workers Organizing Committee (SWOC), and some suffered injuries in the so-called Memorial Day Massacre, an episode in which police fired at picketers demonstrating in a South Chicago steel factory. From contract agreements reached in 1941 with selected plants in Chicago, however, Mexicans received the right to submit formal grievances and have seniority recognized for promotions.[44] Gains elsewhere in the country owed to UCAPAWA's efforts. In California, for instance, it expended time to organize the cannery industry that women workers dominated. A three-month strike protesting poor wages and an atrocious working environment at the California Sanitary Canning Company (Cal-San) met with success in 1939. With this victory, UCAPAWA won influence in the cannery industry and would thus concentrate on organizing it during World War II and the years after.[45]

In Texas, Mexican-American members of the Texas Pecan Shelling Workers Union led the Pecan-Shellers Strike in San Antonio in 1938 after receiving an UCAPAWA charter. They protested the work setting in the plants, low pay, and the exploitation of children. In the face of police intimidation, arrests, red-baiting and other tactics, the strikers still gained concessions, only to see them evaporated by new machine technology adopted by the pecan industry.[46]

Similar strike activity directed by organized labor erupted in the farmlands, especially in California. Among the earliest of such episodes was the Imperial Valley lettuce strike in 1930, led by the Agricultural Workers' Industrial League (AWIL), an affiliate of the Communist party's Trade Union Unity League (TUUL). The strike actually produced no increased wages, nor did it eliminate the use of contract labor and piecework system. This failure hardly demoralized the TUUL, however. It changed the AWIL's name to the Cannery and Agricultural Workers Industrial Union (CAWIU) in 1931, and in 1933 it arrived in El Monte (in the San Gabriel Valley) to assist Mexicans protesting declining wages in the berry fields, lack of housing, and other poor conditions. When the Japanese growers weakened and conceded slight wage increases to the berry pickers, elements among the Mexican strikers decided to negotiate; they severed ties with the CAWIU and launched the aforementioned CUCOM, which won recognition from the Japanese farmers.[47]

Despite the defeat at El Monte, the CAWIU moved on with organizing efforts. It led strikes on several farms, including a prominent one in August 1933 at the Tagus Ranch in the San Joaquin Valley, where peach pickers desired better wages, a shorter work week, and union recognition; when mediators worked out a compromise for wage increases, the CAWIU called off the strike. In October 1933 CAWIU led what emerged as the United States' most massive agricultural strike, this one a walkout in the San Joaquin Valley involving 12,000 cotton pickers (75 percent of them of Mexican descent) protesting growers' decision to set the wage of cotton picked at 60 cents per 100 pounds. But growers responded fiercely, causing much suffering to the strikers until state and federal mediators achieved a compromise granting cotton pickers a 75-cent wage per hundredweight. For the next two years CAWIU played a lead-ing part in farmworkers' struggle in California, but its end came abruptly in 1935, when the Communist party decided to end unionizing activities among agricultural workers.[48]

Sporadic strike activity in the rural regions spread to states outside California. In northern Colorado, the United Front Committee, inspired by left-wing leadership, initiated a statewide work stoppage in May 1932 to protest a newly imposed lower wage scale in the beet fields; the Hispano strikers won nothing as local growers retaliated with red-baiting, arrests, and deportation that deterred further strike activity in the state. In west Texas some 750 Mexican-American members of the Sheep Shearers' Union of North America struck ranches in 1934 for better pay, but the strike also ended in defeat as the wool growers used scabs, threats, and other intimidating tactics.[49]

Between 1930 and 1945, then, efforts by the working class to fulfill aspira-tions for improved living standards produced few significant victories. Several factors intervened. First, a surplus of labor during the era and the willingness of dust bowl farmers from Oklahoma and Arkansas to do what had been regarded as "Mexican work" diluted the bargaining strength of strikers. Also, the federal government did not take the interest in farmworkers that it did in industrial laborers; in fact, government agencies such as the Immigration and Natural-ization Service either harassed or deported Mexico-born labor agitators.[50] Moreover, management wielded immense power to deal with disgruntled work-ers. They had access to local police forces, to strikebreakers, or to newspapers and could mobilize public opinion against the malcontents.

Families in Depression and War

Expectedly, despair, poverty, and unemployment during the depression touched the traditional family structure. Scholars cannot quantify the toll. The historian Richard Griswold del Castillo discerned such problems as offspring leaving the family at a younger age than before and accepted customs such as extended-family obligations deteriorating with continued poverty and the migratory cycles of families. Orphans in Los Angeles once cared for by other family members or *padrinos*, for example, now became the charges of charitable institutions. Aside from economic factors, the example of American life subverted old customs. The rising mass-communications industry (radio and motion pictures, among them) brought modern messages regarding family relations into the enclaves, leading the younger set to ponder the validity of traditional norms.[51]

By no means, however, did the family disintegrate. Old traditions such as *compadrazgo* remained intact, for people still lived in clusters, worked together, and rejected undesirable Anglo influences. The world of Mexican Americans still encompassed concepts about the subordination of women and the responsibility of men as breadwinners. It also retained ideas regarding female modesty and discretion, a preference for midwives, and church consecrated marriages. Mexican Americans still shunned divorce.[52]

Women's participation in the work force hardly improved the economic and social standing of their families; generally women worked to fill in for unemployed males in the family—and during World War II for absent spouses or sons—and the jobs they took ordinarily provided subsistence wages. Many worked as seamstresses, laundresses, midwives, waitresses, and domestics. Many others worked the fields, while still others (the majority of them single teenagers) found openings in the related canning industry. Work in the canneries, albeit seasonal, held some appeal over farm or domestic work, but it paid no better (in California, the average wage stood at $2.50 per day) and could be as arduous. Mexican women received the most punishing tasks at the plants, such as washing the fruit.[53]

Still, a small corps of women did make occupational advances. In some counties in northern New Mexico unprecedented numbers of women became teachers or clerical or health care workers. Also, World War II provided slightly better opportunities for Mexicanas. Many took wartime jobs (by 1943, owing to the labor crisis, this included married women with children and even elderly women) that included drivers of heavy machinery, aircraft assembly-line operatives, medical personnel, office workers, translators, and substitutes in the steel, railroad, and meat-packing industries.[54]

An unprecedented degree of labor activism accompanied work force participation, though such activity did not produce any greater results for women than men. In Los Angeles (where women constituted half of the garment workers) Mexican-American members of the International Ladies Garment Workers Union (ILGWU) immobilized the dress industry for nearly a month in the fall of 1933, and their strike and subsequent picketing bore fruit in the form of security and slight economic gains. In San Antonio women comprised the most active participants in labor unionism, and ILGWU members struck at the Finck Cigar Company between 1933 and 1934, and in 1937 at Shirlee Frock Company, a manufacturer of infant garments. In New Mexico and Colorado women contributed to union organizing by addressing audiences, picketing, and even serving jail time for their participation in demonstrations. Among those achieving fame among Colorado beet-field workers was Monica Tafoya.[55] Other labor leaders during this era included Luisa Moreno and Josefina Fierro de Bright in California. In Texas the counterpart to these labor activists was Emma Tenayuca, called *la Pasionaria* by her co-workers. In 1934 she formed a Communist party organization called the Workers' Alliance in the Alamo City, and four years later led the widely publicized and aforementioned strike against the pecan-shelling plants in San Antonio.[56]

Political activity by women also became more visible by the 1930s. Women everywhere joined men in attacking social wrongs, such as the persistence of police brutality. Others enlisted in such middle class organizations as LULAC, which incorporated women after 1934 through Ladies Councils. For the most part, women activists tended to be middle class and somewhat better educated than the masses, aspired to professional advancements, and belonged to the Mexican-American Generation. Among LULAC's most active members were Mrs. F. I. Montemayor and Mrs. J. C. Machuca of Texas, and Jennie M. González, Susie Chávez, and Mary Baca Romero of New Mexico.[57]

By the end of World War II male society had accepted newer perspectives on women. Increasingly between 1941 and 1945, the more tradition-bound husbands and fathers conceded women's need to work, either because of the necessity to sustain the family while male members fought abroad or because Mexican-American communities felt that women should also contribute to the war effort. By 1945 tradition had also granted to mothers new freedoms to participate in community projects or to further their schooling. Young women profitted from the age of change by gaining freedom to wear the latest fashions and hairstyles.[58]

School Days

Interestingly, the depression era witnessed an upturn in the school attendance of Mexican-American children. There are several reasons for this trend. For one thing, parents retained faith in schooling, recognizing its value as a means to better jobs, as a way to provide security for their families, and as a necessity for penetrating the mainstream. With families not migrating as they had earlier, children had a better opportunity to attend local institutions. The free lunches that the schools offered and the more comfortable atmosphere there, especially in the winter, motivated struggling families to enroll youngsters in school. From the southwestern states to the midwestern cities, a small contingent of Mexican Americans began graduating from high school during the depression years.[59]

In the "Mexican schools" of the age, administrators and teachers continued working under the assumption that Mexican culture lagged behind American civilization. Consequently, they emphasized replacing it with American values, traditions, and the English language. As in the early twentieth century, educators did not reach for training a professional sector within the Mexican-American community as LULAC and other middle class organizations envisioned. They still sought to prepare a group to assume the menial jobs society believed appropriate for Mexicans: in the industrial arts for the boys and in such positions as seamstresses, waitresses, and domestics for girls.[60]

Culture, Community, and Change

The resilience of clubs and societies supported by folks still loyal to *lo mexicano*, the decline of some of these organizations, and the birth of new groups that increasingly expressed a Mexican-American identity all pointed to the cultural transformation unfolding during the era. At the start of the depression, many of the *mutualistas* still took the lead in organizing help within colonias, but the economic dilemma, their persistent emphasis on *lo mexicano,* and newer opportunities for joining other associations, especially during World War II, tested their toughness. During the war years many *mutualistas* witnessed loss in membership. The services they had previously offered now competed with New Deal programs, and the nascent Mexican-American organizations of the age seduced the more politicized among *mutualista* ranks. The durable Alianza Hispano Americana, which retained a large membership until its precipitous fall in the 1960s, proved a major exception.[61]

If Mexican Americans and immigrants had at their disposal a miscellany of mechanisms to deal with community needs, the diversity of newspapers surfacing during the 1930–45 period showed it. On the one hand, there remained the very influential pre-depression newspapers like *La Prensa* and *La Opinión* in San Antonio and Los Angeles, respectively, which continued to express the viewpoint of those tied to the immigrant generation, many of them still in exile in the United States. Ignacio E. Lozano, very much in his prime during these years, still criticized the revolutionary governments in Mexico while simultaneously urging readers to emulate the example of the better Mexican classes in the United States. In encouraging the latter, *La Prensa* urged readers to read its social page; to attend the opera, literary presentations, and the Spanish-language cinema; and to keep abreast of the latest creative works in Spanish that dealt with culture and the history of Mexico.[62]

At the other end of the spectrum stood the likes of Ignacio L. López, editor of *El Espectador*, who symbolized the incipient Mexican-American press. Though born in Mexico, López had received his education in the United States and considered himself American first and Mexican second. He had little interest in the old homeland; he aspired to see the complete integration of Mexican-descent persons into American society. He launched *El Espectador* in the San Gabriel Valley (east of Los Angeles) in 1933 and continued publishing it until 1961. During the 1930s and continuing until the war years, he attacked in print segregationist policies, mistreatment of Mexicans at the hands of the police, and other acts that condemned Mexican Americans to second-class status.[63]

Radio, while not necessarily assuming ideological stands, exposed people to the world beyond the colonias. During the depression era, Anglo-owned radio stations began setting aside time for broadcasting Spanish-language programs (the trend seems to have emerged first in California, then spread elsewhere), providing Mexican-origin listeners with the most popular records in Spanish—among them *corridos, canciones rancheras,* and other types of music popular in Mexico. Mexican Americans, however, also tuned in to hear the latest hit songs in English, to get the latest news, and to heed the disc jockeys' hip talk on matters of interest to teens.[64]

Spanish-language theater continued only sporadically during the 1930s, struggling to continue the mass popularity it had enjoyed during the 1910s and 1920s but ultimately succumbing to the effects of economic hardship, to repatriation drives, and to the growing popularity of motion pictures. Impresarios during the age now converted major stages in cities such as Los Angeles and San Antonio, as well as other minor ones in Chicago, into theaters that showed talking movies featuring Mexican stars such as Dolores del Rio and Lupe Vélez, or that hosted benefit programs and a variety of other performances, including American burlesque shows and boxing and wrestling matches.[65]

Community and church theatrical groups surfaced throughout Mexican-American enclaves to meet the vacuum left by the professional companies; they incidentally provided an outlet for unemployed artists and aspiring actors. Local amateur theater also served as a forum for raising funds for the destitute, local parishes, the community *mutualista*, or civic organizations like LULAC. The *carpa*, in the meantime, weathered the years effectively. As in earlier ages, the *revista* remained a favorite presentation; it now dealt with issues such as repatriation, the continued Americanization of Mexicans in the United States, and the phenomenon of the *pachucos*.[66] *Corridos*, though they remain to this day, seemed to have slipped in prominence during the 1930s. Still, they treated topics of pressing importance to the colonias, among them the impact of the depression and the trauma of confronting law authorities bent on repatriating Mexicans on menial pretexts. Other themes included labor strikes, acculturation, and racial injustice.[67]

Conjunto music (produced by the accordion-led ensemble) came into its own during the 1930s and it gained immense popularity among the lower classes everywhere, from the barrios of Los Angeles to the migrant camps. *Conjuntos* from Texas traveled far afield, visiting the migrant settlements outside the borderlands, bringing with them the most popular tunes, and diffusing Tejano culture. Even without these traveling musicians, there always seemed to be among the itinerant crews someone able to play an accordion or guitar and provide farm crews with the needed entertainment on weekends at improvised dance halls, either in the open air or inside a barn.[68] During the war years a handful of musical artists found national success with both Mexican-American and Anglo audiences. These included Andy Russell (born Andrés Rábago Pérez) from Los Angeles and Lalo Guerrero of Tucson. Both recorded in English and Spanish for companies in the United States and Mexico.[69]

Writers: Creative and Academic

New outlets became available to Mexican-American writers during the 1930s and early 1940s, an interesting occurrence given the fact that Mexican Americans encountered so many limitations during this era. Authors continued turning to newspapers as before, but also to outlets such as the *LULAC News* and other newer periodicals. One essayist, Robert Torres, even published provocative stories on the absurdities of war in the pages of *Esquire*.[70]

Those writing what have become enduring pieces came from the ranks of the educated middle class and tended to write in English. Josephina Niggli, who had begun her literary career in the 1910s, reached her prime in the pre–World War II era. She received her graduate degree from the University of North Carolina in 1931 and resumed writing novels and plays that interpreted Mexican folkways for American audiences. Her 1945 book-length collection of stories, *Mexican Village,* eloquently dileneated Mexico's heritage as an essential feature of the holistic Mexican-American experience. Her long career continued into the 1960s.[71]

Those from New Mexico and California, on the other hand, reiterated the motif of the "Spanish" heritage; writers from New Mexico remained especially faithful to the theme, as many of them traced their ancestry to the pre-1900 era and immigration from Mexico had never become a salient concern in the state (people from Mexico had not found New Mexico attractive between 1900 and 1930). Adelina Otero-Warren, for one, consciously sought to educate all New Mexicans about the state's glorious Spanish legacy, fearing the old heritage would succumb to acculturating influences or other changes occurring during the 1930s. Her book *Old Spain in Our Southwest* (1936) dutifully preserved tales, folk traditions, and songs that appeared of indisputable Iberian origin. Her works and those of such others as Cleofas Jaramillo also recorded the activities of women and serve as valuable sources for learning about the duties, experiences, and personal perceptions that women of New Mexico have historically held.[72]

Scholarship also came into its own during the 1930s, dominated by a handful of university intellectuals who followed in the footsteps of the pioneer scholar Aurelio M. Espinoza, the prolific *nuevomexicano* whose tenure at Stanford University between 1910 and 1947 produced dozens of publications on the folklore and language of Hispanos in the villages of northern New Mexico and southern Colorado.[73] Among the new professors was Dr. Carlos E. Castañeda, a teacher at the University of Texas until 1957, who sought to revise ethnocentric interpretations of Texas history by chronicling the major contributions people of Hispanic descent had made to the history of the United States. His major tome turned out to be the masterful *Our Catholic Heritage in Texas,* a seven-volume series started in 1936 and finished in 1958, but his lifetime record includes 12 books and 78 articles, a notable accomplishment still unmatched by any Chicano historian.[74]

New Mexico–born George I. Sánchez received his doctorate in educational administration at the University of California in 1934. After a distinguished career at the University of New Mexico, he relocated to the University of Texas at Austin and became a champion for educational reforms affecting Mexican Americans. In countless scholarly articles and several books, Sánchez questioned the validity of I.Q. tests in measuring racial intelligence, challenged the belief that Mexican culture and the Spanish language handicapped Mexican students, and denounced segregation as hurtful to Mexican-American youngsters. Sánchez's best-known work, *Forgotten People: A Study of New Mexicans* (1940), was the first book-length social scientific study of the New Mexican Hispanos to be written by a Mexican American.[75]

Arthur Campa joined Castañeda and Sánchez among the most prominent intellectuals of the pre-1945 era. Born in Mexico but raised in New Mexico, Campa held an immense admiration for the plain folks of the Southwest region of his upbringing. With his training in languages (an M.A. from the University of New Mexico in 1930 and a Ph.D. from Columbia University in 1940), he wrote numerous scholarly books and essays on Mexican-American folklore, folk theater, proverbs, and folk tales that he traced not solely to Spain but to Mexico and to the Mexican-American experience in the Southwest.[76]

Jovita González, the first Mexican American to analyze Tejano culture in English, also challenged prevailing views about Mexicans. Raised in Roma,

Texas, from an old Tejano family, she received her M.A. in Spanish from the University of Texas and went on to a lengthy high school teaching career in Corpus Christi. Jovita's many articles on Mexican-American culture conveyed a respect for the people as well as an understanding of the richness of their oral traditions. Her colleagues recognized the significance of her work, and in the 1930s they chose her as the first Tejana to be elected president of the Texas Folklore Society.[77]

Other scholars researched and elaborated on the myriad of social problems that confronted Mexican Americans. Alonso S. Perales, a lawyer who graduated from the National University Law School in Washington, D.C., described the history of Texan/Tejano relations in *El Mexicano Americano y la política de sur de Texas* (1931). His two-volume work *En defensa de mi raza* (1936–37) examined the Mexican-American battle for equal rights. *Are We Good Neighbors?* (1948), Perales's most important work in English, consisted of testimony compiled to convince Anglos of the extent of discrimination against Mexican Americans. This landmark study provided invaluable information for later desegregation lawsuits.[78]

Mexican Americans in Uniform

The nation's call to arms during World War II touched Mexican-American boys in just about every colonia and rural settlement. Some estimates place the figure of Mexican-descent people serving in the war at 400,000; the number represents a higher enlistment of Mexican Americans (in proportion to the total Hispanic population in the country) in combat divisions than other nationalities in the United States. Additionally, a small percentage of women joined the armed forces; some of them served overseas with much merit.[79]

Several reasons explain the Mexican American participation. Obviously, many received draft notices. The ones who volunteered did so believing that democracy stood in peril, or because they wanted to join friends who had just left. Mexican nationals in the United States took seriously Mexico's encouragement to take up the struggle against Hitler and the Japanese.[80]

Proportionately, Mexican Americans achieved the distinction of gaining more decorations for bravery in the battlefield than any other group, and none faced charges of desertion, mutiny, or treason. Moreover, they received more medals of honor (12) in relation to their population than any other ethnic group.[81]

At home, Mexican-American communities joined the war mobilization with unwavering commitment. Colonia organizations in the Southwest and beyond it appealed to people in the barrios for contributions through the purchase of liberty bonds. Common folks participated in Red Cross campaigns. Some Mexican-American women joined clubs patterned after the USO for the benefit of Mexican boys barred from certain public places due to their race.[82] The war also brought Mexican-American civilians in contact with mainstream institutions in the greater society for the first time. It made barrio residents feel vital to the campaign against Hitler and inspired them to display outwardly and patriotically the care for the country that nourished them. The war exposed Mexican-American soldiers to an international setting where men and women of different nationalities and races worked together for a common cause. Servicemen became privy to a more liberal and open society and returned home questioning the racial order and subordination of their community.[83] This "G.I. generation" would lead the cause for Mexican-American equality between 1945 and the 1960s.

A *People in Motion*

The depression sent Mexican Americans reeling, forcing people into wretched livelihoods in the farms and ranches or into colonias to cope as best they could. Paradoxically, the crisis contributed to the beneficial structuring of Hispanic communities. With only moderate pressure on individuals to acculturate, *lo mexicano* coexisted alongside *lo americano*. With so many belonging to a proletariat with much in common, class tension stayed latent. Though the times stifled enlargement of the middle class, adversity inspired leaders to take on initiatives to reverse deteriorating fortunes for the whole. During the 1930s, indeed, Mexican Americans launched initial civil rights crusades.

The post–World War II era, comparatively, enticed people to move out of the rural regions and outside the bounds of the barrios. Expanding cities offered modern amenities, wider employment prospects, and better schooling opportunities. Mexican Americans confronted greater acculturating influences, and some experienced upward mobility and developed cultural tastes that differentiated them from those left in the lower stratum. Class friction and fragmentation surfaced, but so did an invigorated activism, brought on by emboldened war veterans, an expanding and confident middle class, and politicized liberal/Anglo groups wishing to form coalitions with Mexican Americans. In the era after 1945, therefore, Chicanos embarked on new adventures.[84]

seven

Mexican Americans in Postwar America

A fter World War II the United States experienced an unprecedented surge of prosperity, but millions of Mexican Americans did not share in this affluence. While having full employment during the war, Mexican Americans remained at the bottom of the socioeconomic pyramid. They continued to work in low-paying jobs and live in substandard, segregated housing in barrios or colonias throughout the Southwest and outside the borderlands. The Bracero Program, the U.S. government labor strategy, allowed the importation of Mexican workers and, as a result, lowered wages for hundreds of thousands of Mexican-American farm laborers. On the national front a new conservatism emerged, spawning labor and immigration laws that hurt Mexican Americans. At the same time, Mexican Americans organized to fight for civil rights and to abolish segregation in public facilities. Other Mexican Americans organized labor unions and political associations to try to secure a piece of the American pie. The maturation of an educated, articulate Mexican-American political and intellectual leadership in the 1950s prepared the way for a renaissance in the next decade. Generally the Mexican-American middle class had a political and social orientation that differed from that of the thousands of Mexican immigrants who came to the United States either as braceros or as undocumented immigrants. Nevertheless the newly arrived Mexicanos forced the more established and affluent Mexican Americans to confront growing inequities between people of Mexican descent and the general population. A few Mexican-American leaders recognized that by uniting with the immigrants there was the possiblity of advancing the cause of social justice for both groups.

The Bracero Program and "Operation Wetback"

Mexican immigration had a mixed effect on the Mexican Americans of the immediate postwar period. The increased numbers of Mexican-born provided the demographic clout for future political organization. The repatriations of almost a million Mexican undocumented immigrants in the 1950s, even while applauded by many middle-class Mexican-American organizations, created tragic disruptions in family life and damaged the Mexican-American enclave economy that depended on immigrant paychecks. Most of the labor contractors who managed the bracero program and recruited Mexican farmworkers were bilingual Americanized Mexican Americans. Other Mexican Americans, especially those in the working class, felt threatened by the newly arrived Mexican laborers. Mexican-American farm workers knew from experience that these workers took their jobs and were often used to break strikes and to lower wages. This created occasional bitterness between the two groups. But the commonalities of language, history, and culture also nourished close social ties. Many families had immigrant relatives who joined them during this period. Others married immigrants and established families. As historian David Gutiérrez remarked, "Ongoing immigration from Mexico, and Mexican American responses to it, both played crucial roles in shaping the ethnic identity of Mexican Americans."[1] The complex interaction of Mexican immigrants with native-born Mexican American during the 1940s and 1950s became even more intense as the size of the immigrant stream increased. In a sense, the stage was being set for a rediscovery, reinvigoration, and reinterpretation of *lo mexicano*.

As noted in the previous chapter, the Bracero Program originated during World War II when the United States desperately needed farm laborers to take the place of the hundreds of thousands of Mexican Americans who had been drafted or who had volunteered for the armed services. During the 20-year life of the program, many braceros "skipped" their contracts at the end of their period of work and became undocumented immigrants. Of these, an undetermined number settled permanently in the United States. Between 1946 and 1960 braceros far outnumbered legal Mexican immigrants (see Table 7.1). The number of undocumented workers whom officials apprehended rose significantly, suggesting that many more immigrants wanted to come than the country could accommodate. The Bracero Program itself encouraged illegal immigration. The program raised the expectations of millions of Mexico's poor campesinos (farmworkers), causing them to abandon their homes in hope of becoming a bracero. Many more applied than could be accepted, and ultimately the determined agricultural migrant decided to cross illegally.

It was not long before a nativist backlash developed. The noticeable rise in undocumented immigration during the first years of the 1950s led to increased media interest in people who were pejoratively referred to as "wetbacks" and their impact on the American way of life. The newspaper and television coverage consistently termed the undocumented immigrants as "illegal hordes" or their arrival as a "wetback invasion." Increasingly the government considered them a threat to the social and political stability of the country. In 1951, for example, Dwight D. Eisenhower, in writing to William J. Fulbright, a powerful senator on the Foreign Relations Committee, commented that "the rise in illegal border crossings by Mexican wetbacks to a current rate of more than 1,000,000 cases a year has been accompanied by a curious relaxation in ethical standards extending all the way from the farmer-exploiters of this contraband labor to the highest levels of the federal government."[2]

In 1954, reacting to mounting public fears, Attorney General Herbert Brownell prepared to launch a mass roundup of "wetbacks." It was code-named "Operation Wetback" and planned and conducted with all the intricacy of a military operation. The commissioner of immigration, Joseph M. Swing, a retired lieutenant-general, reorganized the Immigration and Naturalization Service (INS) to make the operation more efficient. He marshalled cooperation of the

Table 7.1. Braceros and Mexican Immigration, 1945–1960

Year Apprehended	Braceros[1]	Mexican Immigration[1]	Undocumented[1]
1946	32	6	100
1947	20	7	194
1948	35	8	193
1949	107	8	288
1950	68	6	468
1951	192	6	509
1952	234	9	529
1953	179	9	886
1954	214	18	1,089
1955	338	50	254
1956	417	65	88
1957	450	49	60
1958	419	26	53
1959	448	23	45
1960	427	41	71

[1]In thousands.

Sources: Alejandro Portes and Robert L. Bach, *Latin Journey: Cuban and Mexican Immigrants in the United States* (Berkeley, Los Angeles, and London: University of California Press, 1985), 63; Stanley Ross, ed., *Views Across the Border: The United States and Mexico* (Albuquerque: University of New Mexico Press, 1978), 166.

Mexican authorities, who were also eager to control the flow of their country-men to the United States. Swing carefully orchestrated a media campaign to frighten "illegals" into voluntarily going to Mexico. The government set 1 June 1954 as the beginning of the campaign.

During Operation Wetback the government deported or "repatriated" more than 1 million Mexican immigrants back to Mexico. Under the McCarran-Nixon Internal Security Act (passed in 1950) those immigrants whom the government found to be guilty of subversive activities could be arrested and deported. The government used this provision when carrying out Operation Wetback to get rid of Mexican labor organizers. During the mass roundups (which averaged 2,000 people a day in California), the Immigration and Naturalization Service violated the constitutional protection of hundreds of thousands of persons, illegally entering homes and detaining U.S. citizens without probable cause. The deportations and repatriations continued sporadically for the next few years until the INS claimed victory in controlling the border. In reality, the decline in apprehensions appeared to be more the result of agribusiness's increased pressure on the INS to allow more undocumented immigrants into the country during times of labor shortage.

The big corporate growers in the southwestern states had become avid supporters of the Bracero Program and cheap Mexican labor. When Congress threatened not to renew the program after the war, commercial growers lobbied to continue it. They argued that without it they would go out of business because there were not enough native laborers willing to do the job. Subsequently they succeeded in getting Congress to extend the program repeatedly. In January 1954, just months before the inauguration of Operation Wetback, the Mexican government balked at renewing the bracero agreement because of questions about the certification procedure used for determining bracero wages. In response to growers' complaints that they desperately needed Mexican labor, the INS opened the border to anyone wishing to cross. It then proceeded to help recruit laborers for the farmers by allowing illegal entrants to become legalized as they worked. This strategy pressured Mexico into renewing the agreement on terms favorable to the U.S. growers.[3]

The braceros, along with their undocumented cousins (most of these new immigrants were men) mostly worked in the fields of Texas and California, although they were also recruited to work elsewhere. Labor contractors and growers rounded up braceros to work in the developing agricultural regions in Washington state, Idaho, and Oregon. There the braceros joined Mexican-American immigrants, primarily from New Mexico and Texas, who had been attracted to the region because of labor shortages and higher wages. Ultimately both Mexican immmigrants and Chicano migrants became the nucleus of Spanish-speaking communities in the rural regions of the Pacific Northwest.[4] The government sent many braceros to Michigan, Illinois, and Minnesota, where they augmented the small barrios of Mexicanos that worked in the steel and auto industries in Gary, Indiana, and Detroit. By the end of the bracero years, Mexican communities, composed of "skipped" braceros and their families, could be found scattered throughout the northwestern, western, and midwestern states.

There had been protests about the Bracero Program from the beginning, spearheaded by labor unions and human rights and church oganizations. Included in the opposition were several well-known Mexican-American groups. Both the National Coungress of Spanish-Speaking People and the California Federation of Spanish-speaking voters opposed the program, as did the League of United Latin American Citizens (LULAC), the Bishop's Committee on the Spanish Speaking, and the American G.I. Forum.[5] The labor leader and economist Ernesto Galarza led the fight through the 1940s and 1950s, arguing that the Bracero Program took jobs away from Mexican-American citizens of the United States. He worked to convince Mexican Americans that the program was economically bad for their communities. He and other observers knew that the growers were violating many of the provisions in the original agreement by not actively recruiting native farm laborers and giving employment preference to braceros. Galarza found that, by 1959, braceros were working in nonagricultural occupations, such as lumbering, trucking, light manufacturing, and ranching. He documented how the program lowered wages and depressed working conditions for native workers. The "bracero wage" often became the norm for all agricultural workers. Because of the Bracero Program, growers did not have to consider making improvements in migrant housing in order to retain dependable workers. Sometimes the growers used braceros to break strikes in violation of the federal regulations and workers reported cases of mistreatment and exploitation by the growers. Most often, the braceros complained about unauthorized deductions from their paychecks, excessive charges, substandard housing arrangements, and underemployment.[6] From 1943 to 1947 the Mexican government refused to send braceros to Texas because of incidents of abuse and discrimination.

Bracero workers outside their dormitory in the 1950s. Their employer, Thompson Brothers Farm, north of Mission, Texas, paid $1.50 an hour for 100 pounds of cotton picked and charged them for their accommodations and food. Photograph courtesy of the Special Collections Division, Texas Labor Archives, the University of Texas at Arlington Libraries, Arlington, Texas.

In 1965 the Bracero Program ended by mutual agreement between the two governments. Commercial growers lessened their lobbying efforts to continue the program when they discovered undocumented immigrants to be an even cheaper and more convenient source of labor than the braceros. The program had benefited only a few, big regional corporations. The large growers in California and Texas had been the main beneficiaries of the Bracero Program; only a small percentage of all U.S. farmers had employed the bulk of bracero workers.[7] Union leaders in both Mexico and the United States had called for the abolishment of the program throughout the 1950s. Finally, under the liberal surge of President Lyndon B. Johnson's Great Society, Congress ended the program, but, to soften the impact on the Mexican economy, the two governments negotiated the Border Industrialization Program. This 1965 agreement allowed U.S. industries to employ hundreds of thousands of Mexican laborers in assembly plants along the U.S.–Mexican border and to import finished manufactured goods from Mexico to the United States duty-free. This program created the maquiladora industry, which became a big moneymaker for multinational corporations and threatened the jobs of thousands of U.S. industrial workers.

Geopolitical Diversity and Dispersal

The regional differentiation of Mexican Americans as traced in previous chapters continued but lessened somewhat by the growing influence of American urban consumer culture. Mexican Americans in California were perhaps the most urbanized of those who resided in the old Southwest. Their urban culture was influenced by the contradictory forces of increased Mexican immigration and increased suburbanization of southern California. The Hispanos in New Mexico faced pressure to leave their traditional rural villages to join the migrant labor pool or to move permanently to the big cities in Colorado, Washington state, or California. Those who remained continued to reflect a rural Hispano heritage that identified strongly with a colonial Spanish past. Tejanos retained their rural and small-town solidarity, particularly in the Rio Grande Valley, but economic changes in the Lone Star State also forced them to leave their enclaves to work and live in the larger cities of Texas, to become seasonal migrants, or to leave Texas permanently for jobs in California or the Midwest. The growth of the metropolis of Phoenix and its surrounding irrigated agricultural regions drew many Mexicanos from the small mining and ranching towns of southern Arizona and attracted new migrants from Sonora. A key to promoting the increased migration, both seasonal and permanent, was the rapid growth of an interstate highway system connecting the major job centers of the southwestern states.

Outside the traditional Southwest newcomers steadily streamed into the established colonias and barrios of the big cities and small farming towns such as Yakima, Washington; Medford, Oregon; or Twin Falls, Idaho, all of which had a growing Mexicano and Chicano population after World War II. There was also a noticeable movement into the metropolitan centers of Denver, Colorado, Kansas City, Kansas, and the Chicago–Gary, Indiana, metropolitan area. One of the prime concerns of the new migrants who entered these urban areas was community-building.[8] While the process of establishing cultural and political organizations, Spanish-language churches, and community networks had been undertaken by migrants in previous decades, the deportations and economic decline of the depression had seriously weakened Mexican-American community solidarity. In a sense, the new migrants who came after World War II had to build new communities.[9] Often this meant forging new alliances with other ethnic groups who themselves were new migrants. This was the case in the Midwest, where there had been an influx of thousands of Puerto Ricans as well as African Americans.

Families in Transition

As in previous decades, Mexican Americans depended a great deal on their families for economic and cultural support during these years of rapid economic growth and change. A noticeable trend among Mexican Americans was the decline in the percentage of families whose members were born in Mexico. Permanent, "official" immigration from Mexico reached the lowest levels since 1910 (see Table 8.1 on page 126). There continued to be great differences in family life among Mexican Americans, depending on socioeconomic level, urban/rural residence, and nativity. The vast majority of Mexican immigrants and Mexican Americans lived in working-class families with a minimum amount of financial or job security. Many lived in what could only be termed poverty. In south Texas more than 12,000 families annually had to leave the state to follow the crops in order to earn enough money to survive. The average Mexican-American family income was much below that of Anglo-

Americans. They lived in substandard housing, had inadaquate diets, and their children were forced to leave school in order to join them in the fields or otherwise work to support the family. There really were not many differences in lifestyle between those who were U.S. citizens of Mexican descent and Mexican immigrants. Both groups had family lives that were marked with great economic insecurity and geographic transiency.[10]

Urbanization and employment in industrial work did increase, however, and this changed family life for many rural Mexicans and Mexican Americans. Nowhere was the change greater than in New Mexico, where traditional rural village life changed through massive migration to cities in Colorado, Washington state, California, and Texas. In these cities the older family patterns broke down. Wrote Sigurd Johansen, a social scientist studying the Hispano barrios in Albuquerque, "Family solidarity is decreasing. Lack of parental control and dissatisfaction with prevailing conditions have developed too rapidly for adaptation to take place, and disintegration has started."[11] Variations on this theme probably characterized the stresses in postwar Mexican-American family life.

An indication of changes taking place among Mexican-American families was the loosening of the "ties that bind" in the increasing number of inter-ethnic marriages. After 1945 a number of researchers studied a noticeable increase in Mexican-American intermarriage, a result of new geographic and socioeconomic forces in American society. Outmarriage was generally more prevalent in New Mexico and California and less so in Texas. In the Midwest and Northwest, the incidence of intermarriage appeared to be even higher, almost triple for that of the Southwest.[12]

Urban Mexican-American working-class families had perhaps the greatest challenge. They were being forced to accommodate or adjust to a dynamically changing postwar industrial consumer society. Although tensions between generations and age groups intensified, family solidarity was an important asset. Family unity continued to revolve around the long-suffering mother. This familial tendency—an inheritance from the cultural tradition of Mexico—persisted, but increasingly it would be changed and modified by the "modern" pressures of having to survive in an urban commercial environment.[13]

Another aspect in family life was the growth of a youth subculture that challenged older Mexican values regarding the proper way to behave. This was the aforementioned *pachuco* phenomenon, wherein young men and women created a distinctive style by adopting their own music, language, and dress in rebellion against Mexican as well as middle-class Anlgo-American values. For the young men, as late as the 1950s, the style was to wear a zoot suit, a flamboyant long coat, with baggy pegged pants, a porkpie hat, a long key chain, and shoes with thick soles. The young women wore tight dresses, beehive hairdos, and lots of makeup. To many Mexican parents the *pachuco* phenomenon was alarming proof of the the evil influence of American culture on the young.[14]

The Struggle for Equal Rights

The battle to end the Bracero Program was the economic side of a larger fight to secure equal treatment for Mexican Americans in postwar America. In the late 1940s Mexican-American G.I.s who had been in combat returned to a country where Mexicans continued to lack political representation and to confront segregation in public facilities and in schools. Drawing on their past experience in local Mexican-American associations and in the labor unions they had organized during the 1930s, many of these former G.I.s began to use their associations to confront American racism. These newly confident G.I.s were more aggressive in demanding equality and their civil rights than their Mexican-American predecessors had been in the 1930s.

The historian Mario García, in his landmark study of political leaders from 1930 to 1960, characterized these new Mexican Americans as a generation who wanted political and social integration. In García's words, "Proud of their Mexican origins and of their ability to function in two worlds, Mexican Americans—the term popularized during this period in itself is symbolic— looked to an eventual synthesis and coexistence between the culture of their parents and their desire to be fully accepted as U.S. citizens."[15] These cohorts of the Mexican-American Generation focused their energies on electoral politics and unionizing in an attempt to achieve integration and equality.

The majority of the members of the Mexican-American organizations of these years came from a numerically small middle class. These relatively affluent Mexican Americans believed in the American dream, in the ability of anyone to achieve upward mobility as long as he or she adopted the values of American society. But the vast majority of Mexican Americans were blue-collar workers and had little time or energy to engage in political and legal maneuvers or to theorize over the unfulfilled promises of America. They were too busy struggling to survive on a day-to-day basis. The middle-class men and women of this generation thus became the pioneers in challenging historic systems of subordination in the United States. Anglo-American racial and economic discrimination coupled with the flow of Mexican immigration was renewing the poverty of the barrios, and this would limit the success of the Mexican-American reformist approach. Nevertheless, given the conservative mood of the times, they were remarkably successful in achieving basic political changes.

From the point of view of the Mexican-American Generation, probably the most critical issue in postwar America was the segregation of public facilities. Municipal ordinances in many southwestern towns and cities segregated Mexicans and blacks in special sections of movie theaters, swimming pools, and other public facilities. In southern California, for example, blacks and Mexicans could not use public swimming pools on days reserved for "White Use Only." Some cities, such as Los Angeles, passed miscegenation laws making it a misdemeanor to intermarry. In rural areas of Texas, restaurants and motels often refused service to Mexicans and blacks. Wherever there was a sizable population of Mexican Americans, local authorities passed regulations establishing "Mexican Schools." This kind of segregation died out slowly during the 1950s and 1960s largely through the legal actions brought by various civil rights groups and later because of direct mass protests.

One group in the fight against discrimination was the American G.I. Forum. An incident at a segregated funeral home in a small south Texas town sparked the rapid growth of this organization of Mexican-American veterans. In 1949 a funeral home in Three Rivers, Texas, denied burial to Félix Longoria, a World War II veteran, because of his Mexican descent. Led by Dr. Hector García, Gus García, and a cadre of committed activists, the American G.I. Forum became an active defender of Mexican-American civil rights in the 1950s. The G.I. Forum initiated anti-discrimination lawsuits and voter registration campaigns that increased the Mexican Americans' political clout. Eventually the organization expanded membership to include nonveterans as well as women. The American G.I. Forum, along with other established and newly emerging organizations composed of veterans, launched a legal attack on educational segregation that would eventually do away with de jure segregation throughout the Southwest.[16]

Another influential group in opposing discrimination was the League of United Latin American Citizens. By 1945 LULAC had grown to a national association under the able leadership of Alonso Perales, Carlos Castañeda, and George Sánchez from Texas and Senator Dennis Chávez of New Mexico.[17]

In 1945 a group of Mexican-American parents initiated a class-action lawsuit against several school districts in Orange County, California, intending to challenge these districts' segregationist policies. *Méndez et al. v. Westminster School District of Orange County* would become a landmark case in the long struggle against racial discrimination in schools. This case began in 1943 and was supported by the efforts of the Latin American Organization, a Mexican-American civil rights league that several families had organized for the specific purpose of challenging segregation. Another Mexican-American group from Orange County, the Asociación de Padres de Niños Mexico-Americanos, joined to help the group of families in protesting the segregation policies. Their lawyers argued that segregation violated the equal-protection clause of the Fourteenth Amendment. The court eventually ruled in favor of the Mexican-American plaintiffs; the district court upheld decision on appeal.[18]

The *Méndez* case had wide legal repercussions and became a precedent in the *Brown v. the Board of Education* Supreme Court decision that overturned de jure segregation nationwide in 1954. Gilbert González, who has studied the *Méndez* case extensively, believes that it "inspired renewed anti-segregation efforts by the GI Forum and the League of Latin American Citizens (LULAC) in Arizona and Texas."[19] In Texas these two organizations filed a suit against Bastrop County, charging violation of the children's constitutional rights as well as violation of state laws. Dr. Hector P. García, head of the G.I. Forum, and George Sánchez, the University of Texas educator working with LULAC, led the efforts to bring about a victory in *Delgado v. Bastrop Independent School District* in 1948. This case went beyond the *Méndez* decision by defining segregation and prohibiting even the de facto separation of children by race or ethnicity. The court prohibited the school district "from, in any manner, directly or indirectly, participating in the custom, usage or practice of segregating pupils of Mexican or other Latin American descent in separate schools or classes."[20] Notably the court agreed that both Mexican immigrant children and U.S. citizens of Mexican heritage deserved protection from the evils of segregation.

After the *Delgado* decision, LULAC and the G.I. Forum monitored compliance with this directive and protested the evasion and noncompliance of the school districts. According to Guadalupe San Miguel, Jr., various Mexican American organizations initiated 15 lawsuits against segregated schools in Texas between 1950 and 1957. In addition, Mexican-American groups applied pressure on at least nine school districts by bringing them before special hearings headed by the commissioner of education.[21] Despite some court victories, however, school districts continued to avoid compliance, and segregated schools continued to plague Mexicano and Mexican-American communities, especially in Texas.

Economic and Political Organizations

Other postwar Mexican-American organizations dedicated themselves to the economic and political advancement of La Raza. Again the basic constituency of these groups was the numerically small Mexican-American middle class. As a cohort, they had the education and the knowledge of American society to develop sophisticated strategies to combat racism. In California, Mexican Americans, along with liberal Anglo-Americans, formed the Community Service Organization (CSO) in 1947. Saul Alinsky, a Chicago social activist heading the Industrial Areas Foundation, decided to help Mexican-American communities in California to increase their political power. To do this he sent Fred Ross to organize CSO in Los Angeles. This nonpartisan community association was concerned with issues that affected the urban barrios: civil rights, voter registration, community education, housing discrimination, and police brutality. In Los Angeles, Ross, along with Tony Ríos and a dedicated group of Mexican-American veterans, succeeded in getting more than 12,000 new voters to tip the scales in 1949 and elect Edward R. Roybal, the first Mexican-American member of the Los Angeles City Council since 1881. The CSO supported the new Mexican immigrants and encouraged them to join the organization while simultaneously offering citizenship drives to increase the Mexican community's electoral strength. The CSO was one of the few Mexican-American organizations that provided social services to Mexican immigrants irrespective of legal status.[22]

During the 1950s the CSO expanded its operations outside of Los Angeles to the small towns and medium-size cities of California. They followed Alinsky's organizing techniques, of having house meetings and allowing community members to generate the issues and devise strategies. The CSO soon became the most active Mexican-American civil rights organization in California with more than 20 chapters scattered throughout the state. In 1956 both César Chávez and Dolores Huerta worked as organizers for the CSO, gaining important experience for their later organization efforts for farmworkers. In the late 1950s Chávez worked in Oxnard, California, to organize a protest against the local growers' use of bracero laborers in preference to U.S. citizens. In 1959 Chávez became the national director for the CSO and attempted to get that group to organize a farm labor union. When the CSO leadership balked at this proposal, he resigned and set out to organize his own independent union, which eventually became the United Farm Workers, a flash point for the creation of the Chicano movement in the 1960s.

Another Mexican-American civil rights confederation during the 1950s, organized by middle-class Mexican Americans, was the Civic Unity League, led by Ignacio López, the previously mentioned editor of *El Espectador*. López and the Unity League fought against discrimination in public facilities, swimming pools, theaters, and schools. Working with the Mexican consulate and various Mexican *mutualistas,* López and the Unity League organized boycotts and launched lawsuits against public and private organizations that discriminated against Mexicans. Through the pages of *El Espectador* the Civic Unity League exposed instances of police abuse, discrimination in housing, and the INS's collaboration with agribusiness in using braceros to break strikes.

Like many other Mexican-American associations of the time, López's Civic Unity League encouraged Mexican Americans to become citizens, to vote, and to run for office. Various Unity Leagues in the Southern California towns of Chino, Ontario, Pomona, and San Bernardino sponsored Mexican-American candidates for local elections, and several of them won, largely through an appeal to ethnic solidarity and issues consequential to Mexican Americans. Throughout these political activities López's position was that of a patriotic World War II veteran. He encouraged Mexican Americans to learn English and American history and culture in order to integrate into the mainstream society.[23] Eventually the Civic Unity League declined during the more militant 1960s. Ignacio López went on to a career in government service and worked for federal antipoverty programs in San Bernardino county. President Richard M. Nixon appointed him to a position with the Department of Housing and Urban Development (HUD) in 1972.

Even though their political orientation was moderate, groups like the CSO and the Unity League were attacked by conservatives for having Communist influences or sympathies. The most notable progressive organization of this era, La Asociacíon Nacional México Americana (ANMA), also became a target of anti-Communists. Formed in 1949, ANMA fought for the civil rights of Mexican Americans and Mexican immigrants. Two of its most influential leaders were the aforementioned Josefina Fierro de Bright and Eduardo Quevedo. Quevedo was a New Deal Democrat originally from New Mexico but very active in Mexican Los Angeles's political life. In its newspaper, *Progreso*, ANMA adopted controversial positions. It opposed the Korean War and U.S. interventions in Latin America and denounced INS raids and police brutality. ANMA was one of the few Mexican-American organizations that opposed the deportation and repatriation of Mexican immigrants during Operation Wetback. During the 1950s radicalism was not popular within the Mexican-American communities. After being classified as a subversive organization in 1954, ANMA passed into history.[24]

Women's Emerging Roles

While traditional expectations regarding the woman's role placed her within a family, dependent on men, this ideal was less and less true in the years after 1945, when women became active in the work force and society. True, most women continued to be "traditional," but even then they worked to subvert patriarchy. William Madsen, a sociologist in south Texas during the early 1960s, noted that "the conservative Latin wife is, in fact, a skilled manipulator of her lord and master. The weapons she uses in disguised form are his own self-esteem, his *machismo,* and his role as provider and protector." Or, as one female informant told him, "When a man has to defend himself against you, you get nothing. When he has to protect you, you get everything."[25]

A number of nontraditional women could serve as role models for the "modern" Mexican-American woman. Martha Cotera, in her book *Profile on the Mexican American Woman*, discusses many of these emerging role models. Luisa Moreno, who had been very active in labor organizing in the 1940s, was deported during the McCarthy hysteria of the 1950s. But other women emerged to take her place. Gregoria Montalbo and Sophia González were ILGWU leaders who helped organize the Tex-Son strike in San Antonio in 1959. Isabel Verver set up an experimental school for Mexican-American children, financed by LULAC. It was a tremendous success and eventually became a model program adopted by the Texas Education Agency. Margarita Simón was the editor of *El Demócrata* of Austin, Texas, where she regularly spoke out about the economic and educational problems confronting Mexican Americans.[26]

Hundreds of women worked behind the scenes to support Mexican-American mutual aid societies, LULAC, the G.I. Forum, and a variety of political and social groups. Within LULAC, for example, women were always present and involved in the many conferences and committees that worked to fight against discrimination in education and public facilities.[27] The same could be said about women's auxiliary organizations of the G.I. Forum.

Within some labor unions, women were active as leaders. As studied by historian Vicki Ruiz in her book *Cannery Women/Cannery Lives*, the Mexican women of California's UCAPAWA rose to positions of leadership and responsibility, and through their efforts the cannery union "encompased entire kin and friend networks."[28] Unfortunately their union was undermined during the 1950s by rivalry from the Teamster's union, the importation of union-busting braceros, and the red-baiting of union officials.[29]

The Politics of the Mexican-American Generation

The Mexican-American Generation's drive for acceptance into the American dream extended into electoral politics, where a few members of the middle class succeeded in building political careers in coalition with diverse groups. It would not be until the 1980s, however, that Latino politicians would have the bases to engage in successful grass-roots ethnic politics. Two prominent Mexican-American leaders who won election to national offices are exemplary of the Mexican-American liberal agenda of this era: Edward R. Roybal and Henry B. González.

Probably the most tenacious Mexican-American leader of this era was Roybal of Los Angeles. Originally from Albuquerque, New Mexico, Roybal grew up in Boyle Heights in East Los Angeles and served in the Civilian Conservation Corps during the depression. After attending college and joining the army during World War II, he worked as Los Angeles's public health administrator. In 1947 he and Fred Ross co-founded the CSO in Los Angeles. After an unprecedented voter registration drive and get-out-the-vote campaign by the CSO, Roybal won a historic victory in 1947—a seat on the Los Angeles City Council, where he served for 13 years as an effective advocate for the Mexican-American community. He fought for anti-discrimination measures and increased public housing; he challenged rabid anti-communism and police brutality. In 1957, when the city wanted to elminate a barrio located in Chavez Ravine, the site of the future Dodger Stadium, Roybal was alone in protesting the forcible eviction of Mexican families. He also opposed the redevelopment plans for the Bunker Hill area because of the displacement of seniors and Mexican families.[30] In the 1950s he ran unsuccessfully for lieutenant-governor of California and for county supervisor. In 1962 his district elected him to Congress, where he enjoyed a long and distinguished career. Roybal's career typified the approach of the Mexican-

American Generation. He worked with other groups to achieve what he wanted. His electoral successes were largely because of his appeal to non-Latino voters who shared his liberal agenda of increasing opportunities for all minorities and in challenging the power elite in municipal and national affairs.

In 1960 Henry B. González became the first Texan of Mexican descent to be elected to Congress. González's father worked as the editor of the influential Spanish-language newspaper *La Prensa* in his native San Antonio. González studied law and then worked as chief probation officer for Bexar County. He quit his position because a county judge would not let him hire black staff members at the same pay as whites. In his first attempt at political office he ran for the Texas House of Representatives and lost by a narrow margin in 1950. Three years later, he succeeded in winning a seat on the San Antonio City Council, where he served two terms and succeeded in sponsoring ordinances that ended segregation in San Antonio's recreational facilities. In 1956 he became the first Mexican American to be elected to the Texas Senate; there he won national publicity for his opposition to segregation bills. In 1958 he ran unsuccessfully in the Democratic primary for governor. When Lyndon Johnson ran on the presidential ticket in 1960, González campaigned for Congress and scored an upset over the conservative John Goode, Jr. González's victory owed more to this liberal record on civil rights and the support of Johnson Democrats than to a Mexican-American electorate. He prided himself on representing all the people of his district. In Congress he voted to support most of Kennedy's New Frontier legislation and won reelection in 1962. He voted to abolish the House Un-American Activities Committee, to discontinue the Bracero Program, and to enact the 1964 Civil Rights Bill.

The Mexican-American Generation contributed to the rebirth of political activism by organizing many clubs and associations that would be the training ground for the next generation of activists in the 1960s. During the presidential campaign of 1960, the Democrats organized hundreds of "Viva Kennedy" clubs to mobilize the Mexican-American vote. In Texas the Democrats, in giving prominence and legitimacy to the LULAC members and G.I. Forum members, helped create the expectation of continued participation in national politics. After Kennedy's election, they formed a new association called the Political Association of Spanish-Speaking Organizations (PASSO) in 1961. Drawing on the liberal resurgence generated by Kennedy's leadership, the PASSO leaders began calling for a more radical change in the traditional way of doing things. In the process they attacked the old-style methods of compromise and began to assert an ethnic political agenda.

California Mexican Americans, dissatisfied with their exclusion from mainstream politics, formed the Mexican American Political Association (MAPA) in 1959. Edward Roybal, along with the labor activist Bert Corona, was among its founders, as were women activists, such as Francisca Flores, Dolores Sánchez, and Ramona Morín. Appealing to ethnic identity as the basis for political action, MAPA boosted Kennedy's election in 1960 and went on to support Roybal's election to Congress in 1962. Historian Juan Gómez Quiñones, in his evaluation of MAPA's successes in these years, believed that it was responsible for the election of two Mexican Americans to the California State Assembly and the appointment of six Mexican-American judges before 1965. But MAPA suffered from conservative-liberal divisions and from a "careerist" orientation of some of its officials. Its effectiveness declined as nonelectoral political action took center stage during the latter 1960s.[31]

Mexican-American Labor Unions

Throughout this period more than 80 percent of employed Mexican Americans were blue-collar workers. The vast majority held nonunion jobs, and a declining proportion (less than 20 percent in 1960) worked as farm laborers.[32] The continuation of the Bracero Program and increasing undocumented immigration from Mexico negatively affected the employment and wages of these native-born Mexican Americans. It also made it more difficult for them to organize successful labor unions. In addition, the conservative mood of the country gave Congress the opportunity to pass the Taft-Hartley Labor Act in 1947 that weakened the ability of unions to strike. A new immigration law, the McCarren-Walter Act passed by Congress in 1952, made it possible to deport naturalized citizens whom the government suspected of being subversives. Organized labor was generally on the defensive nationwide as McCarthyite witch hunters branded labor organizers as Communist agitators or racketeers.

Nevertheless, there were several important labor-union organizations and strikes led by Mexican Americans during the postwar years. The conditions for farmworkers were among the worst in the nation. They had virtually no protection from the exploitive demands of labor contractors and growers; they worked long hours at low wages and without any benefits. Mexican and Mexican-American farmworkers lived in substandard housing and had higher rates of illness and mortality than the general working population.

Soon after World War II the AFL attempted to organize a union for farm laborers. They set up the National Farm Labor Union (NFLU), an offshoot of the Southern Tenant Farmers Union. Led by Hank Hasiwar and Ernesto Galarza, the union launched strikes throughout California for wage increases. In 1948 the union began a strike against the Di Giorgio Corporation, a family-run business and one of the largest fruit growers in the United States. The struggle against Di Giorgio lasted two and a half years. The growers eventually broke the strike using a government injunction under the Taft-Hartley Act, braceros as strike breakers, and red-baiting tactics.

One of the NFLU's Mexican-American organizers was Ernesto Galarza, an author, sociologist, and labor expert with a Ph.D. from Columbia University. As a predecessor of César Chávez in organizing farmworkers in California, Galarza developed the strategy of a consumer boycott against Di Giorgio table grapes during the 1940s. He pioneered the idea of organizing picket lines outside supermarkets to encourage mass support for the NFLU farm laborers. Favoring the NFLU boycott, students and clergy from the Bay area lent their support to the grape strike and statewide boycott. Furthermore, as the union's director of research and education, Galarza produced a movie, *Poverty in the Valley of Plenty,* criticizing the conditions farmworkers faced in working on the Di Giorgio farm. But the Di Giorgio family sued and won, and they had the film destroyed. Later, during the 1950s and 1960s, Galarza worked with the AFL-CIO in organizing farm laborers through the Agricultural Workers Organizing Committee (AWOC). This union eventually merged with César Chávez's Farm Workers Association in 1965, and Galarza worked with the UFW for a period of time.[33]

Tejano workers similarly tried to improve their lot through a number of strikes. Employers used undocumented workers to subvert the labor-organizing activities of Mexican-American garment workers in El Paso in 1945 and of the employees of the Rio Grande Valley Gas Company in Harlingen in 1948. Mexican-American women garment workers—members of the ILGWU—stage a walkout in Houston in 1951 when the factory declared itself a closed shop. The longest strike was the 1959 Tex-Son strike by Mexican-American garment workers in San Antonio. It lasted until 1962, when the workers finally gave up in the face of hostile legislation and strike breakers.[34]

On 17 October 1950 a group of predominantly Mexican-American zinc miners working in Hanover, New Mexico, called a work stoppage. They demanded parity in paid holidays with other mines and pay for transit to work. This strike, which lasted until 24 January 1952, became the subject of the award-winning film *Salt of the Earth* (1953). While the film was a dramatization, the cast included the strikers and their families and accurately reflected what happened during the strike. Empire Zinc, owned by a New Jersey corporation, refused to bargain with the miners, who were members of the International Union of Mine, Mill and Smelter Workers. During the strike the company obtained an injunction prohibiting the miners from picketing. In response the miners met and, after much debate, voted to allow the miners' wives to continue the picket-line duty. For the next seven months the women and children of the company town of Hanover endured biting cold, teargas attacks, police provocations, arrests, and jail. The police ran over several of the picketers. The men and women of the union spent 1,148 days in jail and paid more than $100,000 in fines and bails.[35] Sustained by the tenaciousness of the women and donations from sympathetic unions throughout the United States, the miners' union, led by Juan Chacón, won a settlement.

Mexican Americans in the Military

With the outbreak of the Korean War in 1950, thousands of Mexican Americans volunteered for the armed services. As in previous conflicts, many displayed valor in combat. Eight Mexican Americans won the Congressional Medal of Honor during the Korean War, most of them awarded posthumously.[36] For many Mexican Americans, the military served as a means for escaping the discrimination and poverty of the barrio. Unfortunately, all too many found themselves on the front lines and were killed or wounded in action. One of the Congressional Medal winners exemplifies this tragedy. Eugene A. Obregón was born on 12 November 1930 in Los Angeles. He went to school up through the eleventh grade and decided to enlist in the Marines before his graduation from high school. At 17 he went through basic training in San Diego, California. From there the Marines shippped him out to Barstow Supply Depot in the California desert for training as a firefighter. Before reaching the age of 19 he was sent to Korea in the First Provisional Marine Brigade. He saw action in North Korea and participated in the Inchon landing. On 26 September 1950, during the assault to liberate Seoul, he was killed in action while trying to save his comrade, PFC Bert Johnson from Grand Prairie, Texas. Stories of young Mexican Americans sacrificing their lives in heroic action, often to save their Anglo-American buddies, were repeated again and again in the official statements. The larger significance of this self-sacrifice seemed to be lost on an America preoccupied with the threat of Communist aliens and "wetbacks."[37]

The Mexican-American Intelligentsia

In the years after World War II the ranks of Mexican-American intellectuals broadened. Professors, teachers, and creative writers of Mexican descent published their ideas in academic and popular forums. They wrote in English for mixed audiences. Both directly and indirectly they challenged the Anglo-American hegemony in the study of Mexican society within the United States. Many of these Mexican-American scholars had begun their intellectual activity in the 1930s and continued producing for many decades. Either by choice of topic or interpretation, these intellectuals developed a new voice. They were the precursors of the later Chicano academics who produced an explosion of critical and scholarly works after 1965. The Mexican-American perspective was shaped by socioeconomic origins, mainly that of an emerging middle class. It sought to interpret and defend the Mexican-American national origin and culture against Anglo-American detractors.

For years, Anglo-American anthropologists and sociologists had been studying Mexican culture in terms of its supposed deficiencies and pathologies. The Mexican-American intelligentsia made its most significant contributions in challenging the prevailing academic interpretations regarding Mexican Americans. In 1956 Américo Paredes, a young English graduate student from the University of Texas at Austin, received his Ph.D. in English, folklore, and Spanish. He had written his dissertation on a south Texas folk hero of the early twentieth century, Gregorio Cortéz. Two years later his dissertation appeared as a book, *"With a Pistol in His Hand": A Border Ballad and Its Hero.*[38] This work presented a view of the Texas Rangers quite different from that prevailing in the Texas history books. Whereas most Anglo Texans saw the Texas Rangers as heroes, Paredes dared to suggest that their reputation among Mexicans and Tejanos was that of cowardly killers who exaggerated their own prowess. In studying the life and folklore surrounding Cortéz, Paredes presented a view of Texas history as seen by Mexicanos and Tejanos. *"With a Pistol in His Hand"* was a critical success and went through several editions and became a feature movie. In 1962, because of his continued scholarly productivity, Paredes received a Guggenheim fellowship. Over the decades he made many original contributions to Tejano folklore, challenging the perspective of the Texas Mexican offered by Anglo-American folklorists. Through his writings and training of graduate students, Paredes influenced folklore studies of Mexican Americans well into the 1980s. Through his writings and academic reputation, the Mexican-American worldview achieved a powerful validity.

Another person who forced Anglo-Americans to reconsider the morality of U.S. society's treatment of Mexican Americans was Ernesto Galarza. A labor union organizer with the National Farm Workers Labor Union in the 1940s, Galarza was also a scholar and writer. In the 1930s he received his Ph.D. in history (with honors) from Columbia University. His published works in the 1950s and early 1960s reflected his concern with labor conditions and unionization: *Strangers in Our Fields* in 1956, and *Merchants of Labor: The Mexican Bracero Story* in

1964. Both books were heavily researched indictments of the exploitative conditions that Mexican immigrant farmworkers endured. The latter book was
instrumental in helping end the Bracero Program.

Other Mexican-American intellectuals issued criticisms, interpretations,
and perspectives that asserted the value of the contributions of the Spanish-
speaking people in the United States. Julian Samora worked as a sociologist at
the University of Notre Dame, and Raúl Morín wrote the first study of
Mexican-Americans servicemen during World War II and the Korean War,
Among the Valiant (published in 1963). These and other Mexican-American
intellectuals laid the foundation for the later growth of social-scientific and
humanistic studies about Mexican Americans *by* Mexican Americans. The
Mexican-American intelligentsia of the 1950s and early 1960s were among the
first to call attention to the grave social and economic problems confronting
Mexican-American people.

Mexican-American Literature

From 1945 to 1965 Mexican Americans made significant advances in literature, painting, and music. Mexican currents influenced the art of this era, but
ethnic and political sensibilities that would characterize the artistic production
of Chicanos in the 1960s and 1970s were largely absent. Those artists who
found their audience during this era had to accommodate themselves to the
English-speaking consumer culture that surrounded them. Much of their art
reflected the middle-class aspiration to achieve acceptance by other
Americans. As such, they did not emphasize themes of racial and ethnic strife.
Nor did they adopt an overtly critical view of America.

In literature, this period saw the emergence of English-language fiction by
Mexican Americans based on their own experience, without romanticism or
idealization. The first such Mexican-American author of biographically inspired
fiction was Mario Suárez, who wrote a series of short stories in the late 1940s.
The story "El Hoyo" (The Hole) is about life in a Tucson barrio.[39] In it Suárez
uses the term *Chicano* to describe the colorful characters inhabiting the world of
his upbringing. He compares his people to a *capirotada* (a mixture of foods):
"While many seem to the undiscerning eye to be alike it is only because collectively they are referred to as *chicanos*. But like *capirotada*, fixed in a thousand
ways and served on a thousand tables, which can only be evaluated by individual taste, the *chicanos* must be so distinguished."[40] Suárez's other stories were
masterfully developed portraits of various characters from the El Hoyo barrio.
Suárez's view of Mexican-American life appeared honest yet gentle, filled with
a sense of passing.

In 1959 José Antonio Villareal wrote the first modern Mexican-American
novel, *Pocho,* a book largely based on the drama of Mexican immigration and
conflicts in the United States. Published by a major New York commercial press,
it eventually became a best-seller.[41] *Pocho* told the story of a young man, Richard
Rubio, and his coming of age during the 1930s in Santa Clara, California. The
novel's main themes revolved around the conflict of generations and national
cultures. Richard conflicts with his Mexican immigrant parents; his mother and
father differ about the new freedoms allowed in the United States. It ends with
Richard leaving home to join the military. The author modeled this novel on his

own life experiences and portrays the contradictions of Mexican immigrant family life in the United States.

John Rechy, Fray Angélico Chávez, and Sabine R. Ulibarri also made notable literary contributions. Rechy was born in El Paso of Scottish-Mexican parents. He wrote of his experiences in this border city in his essay "El Paso del Norte" (1958) and in his novel *City of Night* (1963), which became a best-seller. Elements of his ethnic experience surfaced in these two works, but more important was the author's search for identity as a homosexual. Developing different themes, Fray Angélico Chávez, a native of New Mexico, wrote poetry, history, essays, and a newspaper column. He worked as a priest, dedicating himself to living with the Pueblo Indians and ministering to poor Hispano communities. Most of his fiction and poetry reflected deeply religious sentiments, as did his poetry collection, *Our Lady of the Conquest* (1948). He had a long and prolific career as a historian of the land and people he loved, producing three monographs between 1970 and 1981. Sabine R. Ulibarri, another New Mexican poet and author, chaired the Department of Modern and Classical Languages at the University of New Mexico in the 1950s. He wrote short stories and poetry in Spanish for local publication. His first published work included a series of short stories about his growing up in a small New Mexican town, *Tierra Amarilla: Cuentos de Nuevo Mexico* (1964).

The Visual and Performing Arts

Mexican-American artists also came of age during the 1950s and early 1960s. Some would contribute to the later Chicano and Latino Renaissance, and all were profoundly influenced by developments in the Mexican arts to one degree or another. The Mexican-American painter Eugenio Quesada traveled from his native Arizona to Mexico and studied the great Mexican mural masters, particularly José Clemente Orozco. These grand works inspired his paintings and drawings reflecting Mexican subjects and themes. The painter Melesio Casas, an El Paso native, received his graduate training in art from the University of the Americas in Mexico City in 1958. He first produced paintings influenced by movies and television images and gradually moved to more political themes during the Chicano movement. A better known Mexican-American artist was Manuel Neri, a sculptor from California. During the 1950s he had many one-man shows in San Francisco, New York, Houston, and Los Angeles and received many honors. He traveled to Mexico and studied the works of Orozco, translating monumental paintings into equally monumental three-dimensional figures. Finally, there were the paintings of Louis Gutiérrez, who exhibited his art at several galleries. Influenced by the easel paintings of the muralist Diego Rivera, Gutiérrez worked with a variety of materials to produce dynamic abstract statements.[42]

Any consideration of the Mexican-American visual arts should include a mention of the pioneering film *The Salt of the Earth,* a compelling depiction of the 1952 New Mexican zinc strike discussed earlier. Even though produced and directed by non–Mexican Americans, this film's genesis and history make it a classic in Mexican-American cinema. The Mexican movie actress Rosaura Revueltas played the leading role of Esperanza, the wife of the union leader Ramón Quintero, who was played by the real-life union organizer Juan Chacón.

Professionals played the antagonists, led by Will Geer as the sheriff, but the rest of the cast were the members of the union and their families.

The scriptwriter, Michael Wilson, spent several months near the end of the strike living with the miners and continued to do so during the months that followed. The workers suggested changes to make the script more accurately reflect the strike. The result was a unique event in film history, what it today called a "docudrama," intimately involving the real-life participants as actors and writers.

Because of the film's pro-union, ethnic message, the Hollywood establishment refused to make it. The producer and director, Paul Jarrico and Herbert Biberman, had to assemble a non-Hollywood staff and produce the film surreptitiously. When they began filming, the *Hollywood Reporter* gossip column reported, "H'wood Reds are shooting a feature-length anti-American racial issue propaganda movie." Before Congress Rep. Donald Jackson declared that "this picture is being made . . . not far from . . . Los Alamos [by] men and women who [are] part of the pro-Soviet secret apparatus in this country."[43] The story of the making of *The Salt of the Earth* is a moving one of overcoming racial prejudice, anti-communism, and government sabotage. The INS deported Rosaura Revueltas near the end of the filming. Many of those involved in making the film were later blacklisted by Hollywood. Nevertheless, the film was finished and went on to win international awards and become a classic that continues to have a strong emotional impact on audiences.

After World War II Mexican music became increasingly popular within Spanish-speaking communities in the United States, owing in part to the Mexican movie musical, where singing cowboys reigned supreme. Jorge Negrete, Pedro Vargas, and Pedro Infante were Mexican movie stars who became the idols of millions of Mexican Americans. As to the home-grown, Texas seemed to be the main place where an authentic Mexican-American music flourished. Small recording companies owned by Texas Mexicans had some success in promoting Tex-Mex *canción ranchera*, an instrumental polka that also featured sung lyrics of a *corrido*. The accordion continued to be the primary instrument of such popular artists as Narciso Martínez and Santiago Jiménez. A musical phenomenon was the career of Lydia Mendoza, who had been a tremendously popular Tejana ballad singer in the 1930s. In the 1950s she staged a comeback, touring the Southwest and Mexico singing original compositions and traditional folk music. Her earthy, hard-hitting style conveyed the sorrows and joys of her people. She made more than 35 albums in this period and earned the title "First Lady of Mexican-American Song."[44]

With records now locally produced and phonographs affordable, Mexican Americans after World War II purchased discs to hear ballads that previously had been limited to regional audiences: the *corridos* of "Gregorio Cortez," "Jacinto Treviño," and "Juan Cortina"—all Tejano folk heroes drawn from the history of conflict with Anglo Texans.[45] With the growing popularity of rock-and-roll, most younger Mexican Americans did not consider the *corrido, conjunto,* or Mexican music "their sound." Nevertheless, there were occasions when traditional forms spanned the generation gap. When Lee Harvey Oswald assassinated President John Kennedy in November 1963, *corridistas* throughout the Southwest began composing ballads based on the president's tragic life. The *corridos* lamented his tragic death and alluded to his importance for Mexicans and

Mexican Americans. More than 100,000 copies of the Kennedy *corridos* sold in the years after his assassination. Their popularity served to remind younger Mexican Americans of the contemporary importance of their musical traditions.[46]

Social class and generational differences in Mexican-American musical tastes could be seen in the development of middle- and upper-class styles. The more affluent classes enjoyed the orchestra form. This phenomenon was especially true in Texas, where the Mexican immigrants and working-class Mexican Americans preferred *rancheras* and *corridos*.[47] The younger generation, however, enjoyed the rock-and-roll music that emerged in the 1950s. A Chicano-style rock-and-roll emerged in Los Angeles as Mexican-American musicians and singers influenced by black rhythm-and-blues began making records for small-label companies. The first hit was "The Pachuco Boogie" (1948), recorded by the Don Tosti Band. The song was a mixture of English, *caló*, and Afro-American rhythms. It sold more than two million copies. Tellingly, many Spanish-language stations refused to play it, considering it offensive to "respectable" Mexican sensibilites. This syncretic type of music continued in the career of L'il Julian Herrera, the first commercially successful rock-and-roll star of Mexican descent. Recording under the name Ron Gregory, his hit song "Lonely, Lonely Nights" mixed Mexican and black vocal styles. The most important Mexican-American early rock star was Ritchie Valens. Born Richard Valenzuela in the San Fernando Valley, Valens and his group the Silhouettes mixed traditional Mexican folk songs, hillbilly ballads, and black rhythm-and-blues to produce a Mestizo rock-and-roll sound. Ritchie Valens became a nationally known star with "La Bamba," "Come On, Let's Go," and "Donna."[48]

In addition to rock-and-roll, Los Angeles was a hot spot for the evolution of the big band sound, Latin jazz, and *musica tropical* (later called salsa), with such notable stars as Lionel Sesma, Trini López, Eddie Cano, and Lalo Guerrero. There were dozens of so-called Latin clubs with names like La Bamba, El Babalú, El Janitzio, and La Capita. Lalo Guerrero, in particular, achieved national recognition as a composer and song writer. Scores of Mexican- and Latin-American musical artists found themselves in Los Angeles during this 1950s, adding to the musical ferment: Tito Puente, Pérez Prado, Luis Alcaraz, and many Mariachi groups found a growing audience in southern California's Mexican-American population.[49]

In the 1950s and 1960s Spanish-language professional theater was revived through the efforts of such producers as Carolina Villalongín and Lalo Astol in San Antonio and Rafael Trujillo Herrera, who managed El Teatro Intimo in Los Angeles.[50] The *tandas de variedad*, or Mexican vaudeville, nourished an ironic and biting humor, expressed by the stock character of the *pachuco* or the *pelado*.[51] It gradually declined but left a legacy. The stylized image of the *pachuco* would be continued in the Mexican movies of Cantinflas and Tin Tan. The *pachuco* as a humorous critic would be re-interpreted by the Mexican-American playwright Luis Valdez during the 1970s.

Mexican popular theater had always been appealing to Mexican Americans and Mexican immigrants regardless of class. As an inexpensive, Spanish-language medium, it maintained cultural, linguistic, and nostalgic ties with the mother country and reinforced common cultural bonds. Mexican immigrants could easily identify with the Mexican-American forms of the *tandas* and *carpas* that were part of a people's theater tradition in Mexico. The decline of this kind of theater was perhaps evidence of the influence of a consumer culture. By the 1960s English-language movies and especially television became the dominant entertainment for most Mexican Americans.

Conclusions

The 20 years after World War II witnessed the further refinement of Mexican-American identity. Coming of age during World War II, the new generation was proud of its patriotism and eager to eliminate barriers to the pursuit of the American dream. Mexican Americans did not reject their ethnicity but used the bonds of language, custom, and heritage to form organizations that could help them in their quest for a better life. As this generation matured, new waves of Mexican immigrants entered the United States. The relationship between these two groups—the *Mexicanos* and the Mexican Americans—was an ambiguous one. Some Mexican Americans endorsed anti-immigration policies like Operation Wetback, if only to prove their complete loyalty to American institutions. Others sought to work with Mexican immigrants and to gain their support in union organizing. At the popular level, Mexican or at least Spanish-language songs, music, dance, and folkways continued, but with diminished force among the more acculturated and urbanized children of middle-class Mexican Americans. There were few Mexican Americans involved in national politics or visible as community leaders. This would change in the next 10 years as another generation, calling themselves Chicanos, sought to redefine their relationship to the Mexican past while challenging the accommodationist approaches of older Mexican Americans. The Mexican-American Generation and the growing immigrant stream from Mexico had laid the foundations for this ethnic revival.

eight

Aztlán Rediscovered: The Chicano Movement

D uring the 1960s the United States underwent a profound social revolution. Chronic poverty, along with the failure of promised reforms affecting America's poor, nonwhite minorities, produced demonstrations, sporadic riots, and violence that shocked the white middle class. The southern civil rights movement led by Dr. Martin Luther King, Jr., evolved into an urban black revolution that exploded in the streets of America's biggest cities. Finally, discontent with a long and frustrating war in Vietnam fueled a growing anti-war movement that challenged the integrity of the government and resulted in mass protests and civil disorder. As a result of these deep divisions, by the mid-1970s a whole generation had grown to distrust institutional authority of all kinds—the officials, the police, school administrators—in a word, the "establishment." The result was a new willingness to experiment with alternative forms of social and political expression.

The standard histories of this turbulent period in American history ignore the protests arising in the Mexican-American barrios of the Southwest. Yet the history of the 1960s would be incomplete without an understanding of the emerging identity of millions of young people who called themselves "Chicanos." The Chicano movement was a radical attempt to redefine the political, social, economic, and cultural status of millions of persons of Mexican descent. It was partly motivated by the convergence of the antiwar and civil rights movements, but it also reflected a new generation's coming to terms with the endemic problems of Mexicans in America. This chapter surveys the most important trends in the history of the Chicano movement, a topic that has received much more lengthy treatment elsewhere.[1] It examines the Chicano movement and seeks to determine how Mexican culture shaped it.

In the early 1960s Chicanos began to articulate a new ethnic position in relation to Mexico and the surge of Mexican immigration that was changing the nature of their communities. The Chicano movement constituted an effort by rural and urban Mexican Americans to redefine their relationship to American society by advocating cultural and political self-determination through radical rhetoric and action. A fundamental aspect of this movement was the attempt to generate pride in being of Mexican descent. As such, Mexican Americans rejected the older euphemisms of "Spanish" or "Latin" and proudly defined themselves as "Chicanos." Mexican Americans themselves had used this term since at least the turn of the century to refer, somewhat disparagingly, to rural Mexican immigrants.[2]

Mexican immigration to the United States began to increase from what it had been previously, augmenting the size of the Spanish-speaking population and creating new social realities that would have long term political consequences. Between 1960 and 1975 more than 700,000 legal Mexican immigrants came to the United States, making Mexico the largest source of legal immigration in this period. These numbers appeared to be lower than the numbers of those who entered illegally. Experts estimated the undocumented immigration from Mexico in this period at about six million.[3] The full political impact of this immigration would be felt in the 1970s. During the years of political activism key leaders saw the important political implications of this flood of new residents. The renewal of a Mexican cultural presence within the barrios and colonias influenced the tone and organization of the Chicano movement (see Table 8.1).

As noted in Chapter 7, middle- and working-class people who believed in peaceful integration into American society made organizing efforts in the Mexican-American barrios during the 1950s. In the 1960s and 1970s a new generation of leaders sought to move beyond assimilationist strategies by advocating what Rodolfo Acuña has called "a renaissance in Mexican consciousness."[4] This meant educating people to be proud of their Mexican heritage. The Chicanos linked the corporate exploitation of Chicanos in the fields and the barrios to the multinationals' domination of Mexico's economy. As had been true during the earlier decades, many of Chicano leaders were from the middle class, or at least aspired to the middle class. The difference was that rather than seek-

Table 8.1. *United States Mexican-Origin Population*[1]
by Region and Foreign Birth, 1930–1990

Census Year	1930	1940	1950	1960	1970	1980	1990
Residing in Southwest[2]							
Number	1,314	1,675	2,290	3,465	4,549	7,028	10,955
Percent	92	90	88	87	83	79	75
Residing outside Southwest							
Number	108	186	294	509	880	1,801	3,541
Percent	8	10	12	13	17	21	25
Total	1,422	1,861	2,584	3,974	5,429	8,829	14,496
Born in Mexico[3]							
Number	639	377	450	573	760	2,199	4,447
Percent	44	20	17	14	14	25	30

[1]In thousands.
[2]Defined as California, Arizona, New Mexico, and Texas.
[3]Does not fully count those who entered illegally or temporary workers in noncensus years.
    Source: U.S. Department of Commerce, *Statistical Abstracts* (Washington D.C.: U.S. Government Printing Office, 1942, 1953, 1973, 1984, 1991, 1992).

ing to distance themselves from the uneducated, impoverished lower-class Mexicans and Mexican Americans, they somewhat idealistically sought to transcend class boundaries and unify all people of Mexican descent under the rubric "Chicano." They deemphasized the persistent geographical, generational, and socioeconomic class differences within the Mexican-origin population and sought to create unity through poetic rhetoric and the glorification of Mexican and Chicano historical figures. This new sense of unity was associated with a reconquest of "Aztlán," the Aztec name for their ancient homeland. It was unimportant that there existed no evidence that the Aztecs had actually lived in the American Southwest. What was important was that Chicanos unite themselves with their Mexican culture and brethren. The creation of Aztlán, as a political symbol, became a spiritual and highly romantic endeavor that would lead Chicanos to champion the cause of undocumented immigrants.[5]

César Chávez

One important catalyst in galvanizing the Chicano revolution was César Chávez, who attempted to gain union recognition for Mexican and Chicano farmworkers.[6] During the 1960s the struggles of the United Farm Workers (UFW) union became one of the most visible expressions of Chicano protest. It was irrelevant that neither Chávez nor most of his union members considered themselves Chicanos or that most of Chávez's early staff and supporters were Anglo-Americans. The UFW black eagle and the pictures of Chávez confronting the police and growers became unifying symbols for the Chicano movement.

Chávez came from a landowning middle-class family in Yuma, Arizona, who had lost everything in the depression and become migrant farmworkers. He found a job working for the Community Service Organization in California during the 1950s. In 1963 he struck out on his own to do what many considered to be an impossible task—to organize a viable union among the thousands of migrant and resident farmworkers in California. Beyond the organizational problems inherent in trying to build a union among farm workers, Chávez had to confront the economic and political power of the growers and their strike-breaking strategy of recruiting Mexican immigrants as strike breakers.

Despite many difficulties, Chávez eventually succeeded in organizing an effective union composed of both immigrants and citizens of Mexican heritage. On 15 September 1965 the Farm Workers Association, as Chávez first called his union, joined the Filipino grape pickers in Delano who had begun a strike to protest low wages and bad housing conditions. Within months Chávez and his union became nationally known. His insistence on nonviolence, his reliance on volunteers from urban universities and religious organizations, his alliance with organized labor and his use of mass mobilizing techniques such as a famous march on Sacramento in 1966 made the UFW grape strike and boycott highly visible as part of a growing protest movement in the United States.

An important event that helped Chávez's union gain support from other unions and from farmworkers was the termination of the Bracero Program. As long as this program operated it was easy for growers to get cheap, docile, and disposable farm laborers from Mexico. It also made it particularly difficult for anyone to organize a farmworkers union. Because of pressures from organized labor and other Mexican-American rights groups, the government canceled the program in 1965.

The Mexican influences within the UFM were manifest. The grape strike and boycott included Mexican immigrants from the beginning. Many of the original members of the Farm Workers Association were legal immigrants or long-term residents, and within the union Spanish was a commonly used language. Symbolically, the day chosen to join the grape strike was 16 September, Mexican Independence Day. Banners of Our Lady of Guadalupe, the patron saint of Mexico, and other Mexican symbols became an integral part of rallies and marches. The Mexican and U.S. flags were prominent in meetings and strikes.

In south Texas the UFW relied on a variety of techniques to counter the grower's importation of strike breakers. In 1966, for example, the UFW organizers in Texas worked with Mexican unions to gain support among border crossers for their strike. The Mexican union, the Confederación de Trabajadores Mexicanos (CTM), organized a picket on the Mexican side of the border opposite Rio Grande City to discourage Mexican green-card holders from crossing to work as scabs, and several UFW supporters joined them.[7] In the summer of 1966 the UFW organized a famous march from the Rio Grande Valley to Austin to dramatize their plight. They assembled on the steps of the state capitol to demand that Governor John Connally help them enact a minimum-wage law. The Texas march took 65 days, covered 490 miles, and included Mexican-born immigrants along with members of LULAC and G.I. Forum. The march brought together thousands of Mexican Americans from all social classes and acted as a stimulus for political activity in Texas for later years. It was the beginning of the Chicano movement in that state.

The UFW undertook the same kind of joint organizational activities with Mexican unions in California as well. In 1968, during a UFW strike, Chávez asked Burt Corona, the longtime activist and labor leader, to go to the Imperial Valley to talk to workers and convince them not to be scabs. On Chávez's recommendation, Corona met with the president of the Mexican local of the Confederación de Trabajadores Mexicanos in Mexicali. Corona asked for and got permission to distribute leaflets on the Mexican side informing workers of the existence of the strike. He also got permission to place ads and stories in the Mexicali newspaper. Corona arranged to make public-service announcements on the Mexicali radio and television stations.[8]

On other occasions UFW organizers tried more direct appeals to Mexican immigrants whom the growers recruited to take the place of strikers. In Yuma, for example, during a 1974 citrus strike, the union stationed members and supporters—many of them Mexican immigrants—along the border to convince illegal crossers not to work as *esquiroles* (scabs).[9] The UFW used the same tactic in the fields as they marched, picketed, and pleaded with Mexican workers to leave the fields to join them.

Decidedly the farmworkers union owed a good deal of its moral force to the horrendous economic plight of migrant workers, many of whom were Mexican immigrants. It was not long before Chávez, although U.S.-born and -raised, became a Chicano leader well known in Mexico. In frequent trips to Mexico, Chávez met with labor leaders and even successive presidents, gaining their moral support for his union. There appeared in Mexico City several feature articles and books on Chávez and the UFW. In 1991, in recognition of his efforts to improve conditions for Mexicans in the United States, the president of Mexico, Salinas de Gotari, awarded him Mexico's highest civilian award, El Aguila de Oro.[10] Chávez died in 1993.

Through the pressure of an international boycott against California table grapes, the UFW eventually succeeded in forcing the major growers to sign a historic agreement. On 29 July 1970, 26 Delano growers filed into the UFW's union hall formally to sign contracts vastly improving the working conditions for thousands of farmworkers. For the first time in the history of farm labor, the growers had settled a negotiated contract with a union representing migrant workers. In years following this victory, Chávez and the UFW had long and bloody jurisdictional fights with the Teamster's Union, which finally agreed to peace in 1974. The next year, because of the lobbying efforts of the UFW, the California legislature passed the first law in the country protecting the rights of farm labor unions. The California Farm Labor Act established a board to review unfair labor practices and to monitor agricultural elections. Unfortunately, under Governor George Deukemejian, during the 1980s, the administration of this law fell into the hands of the growers and conservative Republicans. The net result was to undermine the UFW's gains. By the 1980s Chávez was once again calling for a grape boycott to force the growers to eliminate harmful pesticides in the fields and to sign contracts with the UFW to that effect.

Reies Tijerina

Another prominent leader who helped Mexican Americans articulate a new relationship with Mexico was Reies López Tijerina. Originally a fundamentalist preacher from Texas, Tijerina became part of the struggle of the Hispanos of New Mexico to regain the community land grants that the federal government and land corporations had taken from them after the Mexican War. Claiming that Anglo-Americans had taken the Hispano land grants in violation of the Treaty of Guadalupe Hidalgo, Tijerina attempted in 1964 and 1965 to enlist the support of the Mexican government in his struggle. Ultimately he was unsuccessful, but in the process he interpreted the Chicano's struggle in terms of a key document in Mexican history, the Treaty of Guadalupe Hidalgo. This treaty had promised protection for the civil rights and land grants of former Mexican citizens in the United States. In the years since its enactment in 1848 at the end of the Mexican War, the letter and spirit of the law had beeen repeatedly breached.

During the early 1960s Tijerina traveled throughout New Mexico organizing a land-grant association called La Alianza Federal de Mercedes Libres (the Federal Alliance of Free Land Grants). The organization endeavored "to organize and acquaint the heirs of all Spanish land-grants covered by the Guadalupe Hidalgo Treaty" with their rights. The Alianza became the catalyst for many militant actions by the Hispano villagers: the occupation of Kit Carson National Forest and the proclamation of the Republic of San Joaquín de Chama in 1966; a courthouse raid and shootout at Tierra Amarilla and a massive military manhunt for Tijerina and his followers in 1967; and lengthy legal battles that ended with the federal courts sentencing him to prison in 1970.[11]

Tijerina based his arguments for the reclamation of lost Hispano lands on two documents: the *Recopilación de leyes de las Indias,* a seventeenth-century document that had been the legal framework for the Spanish land grants, and the Treaty of Guadalupe Hidalgo, the 1848 document that had transferred millions of acres of Mexican land to the United States while ostensibly guaranteeing Mexican land grants. Tijerina contended that the United States had violated Articles 8 and 9 of the treaty, the ones that guaranteed property and citizenship rights to Mexicans.[12]

In his land-grant struggles Tijerina sought to forge an alliance with Mexican popular and governmental organizations. Early in January 1964 he and his wife, Patricia, went to Mexico City and met with Mexican officials to explore the possibility of organizing a procession of cars from New Mexico to dramatize the land-grant issue. The Mexican government, in particular the Mexican police, was less than enthusiastic about his radical political rhetoric. Later, when he traveled to Chihuahua in 1964 to promote the upcoming protest, the Mexican Judicial Police arrested him during a speech. Finally Mexico deported him with the threat that if he returned he would be put in prison for 10 years. Tijerina later believed that the U.S. government had set him up. Back in New Mexico with a heavy heart, he called off the protest. Tijerina's activities, in attempting to gain the support of the Mexican people for the plight of the Hispano villagers, had threatened the Mexican government. This episode put an end to Alianza's dream of having the Mexican government act as an advocate. Reies Tijerina's activities did manage to advertise the Chicano movement in Mexico. He rapidly assumed the status of a well-known folk hero fighting for Mexican rights in the United States.[13] Eventually the government secured a conviction of Reies Tijerina for destruction of public property. He spent several years in a U.S. federal prison, which ended his continued leadership of the land-grant struggle in New Mexico.

The Urban Movement: Students

Both Chávez and Tijerina were charismatic leaders whose activities focused on rural problems. They became the inspiration for a movement that would involve thousands of younger urban Chicanos who concerned themselves with other issues—mainly chronically high rates of educational failure and occupational discrimination. Chicanos had some of the highest drop-out rates in the country. In 1960, for example, the median grade attainment for Chicanos stood at 8.1 years, as compared with 9.7 for other nonwhites and 12.0 for Anglo-Americans. Their per capita yearly income remained abysmally low, $968, compared with $2,047 for Anglo-Americans and $1,044 for other nonwhite minorities, such as blacks and American Indians.[14] The statistics appeared even worse for areas of chronic poverty, such as rural New Mexico and south Texas. Viewed from the national level, this condition amounted to a tragedy and a disgrace, a portent of future civil disturbances among the nation's nonwhite minorities.

High school and college students became among the first to abandon the middle-class reformist tactics of their elders. While many of the student leaders came from relatively affluent working- or middle-class families, they sought to create a sense of unity with the laboring masses through militant proposals for liberation. In their speeches they blurred the distinctions between immigrant and the native born, stating again and again that *somos todos Mexicanos,* "we are all Mexicans." In both Texas and California, the two states with the largest Chicano and Mexican immigrant populations, student leaders assumed a key role in mobilizing their communities around themes of pride in Mexican roots and Chicanismo (a sense of brotherhood or ethnic solidarity). It is impossible to determine the numbers of Mexican immigrants who actually participated in the marches, demonstrations, and rallies that the students organized during the 1960s and early 1970s. Many of the participants in the demonstrations were most likely the children of immigrants or legal immigrants.

In Los Angeles and southern California students had been supporting César Chávez and the farmworkers in the grape boycott since 1966. Many resented what they considered racist school policies and the lack of Mexican-American teachers and courses related to the Mexican heritage. Finally, in March 1968, more than 10,000 Mexican-American students at schools in East Los Angeles, a predominantly Mexican-American section of the city, went on strike. Sal Castro was their leader, a high school teacher who had become disillusioned with attempts to reform the system. The students demanded changes in the schools to reflect their awakened cultural pride. The student "Blow Outs," as they were called, galvanized the younger generation's political awareness. Later in the spring of 1968, a student strike broke out at San Francisco State College. The same month Chicano activists occupied the offices of the president of the University of California in Berkeley to denounce racist policies in California's universities.[15] Other strikes in urban schools and universities throughout the Southwest followed the Los Angeles pattern.

The Chicano student strikes in Los Angeles inaugurated a period of intense activism in California. Young activists founded such organizations as the Brown Berets, a paramilitary self-styled barrio defense force patterned after the Black Panthers, and MEChA (Movimiento Estudiantil Chicano de Aztlán), a high school and college student organization dedicated to making educational insti-tutions more responsive to community needs.

The urban Chicano movement gained momentum after a national youth conference took place in Denver in 1969. Rodolfo "Corky" González, the key organizer, was a former middleweight boxer who had started a community self-help organization called the Denver Crusade for Justice. Student activists from all over the Southwest attended this conference to discuss the goals of their movement. The result was the publication of *El Plan Espiritual de Aztlán* (1969), a statement of purpose that relied heavily on the moral and historical ties between the Chicano struggle and Mexican people. The very term *Aztlán* harkened back to the ancient Aztec myth of a homeland somewhere to the north of present-day Mexico City. For the Chicano students, *Aztlán* meant that Chicanos and Mexicans shared a common historical origin and identity. *El Plan Espiritual de Aztlán* defined all Mexican-origin people in the United States as La Raza Bronze (the Bronze People), a Mestizo people proud of their Indian roots. In a poetic passage the students sought to unify all Mexicans, whether immigrant or native-born: "With our heart in our hands and our hands in the soil, we declare the independence of our mestizo nation. We are a bronze people with a bronze culture. Before all of North America, before all our brothers in the bronze conti-nent, we are a nation, we are a union of free pueblos, we are Aztlán. *Por La Raza todo. Fuera de la Raza nada.*"[16]

This call for ethnic unity echoed in high schools and universities as Chicanos began to call for classes and departments that would teach Chicano Studies. Young professors used as texts in these new classes works on Mexican history and translations of Mexican philosophers and writers. Students read and discussed the works of José Vasconcelos, Mariano Azuela, Octavio Paz, and Samuel Ramos. Chicano student organizations took as cultural icons prominent historical figures from Mexico's revolutionary past: Emiliano Zapata, Pancho Villa, Benito Juárez, and Miguel Hidalgo y Costilla. The Mexican flag, Our Lady of Guadalupe, and Aztec images became prominent symbols in marches, demonstrations, and meetings.

In an attempt to carry out *El Espirtual Plan de Aztlán*, at least at the college and university level, the students organized a conference at the University of California at Santa Barbara in 1969. In intense discussions and work groups they agreed to adopt a common terminology for Chicano student organizations, now to be called MEChA. This organization would pressure universities to recruit more Chicanos as students and faculty. It laid out a blueprint to institutionalize the Chicano movement by establishing academic departments and courses that would enable Chicanos to study their heritage. The key idea emerging in *El Plan de Santa Barbara* (1970) was that the universities should serve the interests of the Chicano community. The students believed that institutions of higher education had to be changed accordingly. *El Plan de Santa Barbara* soon became the rallying point for establishing scores of academic departments and programs within California universities. These in turn served to support the political and cultural agendas of Chicanismo.

The Urban Movement: The Community

A dramatic turning point in the Chicano movement was the Chicano Moratorium riot in Los Angeles in August of 1970. The war in Vietnam had polarized American society and created a militant anti-war movement. Within the barrios, disproportionate numbers of young Mexican Americans had been drafted and killed or wounded. While Chicanos were about 10 percent of the population in the Southwest, in 1967 they accounted for almost 20 percent of those killed in the war. The first major mass-protest movement organized by Chicano militants, the Chicano Moratorium was to call for an end to the war in Vietnam. It brought together various organizations: the Brown Berets, MEChA, the participants in the Denver conference, Catholic action groups, returned veterans, and even representatives of some middle-class groups. More than 20,000 people attended the march and rally on 29 August 1970. The march ended in the afternoon at Laguna Park, where the participants relaxed to hear music and speeches. An incident at a nearby liquor store brought a massive response from the police, who surrounded the park and ordered the crowd to disperse. A general riot ensued when hundreds of deputy sheriffs charged the crowd shooting tear gas and clubbing those within their reach. The tumult lasted several hours and ended with three persons being killed, among them Rubén Salazar, a reporter for the *Los Angeles Times* and KMEX, the local Spanish-language television station. In his editorials and stories Salazar had been an outspoken critic of the police. Immediately after the riot, Salazar was sitting in a bar along Whittier Boulevard when a deputy sheriff shot a tear-gas projectile into the structure, striking Salazar in the head. A later coroner's inquest ruled the tragedy an accidental death. The way the government conducted the inquest convinced many Chicano leaders that the police had intentionally killed him.

The Chicano Moratorium riot in 1970 became a rallying point for other Chicano political groups, who started annual commemorations of the march. It also marked intensification of the police efforts to infiltrate and destroy Chicano organizations. Besides police subversion, the young activists had many internal political problems. One of the most divisive issues was an ideological and philosophical one: the degree to which Chicanos should consider themselves Mexican. This problem emerged as a complex and vituperative debate between two factions: the cultural and the revolutionary nationalists. The cultural nationalists argued that Mexican Americans constituted a nation, culturally and politically distinct from Mexico, and that the main struggle remained to unite Chicanos to achieve self-determination and political power. The revolutionary nationalists, on the other hand, felt that Chicanos were actually Mexicans and that they should join with working-class Mexicans to struggle against their common enemies. The revolutionaries believed that Chicanos and Mexicanos constituted *un pueblo sin fronteras,* "a people without borders." This debate over the national and international implications of being Chicano severely divided the Los Angeles Chicano movement and resulted in fierce in-fighting.

One of the most active groups committed to articulating the links between Chicanos and Mexican nationals was CASA (Centro de Acción Social Autónoma; Center for Socially Autonomous Action), based in Los Angeles. Initially led by Burt Corona, a longtime labor activist, CASA, more than any other organization, sought to make the Chicanos politically aware of the political issues raised by Mexican immigration. Corona built an organization of more than 5,000 members in several states primarily to support undocumented immigrants by providing social and economic services. The organizational philosophy was to establish solidarity between the Mexicano and Chicano working classes. Their newspaper, *Sin Fronteras,* published many articles calling on the Chicano community to defend undocumented workers and linking the Chicano movement to organizational struggles in Mexico and Puerto Rico. Historian Juan Gómez Quiñones has called CASA's newspaper "the best militant print organ of the movement." CASA was far in advance of many other Chicano organizations in advocating amnesty for undocumented immigrants and pan-American unity among Chicanos, Mexican immigrants, and Central American refugees. Factionalism eventually undermined CASA's success. More radical members tried to change the organization to take on a more Marxist-Leninist direction, and personal conflicts erupted among the leaders The ensuing internal struggles led to the destruction of the organization by 1977.[17]

Despite CASA's failure, its concern with the plight of the Mexican immigrant and its establishment of trans-border communications and links influenced the direction of the Chicano movement. After CASA's demise, Chicano demonstrations and protests regularly included statements about human rights violations by the INS and the Border Patrol and the corporate exploitation of undocumented immigrants. In San Diego, for example, the CCR (Committee for Chicano Rights), led by Herman Baca, arose as one of the most militant organizations of this period. The CCR sought to organize the Chicano community to protest the treatment of undocumented immigrants. Throughout the 1970s and into the 1980s it organized border marches and conferences to highlight INS abuses. Other immigrant-rights organizations led by Chicanos became common-place. This was a major change from the previous nativist orientations of Mexican-American middle-class groups.

Another effort to define the Chicano's relationship to a Mexican heritage unfolded in Texas. In the early 1970s Chicano student activists there founded a political party called La Raza Unida (the United People). La Raza Unida grew out of a school strike in Crystal City, Texas. José Angel Gutiérrez, a college graduate and former organizer for PASSO (Political Association of Spanish-Speaking Organizations), was the party's key organizer. With Mario Compean, a former migrant worker and student of political science, Gutiérrez founded MAYO in 1968 (Mexican American Youth Organization) to attempt to mobilize student and community power to change the school system in south Texas. In 1970, fresh from an electoral victory in Crystal City, they decided to establish a third party to protest the unresponsiveness of the Republicans and Democrats.[18] As had been true in other Chicano organizations, the leadership of the RUP came primarily from the middle classes—lawyers, teachers, small businesspeople, and social workers. Their ability to appeal to the rank-and-file Chicano, particularly the working classes, varied according to regional conditions.[19]

As a third party, La Raza Unida sought to effect change through electoral pol-itics rather than demonstrations. In that sense it could count on occasional sup-port from the older Mexican-American leadership, especially in Texas. During the early 1970s it enjoyed success in organizing the poverty-stricken rural town-ships in south Texas. It organized small branches in California, New Mexico, and elsewhere, but these were not as successful in appealing to working-class Chicano voters.

Despite all the difficulties, lack of money, distrust of the middle class, and voter conservatism, La Raza Unida managed to survive until the late 1970s. Fearing the gains made by the party, federal and state agencies began a cam-paign of systematic surveillance and harassment. The FBI infiltrated the party and attempted to discredit the membership. More than once opponents got the courts to remove its candidates from the ballot and void election results. Despite this opposition, the party helped open up the local electoral system so that Mexican Americans could win elections as candidates in mainstream parties. With their political programs and candidates coopted, La Raza Unida gradually declined.

During La Raza Unida's last years, its co-founder José Angel Gutiérrez had cultivated politically close relationships with the president of Mexico, Luis Echeverría Alvarez. Gutiérrez hoped to use his Mexican connections to strengthen the economy of Zavala County, where he had established an eco-nomic development corporation (ZCEDC). Luis Echeverría and the next presi-dent, José López Portillo, discussed possibilities of economic programs, and eventually Portillo established a scholarship program for Chicanos to study in Mexican professional schools.

According to Ignacio García, who has written a history of La Raza Unida, the coup de grâce for the party came partially as Gutiérrez refused to unite with other Chicano leaders on the issue of Mexican immigration. In 1977 Gutiérrez got the party involved in a conference on immigration, its purpose being to protest President Carter's immigration reform proposal that called for limited amnesty for illegal Mexican immigrants and employer sanctions for hiring undocumented workers. (This proposal later was enacted into law as the Immigration Reform and Control Act of 1987.) At the conference the various factions of the Chicano movement manifested their division over the immigration issue. The middle-class organizations—represented by LULAC, the G.I. Forum, and MALDEF (Mexican American Legal Defense and Education Fund)—opposed the militant language the younger delegates used to criticize the Carter administration. The Left, represented by the Socialist Workers party and CASA, fought a pitched ideological battle among themselves over control of the conference. Gutiérrez finally threw his support to the Socialist faction (García thinks for political support in an upcoming election) and thus ended up alienating many of his own party members. Conference participants left without any agreement on the immigration issue, and these disagreements fatally divided La Raza Unida.[20]

The Chicano Middle Class

During the militant years of the Chicano movement, the student leaders tended to assume that all Mexican Americans were impoverished, uneducated, and powerless. The rhetoric of the movement tended to encourage this kind of overgeneralization. Of little notice at the time was the presence of a solid group of middle-class "liberal" Mexican Americans who believed in reform rather than revolution. The older generational leadership of LULAC and the G.I. Forum, motivated by the growing unrest within their constituencies, used their connections in Congress to ensure that Mexican Americans benefited from the new social agenda. The result was the establishment of the Service, Employment, and Redevelopment Agency (Project SER), a multi-million-dollar, federally funded job-training and placement service that Chicanos ran and operated. In California a similar middle-class initiative began in 1968, with the founding of the East Los Angeles Community Union (TELACU). A group of enterprising Mexican-American businessmen worked to acquire private and public grants in order to provide social and economic services for predominantly working-class barrio residents. By 1984 TELACU was ranked as the eighth largest Hispanic business in the United States.

Also important in the emerging Chicano middle class were the young law school graduates who came into practice with a new social conciousness. They worked to staff several important groups that sought to use the courts to advance the social and political welfare of the Chicano community. The Mexican American Legal Defense and Education Fund (MALDEF), founded in 1968, targeted Mexican-American community issues. MALDEF attorneys launched scores of lawsuits to challenge vestiges of segregation and discrimination throughout the Southwest. Perhaps the most important of these was *Cisneros v. Corpus Christi Independent School District* (1970). That case produced a decision asserting that Mexican Americans constituted an identifiable ethnic group for desegregation purposes.[21] In 1974 Willie Velásquez founded the Southwest Voter Registration Education Project (SWVRP), whose purpose was to increase

Chicano participation in electoral politics. SWVRP won hundreds of lawsuits throughtout the Southwest, challenging gerrymandered district boundaries and such electoral practices as at-large elections, which undercut Chicano voting strength. In the 1980s the SWVRP legal initiatives would be one of the main causes of a surge in Chicano electoral victories.

Chicanos and the Protestant Denominations

The Catholic Church saw considerable changes during the 1960s and 1970s, ranging from the appointment of Mexican-American bishops, the elaboration of Spanish-language masses, and increased visibility of a social-action agenda and liberation theology among priests within the barrio. This change had often been forced by Chicano militants, such as those in Los Angeles's Católicos Por La Raza, who had actively protested the Church's insentivity to social issues of concern to Chicanos.[22] Priests such as Father Victor Salandini (aka "the Tortilla Priest") had visibility within the UFW, and César Chávez sought to link the Church to the Chicano movement. The vast majority of Latinos remained Catholics, but an important trend since World War II continued to be the growing number of Mexican-American Protestants. A 1960 survey identified about 113,000 Mexican Americans in the United States as being members of Protestant denominations. This was only about 3 percent of the total 1960 Mexican-American population. The most popular denominations for Mexican Americans were the Assemblies of God, the Methodist Church and branches of the Baptist Church.[23] One sociologist speculated that the increased numbers of Chicano Protestants was in response to criticisms raised by the Chicano movement of the Catholic Church's fatalistic approach toward the poverty and oppression of Mexican Americans.[24]

In the 1960s and 1970s many Protestant groups appeared to be more concerned about Mexican Americans than was the Catholic Church. The Migrant Ministry, a group supported by an interdenominational Protestant group, remained active in serving farmworkers. Many of their members became top officials within the UFW, and others remained very active in labor organizing outside of California. The interdenominational group Council on Spanish-American Work (COSAW) assisted Protestant churches in their evangelistic work within the barrios. Many Protestant sects, including the Mormon Church, had long regarded the Southwest as prime missionary territory and had made gains in conversion, particularly among those aspiring to the middle class. In 1971 the American Baptist Convention sought to modernize its approach toward Chicanos by endorsing the concept of "cultural pluralism" and the necessity for militant social action.[25] Some Chicanos sought to bring pressure to bear on the Protestant denominations to be more responsive to the needs of the community. This was the case in the conflict between activists in MAYO and the Presbyterian Church in Houston in 1970 when Chicanos picketed and protested the church's lack of social programs.[26] Others also resented the encroachment of the Protestant faith into Catholic country and foresaw it as leading toward conflict and increased pressure for assimilation. Nevertheless, the growth of non-Catholic Mexican Americans was another sign of the increased diversity of La Raza.

Las Colonias: Mexican Americans beyond Aztlán

After World War II a growing number of Mexican Americans came to live out-side the Southwest. Between 1960 and 1980 more than five million additional Mexicanos and their descendants came to live outside of the four southwest-ern states (see Table 8.1). By 1980 this represented more than 1.8 million Chicanos, or 21 percent of all Chicanos and Mexicanos in the United States. The majority of them resided in such metropolitan areas as Chicago, Detroit, Denver, Seattle, and Gary, Indiana, and in cities and towns throughout the Midwest and Pacific Northwest.[27]

One example of this growing urban population outside the Southwest was the Mexican colony in and around Chicago and Gary, Indiana.[28] In 1960 researchers reported an estimated 67,000 "Mexican-stock" people in these two cities. By 1980 the estimated Mexican-American population numbered more than 400,000.[29] As noted in previous chapters, the majority of these people had come to this area to work in the steel mills in the 1920s. They lived in segre-gated areas of the metropolitan areas, alongside Puerto Rican and black migrants. During the 1960s Mexican Americans left their original colonias and moved to newer more affluent areas, indicating some socioeconomic genera-tional mobility. They nevertheless continued to live in primarily ethnic enclaves; educational achievement remained low, and most lived modest working-class lives. Their feelings of community solidarity were maintained by identification with predominantly Spanish-speaking Catholic parishes and an active social life revolving around pan-Latin organizations (in association with Puerto Ricans), such as the Latin American Bowling League, the Latin American Ladies League, the Latin Civic Political Club, and the like.[30] With the Puerto Rican population, the Mexican Americans of the greater Chicago area forged a new sense of identity as Latino or Latin American. This arose as a response to the long-term discrimination suffered by both these groups and the need to strengthen their collective voice.[31]

A minority of Mexican Americans and Mexicans in the Midwest and Pacific Northwest were farmworkers on farms owned by families and large corpora-tions. More and more Mexican Americans in the Midwest left farming to work in the cities, where they could find better wages and more job security. The increasing mechanization of farmwork also contributed to this trend. Opportunities declined for midwestern farmworkers throughout the period. Following the lead of the UFW struggles in California, midwestern Chicano farmworkers, with the support of the growing urban populations, made their demands for better wages and working conditions known. They organized labor unions following the California model. One of these, Obreros Unidos in Wisconsin, was led by Jesús Salas, an activist from Crystal City, Texas. In the mid-1960s Salas and the Obreros Unidos staff organized marches, walkouts, and strikes to build their union. They won a number of unfair-labor-practice law-suits. The union eventually failed when the AFL-CIO withdrew its support. In subsequent years Chicanos organized the Farm Labor Organizing Committee (FLOC), led by Baldemar Velásquez and other Mexicanos from Ohio. FLOC also had the help of and modeled itself after the UFW in California. Key to FLOC's limited successes in the 1970s were the victories of the UFW in California. The AFL-CIO supported the midwestern farmworkers union as a result.[32]

Chicana Political Activity

The hidden force behind many of the Chicano movement's organizations and protests were the activities of Chicanas. The movement was male-dominated and did not give prominence to female cohorts. An exception was Dolores Huerta, executive vice president of the UFW, who in the 1960s and 1970s became that group's main lobbyist and a key contract negotiator. She traveled constantly to give speeches and secure support for the union's boycott activities. César Chávez came to depend on her as a key negotiator and political strategist during the difficult years of the grape strike and lettuce boycott.

The spouses and families of movement leaders frequently worked in key positions within Chicano organizations. Helen Chávez, César's wife, was treasurer and manager of the credit union within the UFW for many years. Helen González, Rodolfo González's wife, coordinated many of the family activities that the Denver Crusade for Justice organized. Similarly, Reies Tijerina's wife, Patricia, worked with the Alianza organization and helped organize protest activities.[33]

La Raza Unida party gave Chicanas opportunities for political leadership and contributed to the growth of feminist activism. Several women were elected on the party ticket in Crystal City and Zavala County. Many of the party workers were women, and some of them served as the Texas state chairpersons. Under the leadership of Chicanas like Marta Cotera, Maria L. de Hernández, Evey Chapa, and Virginia Múzquiz, the party developed two feminist organizations. In Texas it was called the Federación de Mujeres de la Raza Unida, and in California it was called Mujeres Pro-Raza Unida. They served to give new directions to a male-dominated movement.

By and large Chicanas felt excluded from decision-making power by the traditional outlooks of most of the Chicano leadership. These attitudes, reinforced by rural Mexican culture, subordinated women to roles as wives and mothers. Even in modern times, Mexican and Chicana women were supposed to be submissive and docile, domesticated by the Catholic Church and not encouraged to seek roles outside the family. The ideal woman was embodied in the Virgen de Guadalupe, the model for the passive, obedient woman whose only concern was for the welfare of her children and husband.

In reaction to feelings of exclusion from leadership roles, Chicanas launched their own organizing and political activities. In 1971 more than 600 Chicanas attended a national Chicana conference in Houston. After a highly charged debate, they passed resolutions that reflected their concerns: sexual equality, free legal abortions, and birth control; encouragement of higher education for all women; changes in traditional marriage roles to recognize women as breadwinners; and a denouncement of the Catholic Church's opposition to feminist ideas. Only about half of those attending the conference supported these resolutions, revealing a chronic division among Chicana opinions. A militant contingent felt that the main enemy was sexism and traditional macho attitudes. Another faction believed that issues of sexual politics should be subordinated to the common struggle against capitalist economic and educational oppression.[34]

Sonia López, in her history of the Chicanas in the student movement, identified the period 1971–72 as one when Chicanas began to more openly criticize the male domination of the movement. They formed several alternative organizations on university campuses and in the barrios and held several regional meetings to discuss common problems. Most of the activity took place in California, where feminist activism emerged particularly strong. The Chicana Regional Conference was held in Whittier, California, and La Conferencia Femenil was held in Sacramento, both in 1972. One issue that arose was the relationship of Chicanas and Latinas to the feminist movement. Many prejudices and stereotypes surfaced on both sides. Despite a shared sexist critique and their regard for feminist leadership, some Chicanas distrusted the ethnocentric and reformist directions that the women's movement had taken.[35] Nevertheless, there remained middle-class Mexican-American women who agreed with many of the points made by feminists. In November 1972, for example, the LULAC Women's Affairs Committee met in Houston to discuss ways in which women could enter the political arena. With more than 250 women in attendance, they passed several resolutions to challenge sexist images of passive Mexican womanhood.

Working-class Chicana and Mexican women were more concerned with issues of economic survival. In 1972 the predominantly female and Chicana

Mural entitled *The Birth of La Raza*, painted ca. 1974 at Chicano Park, San Diego. Photograph courtesy of Jane Ferree.

Mural entitled *Chuco/Homeboy*, painted ca. 1974 at Chicano Park, San Diego. Photograph courtesy of Jane Ferree.

employees of the Farah garment factory in El Paso, Texas, went on strike after management refused to recognize their union. After a two-year boycott of the plant, the management relented and signed a contract. The resulting agreement was a victory for the union as much as for Chicanas who had shown their ability and determination to fight for their jobs.

A Chicano Renaissance: The Visual and Performing Arts

The political energies of the Chicano movement found expression in the visual and performing arts. Inspired by a new sense of self-confidence and an ethnic identity born of that era, Chicano artists created a dynamic artistic legacy. A veritable renaissance in Chicano arts exploded on the scene, changing forever the way that America would perceive Mexicans in the United States.

A new force in performance art emerged when Luís Valdez in 1965 organized El Teatro Campesino to support César Chávez's UFW. Initially composed of farmworkers who performed short *actos* (one-act skits) to dramatize the politics of the union's struggle, El Teatro Campesino evolved into a multimedia actors workshop based in San Juan Bautista, California. Valdez trained scores of protégés in acting and playwriting. His plays and films projected strong political messages. Valdez wrote *Los Vendidos* (1967), for example, a humorous play about how Anglos stereotype Mexicans and about the possibility of "faking" being a sellout in order to subvert mainstream society. Valdez and El Teatro Campesino made the first Chicano film, *I Am Joaquín*, based on the poem of the same name written by Rodolfo "Corky" González in 1969. This film presented still images set to music and the words of the poetry. The total effect was to communicate powerful emotions of revolt and resistance, so much so that several school districts prohibited its showing for fear of inciting violence and demonstrations.

Inspired by El Teatro Campesino, student and community groups founded similar *teatros* and produced Valdez's plays as well as their own original compositions. The names of these teatros show the political consciousness underlying their art: El Teatro de la Esperanza (Theater of Hope), El Teatro de la Gente (Theater of the People), Teatro de la Causa de los Pobres (Theater of the Poor People's Cause), El Teatro Mestizo (Mestizo Theater), and Teatro Alma Latina (The Latin Soul Theater). In 1971 these groups joined to form an association called TENAZ (Teatro Nacional de Aztlán), and each year they sponsored an international *teatro* festival. TENAZ also sponsored joint Latin American/Chicano *teatro* exchanges, with performances by student groups from Mexico and other Latin American countries.[36]

A key ingredient in the development of Chicano *teatro* in this era was the use of Mexican legends, symbols, and music. The dynamic of the Chicano *teatro* came from the creative use of Mexican and U.S. cultural elements. Many of the *teatros* used Spanish slang mixed with English. The performance of *corridos* added to the Mexican basis of the *teatro*. The humorous ingredient, so quintessential to this *teatro*, often came from cultural clashes, misunderstandings, and confusions between Mexican and Anglo society. Plays on words, masks, and burlesque, long part of the Mexican popular theater (*carpas* and *tandas*), gained new political meanings when performed in Chicano contexts in English and Spanish slang. Two notable works of this period were *Soldado Razo* (1970), an anti-war play from a Chicano perspective, and *La Carpa de los Rasquachis* (The Tent of the Underdogs) (1974), the first full-length Chicano play.

The *teatro* movement inspired the growth of a Chicano film genre. For years Hollywood had been producing movies that contained derogatory or stereotyped images of Mexicans and Mexican Americans. Until the early 1970s not a single person of Mexican descent had been able to write, direct, or produce a feature film. This began to change when Chicanos started to make their own low-budget documentaries, usually shown first on television, as was *Requiem-29* (1971), about the coroner's inquest into the death of Rubén Salazar, and *Yo Soy Chicano* (1972), a sweeping summary of Chicano history. A growth in funding opportunities and political pressure by Chicano acting groups such as the movie star Ricardo Montalbán's NOSOTROS made it possible for many young film-makers to make their movies.

Young filmmakers took their themes from the Chicano struggle and from Mexican history. Jesús Treviño's *América Tropical* (1971) is about the political controversy surrounding David Alfaro Siquieros's mural in Los Angeles. Ricardo Soto's *A la brava* (1973) tells the story of Chicanos in Soledad prison. And José Luis Ruíz's *The Unwanted* (1974) recounts the exploitation of undocumented immigrants, while Sylvia Morales's *La Chicana* (1979), which she also wrote, surveys Mexican and Chicana women's history.

A important topic for Chicano film remained the experience of the U.S.-Mexican border and Mexican immigration. Chicano filmmakers made several documentaries that had limited distribution. Jesús Treviño was the first to direct a feature-length film on the topic with his *Raíces de Sangre* (1977), which was produced jointly with a Mexican film company. The best film on the Mexican immigrant experience is Robert Young's *Alambrista* (1979), a compelling drama about a young man's travels north.[37]

Perhaps the most noticeable and widespread manifestation of the Chicano movement was in the painting of murals. At first Chicano artists drew their inspiration from the Mexican masters. The Mexican muralists Diego Rivera, David Alfaro Siquieros, and José Clemente Orozco had visualized, on a grand scale, themes of Mexican history and culture. While almost all the Mexican murals had been on public buildings, Chicano artists took it one step further. They painted their murals on the exteriors of private businesses, homes, bridges, freeway overpasses, and even drainage channels. Mexican themes and icons pervaded these murals: images of Our Lady of Guadalupe, the patron saint of Mexico; the Aztec calendar; the eagle and serpent of the Mexican flag; *calaveras* (skeletons); ancient pre-Columbian gods and pyramids; and such revolutionary heroes as Benito Juárez, Miguel Hidalgo, Pancho Villa, and Emiliano Zapata. Again, as in *teatro,* the Chicano murals added perspectives that could only have been visualized by Mexicans or Latinos in the United States: police brutality, the UFW red and black flag, *cholos, vato locos, pachucos,* low riders (all barrio youth with stylized dress), and racial discrimination and solidarity.

Hundreds of Chicano artists produced murals and other kinds of visual art during the Chicano movement. It is estimated that in California alone during this period Chicano artists produced more than 1,500 murals.[38] Chicano mural art developed a certain ironic and critical relationship to Anglo-American (*gaba-cho)* society. Artists created their murals as noncommercial popular art, usually commissioned by government projects, community organizations, or private businesses. As such, Chicano artists felt a responsibility that their art would be of educational, inspirational value to their *raza,* the community.

In the late 1960s artists formed collectives to carry out their work and provide support. José Montoya and Estéban Villa organized the Royal Chicano Air Force (RCAF) in Sacramento. Patricia Rodríguez, Irene Pérez, Graciela Carrillo, and Consuelo Méndez established Mujeres Muralistas, one of the era's many Chicana art groups, in San Francisco. Chicano artists in Los Angeles founded mural art groups such as Los Four, ASCO, and Mechicano Art Center. San Diego artists banded together with students to establish more permanent institutions such as El Centro Cutural de la Raza in Balboa Park and Chicano Park in Barrio

Logan. Organizations outside California included Casa Aztlán (Chicago), Movimiento Artistico del Río Salado (Phoenix), and El Grito Aztlán Art Gallery (Denver).[39]

While street murals emerged as the most visible and dramatic manifestation of Chicano art, many individual painters and sculptors created smaller-scale works. In Texas, Luis Jiménez and Octavio Medellín became well-known sculptors, while Melesio Casas and Amado Peña created paintings with social and political messages. In New Mexico, Felipe Archuleta and Luis Tapia sought to revive the *santero* folk art traditions. Others—Glynn Gómez, for instance—produced more modern and abstract expressions. California produced the emotional explosive paintings of Carlos Almaraz and Glugio Gronk Nicandro (Gronk) along with the realistic representations of John Valadez.

The first large-scale exhibition of Chicano paintings took place at the Guadalupe Culural Arts Center in San Antonio, and other exhibits followed in California. Chicano art slowly began to be recognized by mainstream art critics as an important new development. Chicano artists would later earn national and international recognition for their creative visions.[40]

In the arena of music and dance, Mexican influences abounded, modified and shaped to fit a Chicano reality. The best examples of this were in Texas, where the lively tradition of Tex-Mex *conjunto* music continued to flourish and grow, blending the Mexican *corrido* with German polkas and American rock-and-roll. Artists like Flaco Jiménez, Lydia Mendoza (who staged a comeback from her earlier career), Freddy Fender, and Johnny Rodríguez gained national attention while drawing inspiration from Mexican music and molding it to Chicano realities.

The rock-and-roll contributions of Chicanos in the 1960s continued to reflect a mixture of cultural traditions: African-American rhythm and blues, Mexican folk songs, country and western. Trini López sold four million copies of "If I Had a Hammer," a song that quickly became an anti-war movement song. Sam the Sham and Pharoahs, a Chicano rock group from Dallas, had a hit song in 1965 with "Wooly Booly." The barrios of East Los Angeles spawned a number of notable rock groups. Cannibal and the Headhunters led by Frankie García recorded the hit song "Land of a Thousand Dances." The Midnighters, another Chicano group, produced "Whittier Boulevard," immortalizing the low-riding automobile culture of the barrio. During the activist years a number of groups geared their music toward political causes. Los Lobos recorded their first album to benefit the UFW. The V.I.P.s, a California band, changed their name to El Chicano. Frank Zappa recorded a tribute to the precursors of Chicano rock-and-roll in his album "Zoot Allures." Carlos Santana's band in the 1960s and 1970s probably had the largest impact on Anglo audiences, introducing them to Latin jazz and rock innovations. His appearance at Woodstock in 1969 was the only Latino presence at this landmark event.[41]

Almost every major college or university in the Southwest spawned Mexican folkloric dance groups in response to a new need to identify with Mexican traditions and provide culturally relevant entertainment during mass meetings, conferences, and marches. Many of these groups had both Chicano and Mexican performers. They periodically traveled to Mexico to study "Ballet Folklorico," a re-creation of regional native dances pioneered by Amelia Hernández.

Chicano Literature

The Chicano movement created an explosion of literature that added new dynamic to American letters. Drawing on centuries of literary tradition in Mexico and the old Spanish/Mexican Southwest, the generation of writers in the 1960s and 1970s were self-conscious about their ethnicity and their oppressed position within the United States. Their creative work challenged the literary world to recognize new themes and forms of expression. The earliest published Chicano literature was vivid bilingual poetry that explored themes of conflict and the rejection of Anglo-European values. Literary critics consider the poem "I Am Joaquín" (1968), by Rodolfo "Corky" González, as one of the first-published poems of the Chicano movement. It proclaimed the Chicanos' struggle using simple declarative language and vivid historical images. Its opening lines set the tone for what followed:

> *I am Joaquín,*
> *lost in a world of confusion,*
> *caught up in the whirl of*
> *a gringo society,*
> *confused by the rules,*
> *scorned by attitudes,*
> *suppressed by manipulation,*
> *and destroyed by modern society.*

Chicano poets usually used the verse form to proclaim their emotional life—a life that they believed was shaped by economic and political oppression. Often they mixed the Spanish and English languages or used *caló*, as in the writings of Abelardo "Lalo" Delgado, a Mexican-born poet who lived in El Paso. His first book of poetry, *Chicano: 25 Pieces of a Chicano Mind*, published in 1969, spoke of the frustrations that Chicano artists felt as U.S. society ignored their work. An important movement poet, Ricardo Sánchez drew on his experience in the army, prison, and as a university professor. His prolific output in *Canto y grito mi liberación* (1971) and *HechizoSpells* (1976) were intense personal statements about social protest and the importance of political action. Many other early movement poets—Tino Villanueva, Sergio Elizondo, and Alurista, for instance—created excitement with their vivid images and imaginative language.[42]

While poetry had a limited audience, the contemporary Chicano novel had the greatest literary impact. Writing almost exclusively in English but drawing on a long Spanish-language literary tradition, Chicano novelists used their imagination to probe the dimensions of ethnic identity. The essential theme in Chicano novels is the search for identity in America. Of the scores of Chicano novelists during this era, some of the most important were Rudolfo Anaya, Ron Arías, Rolando Hinojosa-Smith, Miguel Méndez M., Alejandro Morales, and Tomás Rivera.

The most widely read of these was Rudolfo Anaya, a professor of English at the University of New Mexico. His 1972 book *Bless Me, Ultima* won the second annual Premio Quinto Sol National Literary Award and became a best-selling Chicano novel. Anaya tells the story of a young boy growing up and being influenced by the spirituality of a *curandera* (a healer), Ultima, as well as the legends and oral traditions of his community. *Bless Me, Ultima* is a folkloric novel that uses the richness of the native New Mexican people and their traditions. Anaya went on to write other novels and short stories that continued his quest for meaning. He wrote *Heart of Aztlán* (1976) and *Tortuga* (1979), both of which deal with magic, symbolism, and dreams in contrast to the hard realities of life. For Anaya, the essence of what it meant to be a Chicano had something to do with spirtuality and tradition.

Another influential Chicano novelist was Tomás Rivera, a Tejano who received a Ph.D. in Romance languages and literature from the University of Oklahoma and later became the first Latino chancellor in the University of California system. He wrote many works of poetry and short stories, but his most famous work was the short novel *". . . y no se lo tragó la tierra" / And the Earth Did Not Part* (1971). This prize-winning book tells about a migrant Chicano child, his impressions and memories, as he struggles to live in south Texas. Written in a complex form—including dialogues, prayers, memories, and feelings that seem to follow the months of the year—the novel shows how oppression and discrimination shapes a young man's coming of age. The title *And the Earth Did Not Part* refers to the young man's rebellion, provoked by poverty and misfortune, against traditional faith (that the earth would swallow him up if he cursed God).

In a category all by themselves are the novels of Oscar Zeta Acosta. An activist lawyer during the most violent days of the Chicano movement in Los Angeles, Acosta wrote two very influential novels: *The Autobiography of a Brown Buffalo* (1972) and *Revolt of the Cockroach People* (1973). Both books are autobiographical but blend fact and imagination. The engaging and vivid writing style has been compared to Hunter Thompson's Gonzo journalism (fascination with the bizarre promoted by drug use). *Autobiography* follows Acosta's journeys throught the Southwest, his experiments with drugs and alcohol, and his self-discovery in a Mexican border town: "I propose that we call ourselves . . . the Brown Buffalo people . . . because we do have roots in our Mexican past, our Aztec ancestry, that's where we get the *brown* from."[43] In *Revolt of the Cockroach People* Acosta tells of his activities as a revolutionary-lawyer in Los Angeles during 1968–1970. His accounts of the major events and characters of the Chicano movement are perhaps the most engaging of any work of fiction yet produced. Imitating art, as with the main character in his novel, Acosta disappeared mysteriously in the late 1970s.

The immigrant experience appeared as an important theme in many popular Chicano novels. As mentioned, the earliest contemporary Chicano novel was José Antonio Villareal's *Pocho*, published in 1959. Reprinted in many editions, this book enjoyed great popularity during the 1970s. *Pocho* tells about a young boy growing up in Santa Clara, California, beset with cultural conflicts between the Mexican and American societies. The novel depicts intense conflicts between generations, young and old, immigrant and native-born. It is a story of the cultural consequences of immigration. Villareal's other books—*The Fifth Horseman* (1974) and *Clemente Chacón* (1984)—also developed themes of Mexican immigration and cultural conflict. Another popular novel of this period that depicts the conflicts faced by immigrants is Richard Vásquez's *Chicano* (1970), a multigenerational history of a family of Mexicans who come to live in the barrio of East Los Angeles. It was the first published novel to popularize the term *Chicano* in describing the racial prejudices confronted by Mexicans in the United States. Vásquez's later novel, *Another Land* (1982), is an action-packed account of undocumented immigrants and their tribulations in the United States.

Chicanas also wrote novels and short stories during this period, but because they were historically and economically discouraged from writing, very few managed to get their fiction published. Berta Ornelas's *Come Down from the Mound* (1975) presented a feminine view of the Chicano movement as it described the struggle between love and politics. Isabela Ríos's *Victim* (1976) was the first attempt to represent the psychological dimensions of Chicana women. These novels were not well received by Chicano critics and generally did not have much impact. The best of Chicana fiction would be created in the 1980s as Chicana writers developed autobiography-based fiction.

The explosion of creative writing and the visual and performing arts by Chicanos during this period could be termed a renaissance. New energies, forms of expression, and themes emerged as students, community leaders, artists, and poets sought to create a new identity by incorporating and interpreting their Mexican heritage. The tendency to idealize the Mexican past, especially the pre-Columbian and Mexican revolutionary periods, and to simplify and stereotype everything that is Anglo-American marred some of the creative work of this era. Chicano artists tended to subordinate creative literature and the performing arts to political purposes—and usually the message was critical of American institutions and values. Artists did not emphasize the diversity of the Chicano experience concerning generational, gender, or economic class issues. Still, their pursuit of Chicano identity and political action generated an energy and direction that liberated hundreds of people to express themselves through art.

Conclusions

Many of the most exciting and volatile issues raised in the 1960s and early 1970s by the Chicano movement cannot be understood apart from a recognition of the impact that Mexican history, culture, and immigration had on the United States. In many obvious ways, the Chicano movement brought about a revitalization of Mexican identity and culture. In politics and in the arts, Mexican Americans redefined themselves in relation to both U.S. and Mexican society. Movement leaders generally downplayed the great socioeconomic differences that existed between the middle and working classes, the native born Chicanos and Mexican immigrants. The pressure to achieve community and political unity overrode a realistic appraisal of this diversity. A consensus about terminology, particularly about the use of the term *Chicano* never really materialized. Students enthusiastically explored their identity as Chicanos while the middle and working classes continued to think of themselves as Mexican Americans, Mexicans, or just Americans. The vitality of these years waned as the civil rights movement and anti-war movement declined, and as Chicanos won acceptance by mainstream institutions.

The pressures of American consumer culture continued to shape Chicano society. Most Chicanos spoke primarily English and participated much more in American popular culture than had their parents. The newly arrived Mexican or Latin American immigrant lived in a totally different social and economic world. Yet at the base of the power of the Chicano movement was the increased demographic importance of the Spanish-speaking population in the United States and the fact that this was fundamentally related to immigration from Latin America. New social and economic problems caused by increased "new immigration" pressed on the national consciousness with increasing frequency. They gave some of the proposals advanced by the Chicano movement an unexpected legitimacy. Thus the Chicanos, who understood the value of their Mexican heritage, became the logical intermediaries between the immigrant and the larger society.

nine

Latinos and the "New Immigrants"

In the summer of 1983 the *Los Angeles Times* published a series of articles examining the Mexican-American experience in that city. In one article the reporters explored the problem of preferences for ethnic labels and found a lack of unanimity about what Chicanos/Latinos/Hispanics/Mexican Americans/Mexicanos wanted to call themselves. Generally, the native-born preferred *Mexican-American,* followed by *Latino.* The term *Hispanic* was third in preference. Mexican immigrants favored the term *Mexicano,* also followed by *Latino.* While a plurality could agree on the term *Latino,* only a small minority (4 percent) acknowledged that the term *Chicano* fit them.[1]

Sometime during the late 1970s and early 1980s, the term *Latino* became popular among many people of Mexican ancestry in the United States.[2] The older term *Hispanic* enjoyed popularity among the middle class. Its public use sometimes provoked sharp criticism from others who were sensitive to the Indian and Mestizo backgrounds of most Mexican Americans. The occasional confusion and debate over this terminology led to the use of a more neutral term—*Latino*—especially in the newpaper medium. This subtle change indicated an increased recognition of the complexity of the nation's Spanish-speaking population. The term *Latino* referred to a national Spanish-speaking community, with a majority of Mexican ancestry but including large populations of Central and South Americans. Latino communities included the Cuban-American enclaves in Florida and the Puerto Ricans in New York and Chicago. More and more Chicanos recognized the cultural and linguistic bonds they shared with the hundreds of thousands of Latin American immigrants who had been flooding the city and the nation during the decade. Thus the waves of immigration to the United States from Central America and Latin America shaped a concensus for a new terminology in ethnic self-identification.

This chapter examines how new waves of immigration from Latin America have affected the cultural and economic context of Mexican-American history. In the 1980s a dramatic demographic explosion in the Spanish-speaking population, fueled by a new wave of immigration from Latin America and Mexico, underlie the increased visibility of Latino culture. This so-called New Immigration produced ambivalent reactions from the Anglo-American mainstream. Elements of Latino culture gained nationwide popularity, but at the same time Latino immigrants became the targets of discrimination and rejection.

Demographic and Economic Shifts

Between 1975 and 1989 more than eight million immigrants entered the United States legally (see Table 9.1). About a third of these—three million—were Latin Americans. Mexicans comprised about one million of the total. More Asian than Latin American legal immigrants entered the United States during this period. But if the migration of Puerto Ricans to the mainland (not officially counted as immigration) and the millions of undocumented Mexican and Central American immigrants are included, then the Latin Americans undoubtedly comprised the largest group of immigrants during the 1980s.

Rubén Rumbaut, in his 1991 study, noted that this New Immigration from developing regions of the world (Asia and Latin America) was changing the culture of ethnic America: "The American ethnic mosaic is being fundamentally altered, and ethnicity itself being redefined and its new images reified in the popular media and reflected in myriad and often surprising ways. Immigrants from a score of nationalities are told that they are all 'Hispanic,' while far more diverse groups, from India and Laos, China and the Philippines—are lumped together as 'Asians.'"[3]

Latin American immigration caused an upsurge in the Latino population of the United States. A very high Latino birth rate, the highest of any ethnic group in the United States, contributed to this growth as well. Between 1980 and 1988 the Latino population grew from 14.6 millon to 19.4 million, an increase of 34 percent, compared with only a 7 percent increase in the general population. Latin American immigration counted for at least two million of the increase. Another two million could be accounted for by undocumented immigrants who were settlers rather than sojourners, leaving a million explained by the excess of births to deaths. Of almost 20 million Latinos in the United States in 1988, those of Mexican descent accounted for 62 percent of the total. Puerto Ricans were about 13 percent of the mainland Latinos, and Cuban Americans constituted 5 percent; 12 percent of the total came from Central and South America, and the remaining 8 percent were counted as "Other Hispanics."[4]

The 1990 Census showed that the proportion of Mexican immigrants within the larger Latino population declined during the 1980s. This could be explained

Table 9.1. Legal Immigration to the United States, 1960–1990

Region/Country of Birth	Period of Immigration		
	1960–1974	1975–1989	Total
Total Immigration	5,137,182	8,265,992	13,403,154
Latin American	1,990,996	3,188,777	5,180,130
Asian	974,022	3,602,123	4,909,145
By Country			
Mexico	731,857	1,016,746	1,749,603
Cuba	349,788	340,581	690,369
Dominican Republic	147,857	304,399	451,395

Source: Rubén Rumbaut, "Passages to America: Perspectives on the New Immigration," in *America at Century's End: American Society in Transition,* ed. Alan Wolfe (Berkeley: University of California Press, 1991). Printed by permission of University of California Press.

by the relatively large flow of immigrants from Central and South America. For example, by 1990 California had become the most populous state in the union with 29,760,000 people, with about one-fourth of them Latino. About 38 percent of the Los Angeles County's population and 20 percent of San Diego County's were Latino. Projecting a steady high rate of growth, demographers have estimated that the Latino population would reach 30 million by the year 2000. In some states, such as California and Texas, the projected increase would, by the year 2010, make the Latinos almost half their population. Projections were that, by the year 2060, Latinos would become the nation's largest ethnic or racial group.[5]

The use of the word *Latino* to describe immigrant and nonimmigrant Spanish-speaking populations implies a false notion of unity. Not all Latinos regarded the new immigrants welcome additions to the community. The attitudes of Mexican Americans toward this New Immigration varied according to socioeconomic class, education, and generational status. A survey conducted by a research group at Pan American University in South Texas in 1984 disclosed that the more affluent and educated Mexican Americans believed that undocumented immigrants took unfair advantage of social services, particularly public education. They did not regard job competition as serious a problem as did working-class Mexican Americans. Overall, Mexican Americans regardless of socioeconomic class did not think that this immigration from Latin America was having a negative impact on their lives. The more assimilated and educated Mexican Americans, however, supported stricter immigration controls.[6]

Rodolfo de la Garza, a leading analyst of Chicano political opinion regarding Mexico and Mexican immigration, concluded that while Chicanos constituted "the principal group openly defending the Mexican position on the issue of undocumented workers," there was still "historical antipathy between Chicanos and Mexicans."[7] Another study by Christine Sierra pointed out the diversity of Mexican-American responses to proposals for immigration restriction in the 1980s. Native-born Latinos were much more likely to support employer sanctions and stricter enforcement measures than foreign-born Latinos. When compared with other racial and ethnic groups, however, the native-born Latinos tended to be less supportive of strict immigration controls.[8] Apart from these few studies, researchers knew very little about the relationship between Mexican Americans and Mexican immigrants. Anecdotal evidence, gathered from schoolyards and the workplace suggest an ambivalent relationship characterized by antagonism and competition along with a shared language and racial background. Certainly more assimilated Mexican Americans continued to be intermediaries between the recently arrived immigrant and the larger society and economy. Bilingual and bicultural Mexican Americans worked as the bosses, supervisors, and contractors, managing (and sometimes exploiting) monolingual Spanish-speaking Latino immigrants.

A Growing Underclass

The new flood of immigration from Latin America had long-term consequences for the U.S. economy. Between 1980 and 1987 one-fifth of the nation's employment growth was because of increased Latino employment, especially of Latinas. In the 1980s Latinos were the nation's fastest-growing work force.

The non-Latino work force grew by 10 percent, but the number of Latino workers increased by 40 percent. The inflow of Mexican and Latin American immigrants who sought out jobs at the bottom of the American occupational ladder fueled most of this occupational increase. Latino women had a much higher rate of employment gain than men, almost a 50 percent growth rate in the period, two and a half times that of the growth rate for non-Latino women.

Despite the growing numbers of Latinos entering the work force, Latino unemployment, caused by technological innovation, job competition by new immigrants, and business failures, remained about one and a half times above that of the general population but below that of African Americans. Unemployment varied according to national origin: Cuban Americans had the lowest rate of unemployment—about 5 percent—and Puerto Ricans and Mexicans had the highest—about 10 percent. Meanwhile, the unemployment rate for Anglo-Americans ranged from 6 percent to 9 percent. In terms of occupational mobility for all Latinos, there was no significant change in their status during the 1980s. The vast majority remained in lower-paid skilled and unskilled blue-collar jobs. Latino women entered the mid-level sales and technical occupations faster than did Latino men; more than half of all employed Latino men continued to hold blue-collar positions.[9]

Scholars have noted that most of the New Immigrants who entered the United States came from the employed and skilled working classes in their countries of origin. The middle-class Cuban refugees who arrived after 1959 followed this pattern, with heavy representation in the professional classes. (The Cuban immigrants known as *Marielitos* who arrived in the late 1970s did not.) Nevertherless, in comparison to the relatively affluent U.S. working class, the immigrants entered at the bottom of the American socioeconomic pyramid. Native-born Latinos who were U.S. citizens—such as a majority of the Puerto Ricans in New York, Chicanos in the inner-city barrios, Hispanos in New Mexico's small towns, and Tejanos in south Texas—also endured high rates of poverty and educational underachievement.

While immigration continued at a high level, the federal government cut funding for social services. Poverty, high school drop-out rates, and unemployment rose among Latinos. By 1990 Latinos were collectively even worse off than they had been in 1980. At the beginning of 1980, 13 percent of Latino families lived below the poverty line. By the end of the decade the number rose to more than 16 percent. Meanwhile, the Latino median income adjusted for inflation

Table 9.2. Latino Employment Data, 1980–1987[1]

| | Change in Population | | Change in Employment | |
	Latino	Non-Latino	Latino	Non-Latino
Total	3,269 (34.1%)	11,739 (7.4%)	2,263 (40.9%)	10,874 (11.6%)
Men	1,682 (35.9%)	5,819 (7.8%)	1,265 (36.7%)	3,656 (6.8%)
Women	1,587 (32.3%)	5,918 (7.1%)	998 (48.0%)	7,219 (18.0%)

[1]In thousands.

Source: Peter Cattan, "The Growing Presence of Hispanics in the U.S. Work Force," *Monthly Labor Review* (August 1988): 12, table 2.

declined from $23,088 to $21,759. Thus, the Latino experience became more polarized, with some success stories but many more tales of human tragedy and defeat.

The Latino Middle Class

During the late 1970s and 1980s, one of the fastest-growing economic groups in the United States was the Latino middle and upper class. Affluent Latinos—those having annual incomes of more than $50,000—grew from 191,000 in 1972 to 638,000 in 1985, an increase of 234 percent. Most of the expansion during the 1980s came from the growth of the Latino middle class (with incomes between $50,000 and $100,000). The proportion of Latino families living in affluence rose from 7 percent of all households in 1972 to 11 percent in 1988, surpassing the proportion of middle-class blacks (which was 10 percent in 1988) but remaining below the proportion of Anglo-Americans (23 percent). The low average income of all Latinos tended to mask the growth of this small but important group.[10]

Like most well-off Americans, most affluent Latino families had two or more paychecks to support their lifestyles. Unlike the Anglo-American middle class, the Latino families tended be younger, have more children, and have less education than their Anglo counterparts (only 29 percent of the Latino middle class had a college degree versus 50 percent for Anglo-Americans). More of the affluent Latinos lived in metropolitan areas than was true for Anglos. Those cities having the largest Latino middle-class segments in 1989 were Honolulu, Hawaii (25 percent), Washington, D.C. (24 percent), Detroit (18 percent), San Francisco (15 percent), San Jose, California (15 percent), and Orange County, California (14 percent).[11] In the 1980s this group's growth provided an important resource for the mobilization of a new kind of politics. Culturally, this group would be supporters of a more mainstream approach, and this in turn would shape a Latino middle-class market in the visual and performing arts.

Advertising agencies and corporate managers discovered the "Hispanic Market" in the 1980s. They generated a good deal of survey research to investigate the buying habits of Latinos and how they could best exploit this fast-growing group. The collective buying power of Latinos grew to over $171 billion in 1989, increasing at 10 percent per year. Businesses began to expand their promotion of products in the Spanish language, using Latino images that created new opportunities for Latino marketing firms and models, especially in the major southwestern metropolitan areas.[12] The expanded economic clout of Latinos provided Latino political groups with additional weight as they pushed for expanded hiring of Latinos within key companies. In 1985, for example, six national Latino groups led by the League of United Latin American Citizens (LULAC) and the American G.I. Forum signed an agreement with the Adolf Coors Corporation. After a 10-year boycott of Coors by Chicano activists because of its anti-union, anti-Mexican policies, Coors agreed to a minimum hiring level of Latinos and committed its company to invest in the Latino community in proportion to its increased sales.[13]

Some governmental officials and businessmen labeled the 1980s "the Decade of the Hispanic," sounding an optimistic note based on the growing economic and political power of Latinos. Despite the affluence of the Latino middle class, the final record of this decade proved to be mixed concerning overall progress. Latino society became more differentiated, and one could say polarized, with regard to education, socioeconomic status, upward mobility, and assimilation.

Latino Families in the 1990s

By the early 1990s Latino families continued to be diverse in their structure and social meaning, reflecting the complexities of postindustrial America. Mexican immigration served to renew the conservative, rural values associated with family life, whereas within the metropolitan barrios of the Midwest and in Texas and California, Mexican-American families were sometimes indistinguishable from Anglo-American families in terms of their values and structure.

There were some major differences, however. As long as there have been statistics on the phenomenon, the distribution of female headed families has followed a racial pattern: from 1980 to 1991 African Americans had the largest number and whites the least, with Latinos falling in between. For all groups, regardless of ethnicity, there were more children living in homes without fathers present in 1990 than in 1980. For example, the number of Latino children living within a female-headed household rose slightly—from 20 percent to 27 percent of all children—between 1980 and 1990. But among African Americans, 44 percent of all children lived in female-headed households in 1980 and 54 percent in 1990, while whites had 14 percent in these kinds of households in 1980 and 17 percent in 1990.[14]

The implications of these data are open to speculation. The possible negative effects of children being raised without two parents have been outlined by sociologists: higher likelihood of poverty, teenage pregnancies, high school dropouts, and so on. There are exceptions to the trends, however: many Latinas who raised children alone have, despite great odds, avoided these outcomes.[15]

In terms of family structure and living conditions, Latino families continued to be slightly larger and younger than Anglo or black families. Fewer Latinos were reported as being divorced or widowed than blacks or Anglos, and Latinos had about the same proportion of married couples as Anglos. In terms of directional shifts in family and household structure, since 1970 the trend has been toward fewer married couples and more female-headed households.[16]

The most dramatic difference between Hispanic families and other groups was in renting versus owning their homes. The 1990 Census reported that more than two-thirds of Latino families rented their homes as opposed to only about one-third of Anglo-American families and about one half of black families. Similarly, Latinos were less likely to be home owners: only 39 percent of Latino families were home owners, compared with 64 percent of Anglos and 42 percent of African Americans.[17] These statistics, with all their shortcomings, summarize the social realities for millions of religiously and culturally conservative family households condemned to live in poverty.

Regarding the changes that have taken place in family roles and expectations, these generally have varied according to generational, geographic (urban/rural), and socioeconomic determinants. In areas of high living costs and job insecurity, women have been increasingly forced to work for wages outside the home, often over the objections of the husband. As was reported by sociologist Patricia Zavella in her study of the cannery workers in California, "women could not afford to maintain their positions as full-time homemakers."[18] Yet they had to negotiate their working within the context of traditional family obligations, an activity that limited their occupational choices and led to job segregation.

Latino Politics

Obviously there was an important political motive for the widespread adoption of the terms *Hispanic* and *Latino,* particularly among the middle classes. These terms allowed Latino politicians and middle-class organizations to claim that they represented a much larger national constituency than if they had remained identified with ethnic nationalism. In the 1980s scores of Hispanic and Latino political caucuses, professional associations, and business groups organized as political pressure groups. In Congress and in the state governments of Florida, California, Arizona, New Mexico, and Texas Latino legislators formed lobbies and caucuses to push for agendas that would benefit their constituencies.

Two of the most active Latino organizations during this period continued to be the Mexican American Legal Defense and Education Fund (MALDEF) and the Southwest Voter Registration Project (SWVRP). Together they carried on many legal actions to attack impediments to Latino electoral victories. Their attack on the at-large district election system was a tactic that would have profound political consequences. The at-large election system was a structure that forced candidates in local district elections to win their elections at-large or in citywide contests. This political practice handicapped Latino candidates who had limited resources for city-wide campaigns and who lacked political appeal outside their ethnic districts. In the 1980s both MALDEF and SWVRP won hundreds of court victories overturning the at-large electoral system. They won by proving in court that this system discriminated against Latinos, who were protected under the Voting Rights Acts of 1965, 1975, and 1982.

Another front in the political battle for fair representation was redistricting. For decades, Latinos had been victims of gerrymandered electoral zones. Historically, Anglo-American incumbents of both parties had diluted the Latino voting block to create "safe" districts to ensure their reelection. Redistricting occurred every 10 years, after the federal census, to reflect population shifts. In 1981 Latino organizations throughout the southwestern states, spearheaded by MALDEF and SWVRP, launched major efforts to challenge redistricting procedures and overcome Latino political fragmentation. Other Latino groups such as the Puerto Rican Legal Defense and Education Fund (PRLDEF) in New York and the Hispanic Coalition on Reapportionment (HCR) in Michigan and Pennsylvania also lobbied the state reapportionment commissions and presented their own reapportionment plans. In his analysis of the politics of the redistricting struggles in 1981, Richard Santillán argued that hard-won victories in creating Latino electoral districts led to significant Latino electoral gains during the rest of the decade.[19]

Benefiting from the civil rights struggles of the previous decades and the victories against gerrymandering and at-large elections, these new organizations reenergized Latino political life. Latino political organizations had unparalleled success in the 1980s in electing officials. The SWVRP's work in registering new Latino voters was significant in many of these electoral victories. Also important in regional politics in Texas were the efforts of the Communities Organized for Public Service (COPS). In San Antonio this middle-class Latino organization helped register enough voters to elect many Mexican-American officials, including the first Hispanic mayor. COPS, under the able leadership of Ernie Cortés, worked to improve public services and Mexican-American political participation.[20]

The 1980s saw the election of Latino mayors in Denver (Federico Peña) and San Antonio (Henry Cisneros) and Latino governors in New Mexico (Toney Anaya) and Florida (Bob Martínez). The voters elected hundreds of other Latinos to local and state offices, primarily in the Southwest. There were enough Latino elected officials to form a national organization, the National Association of Latino Elected and Appointed Officials (NALEO), which issued annual status reports on the growing electoral strength of Latinos. In 1987 NALEO reported that there were 3,317 elected Latino officials in the United States, a number double the number in 1980.[21] The four southwestern border states—California, Arizona, New Mexico, and Texas—had the majority of elected Latinos, but Florida, New York, and the Midwest also had substantial numbers.

The preponderance of Latinos won elections at the local level, serving on school boards, county offices, and city councils. While Hispanic women remained underrepresented in public offices, a higher proportion of Latinas won election (18 percent), compared with women in the general population (12 percent). Most of the Latino office holders in the 1980s had first entered electoral politics in that decade, but they were not, as a group, particularly young, having an average age of about 44 years. Most Latino elected officials in this decade were native-born citizens (90 percent). These new leaders represented ethnic constituencies, districts of more than 55 percent Latino in population, but the

Table 9.3. Latino Elected Officials by State and Region, 1987[1]

State or Region	Elected Officials
California	466
Arizona	248
New Mexico	577
Texas	1,572
Colorado	167
Midwest	63
Florida	48
New York	68

[1]Partial list.

Source: Harry P. Pachon, "Overview of Hispanic Elected Officials in 1987," *1987 National Roster of Hispanic Elected Officials* ed. National Association of Latino Elected and Appointed Officials (Washington D.C.: NALEO Education Fund, 1987), xiii. Reprinted by permission of the NALEO Educational Fund.

new office holders also appealed to a broader spectrum of nonethnic voters by their articulation of issues.[22]

Representing this new Latino political leadership were people like Gloria Molina, Henry Cisneros, and Federico Peña. Highly educated, committed, and articulate leaders, both had a broad appeal while retaining the solid support of voters within their ethnic communities.

Gloria Molina emerged as a crusading Chicana in East Los Angeles who won her first election in 1982 in an state assembly race against Richard Polanco, a well-entrenched establishment politician. The daughter of a California farm-worker, she lived in the East Los Angeles barrio and had acquired grass-roots political experience during the Chicano movement in the 1960s. She rose to prominence because of her passionate advocacy of women's rights and issues of community development. As an outsider to both the Anglo-dominated political establishment and the old-boy network of Chicano officials, she represented a populist and feminist approach to Latino politics who appealed to a wide variety of middle-class, nonethnic voters.[23]

In the state assembly Molina fought long and hard against the construction of a state prison in her district. She ultimately succeeded by organizing a myriad of local groups and embarrassing the Latino politicos who had supported the prison in hopes of political favors. She ran unsuccessfully against Richard Alatorre in a 1986 Los Angeles City Council race but the next year she won a stunning victory in being elected to a newly created Los Angeles council seat. In 1991 she again ran against Alatorre for the Los Angeles County Board of Supervisors. She won that election with majority support of both men and women, Anglos and Latinos. This was the first time in more than 100 years that the voters had elected a Latino to this powerful office. Most observers predicted that the post provided her with an ideal position to enter national politics.

Henry Cisneros, a young professor of public administration, came much more from a conservative political background. Born in San Antonio, Texas, Cisneros descended from an old-line elite family who had immigrated during the Mexican Revolution. Cisneros attended a Catholic high school and Texas A & M, later earning two master's degrees and a doctorate degree from ivy league universities. When he returned to Texas he worked as a professor at the University of Texas in San Antonio until he won election to the city council in 1975 as part of a multi-ethnic coalition. His youthful optimism and charismatic style along with his management training and fiscal conservatism made him a favorite of the San Antonio Anglo middle class. Also he appealed to San Antonio's working-class Chicanos, who admired his success. He was elected a mayor of the city in 1981 with the support of Anglos and a huge majority (94 percent) of Chicanos. His ability to move in elite circles and his adept manipula-tion of complex issues made him an unusually attractive figure to national politicians. His conservative economic philosophy did not antagonize his Chicano and Mexicano constituency since he also lobbied for more jobs and education. In 1989 Cisneros decided not to run again for mayor, citing personal economic hardships in continuing. In the 1990s he devoted himself to building a Latino-controlled financial management corporation called the Cisneros Group. When Bill Clinton became president in 1992, he appointed Cisneros to head the Department of Housing and Urban Development.

Another new face in Chicano/Latino politics was Federico Peña, the mayor of Denver who, in March 1933, was appointed secretary of transportation by President Clinton. Peña was born in Laredo, Texas, and grew up in Brownsville. He came from an old, middle-class Tejano family and attended parochial schools. Graduating from high school with honors, he attended the University of Texas at Austin and soon got involved in campus politics and liberal causes. He entered the UT law school in 1969 and received his degree in 1972. A year later his brother convinced him to move to Denver and establish a law partnership. As a new lawyer, Federico worked for MALDEF, specializing in poverty law and civil rights issues. He also worked to promote bilingual education and better schooling for Latinos. In 1978 he decided to try for an elected position and won a seat in the Colorado legislature. He was reelected in 1980 and became the minority speaker and was voted the outstanding legislator of the year by his colleagues.

In 1983 he ran for mayor of Denver against heavy odds. Mexican Americans made up only 18 percent of the electorate. Combining his talent for motivating volunteers and appealing to the optimistic and hopeful impulses of the citizens (while his opponent was embroiled in scandals), Peña was able to win in a run-off. He assembled a multi-ethnic coalition of Asian Americans, African Americans, Mexican Americans, women's rights advocates, labor unions, and environmentalists.[24] At 36, he was one of the youngest mayors to be elected in the United States. His main agenda was to develop Denver's infrastructure so that the city could generate new jobs. Fighting tremendous odds and rising unemployment, he tried to get the city to endorse a new convention center and airport. He was barely reelected in 1987, largely with the firm support of Latinos and blacks. During his next term he succeeded in getting approval for the construction of a $2.3 billion airport project and other infrastructure projects. It was because of his visionary leadership that President Clinton chose him to join his cabinet.[25]

Despite these success stories and optimistic trends, Latinos remain underrepresented at all levels of government. In California, for example, where Latinos comprised more than 20 percent of the population, less than 2 percent of the federal, state, and county officials were Latino in 1980. In Texas, where more than 20 percent of the population is Latino, they accounted for less than 6 percent of municipal elected officials in 1983. The same kind of inequity continues to exist everywhere, with the possible exception of New Mexico.

While gains have been made in electoral politics, grass-roots efforts also have remained effective in challenging the status quo. A prominent example is the activities of the Mothers of East Los Angeles (MELA), a group of more than 400 women who organized themselves to oppose the construction of a state prison complex within their community. MELA was composed of low-income, middle-age, Mexican-American women who had a history of being active within Catholic parish organizations. Beginning in 1986, their protests, marches, and lobbying efforts resulted in the defeat of the proposed construction site in 1992. The group went on to lobby against the construction of a toxic-waste incinerator in the community. Again they appeared to be successful when Representative Lucile Roybal-Allard sponsored a law (AB58) protecting the environmental quality of their community.[26] The Mothers of East Los Angeles exem-

Members of the Congressional Hispanic Caucus in 1994: (*right to left, up the stairs*) Estéban E. Torres, Ileana Ros-Lehtinen, Ed Pastor, Luis Gutiérrez, Nydia Velásquez, Robert Underwood, Lucille Roybal-Allard, Frank Tejeda, Henry Bonilla, Lincoln Díaz-Balart, and José E. Serrano (chairman); (*left to right, on balcony*) Solomón P. Ortiz, Robert Menéndez, Ron de Lugo, Bill Richardson, Matthew Martínez (not an official member of the caucus), E. (Kika) de la Garza, and Henry B. González. Not shown are Carlos Romero-Barcelo and Xavier Becerra. Photograph courtesy of the Congressional Hispanic Caucus.

plify how Mexican-American women were able to transform their traditional social networks to affect the political system and improve their community.

Education

The existing educational system remained one of the most important ways that immigrant and native-born Latinos could escape the cycle of poverty and marginalization. There continued to be a devastating drop-out rate in public schools and relatively low numbers of Latinos attending or graduating from college.[27] In the 1980s white Americans "discovered" the educational problem as nationwide reading and math scores declined for all groups. Several best-selling books criticized the failure of secondary schools and colleges to teach basic literacy and numeracy. A well-publicized government study stated that the failures of the educational system was placing the nation at risk.[28]

Chicanos and Mexican immigrants had been "at risk" for many decades, but the influx of hundreds of thousands of New Immigrants made the educational system's failure more visible. Long charged with the task of mainstreaming or "Americanizing" immigrants, the public schools proved unequal to the task as more and more Latino children failed to keep up with their Anglo-American peers.

The Los Angeles City School System illustrated this problem. Perhaps one of the most multiracial, multi-ethnic school systems in the nation, about half of the students were foreign-born in 1980. The largest contingent of the foreign-born, about 80 percent, were Mexican immigrant children, followed by Central Americans and Asians. Between 1970 and 1980 the Latino school population in Los Angeles had doubled to 267,000 students while white enrollment fell to 120,729. By 1990 the school population exceeded 300,000 Latinos while black and Anglo school enrollment continued to decline. Concentrated in segregated regions of the city, the Latino students had a drop-out rate of 48 percent. This compared with a national drop-out rate (in 1980) of 45 percent for Mexican Americans, 28 percent for blacks, and 17 percent for whites.[29]

The educational environment in other school districts having large numbers of Latinos was not much better. There a tradition of segregation led to the inequitable funding of nonwhite schools. In Texas the poorest school districts were invariably Latino or black, yet they were the disticts saddled with the highest property tax rates and the lowest allocation of state funding. In 1973 the Supreme Court ruled in *San Antonio School District* v. *Rodríguez* that this inequity did not violate the Constitution. The problem of unequal funding and increasing educational neglect continued to plague Texas's Latino school districts. In 1984 MALDEF took the plaintif's case to the Texas Supreme Court, and in 1989 that body declared in *Edgewood Independent School District* v. *Kirby* that the state's method of financing public education did in fact violate the state constitution. The state legislature devised a finance formula in the early 1990s that sought to correct the inequities.[30]

In addition, legal discrimination against Mexican children continued. In 1975 the Texas legislature added a statute to the Education Code declaring that only children of U.S. citizens and legal aliens could receive free public education. Many school districts subsequently began charging up to $1,000 a year tuition to children of undocumented workers. In 1977 MALDEF filed a lawsuit to challenge this policy. In *Doe* v. *Plyler* MALDEF argued the state's policy violated the provision of the Fourteenth Amendment that no state shall "deny to any person . . . the equal protection of the laws" of the United States. Furthermore, it argued that the federal government, not the state, was responsible for enforcing immigration laws. In 1980 MALDEF won its case on appeal, thus setting a precedent for the educational rights of undocumented immigrants.[31]

Educational experts appeared much better at describing the dimensions of the problem than at constructing remedies. Educators knew that there existed many reasons for the high drop-out rate for Latinos. The most important was related to the income and educational backgrounds of the parents, the recency of immigration and exclusive use of Spanish at home, and the characteristics of the school itself—class size, school facilities, and teacher motivation and training. The actual reasons for Latinos quitting school before graduation varied tremendously, ranging from pregnancy to boredom, but almost all drop-outs ranked below their grade level in reading and writing skills. This educational lag most often appeared by the third grade, indicating that the most important remedies for the problem (primarily intensive tutoring in reading and writing skills) were to be addressed at the grammar-school level.

Since the 1960s Chicano educators had argued in favor of reform of the elementary school system, in particular, through the institutionalization of bilingual education. Bilingual advocates argued that it was most important to teach Spanish-speaking students how to read in their native language first, and then, when students had mastered reading skills, to turn to English. By using Spanish in the grammar schools to instruct native Spanish speakers, teachers would be able to reinforce the family cultural values of immigrant children and create a more positive learning environment for the teaching of English and other subjects. Almost all Latino immigrant families wanted their children to learn English as they recognized that this skill was important in getting a job.[32]

The bilingual advocates had support from the Supreme Court when the *Lau* v. *Nichols* decision in 1972 directed the schools to address the needs of the non–English-speaking students. The *Lau* decision allowed school districts to determine the methods to be used in fulfilling this mandate. For the next 20 years a wide variety of bilingual programs arose (not all are Spanish-English; some deal with Asian languages), funded by local, state, and federal government. The monies, however, were never sufficient to meet the demand. Moreover, the federal government during the 1980s cut funding for bilingual education by a third. Researchers estimate that by the end of the 1980s less than 3 percent of the Latino school-age population had bilingual education programs.

Yet there was evidence that bilingual programs had an impact on easing the transition from Spanish to English and in preventing drop outs. A 1984 Department of Education study, for example, tracked 2,000 Spanish-speaking grammar school children over four years and found that they achieved skills at the same level as their English-speaking peers. The study confirmed that bilingual programs, if managed correctly, were one way of combating the school's failure to educate. Other studies concluded that bilingual programs improved the self-concept and cognitive functioning of students. Truly bilingual students outperformed their Spanish-speaking peers who had been left to "sink or swim."[33]

Despite these successes, bilingual education came under attack. Many feared the cultural and racial implications of the massive immigration flooding the United States from so-called Third World countries. Nativists worried about the decline of "all-American" values that they linked to the schools' failure linguistically to assimilate foreigners. Bilingual education and its assumptions of multicultural equity bothered those who feared the "balkanization" of American culture. In 1975 Congress amended the Voting Rights Act to require that electoral information and ballots be multilingual. This provoked criticism from conservatives who argued that American citizens should be able to understand English in order to vote.

In 1978 Emmy Shafer, a housewife in Miami, was unable to communicate with any of the Spanish-speaking clerks in the Dade County (Florida) administrative offices. In protest, she organized a local initiative that succeeded in making it illegal to translate official signs into a language other than English. This was the beginning of the English-only movement, a conservative backlash against bilingual education and Spanish-speaking Latinos.

In 1982 Senator S. I. Hayakawa, a California Republican, proposed a constitutional amendment to make English the official language of the United States. When Congress defeated his proposal, Hayakawa formed a private organization called U.S. English to implement English-only laws through initiative procedures and lobbying state legislatures. U.S. English claimed a membership of over 400,000 and engaged in fund-raising and mass mailings to promote its cause, garnering about $6 million annually.[34] For a time the head of U.S. English was Linda Chávez, a young Hispanic Republican from New Mexico who argued that Latinos should embrace the English language to invalidate criticism of their patriotism as Americans and to prevent the "Quebecization" of the United States. She saw herself as a moderate who opposed crank conservatives such as those in the U.S. English organization. In 1988 she resigned as president of U.S. English because of a memo, written by the founder of the organization, John Tanton. The memo stated that the new Latino immigrants were uneducable and that they were corrupting the morality of American public life. He raised the specter of the massive reproductive powers of the immigrants that would soon swamp more desirable American populations. When the memo was made public many notable supporters of the U.S. English organization quit, including Walter Cronkite.[35]

Despite the xenophobic alarms of some of its members, the movement was successful, as more than 17 states voted referenda to make English the official language. The states with the largest Chicano and Mexican immigrant populations, California and Texas, both passed English-only laws. New Mexico, with its long tradition of Spanish language and culture, passed instead an "English Plus" law stating that "proficiency on the part of our citizens in more than one language is to the economic and cultural benefit of our State and Nation."[36] In Arizona an English-as-an-official-language initiative just barely passed by 51 percent to 49 percent. A strong anti–Official English campaign had been under way there, endorsed by both Republican and Democratic senators; it argued that racism was the real issue and that approval of the initiative would lead to a more totalitarian state.

The English-only movement attracted nativists and members of the radical right while generating a good deal of patriotic and linguistic xenophobia. One nativist, Richard Viguerie, mailed a letter to more than 240,000 homes asking for the repeal of federal bilingual education legislation. Included with his letter was a Mexican peso with the message, "I know the peso is worthless in the U.S. but I enclosed it to make an important point about a billion-dollar U.S. government program that's worthless too. It's called the Bilingual Education Act."[37]

Immigration and Nativist Response

The growing tide of immigrant workers flowing into the United States during the 1970s and 1980s led to intense debates over cultural and economic consequences. A large portion of the immigrant influx came as undocumented workers. In 1983, for example, the INS apprehended more than a million illegal entrants from Mexico. This represented only a small fraction of those who actually crossed in that year and was equal to the total number of legal entrants from Mexico during the 1980s.[38] The daily apprehension of thousands of these "illegal aliens" raised the specter of a nation unable to control its borders. In 1977 President Jimmy Carter asked Congress to consider drafting a new immigration law that would impose sanctions on employers for knowingly hiring undocumented workers and would bolster the police powers of the Border Patrol. Included in his message was the suggestion that Congress also draft a program to grant amnesty to undocumented immigrants already residing in the United States. These basic points—employer sanctions, expanded enforcement, and amnesty—became the substance of several immigration bills later introduced into Congress.

The most long-lived proposal was the Simpson-Mazzoli bill, introduced in 1982. The Simpson-Mazzoli bill proposed a fine of $10,000 for employers who hired "illegal aliens" and would have granted amnesty to long-term residents. Additionally, the bill proposed a bracero-like guest-worker program (the H-2 Program) to import seasonal workers from Mexico and the Caribbean in case of a labor shortage. Special interests emerged in the debates in Congress over this bill. S. I. Hayakawa sought to attach an "English as the official language" provision to the bill. Labor unions generally supported the sanctions provisions but were wary of the H-2 Program. Latino human rights groups opposed the penalty provisions fearing that they would be used by employers to justify their discrimination against Latino citizens. Church groups and those against U.S. support for the escalating war in Central America opposed the bill fearing the massive deportation of the thousands of Central American refugees who had fled to the United States to escape political terrorism. Other Latino groups were divided. The G.I. Forum supported the idea of immigration restriction and increased support for the Border Patrol, but groups like the San Diego–based Committee for Chicano Rights oppposed them. Later the G.I. Forum changed its position to support amnesty for immigrants. MALDEF supported immigration reform but opposed many of the provisions of the Simpson-Mazzoli bill. LULAC voted to boycott the Democratic party's convention in 1984 unless the delegates voted to oppose the Simpson-Mazzoli bill.[39] CASA, the oldest advocate for Chicano-Mexicano unity on the immigration issue, formed a National Coalition composed of students, union members, and several middle-class organizations to oppose the bill. The "Latino Lobby," composed of the leaders of the National Council for La Raza, LULAC, MALDEF, and the UFW opposed different aspects of the immigration proposal. The UFW's opposition, in particular, sparked criticism from Chicano immigrant-rights groups, so much so that César Chávez modified the union's support for immigration restrictions.[40]

Eventually, legislators introduced alternative bills to meet the objections of the various lobbies. The result was the passage in 1986 of the Immigration Reform and Control Act (IRCA). This law provided for employer sanctions, a strengthened border patrol, a guest-worker program, and amnesty for undocumented workers who arrived before 1982. It also had provisions to review the implementation of the law to see the extent of violation of the rights of Latino citizens and Central American refugees.

A surge in nativist attitudes accompanied the long debate over various provisions in the immigration bills. Community spokespeople portrayed Mexican and Central American immigrants as a threat to "the American way of life." They believed that the immigrants were responsible for soaring crime rates, disease, unemployment, rising welfare costs, moral decay, and decline in the quality of life. Despite a large body of social scientific studies that contradicted these assertions, a kind of paranoia regarding immigrants swept the country. The Democratic governor of Colorado, Richard Lamm, coauthored *The Immigration Time Bomb* and argued that the United States should curtail immigration from Latin America because it was undermining the nation's economy, corrupting American values, and fragmenting American society.[41] In San Diego, Tom Metzger reorganized the Ku Klux Klan as the White Aryan Resistance. They distributed hate literature in high schools and at public meetings warning Mexicans to go back or face violent consequences. Attacks against undocumented immigrants grew in number, not only by local racists but by Border Patrol officers who had a war-zone mentality. Sadly, many of the attacks also came from Chicano and Mexican thieves (some of them Mexican officials) who preyed on the undocumented crossers. In the 1980s the U.S.-Mexican border region became the most dangerous terrain in America, as every year hundreds of undocumented immigrants were robbed, beaten, raped, and killed as they tried to cross.

Despite the anti-immigrant rhetoric, evidence indicated that the United States needed immigrant labor in order to keep its economy prosperous. The *Wall Street Journal* in 1976 had said that "illegals may well be providing the margin of survival for entire sectors of the economy." By 1985 the *New York Times* reported that respected economists believed that "illegal immigrants" had become the backbone of the economy.[42] Demographers, like Leo Estrada at UCLA, warned that the nation faced a severe labor shortage in the 1990s, particularly in blue-collar occupations, as the general population grew older and had fewer children. A work force augmented by immigration was the only way that the United States could continue to be competitive in a world economy. Undocumented and legal immigration from Mexico and Latin America provided the surplus labor that employers could use to lower their operating costs and expand production. The money spent and taxes paid by the New Immigrants in turn created more jobs and helped fund social services. David Hayes-Bautista, a UCLA scholar, found that in California the population of working younger Latinos, including immigrants, was increasingly responsible for supporting social programs for aged Anglos.[43] Other researchers found that those areas of the country that had the greatest economic growth and the least unemployment were the same areas that had substantial immigration. James Cockcroft's book *Outlaws in the Promised Land* (1986) reviewed the literature on the economic impact of Latin American immigration during the first half of the 1980s and concluded, "In general, U.S. citizens benefit disproportionately from not just the migrants' labor and consumption but all the tax and benefit program checkoffs paid by immigrant workers."[44]

One of the effects of the debates over immigration restriction in the 1980s was to educate millions of U.S. Latinos about the importance of this New Immigration to their political and cultural survival. Latinos joined Central American refugee support groups like CISPES (Committee in Support of the People of El Salvador) and included demands for amnesty for Central American refugees along with demands for police reform and affirmative-action programs. MALDEF and the SWVRP targeted immigrant communities for future citizenship and voter registration drives. The generally anti-Mexican tenor of the debates in Congress mobilized many middle-class Latino organizations to take a stand in favor of immigrant rights.

Chicana/Latina Studies

The post-1975 period saw the emergence of a body of scholarship and creative writing by Chicanas and Latinas as well as the beginnings of the institutionalization of Chicana/Latina studies as an academic field of study. In 1981 the National Hispanic Center in California sponsored a "leadership think thank" gathering to develop an agenda for La Chicana for the 1980s. Meeting in many panel and discussion groups they developed detailed recommendations for action in the areas of employment, political representation, immigration, education, health care, the media, and the law.[45] At the same time a small number of female graduate students and one professor at the University of California at Berkeley established Mujeres en Marcha, an organization dedicated to fighting for the inclusion of women's issues and voices within male-dominated Chicano studies departments and programs. At the 1982 meeting of the National Association for Chicano Studies (NACS) and at subsequent meetings they organized special panels and discussion groups. This activity resulted in establishing the Chicana Caucus within the national organization to lobby for a greater role for and finally an entire annual meeting was devoted to women's issues.[46] Entitled Voces de la Mujer, the NACS conference in Austin, Texas, in 1984 was a landmark in the development of Chicano studies. It drew together more than a thousand, male and female, to hear papers and attend plenary meetings and cultural events devoted to questions of gender in the Mexican-American community.[47]

Another initiative to strengthen Chicana/Latina studies as an academic field was the formation of the Mujeres Activas en Letras y Cambio Social (MALCS) in 1983. This group consisted of university women (students and professors) who sought to support research in the field. They organized annual Chicana/Latina Summer Research Institutes to encourage the intellectual advancement of gender studies. They published a newsletter, a monograph series, and organized conferences to establish a support group for Chicana /Latina research.[48]

Publications in the field of Chicana studies escalated. The first bibliography of works appeared in 1976 and listed several hundred works, many of them dealing with Mexican society and culture.[49] By 1993 the *Chicana Studies Index* listed more than 1,150 journal articles, books, and other material dealing with Chicana/Latina issues.[50] Among the many books that shaped the discourse and defined the issues was Gloria Anzaldúa's, *Borderlands/La Frontera: The New Mestiza*. In this work Anzaldúa argued that old oppressive paradigms and images should be destroyed and be replaced by a dynamic new Mestiza consciousness.[51] In her vision this new consciousness is characterized by a state of perpetual transition and a mixture of cultures. Another theoretical attempt to refine Chicana studies was that of Irene Blea in her book, *La Chicana and the Intersection of Race, Class, and Gender*.[52] Blea critiqued the historical evolution of Mexican women and urged Chicanas to "give definition to cultural values, norms and communicative symbols." For Chicanas, liberation meant "freedom, emancipation from racism and sexism, plus cultural sovereignty."[53] Chicana liberation would involve working with men, not against them. Ultimately she rejects individualism in favor of community liberation.

Maturation of Latino Arts

The demographic, economic, and political prominence of Latinos during the 1980s provided a context for a florescence and maturation in the performing and visual arts. Generally speaking, Latino artists sought to join the mainstream. Bolstered by the new creative energies coming from the Cuban, Puerto Rican, and Latin American cultures, Mexican-American creative artists enjoyed a new popularity. One important aspect in "the boom" in Latino visual and performing arts was the growth of a Latino market. For the first time it was possible for many Latino artists to earn a living from their work by selling their art to other Latinos. The main impetus in the change in Latino arts, however, came from the artists themselves, who made a conscious choice to expand beyond the barrio, to gain acceptance and recognition from the larger society.

Perhaps the most dramatic evidence of the emergence of Latino culture was in the film industry. After decades of Hollywood's exclusion of Latinos from producing and directing jobs, the 1980s saw the exhibition of major motion pictures written, directed, or staring Latinos and based on Latino themes. Perhaps the most artistically powerful statement tying immigration to Latinos was the movie *El Norte* (1983), a moving saga about a Guatemalan brother and sister and their adventures in fleeing through Mexico to the United States. Produced and directed by Gregory Nava, a Chicano, and staring the well-known Mexican actor Pedro Arisméndez, the film made a powerful statement about the tragedies experienced by Latino immigrants in the United States. It also highlighted the competitive and exploitative relationship between the Chicano and the newly arrived immigrant. *El Norte* had limited distribution, however. The first in a series of box office hits was *La Bamba* (1987), written and directed by Luis Valdez. It was a film about the life and tragic death of Ritchie Valens, a popular rock and roll star of the 1950s. Earning more than $55 million, the film showed Hollywood that Latino themes could sell.[54] Next, Cheech Marín starred in the movie *Born in East L.A.* (1987), a comedy with serious undertones about Mexican immigrants and their relationship to Latinos. This also was a modest financial success. In 1988

Hollywood produced three major films staring Latinos and developing Mexican-American cultural themes. Robert Redford with Moctesuma Esparza did *The Milagro Beanfield War* (1988), which had a large Latino cast and starred Rubén Blades, a well-known Latino recording artist. Ramón Menendez directed *Stand and Deliver* (1987), staring James Edward Olmos, based on the true story of a successful barrio high school math teacher and Raúl Julia starred in the film *Romero* (1989), a moving account of the life and assassination of Archbishop Oscar Romero in El Salvador. Raúl Julia and Sonia Braga starred with Richard Dreyfuss in *Moon over Parador* (1989), a satire about a Latin American dictatorship, and Jimmy Smits with Jane Fonda starred in Carlos Fuentes's *Old Gringo*, a story set during the Mexican revolution.

A consequence of these and other films being produced in the 1980s was the promotion of new Latino film stars, many of who had been languishing in sterotypical minor roles. One of the most promising of these was James Edward Olmos, who had grown up in East Los Angeles of Mexican immigrant parents. After several small parts in television series, Olmos was "discovered" by Luis Valdez who cast him as the *pachuco* in the 1978 play *Zoot Suit*. For his acting, Olmos won a Tony nomination and a Los Angeles Drama Critics Circle award, and this led to supporting roles in the films *Wolfen* (1981) and *Blade Runner* (1982). Olmos had a commitment to accept only roles that presented positive images of Latinos. His most important films in this regard were *The Ballad of Gregorio Cortez* (1982), a drama based on Américo Paredes's book, and *Stand and Deliver.* He accepted the role of Lieutenant Martín Castillo on the popular television series *Miami Vice* in 1984 only after promises that he would have creative control of the character. By the end of the decade, Olmos had established his own production company with the goal of making Latino movies that were artistically powerful as well as socially responsible.

In the area of music, a growing Latino population meant more of a domestic market for Latino sounds, but the nonethnic mainstream also picked up on the beat. Latino groups and artists sought to find a popular audience by mixing and crossing over. Los Lobos, an East Los Angeles Chicano group, provided the music for the hit movies *La Bamba* and *Salsa* and sold millions of albums of their unique blend of rock-and-roll, Tex-Mex, and *corridos*. Rubén Blades, the Panama-born recording artist, made his first album in English, *Nothing but the Truth,* keeping the rhythm and style but reaching the non-Latino audience. Linda Ronstadt, from the Tucson-Sonora Ronstadt family, had a big hit with her *Canciones de Mi Padre*, ballads sung in Spanish with the Mariachi Vargas de Tecalitán from Mexico.[55]

Mainstream America began accepting Mexican-American music. In 1983 the Academy of Recording Arts and Sciences added a Latin category to its awards. The first award went to Sheena Easton and Luis Miguel for their duet *Me gustas tal como eres.* In 1985 Vicki Carr won the award for her album *Ay te dejo en San Antonio.* Subsequent winners were Los Tigres del Norte's *Gracias! América sin fronteras* (1987), Linda Ronstadt's *Canciones de mi padre* (1988), and Los Lobos's *La pistola y el corazón* (1989). The Grammys also added a Mexican-American Music category to their annual awards.[56]

While retaining an ethnic tone and message, Latino films and music appealed to large, mixed audiences. The same tendencies were true for the performing arts. Perhaps the best example of this was the play *Zoot Suit* (1978), the first Chicano play to be performed on mainstream stages in Los Angeles and New York. Written and directed by Luis Valdez, *Zoot Suit* was based on the Sleepy Lagoon incident in 1943 (see Chapter 6). Incorporating music and dance of the 1940s, *Zoot Suit* had a sociopolitical message but was entertaining as well. It was immensely popular in Los Angeles and southern California, where it ran for 46 weeks and attracted an audience of over 400,000. It was less popular in New York, perhaps because of the lack of familiarity with Chicano culture. This play and subsequent ones by Valdez—*I Don't Have to Show You No Stinking Badges* and *Corridos,* for instance—entertained larger audiences while remaining faithful to Mexican and Chicano cultural themes.

Aside from Valdez, several Chicano playwrights contributed their talents to producing an authentic Chicano theater that could be appreciated by non-Latinos. Carlos Morton wrote a series of plays and won the Hispanic Playwrights Festival Award and the New York Shakespeare Festival award. Rubén Sierra wrote *La Raza pura o Racial, Racial* (The Pure Race or Racial, Racial) and, with Jorge Huerta, *I Am Celso.* Fausto Avedaño wrote *El corrido de California,* and Estela Portillo Trambely authored *Sor Juana* and *Blacklight*, the latter winning second place in the American Theater Festival in New York.

Jorge Huerta established the nation's first master's in theater arts specializing in Hispanic/Latino theater at the University of California at San Diego. Besides training a cadre of professional actors, directors, and playwrights, he worked with the local Old Globe Theater and San Diego Repertory Theater to produce original Chicano plays of noted Latin American playwrights.

Nicolás Kanellos, a literary critic and historian, aptly summarized the state of Chicano theater in the 1980s: "The days of *teatro* as an arm of revolutionary nationalism are over. The revolutionary aims of the movement have resulted in modest reforms and certain accommodations. Luis Valdez now sits on the California Arts Council. Many other *teatro* and former *teatro* people are members of local arts agencies and boards throughout the Southwest. Former *teatristas* are now professors of drama, authors, and editors of scholarly books and journals on Chicano literature and theater."[57]

If Chicano literature did not produce a wealth of best-sellers or a poet laureate during this era, it was not for lack of talent or productivity. The big publishing houses on the East Coast remained impervious to the literary merits of Latinos. An example of their shortsightedness was Victor Villaseñor's treatment by New York publishers, who insisted on changing the title and character of his family history. He refused to make these changes and took his book to Arte Público Press, a Chicano publishing house in Houston, which then published it as *Rain of Gold* (1991). In a short time it became a best-seller. A major breakthrough for Latino writers occurred in 1989 with the publication of *The Mambo Kings Play Songs of Love* (1989), by Oscar Hijuelos, a Cuban American resident of New York City. Hijuelos's book won the Pulitzer Prize for literature and became a best-seller for Harper & Row Publishers. It is a lyrical and sorrowful story of a couple of Cuban musicians in New York during the 1940s and 1950s as they became part of the Latin music boom of that era. Hijuelos's passionate and rich style evoked a barrage of sensual images. Concurrent with the success of this book, Gabriel García Márquez (Colombia) and Octavio Paz (Mexico) won Nobel Prizes for their literature and this sparked a surge in English-language translations of their works.

Despite this modest Latino "boom" in literature, most Chicano writers did not have large commercial success. Many may have eschewed it. Numerous Chicano writers were university professors whose orientation tended to be away from the marketplace. The Chicano fiction writers of the previous decade continued to publish short stories and novels, but a new group of writers joined them. Nash Candelaria wrote a triology based on New Mexico's history—*Memories of the Alhambra* (1977), *Not by the Sword* (1982), and *Inheritance of Strangers* (1985)—tracing the history of José Rafa's family through 400 years. The main themes of the Rafa trilogy were conquest, conflict, and identity, but the books also underscore Chicanos' links to humanity. In 1984 Arturo Islas published *The Rain God: A Desert Tale,* a historical-autobiographical novel set in El Paso. Lionel García's novel *Leaving Home* (1985) is about a Latino baseball pitcher in the 1930s and 1940s. In 1987 he penned *A Shroud in the Family,* telling of a Tejano searching for his identity in family relations.

Latinas also made important contributions to the development of fiction. Gloria Anzaldúa's *This Bridge Called My Back* (1988) and *Borderlands/Fronteras* (1987) explore issues of gender and cultural politics. Irene Beltrán's *Across the Great River* (1987) deals with the experiences of an undocumented immigrant family as seen through the eyes of a young girl. Denise Chávez's *Face of an Angel* (1990) is about the survival strategies of a career waitress, and Anna Castillo's *Sapagonia* (1990) reflects on the meaning of being a Mestizo in the Americas. Many short-story collections by Latinas have been published by the two most prominent Latino editorial houses, Arte Público Press and Bilingual Review Press.

Modern Chicano literature has continued to be intensely personal. The most controversial and best-selling autobiography of the 1980s was Richard Rodríguez's *Hunger of Memory* (1982). This book, more than any other, perhaps, challenged the values of the Chicano movement. Rodríguez describes his alienation from the main Chicano activists and his willingness to abandon the Mexican culture and embrace Anglo-American values. He stresses the importance of learning a public language (English) rather than preserving a private one (Spanish). He attacks bilingual education, affirmative action, and ethnic politics. Praised by Anglo-American critics for his literary style and power, *Hunger of Memory* came under attack by Chicano intellectuals because of its conservative message. Rodríguez wrote several essays that appeared in national magazines such as *Harper's,* and he narrated television documentaries on Mexican culture. Because of his literary skill he has become, ironically, the most well-known Chicano writer in the United States.

Writing for a smaller audience, Chicano poets turned away from didactic political messages and became more introspective. A major development in these years was the emergence of an energetic group of Chicana and Latina poets. Bernice Zamora published *Restless Serpents* (1976), a piece that explores the contradictory and conflictive feelings about being a woman in a male dominated culture. Zamora links Chicana poetry to American literary works, with frequent allusions to the mainstream tradition. Alma Villanueva's *Bloodroot* and *Poems* in 1977 and *Mother, May I?* in 1978 are intensely personal and confident poetry, powerfully asserting female sexual superiority and creative power while emphasizing her identity as a woman rather than as a Latina. Another prominent

Chicana poet of these years is Lorna Dee Cervantez, whose *Emplumada* (1981) is a complex array of feminist poems dealing with barrio life.[58]

The most prolific and widely acclaimed poet of the 1980s, however, was Gary Soto. Born in the San Joaquin Valley, Soto moved away from the overt political declamations of the Chicano-movement years and explored personal themes using vivid and evocative language. Critics acclaimed his first collection, *The Elements of San Joaquín* (1977), as a masterpiece that captured the essence of rural landscapes and people. *The Tale of Sunlight* (1978) is more psychological in character, and *Father Is a Pillow Tied to a Broom* (1980) evokes more somber and sorrowful tones. *Where Sparrows Work Hard* (1981), *Black Hair* (1985), and *Who Will Know Us, New Poems* (1990) are all major advances in the use of language. Soto won national and international prizes for his work. His collection of short stories, *Living Up the Street* (1985), about his childhood in Fresno, California, won the National Book Award.

Latino visual artists, painters, and sculptors, had somewhat more success than fiction writers in gaining national recognition for their work. The diversity of artistic expression multiplied and mural art declined as the predominant form of artistic expression for Chicanos. In 1987 a national touring exhibition of Latino artists, "Hispanic Art in the United States: Thirty Contemporary Painters and Sculptors," showcased the rich imagery and vitality of modern Latino artists of diverse Latin American backgrounds. Another national touring exhibition, opening in 1990, "CARA: Chicano Art Resistance and Affirmation," interpreted the Chicano art movement (1965–75) within a larger historical and cultural framework. Another historical retrospective organized by the Bronx Museum in 1990, "The Latin American Spirit: Art and Artists in the United States, 1920–1970," focused on the international influences of Latin American art and artists on the United States. These shows, and many other locally organized art exhibits, publicized the emergence of new talent and energies and challenged the conservative dominions of the American art academy. In 1991 the Mexican government organized a major historical and contemporary touring exhibit of visual art entitled "Mexico: Splendors of Thirty Centuries." This exhibit made the public even more aware than ever of the traditions of Latino art.

The main esthetic directions of Chicano art in the 1980s was toward the private and away from the public. Artists sought commercial success in creating canvas paintings, not public murals. A host of new artists sold their work in galleries in Los Angeles, Austin, San Francisco, and San Diego. As art collectors began to bid thousands of dollars for works by artists such as John Valadez, Luis Jiménez, Carmen Lomas Garza, and Carlos Almaraz, Chicano art graduated from the streets to the salons.

Conclusions

Immigration from Latin America and a dramatic growth in the Latino population shaped the years following the decline of the heightened political sensibilities of the Chicano movement (1965–75). The economic, linguistic, and national diversity of the U.S. Spanish-speaking population expanded. The New Immigrants filled an important niche in the American economy, and, at the same time, the general Latino population became more economically polarized. The middle- and upper-class Latino classes grew. So, too, did the Latino under-class. The new wave of immigration led to new political activities. MALDEF and the SWVRP made an intense effort to enlarge Latino representation within the existing political system. Instead of demonstrations they used the courts and the ballot boxes. Latino immigration provoked a nativist backlash that resulted in a new immigration law in 1987 that promised to "cure" the problems attributed to the newcomers. The conservative political and social tone of the Republican-dominated 1980s had its reflection in Latino politics. Large national organizations made deals with multinational corporations to help fund their activities. With some notable exceptions, Latino politicians increasingly joined the mainstream and eschewed radical ethnic approaches. The Chicano renaissance of the 1960s and 1970s became a Latino "boom" in the 1980s. Mainstream America became more aware of the rich cultural expressions of Latino artists in the movies and music. The mood of the 1980s was to commercialize ethnicity and seek ways of selling it. Meanwhile, funda-mental differences remained between the underclass of working-class immi-grant and native-born Latinos and the growing Hispanic middle classes.

As if to confirm the growing differentiation within Latino communities as outlined in this chapter, in the fall of 1992 Rodolfo O. de la Garza and F. Chris García published the results of a nationwide poll entitled *Latino Voices*. Their findings directly challenged some of the assumptions that had been held by Chicano activists during the 1970s. They found that Latinos "do not constitute a political community" and that by and large Hispanics had "positive views on their experience with government" and that "the relationship between these groups and mainstream society is not so harsh as to isolate the 'Hispanic' com-munity and make it easily mobilized around narrow ethnic appeals."[59] Described as the most extensive and complete survey of Hispanics to date, the poll found that a larger percentage of Mexican Americans than non-Hispanic whites believed that there were too many immigrants in the United States and that citi-zens and residents of the United States should learn English. Analyzing the results of the survey they concluded that "there is a growing gulf between the Latino leadership and the community," and that there had been a great deal of assimilation of mainstream American values to the extent that "there has been no real Latino political movement that might have encouraged distinctively Latino views."[60]

This survey is a somber indication of the inability of the activist 1960s to generate a lasting ethnic political consciousness. For those wanting to create national political power for Latinos or Chicanos as a group, it offered a sobering challenge. As they have in the past, Mexican-American leaders continue to have the responsibility to articulate the issues and ideas that can unify the many dif-ferent constituencies that make up the Hispanic population.

ten

Community, Diversity, and Culture:
Some Conclusions

More than 100 years before the first English settlements were established in Virginia and Massachusetts, Spanish conquistadors and Mestizo and Hispanicized Indian settlers established a new civilization throughout a vast area of the Western Hemisphere. The epic proportions of this endeavor have been chronicled by historians and celebrated in literature, poetry, and film. Yet the legacy of *Hispanidad* remains an ambiguous one because it developed from the violent subjugation of millions of native peoples. Ritual human sacrifice practiced by the Aztecs and condemned by the Catholic Iberians paled in comparison to the tens of millions of natives who died of Spanish diseases, starvation, and torture. Thus the birth of the Mestizo people, a mixed race with conflicting cultural heritages, was a painful one—a birthing that has not yet ended as millions of new immigrants and migrants continue the process of multicultural encounter. Mixture and amalgamation, combination and invention, *mestisaje*, throughout the Americas has produced perhaps the most diverse population in the world.

This larger heritage of ethnic and cultural diversity is the parent of the Mexican-American and Latino culture within the United States. It is an inheritance that has brought a rich panoply of ways of living, thinking, and believing to the United States. Along with the Native Americans who assisted them, the Spanish-speaking pioneers west of the Mississippi laid the foundations for a different kind of frontier society. Unlike the English-American frontier, the Spaniards and Mexicans built planned communities that were regulated by autocratic civil and religious authorities. At the same time they developed a democracy born of Iberian individualism and Native American communalism.

The Spanish-speaking settlers' contributions to the development of the present-day American Southwest were many. They named the mountains, rivers, lakes, and harbors after European saints and cities as well as after Native American flora and fauna. Plants and animals brought from Mexico or Spain took root in this far-northern frontier and began an ecological revolution. Wild grasses from Europe along with the cattle, horses, and pigs spread faster than did the migrants.[1] Spanish, Mexican, and Native American *vaqueros* laid the foundation for that all-American type, the cowboy. Mexican foods, songs, music, laws, and customs all persisted beyond the American conquest in 1846–48 and influenced the evolution of American identity.

The most lasting contribution of the Mexicans would come after 1848 as waves of migrants would come north from Mexico to join the descendants of the first Spanish and Mexican pioneers. The rapid development of the western economies in mining, farming, and ranching and in the construction of new cities would be made possible because of this seemingly inexhaustible supply of willing laborers who were able to work long hours for cheap wages. Ironically, only truly appreciated by the bosses who exploited their labor, the Mexican immigrant would remain largely invisible in American society, except during occasional bursts of xenophobic fear during wars and recessions.

Mexican migration and immigration has been a key factor in the shaping of Mexican-American history. The movement of millions of people from Mexico to the United States in the twentieth century has been both a unifying and an fragmenting force for Mexican Americans. Until about 1930 the vast majority of Mexican Americans were Mexican-born, long-term residents of the United States, whose primary language was Spanish and whose cultural reference was primarily Mexican. By 1990 the majority of Mexican Americans were native-born citizens whose dominant language was English. What would be their bond with the newly arriving immigrant? Immigrants have brought with them their language and their regional cultures, thus enriching Mexican-American society. At the same time the Mexican immigrants remain the poorest members of American society, living in urban slums and rural labor camps. Increasing numbers of Mexican Americans are middle-class suburbanites who live in relative affluence. Yet Mexican immigrants and these U.S.-born Mexican Americans are part of the same historical community. They share a common historical destiny. While many Americans have an immigrant experience in their distant ancestry, Mexican Americans are much closer to their immigrant past both generationally and geographically. It is a reality that continues to shape their future.

This ongoing movement of people north to Aztlán, the legendary homeland of the Aztecs, thus has contributed to the differences within the Mexican-American population. A major objective of this book has been to trace the ways in which Mexican-American heterogeneity has been linked to immigration and migration flows as well as to the unique history of geographical regions.

New Mexico and southern Colorado as a cultural region entered the twentieth century with its Hispano population still largely identifying with its Spanish past, unaffected by any appreciable Mexican immigration. As a result the historical experience of the *nuevomexicanos* unfolded out of their contacts with the surrounding native groups and their relative isolation from Mexicans and Anglo-Americans. The most intense changes in New Mexico's Hispano culture came after World War II, when Anglo-American and Mexican migration began to alter the demographic and cultural landscape. Within the state today there is increasing differentiation with respect to socioeconomic and language factors among the Hispano population, and this is not to negate the ever-present differentiation of generation and gender.

The Tejanos have a somewhat different heritage—one shaped by their cultural and familial exchanges with the sizable population of northeastern Mexico for the past 200 years. Added to this has been the experience of their violent incorporation into the Anglo-American Texan Republic beginning in 1836.

Considered by white Texans as being socially on par with Indians and African slaves, Mexican Americans in Texas evolved within a segregated society where lynchings and murder enforced racial order. For Tejanos, language maintenance and cultural loyalty toward their rural and urban communities was necessary if they were to endure as a people. In the twentieth century the Tejano population became more differentiated in class and ideology. Commercial growth and political activism challenged older racist patterns, and Mexican Americans, particularly in urban areas, assumed prominent political positions. Within Texas there remained a great deal of regional variation depending on the economic culture and proportion of Anglo-Americans to Tejanos.

Arizona's Mexican-American history emanated from the political, economic, and cultural influences of Sonora, Mexico. For more than 100 years the Spanish/Mexican people of the region lived in a precarious outpost surrounded by forbidding deserts and deadly Apache bands. The need to ally with Anglo newcomers against these hardships conditioned the tone of their society until statehood in 1912. Thereafter Mexicans in Tucson and in the mining camps and ranches in the southern part of the state became a segregated, marginalized work force. Mexican immigration after 1945 increased their numbers and led to new political and cultural assertions, particularly in the fast-growing metropolitan region of Phoenix. Many of the new Mexican Americans in Arizona migrated there from other southwestern states seeking job opportunities. Internally the Latino population was fragmented, not only along the usual fault lines of gender, generation, and class but also along the newcomer, old-timer division.

California, the last of the U.S. border states having a history in the Spanish and Mexican eras, has had a distinctive Mexican-American history. The forms of land tenure engendered by the missions and *ranchos,* the lack of geographical proximity to mainland Mexico, and the traumatic break with a pastoral culture coming during the gold rush years marked the early formation of Californio culture. In the American era hundreds of thousands and then millions of foreigners streamed into the state and all but extinguished the Californio way of life. Another migration, this time from Mexico beginning in the 1880s, revived, reinvigorated, and eventually overwhelmed native Californios. By the mid-twentieth century the vast majority of California Mexican Americans descended from Mexican immigrants from central Mexico or from migrants from other southwestern states. Perhaps this experience of mobility and transiency and of having to constantly re-create community explains why in the 1960s the Chicano movement, as a revitalization crusade, found its most assertive articulation in California. The extraordinary contrasts within the state also characterized the Chicano population. Here more than any other region of Aztlán, *mestizaje,* particularly in the metropolitan regions of southern California and the Bay area, constantly renews itself: Chicanos, Hispanics, and Mexican immigrants live and work beside large urban populations of Central Americans, African Americans, Asian Americans, and scores of other immigrants. This postmodern "encounter" has led some observers to conclude that the cultural and demographic future of California is that of the United States.[2]

We should not forget the sizable and growing presence of Mexican-origin people living north of Aztlán. Their history belongs to the twentieth century, having an origin in the recruitment of workers to labor on the farms and ranches and in the automobile factories, packing houses, and steel mills. For this reason the key to understanding their history is the economic cycle. Mexican workers were recruited as easily exploited laborers during good times and suffered discrimination, poverty, and a harsh climate and then were fired, deported, or repatriated during recessions or depressions. The diverse working-class enclaves—whether in rural eastern Washington and Oregon or in urban Chicago communities—existed as islands of *Mexicanidad,* surrounded by an English-speaking ocean. Assimilative pressures in school and on the job made for a more Anglicized lifestyle, but Mexican immigration renewed older communities and established newer ones, in Kansas City, Kansas, in Des Moines, Iowa, in Boston, and in New York City. Influenced by the milieu of their region and living with a tremendous diversity of European-stock ethnic Americans, Mexican Americans outside the Southwest are fundamentally connected to their heritage by immigration and internal migration. They are the pioneers of the twenty-first century who are pushing north beyond Aztlán.

This book tells a history of the Mexican-American people but not primarily in terms of the injustices they have suffered within American society. Although inequality and prejudice existed as part of the fabric of life for most Mexican Americans, their history has involved overcoming many obstacles and difficulties so that their culture may persist. The ability to endure incredible hardship and difficulty bolstered by the strength and support of others has been a constant in the history of La Raza. Labor unions, mutual aid societies, artist collectives, musical groups, political parties, religious associations, and humble and impermanent associations of many kinds expressed a historical motif—essentially the need to join with others who shared a common heritage in order to withstand oppression and persist as a people. Thus Mexican-American humanity found form within their attempts to organize community with others. Within this context the variety of La Raza, with its diverse ideologies, generations, classes, and geographical, racial, and gender identities found expression as well.

Women have been important historical actors in all aspects of this history, from the first settlement expeditions to New Mexico to the most recent electoral victories in East Los Angeles. The Latina and Chicana experience has been one of giving, creating, enduring, working, nurturing, and leading, all within the confines of gender discriminations and limitations placed on them by patriarchal societies, whether Spanish, Mexican, or Anglo-American. The story of their struggle to be heard and to work with men to give meaning to life in this county is a continuing one emerging from the writings of Chicana and Latina historians.

Equally as discounted and hidden has been the history of the contributions of Mexican Americans in the creative and performing arts. This book has traced only something of this rich heritage. It stretches from the chronicles and narratives in the sixteenth century to the composition of plays, songs, and poetry in the seventeenth century; from the development of *santero* art in the eighteenth and the publication of newspapers, short stories, and novellas in the nineteenth century; and in our own time, an explosion of talent in the performing and visual arts.

Sometime in the next century the Latino population will become the largest minority group in the United States. This demographic change underscores the importance of America coming to terms with the cultural legacy of this group. Of the projected increase, the overwhelming majority will be of Mexican descent. Mexican immigration will continue to be a major factor accounting for the growth. This movement north to Aztlán has been the subject of hundreds of scholarly studies assessing its economic, social, and political implications. Increasingly, though, if the United States is to become a viable multiracial, multicultural society, more attention will have to be given to cultural and historical perspectives about this group. Historian Ronald Takaki pointed out the need for our society to have "A Different Mirror" with which to see itself, that the older historical lenses no longer project a clear picture of the real America. The old guard may fear diversity, and yet the consequences of America not understanding its historical and cultural differences may prove disastrous.[3]

As has been pointed out by Rubén Rumbaut, like previous immigrant waves, the Latin American immigrants are remaking America, but not in their own image.[4] This means that Latinos are to be one of the main architects in the re-invention of America in the twenty-first century but that they will not be alone in determining the final product. What is taking place is not a Mexicanization or Latinization of the United States but a continuation of the historical processes of *mestizaje*—a complex, often conflictive project of amalgamation and invention. As Carlos Fuentes in his book *The Buried Mirror* suggested, this confrontation with the "Other" has been the unfinished project of the Latin American peoples. It will also be the major challenge for the United States in the next century. The moral, intellectual, and esthetic record of Mexican Americans spanning the experience from indigenous to immigrant, white to dark, and rich to poor constitutes an inheritance for future generations who are to confront this challenge.

Chronology

1521	Fall of Tenochtitlán to Cortez and the Spanish conquistadores.
1528–1536	First Europeans enter the Southwest: Alvar Núñez Cabeza de Vaca, Estevanico, and others.
1540–1542	Francisco Vásquez de Coronado leads major expedition into area exploring portions of what is now Arizona, New Mexico, Texas, Kansas, Nebraska, and Oklahoma.
1598	Juan de Oñate leads expedition to New Mexico. Gaspar de Villagrá writes *La Historia de nuevo mexico.*
1609	Santa Fe, New Mexico, is founded.
1659	El Paso, Texas, is founded.
1680	Pueblo Indians revolt agains the Spanish in New Mexico.
1718	San Antonio, Texas, is founded; the community is given *villa* status in 1731.
1765	Bourbon Reforms introduced into New Spain.
1769	San Diego, Alta California, is founded as a mission and presidio.
1775	Tucson, Pimería Alta (Arizona), is established as a presidio.
1781	El Pueblo de la Reina de Los Angeles, Alta California, is settled.
1810	Miguel Hidalgo y Costilla leads War of Independence in Mexico.
1819	Adams-Onís Transcontinental Treaty is signed. United States and Spain agree on the eastern boundary of the Far North.
1821	Mexico gains independence from Spain. The Santa Fe trade begins between Missouri and New Mexican merchants.
1825	Mexico opens the state of Texas-Coahuila to immmigration from the United States. More than 30,000 Americans move to Texas.
1831	Fray Geronimo Boscana chronicles the life of the native tribes at the mission of San Juan Capistrano.

1833	California missions are secularized.
1836	Texas War of Independence. The Alamo falls to Mexican forces. At San Jacinto, Santa Anna agrees that Texas no longer belongs to Mexico.
1845	United States annexes Texas.
1846	U.S.–Mexican War begins in south Texas.
1847	U.S. troops occupy Mexico City, California, and New Mexico.
1848	Treaty of Guadalupe Hidalgo ends the war.
1851	Juanita is lynched in Downieville, California, for murdering an Anglo miner who made unwanted advances toward her. She is the first and only women lynched in California.
1859	Juan "Cheno" Cortina begins rebellion in south Texas.
1862	Confederates invade New Mexico and Arizona and are driven back by Anglo and Mexican-American troops.
1867	Death of Padre José Antonio Martínez of Taos, New Mexico.
1877	El Paso Salt War.
1880–1890s	Las Gorras Blancas (the White Caps) continue resistance in New Mexico against developers and corporations that have infringed on traditional lands.
1884	María Amparo Ruiz de Burton writes *The Squatter and the Don*, the first novel by a Mexican American to be written in English.
1891–1892	Catarino Garza launches invasion from south Texas trying to overthrow President Porfirio Díaz of Mexico.
1894	La Alianza Hispano-Americana (a *mutualista*) is founded in Arizona.
1898	Maximiliano Luna of New Mexico fights with distinction at the Battle of San Juan Hill in the Spanish–American War.
1901	Gregorio Cortez becomes the object of a massive manhunt after killing (in self-defense) an Anglo lawman in central Texas.
1910	Mexican Revolution begins, led by Francisco Madero who is based in San Antonio. Ricardo and Enrique Flores Magón begin publishing *La Regeneración* in Los Angeles.
1913	*La Prensa* is founded in San Antonio by Ignacio E. Lozano, a Mexican immigrant.
1913–1914	Mexican and Anglo miners strike in Ludlow, Colorado.
1915	El Plan de San Diego, Texas, calls for popular insurrection among Mexicans in the Southwest. Mariano Azuela's *Los de abajo* is published in El Paso.
1916	Pancho Villa raids Columbus, New Mexico; United States sends an expeditionary force into Mexico in pursuit.

1921 La Orden Hijos de America is founded in San Antonio to promote citizenship and voting.

1927–1929 La Confederación de Uniones Obreras Mexicanas (CUOM) is founded in Southern California; it is the first stable union of Mexican workers.

1928 La Unión de Trabajadores del Valle Imperial in California calls for strike in the cantaloupe fields. Daniel Venegas's *Las Aventuras de don Chipote o cuando los pericos mamen* is published in Los Angeles.

1929 League of United Latin American Citizens (LULAC) organizes in Corpus Christi, Texas. Depression begins.

1930 Mexican-American parents sue Lemon Grove school district in first anti-segregation case and win a decision the next year. Repatriation drives begin. Thousands of Mexicans are pressured into leaving the United States.

1932–1933 The Cannery and Agricultural Workers Industrial Union organizes in California and leads the San Joaquin Valley cotton strike. El Monte berry strike in California.

1935 Dennis Chávez is elected U.S. senator from New Mexico.

1938 Pecan-shellers' strike in San Antonio led by Emma Tenayuca. First national conference of Spanish-speaking peoples (El Congreso del Pueblo de Habla Español), organized by Luisa Moreno and Bert Corona, meets in Los Angeles.

1941–1945 More than 100,000 Mexican Americans serve in U.S. armed services during World War II.

1943 The Bracero Program is enacted by Congress. Zoot Suit Riots in Los Angeles.

1945–1948 More than 15 lawsuits against segregation of Mexican Americans are filed by the G.I. Forum and LULAC.

1945 *Méndez et al. v. Westminster School District of Orange County,* a landmark case challenging racial discrimination in schools.

1947 The Community Service Organization (CSO) is formed in Los Angeles.

1950 Ignacio López, editor of *El Espectador,* founds Unity Leagues in California.

1952 César Chávez begins working for the CSO in California.

1959 José Antonio Villarreal publishes *Pocho,* the first modern Chicano novel.

1960 The Political Association of Spanish-Speaking Organizations (PASSO) is founded by Hector P. García in Texas.

1962 The Farm Workers Association (FWA) is founded by César Chávez and Dolores Huerta; Edward Roybal is elected to Congress.

1963 Reies Tijerina forms the Alianza Federal de Mercedes Libres in New Mexico.

1965 California farmworkers begin grape strike led by César Chávez.

1966 Rodolfo "Corky" González founds the Denver Crusade for Justice.

1967 Tierra Amarilla shoot out; Reies Tijerina is arrested. Students organize for civil rights (MAYO in San Antonio; UMAS in Los Angeles).

1968 High School "blowouts" in Los Angeles. Chicano students boycott school system.

1969 *El Plan Espitual de Aztlán* issued as a result of National Chicano Youth Liberation Conference in Denver. *El Plan de Santa Barbara* issued, calling for Chicano Studies departments in higher education.

1970 National Chicano Moratorium is organized in Los Angeles. Rubén Salazar is killed. Chicana feminists organize Comisión Femenil Mexicana Nacional. La Raza Unida party is founded in Texas.

1971 First National Conference of La Raza Women meets in Houston with 600 delegates.

1972 In *Lau* v. *Nichols* the Supreme Court directs schools to address the needs of non–English-speaking students.

1972–1974 Farah strike by Mexican and Chicana workers in El Paso.

1974 Southwest Voter Registration Project is launched.

1977 In *Doe* v. *Plyler* MALDEF successfully challenges a Texas statute that had withheld education from children of undocumented immigrants.

1978 *Zoot Suit* by Luis Valdez is performed in Los Angeles and New York.

1980 Chicanos are elected to prominent offices: Toney Anaya (governor of New Mexico), Federico Peña (mayor of Denver), and Henry Cisneros (mayor of San Antonio). Gloria Molina wins election to the California Assembly.

1982 Senator S. I. Hayakawa forms U.S. English to promote English-only laws. Simpson-Mazzoli immigration bill is introduced to Congress. The film *The Ballad of Gregorio Cortez,* based on Américo Paredes's book, is released. Richard Rodríguez's *Hunger of Memory* is published.

1983   Formation of Mujeres Activas en Letras y Cambio Social (MALCS) in 1983. The film *El Norte,* directed by Gregory Nava, is released.

1984   LULAC votes to boycott the Democratic Convention in opposition to immigration restriction. NACS conference, *Voces de la Mujer,* is held in Austin.

1986   Mothers of East Los Angeles organizes 400 women to protest construction of state prison complex within their community. Immigration Reform and Control Act (IRCA) passes Congress.

1987   The film *La Bamba,* written and directed by Luis Valdez, is released. Los Tigres del Norte win national music award. Gloria Anzaldúa's *Borderlands/Fronteras* is published.

1988   The film *Stand and Deliver,* directed by Ramón Menendez and starring Edward James Olmos, is released.

1989   The group Los Lobos win a Grammy award for their album *La Pistola y el corazón.*

1990   The touring exhibition "CARA: Chicano Art Resistance and Affirmation" opens in Los Angeles.

1991   The touring exhibition "Mexico: Splendors of Thirty Centuries" opens in New York.

1993   César E. Chávez dies; more than 70,000 participate in memorial march in Delano, California.

1994   The North American Free Trade Agreement (NAFTA) is ratified; Proposition 187, an anti-immigrant measure, passes in California.

Notes and References

one

1. Geoffrey Turner, *Indians of North America* (Dorset, England: Blandford Press, 1979), 189–96.

2. Alfred Crosby, *The Colombian Exchange: Biological and Cultural Consequences of 1492* (Westport, Conn.: Greenwood Press, 1977).

3. Colin M. MacLachlan and Jaime E. Rodríguez-O, *The Forging of the Cosmic Race: A Reinterpretation of Colonial Mexico* (Berkeley, Los Angeles, and London: University of California Press, 1980), 201–202.

4. Douglas H. Ubelaker, "North American Indian Population Size, A.D. 1500 to 1985," *American Journal of Physical Anthropology* 77 (1988): 292.

5. David J. Weber, *The Spanish Frontier in North America* (New Haven, Conn., and London: Yale University Press, 1992), 264–65; 280–82.

6. Edward H. Spicer, *Cycles of Conquest: The Impact of Spain, Mexico, and the United States on the Indians of the Southwest, 1533–1960* (Tucson: University of Arizona Press, 1962), 221–29; Ramón Gutiérrez, *When Jesus Came, the Corn Mothers Went Away: Marriage, Sexuality, and Power in New Mexico, 1500–1846* (Palo Alto, Calif.: Stanford University Press, 1991), 149–56.

7. Antonia I. Castañeda, *"Presidarias y Pobladores:* Spanish-Mexican Women in Frontier Monterey, Alta California, 1770–1821," Ph.D. diss., Stanford University, 1990, chap. 2.

8. Spicer, *Cycles of Conquest,* 585.

9. Oakah L. Jones, Jr., *Los Paisanos: Spanish Settlers on the Northern Frontier of New Spain* (Norman: University of Oklahoma Press, 1979), 128.

10. Seymour V. Connor, *Texas: A History* (Arlington Heights, Ill.: Harlan Davidson, 1971), 57

11. Jones, *Los Paisanos,* 177.

12. James Officer, *Hispanic Arizona, 1536–1856* (Tucson: University of Arizona Press, 1987), 8–24; 71, 80. Arizona means "small springs" in the Pima language.

13. Douglas Monroy, *Thrown among Strangers: The Making of Mexican Culture in Frontier California* (Berkeley and Los Angeles: University of California Press, 1990), 79.

14. Jones, *Los Paisanos,* 217.

15. Gilbert R. Cruz, *Let There Be Towns: Spanish Municipal Origins in the American Southwest, 1610–1810* (College Station: Texas A & M University, 1988), 169. An

excellent study of the vitality of the early town governments is Gilberto Miguel Hinojosa, *A Borderlands Town in Transition: Laredo, Texas, 1775–1870* (College Station: Texas A & M University, 1983). See also Antonio Ríos-Bustamante, "New Mexico in the Eighteenth Century: Life, Labor and Trade in la Villa de San Felipe de Albuquerque, 1706–1790," *Aztlán* 7 (Fall 1976): 375; Sarah Deutsch, *No Separate Refuge: Culture, Class, and Gender on an Anglo-Hispanic Frontier in the American Southwest, 1880–1940* (New York: Oxford University Press, 1987), 14; Weber, *The Spanish Frontier in North America*, 177, 193.

16. For a discussion of the Bourbon reforms and their effects on the frontier of New Spain, see Thomas D. Hall, *Social Change in the Southwest, 1350–1880* (Lawrence: University of Kansas Press, 1989), 138–47.

17. Ríos-Bustamante, "New Mexico in the Eighteenth Century," 351, 359, 369–76; Weber, *The Spanish Frontier in North America*, 234–35, 310; Gutiérrez, *When Jesus Came*, 303–304, 319, 320–22, 327; Gerald E. Poyo and Gilberto M. Hinojosa, "Spanish Texas and Borderlands Historiography in Transition," *Journal of American History* 75 (September 1988): 411–12.

18. The rate of intermarriage with the native population was probably similar to or slightly higher than that in central Mexico. See Castañeda, "Presidarias y Pobladores," 250–58.

19. Ramón Gutiérrez found that a fairly low percentage of *españoles* (13 percent) married outside their caste but that the widespread practice of concubinage and slavery increased the mestizo population considerably. His analysis of the 1790 census of New Mexico shows about 67 percent as *español*. He agrees with estimates that about one-third of New Mexico's population were *genízaro* (detribalized Indians). An exact count of mestizos in New Mexico is rendered difficult by the political blurring of the term *español*. See Gutiérrez, *When Jesus Came*, 197–204.

20. Bill Mason, "The Garrisons of San Diego Presidio: 1770–1794," *Journal of San Diego History* 24, no. 4 (Fall 1978): 419. There were 25 persons of African ancestry and seven of mixed Indian, Spanish background. Mason found that of the 49 *españoles*, seven had been classified as *mestizo* in earlier church records. See also Jones, *Los Paisanos*, 50–51, 130. Antonia Castañeda suggests that rape and concubinage were probably statistically more important sources of *mestizaje* than intermarriage ("*Presidarias y Pobladoras*," 286–87). See also David J. Weber, *The Mexican Frontier, 1821–1846: The American Southwest under Mexico* (Albuquerque: University of New Mexico Press, 1982), 214.

21. For a detailed discussion of the Iberian family values on the Spanish frontier, especially New Mexico, see Gutiérrez, *When Jesus Came*, chaps. 5 and 6.

two

1. MacLachlan and Rodríguez-O, *The Forging of the Cosmic Race*, 294, 293, 292.

2. Ibid., 291, 292.

3. Ibid., 296, 297, 298; David J. Weber, *The Mexican Frontier, 1821–1846: The American Southwest under Mexico* (Albuquerque, University of New Mexico Press, 1982), chap. 5; Poyo and Hinojosa, "Spanish Texas and Borderlands Historiography in Transition," 414.

4. Gutiérrez, *When Jesus Came*, 337; Richard L. Nostrand, *The Hispano Homeland* (Norman: University of Oklahoma Press, 1992), 46–47; James E. Officer, *Hispanic Arizona, 1536–1856* (Tucson: University of Arizona Press, 1987), 84.

5. Jesús F. de la Teja, "Rebellion in the Frontier" (unpublished paper in files of Arnoldo De León); Weber, *The Mexican Frontier*, 9–10.

6. Weber, *The Mexican Frontier*, 20, 22, 24, 25, 28.

7. Ibid., 32, 35–36, 40, 41, 280.

8. Weber, *The Mexican Frontier*, 158–61, 164; David J. Weber, "Refighting the Alamo: Mythmaking and the Texas Revolution," in *Myth and the History of the Hispanic Southwest,* ed. David J. Weber (Albuquerque: University of New Mexico Press, 1988), 140–51.

9. Weber, *The Mexican Frontier*, 261–65, 270.

10. Ibid., 255–60, 269–70; Leonard Pitt, *The Decline of the Californios: A Social History of the Spanish-Speaking Californians, 1846–1900* (Berkeley: University of California Press, 1966), 7.

11. Weber, *The Mexican Frontier*, 265, 272, 274; Roxanne Dunbar Ortiz, *Roots of Resistance: Land Tenure in New Mexico, 1680–1980* (Los Angeles: Chicano Studies Research Center Publications and American Indian Studies Center, 1980), 86–87.

12. Weber, *The Mexican Frontier*, 13, 161, 162.

13. Officer, *Hispanic Arizona*, 106, 108, 110; Thomas E. Sheridan, *Los Tucsonenses: The Mexican Community in Tucson, 1854–1941* (Tucson: University of Arizona Press, 1986), 13–14; Weber, *The Mexican Frontier*, 183–84.

14. Monroy, *Thrown among Strangers,* 109–10, 157–58; Richard Griswold del Castillo, *The Los Angeles Barrio, 1850–1890: A Social History* (Berkeley: University of California Press, 1979), 6–7; Weber, *The Mexican Frontier*, 186, 190, 196, 205.

15. Janet Lecompte, "Manuel Armijo and the Americans," *Journal of the West* 19 (July 1980): 57–59; Marianne L. Stoller, "Grants of Desperation, Lands of Speculation: Mexican Period Land Grants in Colorado," *Journal of the West* 19 (July 1980), 22–39; Nostrand, *The Hispano Homeland*, 157; Weber, *The Mexican Frontier*, 190.

16. Officer, *Hispanic Arizona*, 5; Sheridan, *Los Tucsonenses*, 18.

17. Nostrand, *The Hispano Homeland*, 47, 48, 77, 92; Gutiérrez, *When Jesus Came*, 170.

18. Weber, *The Mexican Frontier*, 1, 4, 5, 6, 183, 191, 196, 198, 206; Pitt, *The Decline of the Californios*, 7–8, 10; Albert Camarillo, *Chicanos in a Changing Society: From Mexican Pueblos to American Barrios in Santa Barbara and Southern California, 1848–1930* (Cambridge: Harvard University Press, 1979), 9.

19. Weber, *The Mexican Frontier*, 195, 206, 184; Officer, *Hispanic Arizona*, 4, 214; Nostrand, *The Hispano Homeland*, 157; Gutiérrez, *When Jesus Came*, 167, 169, 327.

20. John Francis Bannon, *The Spanish Borderlands Frontier, 1513–1821* (New York: Holt, Rhinehart & Winston, 1970), 209, 215, 216–18.

21. Gutiérrez, *When Jesus Came,* 320–21; David Sandoval, "Gnats, Goods, and Greasers: Mexican Merchants on the Santa Fe Trail," *Journal of the West* 28 (April 1989): 22–23, 24, 27–28; Weber, *The Mexican Frontier*, 129, 130, 329n16; John M. Townley, "El Placer: A New Mexican Mining Boom before 1846," *Journal of the West* 10 (January 1971): 102, 104–105; Rebecca McDowell Craver, *The Impact of Intimacy: Mexican-Anglo Intermarriage in New Mexico, 1821–1846* (El Paso: Texas Western Press, 1982), 18–19.

22. Weber, *The Mexican Frontier*, 13–14, 129, 130; Officer, *Hispanic Arizona*, 104–106; Sheridan, *Los Tucsonenses*, 23.

23. Monroy, *Thrown among Strangers*, 154–55, 157, 158, 171–72; Weber, *The Mexican Frontier*, 13–14, 133–34, 135.

24. Raymund A. Paredes, "The Mexican Image in American Travel Literature, 1831–1869," *New Mexico Historical Review* 52 (January 1977): 5–13; Pitt, *The Decline of the Californios*, 14–18; Reginald Horsman, *Race and Manifest Destiny: The Origins of*

American Racial Anglo-Saxonism (Cambridge: Harvard University Press, 1981), 208–10.

25. Craver, *The Impact of Intimacy*, 3, 7.

26. Ibid., 4–5, 14; Pitt, *The Decline of the Californios*, 18–19.

27. Craver, *The Impact of Intimacy*, 27, 29, 30, 31–32, 38; Griswold del Castillo, *The Los Angeles Barrio*, 22.

28. Carver, *The Impact of Intimacy*, 16–17, 18–19; Monroy, *Thrown among Strangers*, 158.

29. Monroy, *Thrown among Strangers*, 158–59, 160–61; Craver, *The Impact of Intimacy*, 10–11, 13, 15, 17, 18–19, 22; Jane Dysart, "Mexican Women in San Antonio, 1830–1860: The Assimilation Process," *Western Historical Quarterly* 7 (October 1976): 370, 371; David Montejano, *Anglos and Mexicans in the Making of Texas, 1836–1986* (Austin: University of Texas Press, 1987), 34–37.

30. Weber, *The Mexican Frontier*, 179, 196, 198; Pitt, *The Decline of the Californios*, 19.

31. John R. Chávez, *The Lost Land: The Chicano Image of the Southwest* (Albuquerque: University of New Mexico Press, 1984), 35–41; Weber, *The Mexican Frontier*, 275.

three

1. Oscar J. Martínez, "On the Size of the Chicano Population: New Estimates, 1850–1900," *Aztlán* 6 (Spring 1975): 50–56.

2. Arthur F. Corwin, ed., *Immigrants—and Immigrants: Perspectives on Mexican Labor Migration to the United States* (Westport, Conn.: Greenwood Press, 1978), 25–26, 27, 29; Richard Griswold del Castillo, *La Familia: Chicano Families in the Urban Southwest, 1848 to the Present* (Notre Dame, Ind.: University of Notre Dame Press, 1984), 57–58; Nostrand, *The Hispano Homeland,* 159, 161; Erasmo Gamboa, "The Mexican Mule Pack System of Transportation in the Pacific Northwest and British Columbia," *Journal of the West*, 29 (January 1990): 20.

3. Griswold del Castillo, *The Los Angeles Barrio,* 133–34, 139.

4. Monroy, *Thrown among Strangers,* 206; Montejano, *Anglos and Mexicans in the Making of Texas,* 84; Darlis A. Miller, "Hispanos and the Civil War in New Mexico: A Reconsideration," *New Mexico Historical Review* 54 (April 1979): 105.

5. Montejano, *Anglos and Mexicans in the Making of Texas,* 316; Nostrand, *The Hispano Homeland*, 71, 80, 81, 82, 84–98; Sheridan, *Los Tucsonenses,* 33; Monroy, *Thrown among Strangers,* 206; Arthur L. Campa, *Hispanic Culture in the Southwest* (Norman: University of Oklahoma Press, 1979), 143–44, 148–49.

6. Montejano, *Anglos and Mexicans in the Making of Texas,* 316; Nostrand, *The Hispano Homeland,* 96, 112–14; Monroy, *Thrown among Strangers,* 206; Sheridan, *Los Tucsonenses,* 31, 33, 42.

7. Montejano, *Anglos and Mexicans in the Making of Texas,* 34, 37, 41, 310–11, 314; Griswold del Castillo, *La Familia,* 67–68, 69; Monroy, *Thrown among Strangers,* 206, 222; Sheridan, *Los Tucsonenses,* 42, 43; Robert J. Rosenbaum, *Mexicano Resistance in the Southwest: "The Sacred Right of Self-Preservation"* (Austin: University of Texas Press, 1981), 25; Pitt, *Decline of the Californios,* 131–32.

8. Sheridan, *Los Tucsonenses,* 41–42; Manuel G. Gonzales, *The Hispanic Elite of the Southwest* (El Paso: University of Texas at El Paso Press, 1989), 14–15, 16, 17; Pitt, *Decline of the Californios,* 271–72.

9. Montejano, *Anglos and Mexicans in the Making of Texas,* 52, 311; Pitt, *Decline of the Californios,* 101.

10. Jay J. Wagoner, *Early Arizona: Prehistory to the Civil War* (Tucson: University of Arizona Press, 1975), 162–63.

11. Montejano, *Anglos and Mexicans in the Making of Texas*, 311; Monroy, *Thrown among Strangers*, 203, 204–205; Pitt, *Decline of the Californios*, 91, 95, 98, 107–108, 250–51.

12. Pitt, *Decline of the Californios*, 98–99; Monroy, *Thrown among Strangers*, 159.

13. Montejano, *Anglos and Mexicans in the Making of Texas*, 51, 60, 313–14, 312–13; Monroy, *Thrown among Strangers*, 224–25; Pitt, *Decline of the Californios*, 99–100, 108–109, 250–51.

14. Monroy, *Thrown among Strangers*, 230–32; Pitt, *Decline of the Californios*, 244–48; Montejano, *Anglos and Mexicans in the Making of Texas*, 58, 59.

15. Montejano, *Anglos and Mexicans in the Making of Texas*, 76–77, 79–86, 313; Monroy, *Thrown among Strangers*, 183, 185, 187; Nostrand, *The Hispano Homeland*, 75, 76; Miller, "Hispanos and the Civil War in New Mexico," 108, 117; George I. Sánchez, *Forgotten People: A Study of New Mexicans* (Albuquerque: C. Horn, 1967), 58–59.

16. Camarillo, *Chicanos in a Changing Society,* 129, 132.

17. Arnoldo De León and Kenneth L. Stewart, *Tejanos and the Numbers Game: A Socio-Historical Interpretation from the Federal Censuses, 1850–1900* (Albuquerque: University of New Mexico Press, 1989), 33–35; Camarillo, *Chicanos in a Changing Society*, 127, 129, 135; Sheridan, *Los Tucsonenses*, 35–36.

18. Griswold del Castillo, *La Familia*, 34, 36.

19. Arnoldo De León and Kenneth L. Stewart, "A Tale of Three Cities: Comparative Analysis of the Socio-Economic Conditions of Mexican Americans in Los Angeles, Tucson, and San Antonio, 1850–1900," *Journal of the West* 24 (April 1985): 58–69.

20. Nostrand, *The Hispano Homeland*, 106; Arnoldo De León, *They Called Them Greasers: Anglo Attitudes Toward Mexicans in Texas, 1821–1900* (Austin: University of Texas Press, 1983), chaps. 3 and 4; Monroy, *Thrown among Strangers*, 206; Sheridan, *Los Tucsonenses*, 32, 33; Pitt, *Decline of the Californios*, 71; Darlis A. Miller, "Cross-Cultural Marriages in the Southwest: The New Mexico Experience, 1846–1900," *New Mexico Historical Review* 57 (October 1982): 340.

21. Montejano, *Anglos and Mexicans in the Making of Texas*, 64–85; Monroy, *Thrown among Strangers*, 207, 222; Pitt, *Decline of the Californios*, 53, 68, 69; Sheridan, *Los Tucsonenses*, 23, 34, 42; Nostrand, *The Hispano Homeland*, 96, 112–14.

22. Montejano, *Anglos and Mexican in the Making of Texas*, 28–30, 32–33, 53; De León, *They Called Them Greasers*, chaps. 7 and 8.

23. Rosenbaum, *Mexicano Resistance in the Southwest*, 90–98.

24. Virginia Culin Roberts, "Francisco Gándara and the 'War on the Gila,'" *Journal of Arizona History* 24 (Autumn 1983): 221–32; Sheridan, *Los Tucsonenses*, 36; Andrés E. Jiménez Montoya, "Political Domination in the Labor Market: Racial Division in the Arizona Copper Industry" (Berkeley: Institute for the Study of Social Change, 1977), 18–19.

25. Monroy, *Thrown among Strangers*, 218–19; Pitt, *Decline of the Californios*, 70–74, 229; Rosenbaum, *Mexicano Resistance in the Southwest*, 61–63.

26. Rosenbaum, *Mexicano Resistance in the Southwest*, 25–26, 27; Montejano, *Anglos and Mexicans in the Making of Texas*, 40.

27. Montejano, *Anglos and Mexicans in the Making of Texas*, 40–41; Rosenbaum, *Mexicano Resistance in the Southwest*, 27; Pitt, *Decline of the Californios*, 131–32; Sheridan, *Los Tucsonenses*, 46; Gonzales, *Hispanic Elite of the Southwest*, 19–28.

28. Montejano, *Anglos and Mexicans in the Making of Texas*, 39–40; Sheridan, *Los*

Tucsonenses, 46; Pitt, *Decline of the Californios*, 133–34; Gonzales, *Hispanic Elite of the Southwest*, 9–11, 22–25.

29. Sheridan, *Los Tucsonenses*, 42–46; Campa, *Hispanic Culture in the Southwest*, 151–52.

30. Pitt, *Decline of the Californios*, 131, 134–47, 197; Rosenbaum, *Mexicano Resistance in the Southwest*, 26, 27; Gonzales, *Hispanic Elite of the Southwest*, 12–15; Maurilio Vigil, *Los Patrones: Profiles of Hispanic Political Leaders in New Mexico History* (Washington, D.C.: University Press of America, 1980), 45–47, 29–31.

31. Jerry Don Thompson, *Vaqueros in Blue and Gray* (Austin: Presidial Press, 1976), 5–24; Miller, "Hispanos and the Civil War in New Mexico," 112–17.

32. Rosenbaum, *Mexicano Resistance in the Southwest*, 42–45; Montejano, *Anglos and Mexicans in the Making of Texas*, 32–33; Jerry D. Thompson, "The Many Faces of Juan Nepomuceno Cortina," in *Conference on South Texas Studies*, vol. 2 (Victoria: Victoria College Press, 1991), 85–98.

33. Pitt, *Decline of the Californios*, 77–81; Rosenbaum, *Mexicano Resistance in the Southwest*, 53, 55, 58–59.

34. Rosenbaum, *Mexicano Resistance in the Southwest*, 53, 55–58; Pitt, *Decline of the Californios*, 262.

35. Rosenbaum, *Mexicano Resistance in the Southwest*, 61–64; Pitt, *Decline of the Californios*, 167–71.

36. Mary Romero, "El Paso Salt War: Mob Action or Political Struggle?" *Aztlán* 16, nos. 1–2 (1985): 119–43.

37. Griswold del Castillo, *La Familia*, 38–39; Miller, "Cross-Cultural Marriages in the Southwest," 344, 346.

38. Griswold del Castillo, *La Familia*, 42, 78; Deutsch, *No Separate Refuge*, 42–44.

39. Miller, "Cross-Cultural Marriages in the Southwest," 339, 340, 341, 342; Deena L. González, "Widowed Women of Santa Fe: Assessments on the Lives of Unmarried Population, 1850–1880," in *On Their Own: Widows and Widowhood in the American Southwest, 1848–1939*, ed. Arlene Scadron (Urbana: University of Illinois Press, 1988), 80; Pitt, *Decline of the Californios*, 268; Monroy, *Thrown among Strangers*, 222.

40. Miller, "Cross-Cultural Marriages in the Southwest," 344; Susan L. Johnson, "Sharing Bed and Board: Cohabitation and Cultural Differences in Central Arizona Mining Towns, 1863–1873," in Susan H. Armitage and Elizabeth Jameson, *The Women's West* (Norman: University of Oklahoma Press, 1987), 78, 82, 88.

41. Griswold del Castillo, *La Familia*, 31–32, 38, 68.

42. Miller, "Cross-Cultural Marriages in the Southwest," 347, 352–53; Johnson, "Sharing Bed and Board," 81; Janet Lecompte, "The Independent Women of Hispanic New Mexico, 1821–1846," *Western Historical Quarterly* 12 (January 1981): 35.

43. Pitt, *Decline of the Californios*, 215; Nostrand, *The Hispano Homeland*, 109; Griswold del Castillo, *La Familia*, 81, 83; Griswold del Castillo, *The Los Angeles Barrio*, 161, 169; Campa, *Hispanic Culture in the Southwest*, 149, 150.

44. Pitt, *Decline of the Californios*, 215; Nostrand, *The Hispano Homeland*, 109; Griswold del Castillo, *The Los Angeles Barrio*, 169; Paul Horgan, *Lamy of Santa Fe: His Life and Times* (New York: Farrar, Straus & Giroux, 1975), 152, 240, 243, 250–61.

45. R. Douglas Brackenridge and Francisco O. García-Treto, *Iglesia Presbiteriana: A History of Presbyterians and Mexican Americans of the Southwest* (San Antonio: Trinity University Press, 1974), 12–13, 38–46, 63, 74, 79.

46. Sheridan, *Los Tucsonenses*, 46–47; Dianna Everett, "The Public School Debate in New Mexico, 1850–1891," *Arizona and the West* 26 (Summer 1984): 107–10; Guadalupe San Miguel, Jr., "Culture and Education in the American Southwest: Towards an Explanation of Chicano School Attendance, 1850–1940," *Journal of American Ethnic History* 7 (Spring 1988): 5–15; Arnoldo De León, *The Tejano Community, 1836–1900* (Albuquerque: University of New Mexico Press, 1982), 189; De León and Stewart, *Tejanos and the Numbers Game*, 85–86; Griswold del Castillo, *The Los Angeles Barrio*, 86–87.

four

1. Howard Robert Lamar, *The Far Southwest, 1846–1912: A Territorial History* (New Haven, Conn.: Yale University Press, 1966), 462–63; Nostrand, *The Hispano Homeland*, 116–17; Sheridan, *Los Tucsonenses*, 56.

2. Lawrence A. Cardoso, *Mexican Emigration to the United States, 1897–1931* (Tucson: University of Arizona Press, 1980), 19–20; Camarillo, *Chicanos in a Changing Society*, 81; Cletus E. Daniel, *Bitter Harvest: A History of California Farmworkers, 1870–1941* (Ithaca, N.Y.: Cornell University Press, 1981), 19, 21, 35.

3. Cardoso, *Mexican Emigration to the United States*, 19.

4. Montejano, *Anglos and Mexicans in the Making of Texas*, 103, 104, 109; Lamar, *The Far Southwest*, 467; Camarillo, *Chicanos in a Changing Society*, 81.

5. Cardoso, *Mexican Emigration to the United States*, 1, 5–7.

6. Ibid., 9–10.

7. Ibid., 2, 14–15.

8. Ibid., 18, 22, 28–30; Camarillo, *Chicanos in a Changing Society*, 137–38; Nostrand, *The Hispano Homeland*, 161–62.

9. Sheridan, *Los Tucsonenses*, 99, 106–107.

10. James A. Sandos, *Rebellion in the Borderlands: Anarchism and the Plan of San Diego, 1904–1923* (Norman: University of Oklahoma Press, 1992), 8–9.

11. Mario Barrera, *Race and Class in the Southwest: A Theory of Racial Inequality* (Notre Dame, Ind.: University of Notre Dame Press, 1979), 66, citing *Mexicans in California*, Report of Governor C. C. Young's Mexican Fact-Finding Committee, October 1930, Table 9, 31. Oscar Martínez, a border historian, puts the number as high as 381,000 to 562,000 for 1900 but does not break down figures by state for that decennial year, nor does he provide an estimate for the overall 1910 population. Oscar J. Martínez, "On the Size of the Chicano Population: New Estimates, 1850–1900," *Aztlán* 6 (Spring 1975): 56, Table 4.

12. Erlinda Gonzales-Berry, ed., *Pasó Por Aquí: Critical Essays on the New Mexican Literary Tradition, 1542–1988* (Albuquerque: University of New Mexico Press, 1989), 10n7.

13. Deutsch, *No Separate Refuge*, 75, 77.

14. Ibid., 38–39; Nostrand, *The Hispano Homeland*, 123; Pitt, *Decline of the Californios*, 267–68; Griswold del Castillo, *The Los Angeles Barrio*, 171–72; De León, *The Tejano Community*, 205–206.

15. De León, *They Called Them Greasers*, 60–61; Deutsch, *No Separate Refuge*, 39, 86; Camarillo, *Chicanos in a Changing Society*, 65; De León, *The Tejano Community*, 205–206; Sheridan, *Los Tucsonenses*, 109–10.

16. Deutsch, *No Separate Refuge*, 4, 31–35, 88; Nostrand, *The Hispano Homeland*, 131, 143, 148, 193–96.

17. Cardoso, *Mexican Emigration to the United States*, 24–25, 26, 27, 29; Griswold del Castillo, *La Familia*, 58; Michael M. Smith, "Beyond the Borderlands: Mexican Labor in the Central Plains, 1900–1930," *Great Plains Quarterly* (Fall 1981): 242.

18. Terry G. Jordan, "A Century and a Half of Ethnic Change in Texas, 1836–1986," *Southwestern Historical Quarterly* 89 (April 1986): 398–99; Montejano, *Anglos and Mexicans in the Making of Texas*, 104.

19. Nostrand, *The Hispano Homeland*, 119–27; Deutsch, *No Separate Refuge*, 19.

20. Pitt, *The Decline of the Californios*, 249–50, 274–75.

21. Sheridan, *Los Tucsonenses*, 50; Lamar, *The Far Southwest*, 465, 467; Suzanne Forrest, *The Preservation of the Village: New Mexico's Hispanics and the New Deal* (Albuquerque: University of New Mexico Press, 1989), 64; De León, *They Called Them Greasers*, 45.

22. Sheridan, *Los Tucsonenses*, 149–50; Pitt, *Decline of the Californios*, 268; Montejano, *Anglos and Mexicans in the Making of Texas*, 92.

23. Pitt, *Decline of the Californios*, 254, 275–76; Deutsch, *No Separate Refuge*, 28–29; Sheridan, *Los Tucsonenses*, 70–71.

24. Sheridan, *Los Tucsonenses*, 53–54, 99; Pitt, *The Decline of the Californios*, 268–69; Mario T. García, *Desert Immigrants: The Mexicans of El Paso, 1880–1920* (New Haven, Conn.: Yale University Press, 1981), 79–84; De León, *The Tejano Community*, 96, 97.

25. De León, *The Tejano Community*, 96, 97; Sheridan, *Los Tucsonenses*, 48–49, 50–52, 96–97, 102–103.

26. Sheridan, *Los Tucsonenses*, 48, 53, 73; Deutsch, *No Separate Refuge*, 19, 21; Lamar, *The Far Southwest*, 488; Pitt, *Decline of the Californios*, 275; Montejano, *Anglos and Mexicans in the Making of Texas*, 92, 94.

27. William B. Taylor and Elliott West, "Patrón Leadership at the Crossroads: Southern Colorado in the Late Nineteenth Century," in *The Chicano*, ed. Norris Hundley, Jr. (Santa Barbara: Clio Press, 1975), 75–80, 94–95; Camarillo, *Chicanos in a Changing Society*, 94–95; Montejano, *Anglos and Mexicans in the Making of Texas*, 110, 314–15; Deutsch, *No Separate Refuge*, 22–23.

28. Cardoso, *Mexican Emigration to the United States*, 19–20; Smith, "Beyond the Borderlands," 248.

29. Pitt, *Decline of the Californios*, 255–56; Smith, "Beyond the Borderlands," 243, 246; Cardoso, *Mexican Emigration to the United States*, 26–27; Nostrand, *The Hispano Homeland*, 140.

30. Camarillo, *Chicanos in a Changing Society*, 98–99, 136–39; Sheridan, *Los Tucsonenses*, 29; Smith, "Beyond the Borderlands," 243, 246; García, *Desert Immigrants*, chap. 4; De León, *The Tejano Community*, chap. 4.

31. Camarillo, *Chicanos in a Changing Society*, 53–54; Nostrand, *The Hispano Homeland*, 116.

32. Sheridan, *Los Tucsonenses*, 126–27, 150; Cardoso, *Mexican Emigration to the United States*, 27; García, *Desert Immigrants*, 135–36, 139–41; Nostrand, *The Hispano Homeland*, 143, 195–96; Griswold del Castillo, *The Los Angeles Barrio*, 145–46.

33. Sheridan, *Los Tucsonenses*, 80, 99; Griswold del Castillo, *The Los Angeles Barrio*, 149–50.

34. Lamar, *The Far Southwest*, 491, 493–94; Sheridan, *Los Tucsonenses*, 125; Camarillo, *Chicanos in a Changing Society*, 77; Deutsch, *No Separate Refuge*, 37, 102; José E. Limón, "El Primer Congreso Mexicanista de 1911: A Precursor to Contemporary Chicanismo," *Aztlán* 5 (Spring and Fall 1974): 89.

35. Monroy, *Thrown among Strangers*, 259–71; Camarillo, *Chicanos in a Changing Society*, 70; Chávez, *The Lost Land*, 259–71.

36. Chávez, *The Lost Land*, 92; Gonzales-Berry, *Pasó Por Aquí*, 3–4, 10n7.

37. Jean F. Riis, "The Lynching of Francisco Torres," *Journal of Mexican American History* 2 (Spring 1972): 90–121; De León, *They Called Them Greasers*, 104–105.

38. Sheridan, *Los Tucsonenses*, 91; Griswold del Castillo, *The Los Angeles Barrio*, 117–19; Edward J. Escobar, "Mexican Revolutionaries and the Los Angeles Police: Harassment of the Partido Liberal Mexicano, 1907–1910," *Aztlán* 17 (Spring 1986): 1–46.

39. Pitt, *Decline of the Californios*, 273–74; Sheridan, *Los Tucsonenses*, 121; Deutsch, *No Separate Refuge*, 29.

40. Montejano, *Anglos and Mexicans in the Making of Texas*, 143; Taylor and West, "Patrón Leadership at the Crossroads," 78–79, 94–95.

41. Deutsch, *No Separate Refuge*, 28–29.

42. Sheridan, *Los Tucsonenses*, 50, 109; De León, *The Tejano Community*, 32–33, 40–41; Rosenbaum, *Mexicano Resistance in the Southwest*, 146–47.

43. Sheridan, *Los Tucsonenses*, 114–15; De León, *The Tejano Community*, 39; Fernando V. Padilla and Carlos B. Ramírez, "Patterns of Chicano Representation in California, Colorado, and Nuevo Mexico," *Aztlán* 5 (Spring and Fall 1974): 222, 224.

44. Tobías Durán, "Francisco Chávez, Thomas B. Catron, and Organized Political Violence in Santa Fe in the 1890s," *New Mexico Historical Review* 59 (July 1984): 291; Sheridan, *Los Tucsonenses*, 106; Jerry D. Thompson, *Warm Weather and Bad Whiskey: The 1886 Laredo Election Riot* (El Paso: Texas Western Press, 1991).

45. De León, *They Called Them Greasers*, 61–62; Chávez, *The Lost Land*, 72–75; Richard Melzer and Phyllis Ann Mingus, "Wild to Fight: The New Mexico Rough Riders in the Spanish American War," *New Mexico Historical Review* 59 (April 1984): 109–136; Graeme S. Mount, "Nuevo Mexicanos and the War of 1898," *New Mexico Historical Review* 58 (October 1983): 381–96.

46. Sheridan, *Los Tucsonenses*, 117–20; Arnoldo De León, *Mexican Americans in Texas: A Brief History* (Arlington Heights, Ill.: Harlan Davidson, 1993), 55–56; Pitt, *Decline of the Californios*, 272–73.

47. Lamar, *The Far Southwest*, 500; Deutsch, *No Separate Refuge*, 29; Sheridan, *Los Tucsonenses*, 49, 50; Chávez, *The Lost Land*, 57–58, 60, 61; Lynn I. Perrigo, *Hispanos: Historic Leaders in New Mexico* (Santa Fe: Sunstone Press, 1985), 54, 56, 62–64, 70–71; Padilla and Ramírez, "Patterns of Chicano Representation," 190–91, 203, 210. On Miguel A. Otero, see further the special issue of the *New Mexico Historical Review* 67 (January 1992).

48. Vigil, *Los Patrones*, 87–93.

49. Padilla and Ramírez, "Patterns of Chicano Representation," 218.

50. Larry D. Ball, *Elfego Baca in Life and Legend* (El Paso: University of Texas Press, 1992); Sheridan, *Los Tucsonenses*, 99–100.

51. Rosenbaum, *Mexicano Resistance in the Southwest*, 68–70, 72–90.

52. Ibid., 99–124; Deutsch, *No Separate Refuge*, 26; Robert W. Larson, "The Knights of Labor and Native Protest in New Mexico," in *Labor in New Mexico: Unions, Strikes, and Social History since 1881*, ed. Robert Kern (Albuquerque: University of New Mexico Press, 1983), 31–52.

53. Rosenbaum, *Mexicano Resistance in the Southwest*, 125–48; Larson, "Knights of Labor and Native Protest in New Mexico," 31–52.

54. García, *Desert Immigrants*, 97; Emilio Zamora, *The World of the Mexican Worker in Texas* (College Station: Texas A & M University Press, 1993), 56–57, 119–22, 71–81; Mario T. García, "Racial Dualism in the El Paso Labor Market, 1880–1920," *Aztlán* 6 (Summer 1975): 213.

55. Charles Wollenberg, "Working on El Traque: The Pacific Electric Strike of 1903," in *The Chicano*, 96–107.

56. Camarillo, *Chicanos in a Changing Society*, 170–71; Juan Gómez-Quiñones, "The First Steps: Chicano Labor Conflict and Organizing, 1900–1920," *Aztlán: Chicano Journal of Social Sciences and the Arts* 3 (Spring 1972): 24–26, 28.

57. Joseph F. Park, "The 1903 'Mexican Affair' at Clifton," *Journal of Arizona History* 18 (Summer 1977): 135–46; Gómez-Quiñones, "The First Steps," 23, 24; Phil Mellinger, "'The Men Have Become Organizers': Labor Conflict and Unionization in the Mexican Mining Communities of Arizona, 1900–1915," *Western Historical Quarterly* 23 (August 1992): 323–47.

58. Sandos, *Rebellion in the Borderlands*, 8–11; Escobar, "Mexican Revolutionaries and the Los Angeles Police," 11; Gómez-Quiñones, "The First Steps," 28.

59. Sheridan, *Los Tucsonenses*, 135–41, 145; Griswold del Castillo, *La Familia*, 42–43.

60. Sheridan, *Los Tucsonenses*, 141–42; Deutsch, *No Separate Refuge*, 5; Griswold del Castillo, *La Familia*, 86–87.

61. Sheridan, *Los Tucsonenses*, 136–38; De León and Stewart, *Tejanos and the Numbers Game*, 63–65.

62. Deutsch, *No Separate Refuge*, 74–76.

63. Camarillo, *Chicanos in a Changing Society*, 90–93, 99; Sheridan, *Los Tucsonenses*, 129; Deutsch, *No Separate Refuge*, 34; García, *Desert Immigrants*, 74–79; Griswold del Castillo, *La Familia*, 34.

64. Camarillo, *Chicanos in a Changing Society*, 90–93, 99; Sheridan, *Los Tucsonenses*, 129; Deutsch, *No Separate Refuge*, 34, 35, 56; García, *Desert Immigrants*, 74–79.

65. Griswold del Castillo, *La Familia*, 44; Zamora, "Mexican Labor Activity in South Texas," 98–100; Sheridan, *Los Tucsonenses*, 142; Deutsch, *No Separate Refuge*, 102.

66. Sandra L. Stephens, "The Women of the Amador Family," in Joan M. Jensen and Darlis A. Miller, eds., *New Mexico Women: Intercultural Perspectives* (Albuquerque: University of New Mexico Press, 1986), 261, 263, 264; Jovita González, "America Invades the Border Towns," *Southwest Review* 15 (Summer 1930): 469.

67. Darlis A. Miller, "The Women of Lincoln County, 1860–1900," in *New Mexico Women*, 182, 184.

68. Griswold del Castillo, *La Familia*, 90–91; Griswold del Castillo, *The Los Angeles Barrio*, 169; De León, *The Tejano Community*, 152–54.

69. Sheridan, *Los Tucsonenses*, 151, 158–63; García, *Desert Immigrants*, 222–23.

70. Brackenridge and García-Treto, *Iglesia Presbiteriana*, 22, 23, 31, 62; García, *Desert Immigrants*, 219–20.

71. García, *Desert Immigrants*, 112–13; Dianna Everett, "The Public School Debate in New Mexico, 1850–1891," *Arizona and the West* 26 (Summer 1984): 133–34; San Miguel, "Culture and Education in the American Southwest," 10–11, 13–14.

72. San Miguel, "Culture and Education in the American Southwest," 7, 12.

73. Deutsch, *No Separate Refuge*, 64, 75; San Miguel, "Culture and Education in the American Southwest," 8–9, 12.

74. Perrigo, *Hispanos: Hispanic Leaders in New Mexico*, 58, 62–63.

75. Sheridan, *Los Tucsonenses*, 107–109; Griswold del Castillo, *The Los Angeles Barrio*, 135–38; Garcia, *Desert Immigrants*, 223–24; De León, *The Tejano Community*, 195–96; José Amaro Hernández, *Mutual Aid for Survival: The Case of the Mexican American* (Malabar, Fla.: Robert E. Krieger Publishing Co., 1983).

76. Sheridan, *Los Tucsonenses*, 108–109, 111–13; Manuel G. Gonzales, "Carlos I. Velasco," *Journal of Arizona History* 25 (Autumn 1984): 276–79; Olivia Arrieta, "The Alianza Hispano Americana in Arizona and New Mexico: The Development and Maintenance of a Multifunctional Ethnic Organization," 7 Series 1989–1990, *Renato Rosaldo Lecture Series Monograph* (Tucson: Mexican American Studies and Research Center, University of Arizona, 1991), 59–82.

77. Griswold del Castillo, *The Los Angeles Barrio*, 135–38.

78. Marcienne Rocard, *The Children of the Sun: Mexican Americans in the Literature of the United States* (Tucson: University of Arizona Press, 1989), 83–86, 104–105; Raymund A. Paredes, "The Evolution of Chicano Literature," in *Three American Literatures: Essays in Chicano, Native American, and Asian-American Literature for Teachers of American Literature*, ed. Houston A. Baker, Jr. (New York: Modern Languages Association of America, 1982); José E. Limón, "Healing the Wounds: Folk Symbols and Historical Crisis," *Texas Humanist* 6 (March–April 1984): 23.

79. Francisco Lomelí, "A Literary Portrait of Hispanic New Mexico: Dialectics of Perspective," in *Pasó Por Aquí*, 140.

80. Sheridan, *Los Tucsonenses*, 102–107, 148; Doris L. Meyer, "Early Mexican-American Responses to Negative Stereotyping," *New Mexico Historical Review* 53 (January 1978): 77, 79–85; Gonzales, "Carlos I. Velasco," 255–76; Clara Lomas, "The Articulation of Gender in the Mexican Borderlands, 1900–1915," in Ramón Gutiérrez and Genaro Padilla, eds., *Recovering the U.S. Hispanic Heritage* (Houston: Arte Público Press, 1993), 295, 296.

81. Rosembaum, *Mexicano Resistance in the Southwest*, 131–32.

82. Porter A. Stratton, *The Territorial Press of New Mexico, 1834–1912* (Albuquerque: University of New Mexico Press, 1969), 130–37, 90; De León, *The Tejano Community*, 197–201; Meyer, "Early Mexican-American Responses to Negative Stereotyping," 75–91; Lomas, "Articulation of Gender," 299–302; Nicolás Kanellos, "A Socio-Historic Study of Hispanic Newspapers in the United States," in *Recovering the U.S. Hispanic Literary Heritage*, 117.

83. Lomelí, "A Literary Portrait of Hispanic New Mexico: Dialectics of Perspective," in *Pasó Por Aqui*, 140–42; Rocard, *Children of the Sun*, 68–69; Paredes, "Evolution of Chicano Literature," 47–48; Emilio Zamora, Jr., "Sara Estela Ramírez: Note on Research," *Hembra* (Spring 1976): 4–6; Luis Leal, "Truth Telling Tongues: Early Chicano Poetry," in *Recovering the U.S. Hispanic Literary Heritage*, 91–105.

84. Charles M. Tatum, *Chicano Literature* (Boston: Twayne Publishers, 1982), 30–31.

85. Lomelí, "A Literary Portrait of Hispanic New Mexico: Dialectics of Perspective," in *Pasó Por Aquí*, 149–64.

86. E. A. Mares, "The Wraggle-Taggle Outlaws: Vicente Silva and Billy the Kid as Seen in Two Nineteenth Century Documents," in *Pasó Por Aquí*, 169–74; Tatum, *Chicano Literature*, 30–32.

87. Kathleen Crawford, "María Amparo Ruíz Burton," *Journal of San Diego History* (Spring 1990), 188–21.

88. Lomelí, "A Literary Portrait of Hispanic New Mexico: Dialectics of Perspective," in *Pasó Por Aquí*, 142.

89. Paredes, "Evolution of Chicano Literature," 48; Genaro M. Padilla, "The Recovery of Chicano Nineteenth-Century Autobiography," *American Quarterly* 40 (September 1988): 290; Genaro M. Padilla, "Recoverinq Mexican-American Autobiography," in *Recovering the U.S. Hispanic Literary Heritage*, 164; Jacqueline Dorgan Meketa, ed., *Legacy of Honor: The Life of Rafael Chacón, a Nineteenth-Century New Mexican* (Albuquerque: University of New Mexico Press, 1986).

90. Nicolás Kanellos, *A History of Hispanic Theatre in the United States* (Austin: University of Texas Press, 1990), 14–15, 21, 71–73, 184–85; De León, *The Tejano Community*, 144–45; Griswold del Castillo, *La Familia*, 85–86.

five

1. Cletus Daniel, *Bitter Harvest: A History of California Farm Workers, 1870–1941* (Ithaca, N.Y.: Cornell University Press, 1981), 108; Mark Reisler, *By the Sweat of Their Brow: Mexican Immigrant Labor in the United States, 1900–1940* (Westport, Conn.: Greenwood Press, 1976), 6–7, 78–79; Sheridan, *Los Tucsonenses*, 166–67; Dennis Nodín Valdes, *Al Norte: Agricultural Workers in the Great Lakes Region, 1917–1970* (Austin: University of Texas Press, 1991), 3–4.

2. Michael P. Malone and Richard W. Etulain, *The American West: A Twentieth-Century History* (Lincoln: University of Oklahoma Press, 1989), 36–45.

3. Sheridan, *Los Tucsonenses*, 166; Malone and Etulain, *The American West*, 23; Michael M. Smith, *The Mexicans in Oklahoma* (Norman: University of Oklahoma Press, 1980), 45.

4. Francisco Arturo Rosales and Daniel T. Simon, "Mexican Immigrant Experience in the Urban Midwest: East Chicago Indiana, 1919–1945," in *Forging a Community: The Latino Experience in Northwest Indiana, 1919–1975*, ed. James B. Lane and Edward J. Escobar (Chicago: Cattails Press, 1987), 138.

5. Cardoso, *Mexican Emigration to the United States*, 28–29, 38, 47, 51–52, 71, 84, 85; Deutsch, *No Separate Refuge*, 109, 120; Gilberto Cárdenas, "United States Immigration Policy towards Mexico: A Historical Perspective," *Chicano Law Review* 2 (Summer 1975): 67–69; Valdes, *Al Norte*, 8–11.

6. Ricardo Romo, "The Urbanization of Southwestern Chicanos in the Early Twentieth Century," in *New Directions in Chicano Scholarship*, ed. Ricardo Romo and Raymund A. Paredes (La Jolla: University of California at San Diego, 1978), 194.

7. Cardoso, *Mexican Emigration to the United States*, 82; Ricardo Romo, *East Los Angeles: History of a Barrio* (Austin: University of Texas Press, 1983), 52; *Immigrants—and Immigrants*, 117; Richard A. García, *Rise of the Mexican American Middle Class: San Antonio, 1929–1941* (College Station: Texas A & M University Press, 1991), 34.

8. Cardoso, *Mexican Emigration to the United States*, 41; Sheridan, *Los Tucsonenses*, 166.

9. Daniel D. Arreola, "Mexico Origins of South Texas Mexican Americans, 1930," *Journal of Historical Geography* 19 (1993): 49, 55, 61; Romo, *East Los Angeles*, 52; Michael M. Smith, "Mexicans in Kansas City: The First Generation, 1900–1920," in *Perspectives in Mexican American Studies*, vol. 2, ed. Juan R. García et al. (Tucson: Mexican American Studies and Research Center, 1989), 30.

10. García, *Rise of the Mexican American Middle Class*, 35; Michael M. Smith, "Social and Political Dynamics of the Kansas City Colonia during the Mexican Revolution: The Role of the Unión Mexicana Benito Juárez and Middle Class

Leadership," in *Five Centuries of Mexican History,* ed. Virginia Guedea and Jaime E. Rodríguez-O (Irvine: University of California, 1991), 387, 388.

11. Juan Gómez-Quiñones, *Sembradores: Ricardo Flores Magón and El Partido Liberal Mexicano: A Eulogy and a Critique* (Los Angeles: Aztlán Publications, 1973), 41–52, 57–60, 68; Sandos, *Rebellion in the Borderlands,* 18, 27, 33, 36, 44, 133–34, 169–70.

12. Romo, *East Los Angeles,* 12, 149–150, 155–56; García, *Desert Immigrants,* 202–203; Reisler, *By the Sweat of Their Brow,* 111–13; Smith, "Social and Political Dynamics of the Kansas City Colonia," 387, 388; F. Arturo Rosales, "Mexicans, Interethnic Violence, and Crime in the Chicago Area during the 1920s and 1930s: The Struggle to Achieve Ethnic Consciousness," in *Perspectives in Mexican American Studies,* 63, 64–65.

13. García, *Desert Immigrants,* 211–12; Juan R. García and Angel Cal, "El Círculo de Obreros Católicos 'San Jose,' 1925 to 1930," in *Forging a Community,* 104; Smith, *Mexicans in Oklahoma,* 53; Vicki Ruiz, *Cannery Women, Cannery Lives: Mexican Women, Unionization, and the California Food Processing Industry, 1930–1950* (Albuquerque: University of New Mexico Press, 1987), 10–13, 17–18; Zaragosa Vargas, *Proletarians of the North: A History of Mexican Industrial Workers in Detroit and the Midwest, 1917–1933* (Berkeley: University of California Press, 1993), 165–66, 138; Douglas Monroy, "'Our Children Get So Different Here': Film, Fashion, Popular Culture, and the Process of Cultural Syncretization in Mexican Los Angeles, 1900–1935," in *Aztlán: A Journal of Chicano Studies* 19 (Spring 1988–90): 79, 80, 83, 86, 102; Vicki L. Ruiz, "'Star Struck': Acculturation, Adolescence, and the Mexican American Woman, 1920–1950," in *Building with Our Hands: New Directions in Chicana Studies,* ed. Adela de la Torre and Beatriz M. Pesquera (Berkeley: University of California Press, 1993), 110–17.

14. García, *Desert Immigrants,* 218; Deutsch, *No Separate Refuge,* 107, 111–14.

15. Romo, *East Los Angeles,* 130, 132, 133; Albert Camarillo, *Chicanos in a Changing Society,* 160–61; García, *Desert Immigrants,* 149–50; Ruth Hutchinson Crocker, "Gary Mexicans and 'Christian Americanization': A Study in Cultural Conflict," in *Forging a Community,* 115–34; George I. Sánchez, *Go after the Women: Americanization and the Mexican Immigrant Woman, 1915–1929* (Stanford, Calif.: Stanford Center for Chicano Research, 1984), 1, 2, 9–12, 24–25.

16. Crocker, "Gary Mexicans," 128, 127, 118; Sánchez, *Go after the Women,* 22–23; Guadalupe San Miguel, Jr., "The Struggle against Separate and Unequal Schools: Middle Class Mexican Americans and the Desegregation Campaign in Texas, 1929–1957," *History of Education Quarterly* 23 (February 1983): 344.

17. Chávez, *The Lost Land,* 82, 84–85, 92, 93, 94, 96; Camarillo, *Chicanos in a Changing Society,* 188; Ramón A. Gutiérrez, "Nationalism and Literary Production: The Hispanic and Chicano Experiences," in *Recovering the U.S. Hispanic Literary Heritage,* 244; Phillip G. Gonzales, "The Political Construction of Latino Nomenclatures in Twentieth-Century New Mexico," *Journal of the Southwest* 35 (Summer 1993): 158–85.

18. Zamora, *The World of the Mexican Worker in Texas,* 86, 92, 108, 206–207.

19. Deutsch, *No Separate Refuge,* 35; Smith, "Mexicans in Kansas City," 35; Zaragosa Vargas, "Armies in the Fields and Factories: The Mexican Working Classes in the Midwest in the 1920s," *Mexican Studies/Estudios Mexicanos* 7 (Winter 1991): 47–71.

20. Cardoso, *Mexican Emigration to the United States,* 86–87; Valdes, *Al Norte,* 3, 4, 10; García, *Desert Immigrants,* 62, 91; Gilbert Cárdenas, "Los Desarraigados: Chicanos in the Midwestern Region of the United States," *Aztlán* 7 (Summer

1976): 155, 159, 161–62; Reisler, *By the Sweat of Their Brow*, 99–103; Romo, "Urbanization of the Southwestern Chicano," 195; Vargas, *Proletarians of the North*, chap. 1.

21. Michael M. Smith, "The Mexican Immigrant Press beyond the Borderlands: The Case of *El Cosmópolita*," *Great Plains Quarterly* 10 (Spring 1990): 242, 243.

22. Deutsch, *No Separate Refuge*, 132, 136, 153, 160; Nostrand, *The Hispano Homeland*, 147–48; Reisler, *By the Sweat of Their Brow*, 88.

23. Erasmo Gamboa, *Mexican Labor and World War II: Braceros in the Pacific Northwest* (Austin: University of Texas Press, 1990), 6, 8–9.

24. Cardoso, *Mexican Emigration to the United States*, 48; Reisler, *By the Sweat of Their Brow*, 100–101.

25. Romo, *East Los Angeles*, 89–91.

26. Valdes, *Al Norte*, 19; Vargas, *Proletarians of the North*, 87–88, 109–12, 129–33; Deutsch, *No Separate Refuge*, 114, 119, 137, 140, 151; Camarillo, *Chicanos in a Changing Society*, 183, 188, 191–92; Reisler, *By the Sweat of Their Brow*, 140; Daniel, *Bitter Harvest*, 105–106; Montejano, *Anglos and Mexicans in the Making of Texas*, 114, 115, 162–63, 223, 225, 227, 315; Smith, "Mexicans in Kansas City," 33, 39; Edward J. Escobar, "The Forging of a Community," in *Forging a Community*, 6–7; Arthur G. Pettit, *Images of the Mexican American in Fiction and Film* (College Station: Texas A & M University Press, 1980), 132–33; Blaine P. Lamb, "The Convenient Villain: The Early Cinema Views the Mexican American," *Journal of the West* 14 (October 1975).

27. Dennis Nodín Valdes, "The New Northern Borderlands: An Overview of Midwestern Chicano History," in *Perspectives in Mexican American Studies*, 7–8; Camarillo, *Chicanos in a Changing Society*, 193; Deutsch, *No Separate Refuge*, 134; Reisler, *By the Sweat of Their Brow*, 86, 141; Montejano, *Anglos and Mexicans in the Making of Texas*, 167, 168, 315; Smith, "Mexicans in Kansas City," 33, 39; Vargas, *Proletarians of the North*, 131–33.

28. Romo, *East Los Angeles*, 89–90, 92, 94, 96–97, 100–102; Deutsch, *No Separate Refuge*, 121.

29. Cárdenas, "United States Immigration Policy toward Mexico," 73–74; Juan Gómez-Quiñones, "Mexican Immigration to the United States, 1848–1980: An Overview," in *Chicano Studies: A Multidisciplinary Approach*, ed. Eugene E. García and Francisco A. Lomelí (New York: Teachers College Press, 1984), 67–68; Montejano, *Anglos and Mexicans in the Making of Texas*, 180–90; Corwin, *Immigrants—and Immigrants*, 142–48; Cardoso, *Mexican Emigration to the United States*, 83–84, and chap. 7.

30. Griswold del Castillo, *La Familia*, 94–96; Cardoso, *Mexican Emigration to the United States*, 93.

31. Reisler, *By the Sweat of Their Brow*, 106; Francisco Arturo Rosales, "The Regional Origins of Mexicano Immigrants to Chicago During the 1920s," *Aztlán* 7 (Summer 1976): 189–90; Romo, *East Los Angeles*, 78–80; Smith, "Mexicans in Kansas City," 36; Vargas, *Proletarians of the North*, 64.

32. Reisler, *By the Sweat of Their Brow*, 85–86, 106, 107; Romo, *East Los Angeles*, 69, 72; Smith, "Mexicans in Kansas City," 36; Juan R. García, "History of Chicanos in Chicago Heights," *Aztlán* 7 (Summer 1976): 295–96; Vargas, *Proletarians of the North*, 39–40, 46, 68, 128–29; Deutsch, *No Separate Refuge*, 154; Gilbert González, *Chicano Education in the Era of Segregation* (Philadelphia: Balch Institute Press, 1990), 20; García, *Desert Immigrants*, 145–46.

33. Romo, *East Los Angeles*, 148–49; Rosales, "Regional Origins," 191; Escobar, "The Forging of a Community," 3, 16; Reisler, *By the Sweat of Their Brow*, 108; Sheridan, *Los Tucsonenses*, 99; Vargas, *Proletarians of the North*, 42, 50, 139–42.

34. Barrera, *Race and Class in the Southwest,* 91–93; García, *Desert Immigrants,* 79–84; Smith, "Social and Political Dynamics of the Kansas City Colonia," 387–88; Richard A. García, "The Mexican American Mind: A Product of the 1930s," in *History, Culture, and Society: Chicano Studies in the 1980s,* ed. Mario T. García (Ypsilanti, Mich.: Bilingual Press/Editorial Bilingue, 1983), 70; Sheridan, *Los Tucsonenses,* 96–98; Kanellos, *A History of Hispanic Theatre in the United States,* 198.

35. Romo, *East Los Angeles,* 120; Camarillo, *Chicanos in a Changing Society,* 176; Manuel Peña, *The Texas Mexican Conjunto: A History of a Working-Class Music* (Austin: University of Texas Press, 1985), 126–27; Barrera, *Race and Class in the Southwest,* 95, 96–97.

36. Barrera, *Race and Class in the Southwest,* 86–87, 89; Camarillo, *Chicanos in a Changing Society,* 155–56, 211, 221; Romo, *East Los Angeles,* 68–69, 116–18; García, *Desert Immigrants,* 69, 71; Reisler, *By the Sweat of Their Brow,* 96, 97, 100, 103; Smith, "The Immigrant Press beyond the Borderlands," 246; Valdes, "The New Northern Borderlands," 7–8; Vargas, *Proletarians of the North,* 41–53, and chap. 3.

37. Barrera, *Race and Class in the Southwest,* 83–85; Sheridan, *Los Tucsonenses,* 181; Romo, *East Los Angeles,* 71–72; Reisler, *By the Sweat of Their Brow,* 97–99; Vargas, *Proletarians of the North,* 34–41; Zamora, *World of the Mexican Worker,* 20–21; Smith, *Mexicans in Oklahoma,* 45–47.

38. Barrera, *Race and Class in the Southwest,* 77; Camarillo, *Chicanos in a Changing Society,* 157–58, 166, 177; Reisler, *By the Sweat of Their Brow,* 6–7, 77, 78, 82, 88; Montejano, *Anglos and Mexicans in the Making of Texas,* 114; Smith, "The Immigrant Press beyond the Borderlands," 245, 248; Valdes, *Al Norte,* 15–18; Zamora, *World of the Mexican Worker,* 20–21.

39. Camarillo, *Chicanos in a Changing Society,* 157–58, 159, 160, 166, 177; Reisler, *By the Sweat of Their Brow,* 6–7, 77, 78, 82, 88; Smith, "The Immigrant Press beyond the Borderlands," 248; Smith, *Mexicans in Oklahoma,* 17–34; Valdes, *Al Norte,* 14; Romo, *East Los Angeles,* 72; Gilbert González, "Labor and Community: The Camps of Mexican Citrus Pickers in Southern California," *Western Historical Quarterly* 22 (August 1991): 289–312; Vargas, *Proletarians of the North,* 24–34.

40. Montejano, *Anglos and Mexicans in the Making of Texas,* 174, 198, 201; Barrera, *Race and Class in the Southwest,* 77–78; Reisler, *By the Sweat of Their Brow,* 80–81, 88–89; Camarillo, *Chicanos in a Changing Society,* 213, 215; Valdes, *Al Norte,* 12–18.

41. Camarillo, *Chicanos in a Changing Society,* 168; Escobar, "The Forging of a Community," 6, 10–11, 14.

42. Forrest, *The Preservation of the Village,* 30–31.

43. Garcia, *Desert Immigrants,* 170–71; Montejano, *Anglos and Mexicans in the Making of Texas,* 112, 143.

44. Vigil, *Los Patrones,* 32, 37, 116–18, 124–27, 143–44, 147; Chávez, *The Lost Land,* 102–103; Joan M. Jensen, "'Disfranchisement is a Disgrace': Women and Politics in New Mexico, 1940–1960," in *New Mexico Women,* 322–23.

45. Limón, "El Primer Congreso Mexicanista de 1911," 85–117; Zamora, *World of the Mexican Worker,* 97–99.

46. Romo, *East Los Angeles,* 94, 99–100; Sandos, *Rebellion in the Borderlands,* xv–xvi, 43, 59, 72–74, 126–27, 172–73, and chap. 5; Zamora, *World of the Mexican Worker,* 81–85.

47. Deutsch, *No Separate Refuge,* 13.

48. Ibid., 155; Carole E. Christian, "Joining the American Mainstream: Texas' Mexican Americans during World War I," *Southwestern Historical Quarterly* 93 (April 1989): 589, 590; García, *Rise of the Mexican American Middle Class,* 255–58; Zamora, *World of the Mexican Worker,* 89–90; Benjamin Márquez, *LULAC: The Evolution of a*

Mexican American Political Organization (Austin: University of Texas Press, 1993), 15–17.

49. Barrera, *Race and Class in the Southwest*, 80; Camarillo, *Chicanos in a Changing Society*, 172.

50. Zamora, *World of the Mexican Worker*, 7, 35, 86, 88–90, 93–94, 97, 207–10, 219n9.

51. Ibid., 36–38, 66, 69.

52. Ibid., 4, 7, 15, 56, 59, 62–63, 72, 81–84, 191, 192, 198–99, 210.

53. García, *Desert Immigrants*, 107–108; Camarillo, *Chicanos in a Changing Society*, 172; Gómez-Quiñones, "The First Steps," 29; Deutsch, *No Separate Refuge*, 158; Reisler, *By the Sweat of Their Brow*, 234–36; Daniel, *Bitter Harvest*, 105; Vargas, *Proletarians of the North*, 157.

54. García, *Desert Immigrants*, 107–109; Camarillo, *Chicanos in a Changing Society*, 171; Gómez-Quiñones, "The First Steps," 28, 35–36.

55. Daniel, *Bitter Harvest*, 72, 108–109; Gómez-Quiñones, "The First Steps," 36; Charles Wollenberg, "Huelga, 1928 Style: The Imperial Valley Cantaloupe Workers' Strike," *Pacific Historical Review* 38 (February 1969): 45–59.

56. Sheridan, *Los Tucsonenses*, 182–83.

57. Zamora, *World of the Mexican Worker*, 62–63, 179, 187–88, 193, 202, 206, 209; García, *Desert Immigrants*, 99–100; Daniel, *Bitter Harvest*, 76, 79–81; Gómez-Quiñones, "The First Steps," 28–29; Deutsch, *No Separate Refuge*, 158.

58. Daniel, *Bitter Harvest*, 76, 81; Deutsch, *No Separate Refuge*, 158; Zamora, *World of the Mexican Worker*, 133–39, 200–201; Vargas, *Proletarians of the North*, 156.

59. García, *Desert Immigrants*, 98–99; Zamora, *World of the Mexican Worker*, 58–59; Vargas, *Proletarians of the North*, 156; Gómez-Quiñones, "The First Steps," 29–30; Daniel, *Bitter Harvest*, 88–90.

60. Deutsch, *No Separate Refuge*, 103–105, 156–57; Gómez-Quiñones, "The First Steps," 32–34, 35; James R. Kluger, *The Clifton-Morenci Strike: Labor Difficulty in Arizona, 1915–1916* (Tucson: University of Arizona Press, 1970), 20, 23, 24, 31, 32, 66–68, 69, 75; Mellinger, "'The Men Have Become Organizers,'" 323–48.

61. Daniel, *Bitter Harvest*, 76–77, 79–80, 87.

62. García, *Desert Immigrants*, 75, 201; Monroy, "'Our Children Get So Different Here,'" 82, 87, 100, 102, 103; Emma Pérez, "'A La Mujer': A Critique of the *Partido Liberal Mexicano*'s Gender Ideology on Women," in *Essays on Mexicana/Chicana History,* ed. Adelaida R. del Castillo (Encino, Calif.: Floricanto Press, 1990), 459, 464, 473.

63. Barrera, *Race and Class in the Southwest*, 98–99; Camarillo, *Chicanos in a Changing Society*, 177–79, 221; García, *Desert Immigrants*, 75–79; Valdes, "The New Northern Borderlands," 9; Vargas, *Proletarians of the North*, 132–39.

64. Pérez, "'A La Mujer,'" 470–73.

65. García, *Desert Immigrants*, 200–202; Ruiz, *Cannery Women, Cannery Lives*, 11–12, 17; Ruiz, "'Star Struck,'" 110–17; Monroy, "'Our Children Get So Different Here,'" 88; Vargas, *Proletarians of the North*, 138, 155–66.

66. Deutsch, *No Separate Refuge*, 67–68, 115; Camarillo, *Chicanos in a Changing Society*, 178, 179, 211, 221; García, *Desert Immigrants*, 70, 76, 78; Perrigo, *Hispanos: Historic Leaders in New Mexico*, 75–77; Romo, *East Los Angeles*, 118.

67. San Miguel, "*Let All of Them Take Heed*," 20–22, 23, 32–33, 39; García, *Desert Immigrants*, 110, 114–15, 117–21; Romo, *East Los Angeles*, 137, 138, 140, 141; González, *Chicano Education in an Era of Segregation*, 30, 35, 36–38, 41, 47–49, 67, 82–90; Irving I. Hendricks, "Early Schooling for Children of Migrant Farm Workers

in California: The 1920s," *Aztlán* 8 (Fall 1977); Vargas, *Proletarians of the North*, 73; Charles Wollenberg, *All Deliberate Speed: Segregation and Exclusion in California Schools* (Berkeley: University of California Press, 1976), 113–14.

68. Doris L. Meyer, "The Language Issue in New Mexico, 1880–1900: Mexican American Resistance against Cultural Erosion," *Bilingual Review* 4 (1977): 103; García, *Desert Immigrants*, 124; San Miguel, *"Let All of Them Take Heed,"* 23, 54–56; Wollenberg, *All Deliberate Speed*, 111–18; Romo, *East Los Angeles*, 139–40; Montejano, *Anglos and Mexicans in the Making of Texas*, 228.

69. San Miguel, "Culture and Education in the American Southwest," 9, 11, 14, 16; García, *Desert Immigrants*, 125, 216; Nelson A. Pichardo, "The Establishment and Develoment of Chicano Voluntary Associations in California, 1910–1930," *Aztlán* 19 (Fall 1988–90): 107.

70. Sheridan, *Los Tucsonenses*, 156–57; Deutsch, *No Separate Refuge*, 144; Vargas, *Proletarians of the North*, 70–78, 143–46.

71. Sheridan, *Los Tucsonenses*, 153, 155; Hernández, *Mutual Aid for Survival*, chap. 1.

72. García, *Desert Immigrants*, 219, 220; Deutsch, *No Separate Refuge*, 144; Cardoso, *Mexican Emigration to the United States*, 90–91; Crocker, "Gary Mexicans," 118; Vargas, *Proletarians of the North*, 146–48.

73. García, *Desert Immigrants*, 225, 227; Sheridan, *Los Tucsonenses*, 167, 169; Deutsch, *No Separate Refuge*, 154; Rosales, "Regional Origins," 191; Smith, "Mexicans in Kansas City," 44–46; Vargas, *Proletarians of the North*, 149–55; Camarillo, *Chicanos in a Changing Society*, 148, 149, 153; Romo, *East Los Angeles*, 149; Reisler, *By the Sweat of Their Brow*, 107; Pichardo, "Establishment and Development of Voluntary Associations in California," 93–155.

74. Sheridan, *Los Tucsonenses*, 169–75; James D. McBride, "The Liga Protectora Latina: A Mexican Benevolent Society in Arizona," *Journal of the West* 14 (October 1975): 83–88.

75. Romo, *East Los Angeles*, 151–53; García, *Desert Immigrants*, 226–27; Antonio Ríos-Bustamante and Pedro Castillo, *An Illustrated History of Mexican Los Angeles* (Los Angeles: Chicano Studies Center, UCLA, 1986), 124–27; Arrieta, "The Alianza Hispano Americana in Arizona and New Mexico, 55–82.

76. Camarillo, *Chicanos in a Changing Society*, 153; Romo, *East Los Angeles*, 153–54; Deutsch, *No Separate Refuge*, 154; Valdes, "The New Northern Borderlands," 10.

77. Kanellos, *A History of Hispanic Theatre in the United States*, 18, 23, 46, 50, 177, 187, 199–200.

78. Ibid., 179, 184–87, 189, 192; Vargas, *Proletarians of the North*, 152.

79. Ibid., 19–20, 60, 61, 97, 98, 100–101, 177.

80. Rocard, *Children of the Sun*, 82–105; Paredes, "The Evolution of Chicano Literature," 41–44; Steven Loza, *Barrio Rhythm: Mexican American Music in Los Angeles* (Urbana: University of Illinois Press, 1993), 20–21.

81. Sheridan, *Los Tucsonenses*, 189–91, 198.

82. Tatum, *Chicano Literature*, 24–30, 44, 45, 47; Onofre di Stefano, "'Venimos a Luchar': A Brief History of *La Prensa*'s Founding," *Aztlán* 16 (1985): 113; Francine Medeiros, *"La Opinión*: A Mexican Exile Newspaper," *Aztlán* 11 (Spring 1980): 67, 68, 69, 77–78, 80; Kanellos, "A Socio-Historic Study of Hispanic Newspapers in the United States," 114, 116–17; Lomas, "The Articulation of Gender," 306.

83. Kanellos, "A Socio-Historic Study of Hispanic Newspapers in the United States," 114.

84. *Pasó Por Aquí*, 185–89, 194, 197; Doris Meyer, "Felipe Maximiliano Chacón: A Forgotten Mexican American Author," in *New Directions in Chicano Scholarship*, 111–13; Raymund A. Paredes, "Mexican American Literature: An Overview," in *Recovering the U.S. Hispanic Literary Heritage*, 36–37.

85. Tatum, *Chicano Literature*, 32–33, 35.

86. Genaro Padilla, "Recovering Mexican-American Autobiography," in *Recovering the U.S. Hispanic Literary Heritage*, 164.

87. Paredes, "Evolution of Chicano Literature," 49, 53.

88. Ramón D. Chacón, "The Chicano Immigrant Press in Los Angeles: The Case of *El Heraldo de México*, 1916–1920," *Journalism History* 4 (Summer 1977): 49; Richard Griswold del Castillo, "The Mexican Revolution and Spanish-Language Press in the Borderlands," *Journalism History* 4 (Summer 1977): 42–43; di Stefano, "'Venimos a Luchar,'" 105; Ríos-Bustamante and Castillo, *Illustrated History of Mexican Los Angeles*, 119–22; García, *Rise of the Mexican American Middle Class*, 35; Smith, "Mexicans in Kansas City," 48; Kanellos, "A Socio-Historic Study of Hispanic Newspapers in the United States," 110–12; Pichardo, "The Establishment and Development of Chicano Voluntary Associations in California," 104–105.

89. Chacón, "Chicano Immigrant Press," 50, 62, 64; Smith, "Mexicans in Kansas City," 48–49; García and Cal, "El Círculo de Obreros Católicos 'San José,'" 101–106; Rios-Bustamante and Castillo, *Illustrated History of Mexican Los Angeles*, 119–22; Medeiros, "*La Opinión*," 67, 68, 69, 77–78, 80; di Stefano, "'Venimos a Luchar,'" 110, 113; Mario T. García, "*La Frontera*: The Border as Symbol and Reality in Mexican American Thought," *Estudios Mexicanos/Mexican Studies* 1 (Summer 1985): 198–205; Kanellos, "A Socio-Historic Study of Hispanic Newspapers in the United States," 110–12.

90. Griswold del Castillo, "The Mexican Revolution and Spanish-Language Press," 43, 44, 46, 47; Medeiros, "La Opinión," 71–72.

91. Valdes, *Al Norte*, 24–25, 29; Vargas, *Proletarians of the North*, 57, 88, 132–33.

SIX

1. Corwin, *Immigrants—and Immigrants*, 225.

2. Ibid., 117, 149.

3. Francisco Balderrama, *In Defense of La Raza: The Los Angeles Mexican Consulate and the Mexican Community, 1929–1936* (Tucson: University of Arizona Press, 1982), 57–61.

4. García, "The Mexican American Mind," 68, 71, 72, 75–78, 87; García, *Rise of the Mexican American Middle Class*, 96–97, 115, 222, 225–26.

5. Corwin, *Immigrants—and Immigrants*, 116; Chávez, *The Lost Land*, 119; García, "Making of the Mexican American Mind," 84; González, *Chicano Education in the Era of Segregation*, 36; Francisco Arturo Rosales and Daniel T. Simon, "Mexican Immigrant Experience in the Urban Midwest: East Chicago, Indiana, 1919–1945," in *Forging a Community*, 149, 152–53; Carlos Muñoz, Jr., *Youth, Identity, Power: The Chicano Student Movement* (New York: Verso, 1989), 29–31, 43; Deutsch, *No Separate Refuge*, 188–89; Richard Santillán, "Rosita the Riveter: Midwest Mexican American Women During World War II, 1941–1945," in *Perspectives in Mexican American Studies*, 121, 126; Louise Año Nuevo Kerr, "The Chicano Experience in Chicago: 1920–1970," Ph.D. diss., University of Illinois, Chicago, 1976, 98–102.

6. García, "Making of the Mexican American Mind," 68–73, 84, 89; Muóoz, *Youth, Identity, Power*, 32; Guadalupe San Miguel, Jr., "The Struggle against Separate

and Unequal Schools," 344; Peña, *The Texas-Mexican Conjunto,* 126; Sheridan, *Los Tucsonenses,* 212.

7. García, "Making of the Mexican American Mind," 73; García, *Rise of the Mexican American Middle Class,* 42–43; Griswold del Castillo, *La Familia,* 102, 104.

8. Corwin, *Immigrants—and Immigrants,* 117.

9. Juan R. García, "History of Chicanos in Chicago Heights," *Aztlán* 7 (Summer 1976): 299; Erasmo Gamboa, *Mexican Labor and World War II: Braceros in the Pacific Northwest* (Austin: University of Texas Press, 1990), 11–14, 20; Juan R. García, Introduction, *Perspectives in Mexican American Studies,* xiii–xiv; Valdes, "The New Northern Borderlands," 2: 14–16; Valdes, *Al Norte,* 52, 73, 99.

10. Deutsch, *No Separate Refuge,* 164, 165–66; Nostrand, *The Hispano Homeland,* 150–54, 175.

11. Corwin, *Immigrants—and Immigrants,* 227–29, 233–34; Escobar, "The Forging of a Community," 13; Rosales and Simon, "Mexican Immigrant Experience in the Urban Midwest," 146–49; Kerr, "The Chicano Experience in Chicago," 72–75; Vargas, *Proletarians of the North,* chap. 5; Balderrama, *In Defense of La Raza,* chap. 2; Lorraine Esterly Pierce, "Mexican Americans on St. Paul's Lower West Side," *Journal of Mexican American History* 4 (1974): 3.

12. Corwin, *Immigrants—and Immigrants,* 234–35; Balderrama, *In Defense of La Raza,* chap. 2; Vargas, *Proletarians of the North,* chap. 3; Dennis Nodín Valdes, "Mexican Revolutionary Nationalism and Repatriation During the Great Depression," *Mexican Studies/Estudios Mexicanos* 4 (Winter 1988): 1–24.

13. Corwin, *Immigrants—and Immigrants,* 232; Abraham Hoffman, *Unwanted Mexican Americans in the Great Depression: Repatriation Pressures, 1929–1939* (Tucson: University of Arizona Press, 1974), 126–27, 174–75.

14. Deutsch, *No Separate Refuge,* 175; Gamboa, *Mexican Labor and World War II,* 16; Reisler, *By the Sweat of Their Brow,* 246–47.

15. Sheridan, *Los Tucsonenses,* 245; Chávez, *The Lost Land,* 118–20; Mauricio Mazón, *The Zoot-Suit Riots: The Psychology of Symbolic Annihilation* (Austin: University of Texas Press, 1984), 3–5, 20–24, 28–29, 58–60, 69–72, 75–79, 85–87; Arnoldo De León, *Ethnicity in the Sunbelt: A History of Mexican Americans in Houston* (Houston: Mexican American Studies Program, 1989), 105–10.

16. Montejano, *Anglos and Mexicans in the Making of Texas,* 227; Smith, *The Mexicans in Oklahoma,* 61; García, *Rise of the Mexican American Middle Class,* 39–40, 72–73; Pierce, "Mexican Americans on St. Paul's Lower West Side," 6–7; Shirley J. Roberts, "Minority Group Poverty in Phoenix," *Journal of Arizona History* 14 (Winter 1973): 355–56.

17. Deutsch, *No Separate Refuge,* 197–98; Forrest, *The Preservation of the Village,* 15, chaps. 6 and 7.

18. Rosales and Simon, "Mexican Immigrant Experience in the Urban Midwest," 146; Smith, *Mexicans in Oklahoma,* 51; Deutsch, *No Separate Refuge,* 168–69; Sheridan, *Los Tucsonenses,* 212–13; García, *Rise of the Mexican American Middle Class,* 87; Balderrama, *In Defense of La Raza,* chap. 3.

19. Forrest, *The Preservation of the Village,* 11, 15, 79, 151.

20. Montejano, *Anglos and Mexicans in the Making of Texas,* 176–77, 212–13; Reisler, *By the Sweat of Their Brow,* 229; Valdes, *Al Norte,* 53–54, 55–56.

21. Valdes, *Al Norte,* 64–67, 79–80.

22. Reisler, *By the Sweat of Their Brow,* 247. For a description of life in the citrus camps of California during this era, see Gilbert C. González, "Labor and Community: The Camps of Mexican Citrus Pickers in Southern California," *Western Historical Quarterly* 22 (August 1991): 289–312.

23. Corwin, *Immigrants—and Immigrants*, 53–54; Gilberto Cárdenas, "United States Immigration Policy towards Mexico: A Historical Perspective," *Chicano Law Review* 2 (Summer 1975): 75–77; Gómez-Quiñones, "Mexican Immigration to the United States, 1848–1980," 69; Richard B. Craig, *The Bracero Program: Interest Group and Foreign Policy* (Austin: University of Texas Press, 1971), 42–45; Gamboa, *Mexican Labor and World War II*, xi, xii, 41, 90, 91, 92–93, 129; Valdes, *Al Norte*, chap. 5; Kerr, "The Chicano Experience in Chicago," 121–25. The classic analysis of the bracero program is Ernesto Galarza, *Merchants of Labor: The Mexican Bracero Story* (Santa Barbara and Charlotte: McNally & Loftin Publishers, 1964).

24. Emilio Zamora, "The Failed Promise of Wartime Opportunity for Mexicans in the Texas Oil Industry," *Southwestern Historical Quarterly* 95 (January 1992): 323–50; Montejano, *Anglos and Mexicans in the Making of Texas*, 269; Juan Gómez-Quiñones, *Chicano Politics: Reality and Promise, 1940–1990* (Albuquerque: University of New Mexico Press, 1990), 35–36, 37–38.

25. Gómez-Quiñones, *Chicano Politics*, 31; García, *Rise of the Mexican American Middle Class*, 206, 271–72.

26. Gómez-Quiñones, *Chicano Politics*, 45–48; Phillip B. Gonzales, "Spanish Heritage and Ethnic Protest in New Mexico: The Anti-Fraternity Bill of 1933," *New Mexico Historical Review* 61 (October 1986): 281–99; Deutsch, *No Separate Refuge*, 179; Perrigo, *Hispanos: Historic Leaders of New Mexico*, 85–87.

27. San Miguel, "The Struggle against Separate and Unequal Schools," 344; García, "Making of the Mexican American Mind," 68, 79.

28. García, *Rise of the Mexican American Middle Class*, 260, 264, 274; Márquez, *LULAC: The Evolution of a Mexican American Political Organization*.

29. García, *Rise of the Mexican American Middle Class*, 272; De León, *Ethnicity in the Sunbelt*, chap. 5.

30. Balderrama, *In Defense of La Raza*, 59; García, *Rise of the Mexican American Middle Class*, 271–72; De León, *Ethnicity in the Sunbelt*, 90.

31. García, "Making of the Mexican American Mind," 70, 80, 82–89; San Miguel, "The Struggle against Separate and Unequal Schools," 345.

32. Rosales and Simon, "Mexican Immigrant Experience in the Urban Midwest," 150–51; Rosales, "Mexicans, Interethnic Violence, and Crime in the Chicago Area during the 1920s and 1930s," 87.

33. Muñoz, *Youth, Identity, Power*, 29, 30–32, 35–43.

34. Mario T. García, *Mexican Americans: Leadership, Ideology, and Identity, 1930–1960* (New Haven, Conn.: Yale University Press, 1989), chap. 6.

35. Ibid., 176.

36. Kerr, "The Chicano Experience in Chicago," 85–87, 90; García, *Rise of the Mexican American Middle Class*, 55, 60–63; Reisler, *By the Sweat of Their Brow*, 238, 246; Rodolfo Acuña, *Occupied America: A History of Chicanos*, 2d ed. (New York: Harper & Row, 1981), 220, 228, 229.

37. Acuña, *Occupied America*, 2d ed., 228–30; Reisler, *By the Sweat of Their Brow*, 236, 246; Cletus Daniel, *Bitter Harvest: A History of California Farmworkers, 1870–1941* (Ithaca, N.Y.: Cornell University Press, 1981), 111, 112; Victor B. Nelson-Cisneros, "UCAPAWA Organizing Activities in Texas, 1935–1950," *Aztlán* 9 (Spring, Summer, Fall 1978): 73–74; García, *Rise of the Mexican American Middle Class*, 60.

38. Gamboa, *Mexican Labor and World War II*, 74–77, 80–82.

39. Reisler, *By the Sweat of Their Brow*, 248, 233; Daniel, *Bitter Harvest*, 142.

40. Vargas, *Proletarians of the North*, 196–97; Luis Leobardo Arroyo, "Chicano Participation in Organized Labor: The CIO in Los Angeles, 1938–1950: An Extended Research Note," *Aztlán* 6 (Summer 1975): 277, 280–83; Rosales and Simon, "Mexican Immigrant Experience in the Urban Midwest," 151; Kerr, "The Chicano Experience in Chicago," 91–92.

41. García, *Mexican Americans*, chap. 7.

42. García, *Rise of the Mexican American Middle Class*, 60, 63; Daniel, *Bitter Harvest*, 279–80; Victor B. Nelson-Cisneros, "UCAPAWA and Chicanos in California: The Farm Worker Period, 1937–1940," *Aztlán* 7 (Fall 1976): 468.

43. Valdes, *Al Norte*, 42–50; Daniel, *Bitter Harvest*, 277–81; Nelson-Cisneros, "UCAPAWA and Chicanos in California," 470–73; Nelson-Cisneros, "UCAPAWA Organizing Activities in Texas, 1935–1950," 73–74.

44. Vargas, *Proletarians of the North*, 197; Rosales and Simon, "Mexican Experience in the Urban Midwest," 152.

45. Nelson-Cisneros, "UCAPAWA and Chicanos in California," 463; Ruiz, *Cannery Women, Cannery Lives*, 69–77.

46. García, *Rise of the Mexican American Middle Class*, 60–63; Nelson-Cisneros, "UCAPAWA Organizing Activities in Texas, 1935–1950," 80–81.

47. Reisler, *By the Sweat of Their Brow*, 236, 237–38; Daniel, *Bitter Harvest*, 111–17, 146–47; Balderrama, *In Defense of La Raza*, chap. 6.

48. Reisler, *By the Sweat of Their Brow*, 239–43; Daniel, *Bitter Harvest*, 155–58, and chaps. 6 and 7.

49. Deutsch, *No Separate Refuge*, 171–73; Arnoldo De León, "*Los Tasinques* and the Sheep Shearers' Union of North America: A Strike in West Texas, 1934," *West Texas Historial Association Yearbook* 55 (1979): 3–16.

50. D. H. Dinwoodie, "Deportation: The Immigration Service and the Chicano Labor Movement in the 1930s," *New Mexico Historical Review* 52 (July 1977): 193–206.

51. Griswold del Castillo, *La Familia*, 100–101, 105; García, *Rise of the Mexican American Middle Class*, 51, 124–26, 128–29.

52. Griswold del Castillo, *La Familia*, 110–11, 105; García, *Rise of the Mexican American Middle Class*, 136, 145, 148.

53. García, *Rise of the Mexican Ameican Middle Class*, 123–26; Ruiz, *Cannery Women, Cannery Lives*, 14, 25, 27; Ríos-Bustamante and Castillo, *An Illustrated History of Mexican Los Angeles*, 144–45.

54. Deutsch, *No Separate Refuge*, 179; Vargas, *Proletarians of the North*, 137; Santillán, "Rosita the Riveter," 115–16, 118, 124, 130, 131–33, 138–39.

55. Douglas Monroy, "*La Costura en Los Angeles*, 1933–1939: The ILGWU and the Politics of Domination," in *Mexican Women in the United States: Struggles Past and Present*, ed. Magdalena Mora and Adelaida R. Del Castillo (Los Angeles: Chicano Studies Research Center Publications, 1980), 171–78; García, *Rise of the Mexican American Middle Class*, 60, 62–63, 64, 207–208; Deutsch, *No Separate Refuge*, 170; Ruiz, *Cannery Women, Cannery Lives*, 45; Melissa Hield, "Union Minded: Women in Texas ILGWU, 1937–1950," in Richard Croxdale, *Women in the Texas Workforce Yesterday and Today* (Austin: People's History in Texas, 1979), 8–11, 13.

56. Nelson-Cisneros, "UCAPAWA Organizing Activities in Texas, 1935–1950," 80–81; Kenneth P. Walker, "The Pecan Shellers of San Antonio and Mechanization," *Southwestern Historical Quarterly* 69 (July 1965): 44–58; García, *Rise of the Mexican American Middle Class*, 60, 62–63, 64.

57. García, "Making of the Mexican American Mind," 82; García, *Rise of the*

Mexican American Middle Class, 261; García, *Mexican Americans*, 38–39; Deutsch, *No Separate Refuge*, 170.

58. Santillán, "Rosita the Riveter," 125–26, 138–39.

59. San Miguel, "Culture and Education in the American Southwest," 14–15, 17; Deutsch, *No Separate Refuge*, 169, 197; Rosales and Simon, "Mexican Immigrant Experience in the Urban Midwest," 149; Kerr, "The Chicano Experience in Chicago," 96–97; García, *Rise of the Mexican American Middle Class*, 180, 194–98, 201.

60. Gonzales, *Chicano Education in the Era of Segregation*, 36, 45, 49, 93; García, *Rise of the Mexican American Middle Class*, 176, 178, 180.

61. Sheridan, *Los Tucsonenses*, 213; Rosales and Simon, "Mexican Immigrants in the Urban Midwest," 146; Mario Barrera, "The Historical Evolution of Chicano Ethnic Goals: A Bibliographic Essay," *Sage Race Relations Abstracts* 10 (February 1985): 6–7; Gómez-Quiñones, *Chicano Politics*, 63–64; Manuel P. Servín, "The Role of Mexican-Americans in the Development of Early Arizona," in *An Awakened Minority: The Mexican Americans*, ed. Manuel P. Servín (Beverly Hills: Glencoe Press, 1970), 35; Hernández, *Mutual Aid for Survival*, 48–49.

62. García, *Rise of the Mexican American Middle Class*, 167, 225–26, 233–34.

63. García, *Mexican Americans*, chap. 4.

64. Loza, *Barrio Rhythm*, 21; Nelson A. Pichardo, "The Establishment and Development of Chicano Voluntary Associations in California, 1910–1930," *Aztlán* 19 (Fall 1988–90): 105–106; García, *Rise of the Mexican American Middle Class*, 83; Félix F. Gutiérrez and Jorge Reina Schement, *Spanish-Language Radio in the Southwestern United States* (Austin: Center for Mexican American Studies, 1979), 5–9.

65. Kanellos, *A History of Hispanic Theatre in the United States*, 27, 29, 32, 34, 85, 86, 191.

66. Ibid., 60–62, 66–67, 70, 90, 100, 182, 187, 188, 190, 195–96.

67. Luis Leal and Pepe Barrón, "Chicano Literature: An Overview," in *Three American Literatures: Essays on Chicano, Native American, and Asian American Literatures for Teachers of American Literature*, ed. Houston A. Baker, Jr. (New York: Modern Language Association, 1982), 21; Paredes, "The Evolution of Chicano Literature," 44–45; García, *Rise of the Mexican American Middle Class*, 82–83; Cardoso, *Mexican Emigration to the United States*, 145, 147; Loza, *Barrio Rhythm*, 20–26.

68. Valdes, *Al Norte*, 71–72; Peña, *The Texas Mexican Conjunto*, chapter 2; Loza, *Barrio Rhythm*, 20–26.

69. Loza, *Barrio Rhythm*, 142–50, 158–67, 180.

70. Paredes, "The Evolution of Chicano Literature," 50.

71. Chávez, *The Lost Land*, 101; Paredes, "The Evolution of Chicano Literature," 53–55.

72. Chávez, *The Lost Land*, 96–101; Paredes, "The Evolution of Chicano Literature," 51–52; *Pasó Por Aquí*, 200–201, 202–203, 205–206; Genaro M. Padilla, "Recovering Mexican-American Autobiography," in *Recovering the U.S. Hispanic Literary Heritage*, 165–66.

73. Aurelio M. Espinosa, *The Folklore of Spain in the American Southwest: Traditional Spanish Folk Literature in Northern New Mexico and Southern Colorado*, ed. J. Manuel Espinoza (Norman: University of Oklahoma Press, 1985), 3–25.

74. García, *Mexican Americans*, chap. 9.

75. Ibid., chap. 10.

76. Ibid., chap. 11.

77. Alfredo Mirandé and Evengelina Enríquez, *La Chicana: The Mexican-American Woman* (Chicago: University of Chicago Press, 1979), 225.

78. García, *Rise of the Mexican American Middle Class*, 282–89.

79. Gómez-Quiñones, *Chicano Politics*, 34; Chávez, *The Lost Land*, 117; Ríos-Bustamante and Castillo, *An Illustrated History of Mexican Los Angeles*, 158; Santillán, "Rosita the Riveter," 116; Smith, *Mexican in Oklahoma*, 61; Robin Fitzgerald Scott, "Wartime Labor Problems and Mexican-Americans in the War," in *An Awakened Minority*, 137.

80. Chávez, *The Lost Land*, 117; Santillán, "Rosita the Riveter," 122–23.

81. Chávez, *The Lost Land*, 117; Gómez-Quiñones, *Chicano Politics*, 34; *Hispanic Magazine* (August 1993): 34–40.

82. Rosales and Simon, "Mexican Immigrant Experience in the Urban Midwest," 153; Santillán, "Rosita the Riveter," 116; Christine Marín, "Mexican Americans on the Home Front: Community Organizations in Arizona during World War II," *Perspectives in Mexican American Studies,* vol. 4 (Tucson: Mexican American Studies and Research Center, 1993), 77, 81–82, 84–86.

83. Rosales and Simon, "Mexican Immigrant Experience in the Urban Midwest," 153.

84. Peña, *The Texas-Mexican Conjunto*, 114–19.

seven

1. David G. Gutiérrez, "Ethnicity, Ideology, and Political Development: Mexican Immigration as a Political Issue in the Chicano Community, 1910–1977," Ph.D. diss., Stanford University, 1988, 6.

2. Juan Ramón García, *Operation Wetback: The Mass Deportation of Mexican Undocumented Workers in 1954* (Westport, Conn.: Greenwood Press, 1980), 165.

3. James D. Cockcroft, *Outlaws in the Promised Land: Mexican Immigrant Workers and America's Future* (New York: Grove Press, 1986), 78.

4. Erasmo Gamboa, "Mexican Migration into Washington State: A History, 1940–1950," *Pacific Northwest Quarterly* 72, no. 3 (July 1981): 121–31; Gamboa, "Chicanos in the Northwest: An Historical Perspective," *El Grito* 6 (Summer 1973): 57–70; Richard Slatta, "Chicanos in the Pacific Northwest: An Historical Overview of Oregon's Chicanos," *Aztlán* 6 (1975): 327–40. See also Gamboa, *Mexican Laborers in World War II.*

5. Gutiérrez, *"Ethnicity, Ideology, and Political Development,"* 245; Vernon Carl Allsup, "The American G.I. Forum: A History of an American Organization," Ph.D. diss., University of Texas, 1976, 149.

6. Galarza, *Merchants of Labor*, 182–84.

7. Harvey Levenstein, "Sindicalismo norteamericano, braceros y 'espaladas mojadas,'" *Historia Mexicana* 28, no. 2 (1978): 172–80.

8. For a full discussion of this process see Escobar, "The Forging of a Community," 3–24.

9. See for example the study of Aurora, Illinois, by Ralph Clintron in "Divided, Yet a City: A Brief History," *Perspectives in Mexican American Studies: Community, Identity and Education* 3 (1992): 39–43.

10. Griswold del Castillo, *La Familia,* 98–104.

11. Sigurd Johansen, "Family Organization in a Spanish-American Cultural Area," *Sociology and Social Research* 28, no. 2 (November–December 1943): 131.

12. Griswold del Castillo, *La Familia,* 120–21.

13. Margaret Clark described how the traditional Mexican family customs were mixed with more modern practices in her study of the San Jose barrio *Sal Si Puedes*. See her *Health in the Mexican-American Culture* (Berkeley and Los Angeles: University of California Press, 1959,) 118–61.

14. The classic critique of the Pachuco appears in Octavio Paz, *The Labyrinth of Solitude: Life and Thought in Mexico* (New York: Grove Press, 1961), chap. 1. For contemporary interpretations of this phenomenon see Beatrice Griffith, *American Me* (Boston: Houghton Mifflin, 1948), 15–28; George I. Sanchez, "Pachucos in the Making," *Common Ground* 5 (Autumn 1943): 13–20; Ruth D. Tuck, *Not with the Fist: Mexican-Americans in a Southwest City* (New York: Arno Press, 1974); also Ralph H. Turner and Samuel J. Surace, "Zoot-Suiters and Mexicans: Symbols in Crowd Behavior," *American Journal of Sociology* 62 (1956): 14–24.

15. García, *Mexican Americans: Leadership, Ideology, and Identity,* 21.

16. Allsup details many of the organization's activities in fighting against discrimination, 89–139.

17. These efforts are analyzed in detail by Márquez, *LULAC: Evolution of a Mexican American Political Organization,* 39–60.

18. San Miguel, *"Let All of Them Take Heed,"* 118–19; Márquez (*LULAC: Evolution of a Mexican American Political Organization,* 51–60) outlines other LULAC iniatives similar to those in California. See also González, *Chicano Education in the Era of Segregation,* 136–56.

19. González, *Chicano Education in the Era of Segregation,* 155.

20. San Miguel, *"Let All of Them Take Heed,"* 125; Márquez, *LULAC: Evolution of a Mexican American Political Organization,* 54.

21. Márquez, *LULAC: Evolution of a Mexican American Political Organization,* 133.

22. Gutiérrez, "Ethnicity, Idealogy, and Political Development," 273–75.

23. García, *Mexican Americans: Leadership, Ideology, and Identity,* 84–111.

24. García, *Mexican Americans: Leadership, Ideology, and Identity,* 154–57; Gomez-Quiñones, *Chicano Politics: Reality and Promise*, 50–52.

25. William Madsen, *Mexican-Americans of South Texas* (New York: Holt, Rinehart & Winston, 1967), 53.

26. Martha Cotera, *Profile on the Mexican American Women* (Austin: National Educational Laboratory Publishers, 1976), 97–98.

27. Márquez, *LULAC: Evolution of a Mexican American Political Organization,* 37–60.

28. Ruiz, *Cannery Women, Cannery Lives,* 121.

29. Ibid., 121–23.

30. Rodolfo Acuña, *Occupied America: A History of Chicanos,* 3d rev. ed. (New York: Harper & Row, 1988), 296, 297.

31. Gomez-Quiñones, *Chicano Politics,* 67–69.

32. Leo Grebler, Joan W. Moore, and Ralph Guzmán, *The Mexican-American People: The Nation's Second Largest Minority* (New York: Free Press, 1970), 209–10. According to Table 9.2, 16 percent of Spanish-surnamed adult males were classified as being farm laborers by the 1960 census. Table 9.3 lists 16.1 percent as being employed in white-collar occupations.

33. Jacques Levy, *Cesar Chavez: Autobiography of La Causa* (New York: W. W. Norton, 1975), 78–79.

34. De León, *Mexican Americans in Texas,* 111.

35. Michael Wilson, *Salt of the Earth* (Old Weatherbury, N.Y.: Feminist Press, 1978), 124.

36. Lt. Col. Miguel A. García, "Roots of the Hispanic Serviceman," *La Luz,* September 1978, 26–27. Thirty-eight Congressional Medal of Honor Winners have been Hispanic.

37. Raúl Morín, *Among the Valiant: Mexican-Americans in World War II and Korea* (Los Angeles: Borden Publishing, 1963), 261.

38. Américo Paredes, *"With a Pistol in His Hand": A Border Ballad and Its Hero* (Austin: University of Texas Press, 1958).

39. Mario Suárez, "El Hoyo," *Arizona Quarterly* 3 (Summer 1947): 114–15.

40. Carl R. Shirley and Paula W. Shirley, *Understanding Chicano Literature* (Columbia: University of South Carolina Press, 1988), 97.

41. José Antonio Villareal, *Pocho* (Garden City, N.Y.: Doubleday, 1959).

42. Jacinto Quirarte, *Mexican American Artists* (Austin and London: University of Texas Press, 1973), 77–89.

43. Ibid., 131–32.

44. Carlos B. Gil, "Lydia Mendoza: Houstonian and First Lady of American Song," *Houston Review* 3, no. 2 (Summer 1981).

45. Peña, *The Texas Mexican Conjunto,* 75–78.

46. Dan William Dickey, *The Kennedy Corridos: A Study of the Ballads of a Mexican American Hero* (Austin: Center for Mexican American Studies, 1978).

47. Peña, *The Texas Mexican Conjunto.*

48. George Lipsitz, "Land of a Thousand Dances: Youth, Minorities, and the Rise of Rock and Roll," in *Recasting America: Culture and Politics in the Age of Cold War,* ed. Lary May (Chicago and London: University of Chicago Press, 1989), 271–75.

49. The best discussion of Mexican American musical history in Los Angeles is Loza, *Barrio Rhythm,* 70–72, 158–65. See also Sheridan, *Los Tucsonenses,* 246–47.

50. Nicolás Kanellos, *Two Centuries of Hispanic Theater in the Southwest,* program guide (Revista Chicano Riqueña, 1982), 19.

51. Nicolás Kanellos, *Hispanic Theatre in the United States* (Houston: Arte Público Press, 1984), 59; see also selected portions of Kanellos, *A History of Hispanic Theater in the United States.*

eight

1. Muñoz, *Youth, Identity, Power;* Gómez Quiñones, *Chicano Politics;* and Mario Barrera, *Beyond Aztlán: Ethnic Autonomy in Comparative Perspective* (New York, London, and Westport, Conn.: Praeger, 1988).

2. See Manuel Gamio, *Mexican Immigration: The Life Story of the Mexican Immigrant,* 2d ed. (New York: Dover, 1971), for an early sense of the term as describing Mexican immigrants in the United States. Use of the term "Chicano" can be found in the early novel by Daniel Venegas, *Las aventuras de Don Chipote: ó cuando los péricos mamen* (Mexico: SEP, CEFROMEX, 1984).

3. See Rubén Rumbaut, "Passages to America: Perspectives on the New Immigration," in *America at Century's End: American Society in Transition,* ed. Alan Wolfe (Berkeley: University of California Press, 1991); F. Ray Marshall, "Economic Factors Influencing the International Migration of Workers," in *Views across the Border: The United States and Mexico,* ed. Stanley Ross (Albuquerque: University of New Mexico Press, 1978), 167. The estimated number of undocumented aliens is usually determined by multiplying the number apprehended. Between 1960 and 1973 more than 2.5 million undocumented Mexican workers were apprehended or deported.

4. Acuña, *Occupied America,* 3d ed., 320. It should be noted that not all people of this generation endorsed the Chicano label and strategies. The continuation of a middle-class caution and desire to work within established institutions continued. See De León, *Ethnicity in the Sunbelt.*

5. The best statement of this concept is in Chávez, *The Lost Land,* 152–55.

6. For a history of Chávez's labor movement see Jacques E. Levy, *Cesar Chavez: Autobiography of La Causa* (New York: W. W. Norton, 1975); Joan London and Henry Anderson, *So Shall Ye Reap: The Story of Cesar Chavez and the Farm Worker's Movement* (New York: Thomas Crowell, 1970); and Dick Meister and Anne Loftis, *A Long Time Coming: The Struggle to Unionize America's Farm Workers* (New York: Macmillian, 1977).

7. San Antonio to Director, FBI Memo, 5/16/67, Bureau File 100-44444762-105, F.B.I. Files, Washington, D.C.

8. Personal interview with Burt Corona, 23 May 1989.

9. *Los Angeles Times,* 8 October 1974, p. 3 col. 4.

10. *Replica* 21 (December 1990): 4–6.

11. For a history of Reies Tijerina and the land-grant movement in New Mexico see Patricia Bell Blawis, *Tijerina and the Land Grants* (New York: International Publishers, 1970); Richard Gardner, *Grito!: Reies Tijerina and the New Mexican Land Grant Wars of 1967* (New York: Harper & Row, 1970); and Peter Nabokov, *Tijerina and the Courthouse Raid* (Albuquerque: University of New Mexico Press, 1969). For Tijerina's own account of the trip and the Alianza, see Reies Tijerina, *Mi lucha por tierra* (Mexico: Fondo de Cultura y Economia, 1978).

12. For a discussion of Tijerina's legal struggles see Richard Griswold del Castillo, *Treaty of Guadalupe Hidalgo: A Legacy of Conflict* (Norman: University of Oklahoma Press, 1990), 132–38.

13. A detailed account of his attempts to organize this caravan appears in Tijerina, 104–10.

14. Acuña, *Occupied American,* 311.

15. Muñoz, *Youth, Identity, Power,* 65–75.

16. *Documents of the Chicano Struggle* (New York: Pathfinder Press, 1971), 4. Spanish translantion: "For my people everything. Outside of my people nothing."

17. Barrera, *Beyond Aztlán,* 49–50; for a firsthand account see Juan Gómez-Quiñones, *Chicano Politics,* 150–53.

18. Ignacio M. García, *United We Win: The Rise and Fall of La Raza Unida Party* (Tucson: University of Arizona Press, 1989), 37–58.

19. For an interpretation of the Raza Unida party as part of a legacy of attacks on Jim Crow practices in Texas arising from the increased urbanization of the state see Montejano, *Anglos and Mexicans in the Making of Texas,* 284–85.

20. Montejano, *Anglos and Mexicans in the Making of Texas,* 289–91, describes the end of the Raza Unida party as a result of the old conflict between middle-class and working-class activists.

21. De León, *Ethnicity in the Sunbelt,* 186.

22. Acuña, *Occupied America,* 345.

23. Grebler, Moore, and Guzman, *The Mexican American People,* 487–88.

24. Irene Blea, *Bessemere: A Sociological Perspective of the Chicano Barrio* (New York: AMS Press, 1991), 145.

25. See the polemic by E. C. Orozco, *Republican Protestantism in Aztlán: The Encounter Between Mexicanism and Anglo-Saxon Secular Humanism in the United States Southwest* (Petereins Press, 1980), 199.

26. De León, *Ethnicity in the Sunbelt,* 178–79.

27. U.S. Department of Commerce, *Statistical Abstracts of the United States,* 1984. In the 1980 census 1.8 million people of "Spanish origin" were reported as living in the Southwest. Of this number, more than half were of Mexican descent.

28. For a brief summary of the historical scholarship regarding Chicanos in the Midwest during this period see Juan R. García, "Select Bibliography on Mexicans and Mexican Americans in the Midwest," *Perspectives in Mexican American Studies: Mexicans in the Midwest,* 2 (1989): 181–85. Within this publication see also Valdes, "The New Northern Borderlands," 1–29.

29. Julian Samora and Richard A. Lamanna, "Mexican-Americans in a Midwest Metropolis: A Study of East Chicago," *Mexican-Study Project: Advance Report 8* (Los Angeles: UCLA, Graduate School of Business Administration, 1967), 4.; U.S. Department of Commerce, *Characteristics of the Population, Illinois: 1990 Census,* vol. 1 (Washington D.C.: U.S. Government Printing Office, 1982), 15–48. Louise Año Nuevo Kerr, "Chicanos in Chicago: A Brief History," *Journal of Ethnic Studies* 2, no. 1 (1975): 22–32.

30. Kerr, "Chicanos in Chicago: A Brief History," 85.

31. See Félix Padilla, *Latino Ethnic Consciousness: The Case of Mexican Americans and Puerto Ricans in Chicago* (Notre Dame, Ind.: University of Notre Dame Press, 1985), 52–59. For a discussion of the problems involved as successive waves of immigrants entered this region, see Ralph Cintron, "Divided, Yet a City: A Brief History," *Perspectives in Mexican American Studies: Community, Identity, and Education* 3 (1992): 43–50.

32. Valdes, *Al Norte,* 163–64, 191–92, 197–98.

33. Martha P. Cotera, *Diosa y Hembra: The History and Heritage of Chicanas in the United States* (Austin, Texas: Information Systems Development, 1976), 110–12.

34. Sonia A. López, "The Role of the Chicana within the Student Movement," in *Essays on La Mujer,* ed. Rosaura Sánchez and Rosa Martínez Cruz (Los Angeles: Chicano Studies Center Publications, 1977), 24–25.

35. See Adelaida R. Del Castillo, "Mexican Women in Organizations," in *Mexican Women in the United States: Struggles Past and Present,* ed. Magdalena Mora and Adelaida Del Castillo (Los Angeles: Chicano Studies Research Center Publications, 1980), 7–16.

36. Nicolás Kanellos, *Mexican American Theater: Legacy and Reality* (Pittsburgh: Latin American Literary Review, 1987), 11–12.

37. See various essays on Chicano film in *Chicano Cinema: Research, Reviews, and Resources,* ed. Gary D. Keller (Binghamton, N.Y.: Bilingual Review Press, 1985).

38. Shifra Goldman, "How, Why, Where, and When It All Happened: Chicano Murals of California," in *Signs from the Heart: California Chicano Murals,* ed. Eva Sperling Cockcroft and Holly Barnet-Sánchez (Venice: Social and Political Art Resource Center, 1990), 24.

39. Tomás Ybarra Frausto and Shirfra Goldman, Introduction, *Arte Chicano: A Comprehensive Annotated Bibliography of Chicano Art, 1965–1981* (Berkeley: Chicano Studies Publications, 1985).

40. Museum of Fine Arts, *Hispanic Art in the United States: Thirty Contemporary Painters and Sculptors* (New York: Abbeville Press, 1987), has biographies as well as representative color photos of the works of these artists. See also Jacinto Quirarte's essay "Mexican and Mexican American Artists in the United States, 1920–1970," in the Bronx Museum of the Arts, *The Latin American Spirit: Art and Artists in the United States, 1920–1970* (New York: Harry N. Abrams, 1989), 14–71.

41. Lipsitz, "Land of a Thousand Dances," 279. For a definitive study of Chicano music of this period see Loza, *Barrio Rhythm.* For a discography of Chicano rock and roll in East Los Angeles in these years see, George Lipsitz, "Chicano Rock and Roll from East Los Angeles: A Research Discography," in *Chicano Studies: Nuevos Horizontes/Midwest Foco Proceedings,* ed. Guillermo Rojas (Minneapolis: Prisma Institute, 1987), 67–71.

42. For a good introduction to Chicano poetry see Cordelia Candelaria, *Chicano Poetry: A Critical Introduction* (Westport, Conn.: Greenwood Press, 1986).

43. Quoted in Shirley and Shirley, *Understanding Chicano Literature,* 196.

nine

1. Frank Sotomayor, "A Box Full of Ethnic Labels," *Southern California's Latino Community* (Los Angeles: Times Mirror Co., 1983), 27–28.

2. There were many exceptions to the spread of Latino nomenclature. For an analyis of the problem, see Phillip B. Gonzales, "The Political Construction of Latino Nomenclatures in Twentieth-Century New Mexico," *Journal of the Southwest* 35, no. 2 (Summer 1993): 158–79. Gonzales points out that terminologies have a political dimension in that they are developed for gaining institutional resources as well as "forming part of the arsenal for gaining and sustaining leadership within the ethnic political community" (159). The term *Latino* he found was emerging in New Mexico but not yet as popular as the term *Hispanic* or *Spanish.* For another discussion of *Latino* terminology, see Earl Shorris, *Latinos: A Biography of the People* (New York and London: W.W. Norton, 1992), xv–xvii.

3. Rubén Rumbaut, "Passages to America: Perspectives on the New Immigration," in *America at Century's End: American Society in Transition,* ed. Alan Wolfe (Berkeley: University of California Press, 1991).

4. *La Red/The Net* 2, no. 2 (1989): 20.

5. "U.S. Hispanic Population: The Year 2080," *Hispanic Business* 9, no. 3 (March 1987): 50.

6. Lawrence W. Miller, Jerry L. Polinard, and Robert D. Wrinkle, "Attitudes toward Undocumented Workers: The Mexican American Perspective," *Social Science Quarterly* 65, no. 2 (June 1984): 483–93.

7. Rodolfo O. de la Garza, "Chicanos and U.S. Foreign Policy: The Future of Chicano-Mexican Relations," in *Mexican-U.S. Relations: Conflict and Convergence,* ed. Carlos Vásquez and Manuel García y Griego (Los Angeles: UCLA Chicano Studies Reseach Center and UCLA Latin American Center Publications, 1983), 401–403.

8. Christine Marie Sierra, "Latinos and the 'New Immigration': Responses from the Mexican American Community," *Renato Rosaldo Lecture Series 3: 1985–1986,* ed. Ignacio Garcia (Tucson: Mexican American Studies and Research Center, University of Arizona, 1987), 42–55.

9. Peter Cattan, "The Growing Presence of Hispanics in the U.S. Work Force," *Monthly Labor Review* (August 1988): 9–13.

10. For a detailed analysis of middle-class growth, see W. O'Hare, "The Rise of Hispanic Affluence," *American Demographics* (August 1990): 40–43. An analysis of this trend by Rochín and Soberanis in *The Thomás Rivera Center Policy Brief* (December 1992) concludes that while "the number of 'higher income' Latino households, has increased over the past 20 years . . . [the increase] has not been enough to counteract the income drops experienced by larger segments of the Latino community" (1).

11. O'Hare, "Rise of Hispanic Affluence."

12. George Swisshelm, "U.S. Hispanics Move to Rediscover Their Ethnic Roots," *Television/Radio Age* 36 (July 1989): A1-A47.

13. Tom Díaz, "Coors Gets on Board Hispanic Trend," *Nuestro* (January–February 1985): 12–18.

14. *Statistical Abstracts of the United States,* no. 69 (1992): 55. The census summaries dealing with household and family data did not distinguish between Puerto Rican, Cuban, Latin-American, and Mexican-American groups. The increase in the number of children in homes without fathers was paralleled with increases in the number of female householders: for Hispanics, 20 percent female-headed in 1980 and 24 percent in 1991; for blacks, 40 percent in 1980 and 46 percent in 1991; for whites, 12 percent in 1980 and 13 percent in 1991. See *Statistical Abstracts of the United States,* no. 70 (1991): 55.

15. Irene Blea, for example, found that single parents of Bessemer, Colorado, were subject to negative social stereotypes by the Mexican-American community. They considered them as "loose, unethical, immoral, incompetent and bad mothers." Irene Blea, *Bessemer: A Sociological Perspective of the Chicano Barrio* (New York: AMS Press, 1991), 125.

16. *Statistical Abstracts of the United States (1992),* no. 57: 47: the proportion of married couples of all Hispanic families has declined from 81 percent in 1970 to 69 percent in 1991.

17. *Statistical Abstracts of the United States (1992),* no. 59: 48.

18. Patricia Zavella, *Women's Work and Chicano Families: Cannery Workers of the Santa Clara Valley* (Ithaca, N.Y., and London: Cornell University Press, 1987), 98.

19. Richard Santillán, "The Latino Community in State and Congressional Redistricting, 1961–1985," *Journal of Hispanic Policy* 1, no. 1 (1985): 52–65.

20. For a good summary of COPS activities in San Antonio, see Acuña, *Occupied America,* 3d rev. ed., 433–34.

21. Harry P. Pachon, "Overview of Hispanic Elected Officials in 1987," *1987 National Roster of Hispanic Elected Officials,* ed. National Association of Latino Elected and Appointed Officials (Washington D.C.: NALEO Education Fund, 1987).

22. Pachon, "Overview of Hispanic Elected Officials in 1987," xv–xxiv.

23. *Los Angeles Times,* 20 February 1991, A18.

24. "Federico Peña," *Current Biography* (October 1993): 36–40.

25. *Denver Post,* 24 July 1983 and 11 April 1993; *Washington Post,* 25 December 1992, 24.

26. Mary Pardo, "Mexican American Women Grassroots Community Activists: Mothers of East Los Angeles," *Frontiers* 11, no. 1 (1990): 2. See also Rodolfo F. Acuña, "Forming the Debate: The Present Interprets the Past," *Renato Rosaldo Lecture Monograph Series* (1992): 80–81.

27. See for example Charles Kyle, "The Magnitude of and Reasons for Chicago's Hispanic Drop-Out Problem: A Case Study of Two Public High Schools," *Renato Rosaldo Lecture Series Monograph* (1990): 25–60; Laurence Steinberg et al., *Dropping Out among Language Minority Youth: A Review of the Literature,* report 81-3W (Los Alamitos, Calif.: National Center for Bilingual Research, 1982).

28. See *A Nation at Risk: The Imperative for Educational Reform* (Washington D.C.: National Commission on Excellence in Education, 1983) and E. D. Hirsh, *Cultural Literacy: What Every American Needs to Know* (Boston: Houghton Mifflin, 1987); Charles Sykes, *Profscam: Professors and the Demise of Higher Education* (Washington D.C.: Regnery Coteway, 1988).

29. Thomas Muller and Thomas J. Sepenshade et al., *The Fourth Wave: California's Newest Immigrants* (Washington, D.C.: Urban Institute, 1985), 80, 82.

30. Acuña, *Occupied America*, 3d rev. ed., 389–90; Arnoldo De León, *Mexican Americans in Texas*, 141–42, discusses the subsequent court rulings on this issue.

31. *MALDEF Newsletter* 10, no. 4 (Fall 1980): 1.

32. For an excellent discussion of drop-outs and educational statistics, see selected essays in *Hispanics in the United States: A New Social Agenda*, ed. Pastora San Juan Cafferty and William C. McCready (New Brunswick, N.J.: Transaction Books, 1985).

33. San Juan Cafferty, "Language and Social Assimilation," in *Hispanics in the United States*, 102–104, describes the evaluation of bilingual programs. For a more recent study see "Bilingual Students Held to Do Well," *Los Angeles Times*, 12 February 1991, 1.

34. Linda Chávez, *Out of the Barrio: Toward a New Politics of Hispanic Assimilation* (New York: Basic Books, 1991), 88.

35. Chávez, *Out of the Barrio*, 91–92.

36. Mark R. Halton, "Legislating Assimilation: The English-Only Movement," *Christian Century* 106 (29 November 1989): 1119.

37. Raúl Yzaguirre, "The Perils of Pandora: An Examination of the English-Only Movement," *Journal of Hispanic Policy* 2 (1986–87): 5.

38. David Reimers, *Still the Golden Door: The Third World Comes to America* (New York: Colombia University Press, 1985), 203.

39. James D. Cockcroft, *Outlaws in the Promised Land: Mexican Immigrant Workers and America's Future* (New York: Grove Press, 1986), 218–27.

40. Sierra, "Latinos and the 'New Immigration,'" 51; Gutiérrez, "Ethnicity, Ideology, and Political Development," 334–39.

41. Richard D. Lamm and Gary Imhoff, *The Immigration Time Bomb: The Fragmenting of America* (New York: Truman Talley Books, 1986).

42. Cockcroft, *Outlaws in the Promised Land*, 130.

43. David E. Hayes-Bautista, Werner O. Schinek, and Jorge Chapa, "Young Latinos in an Aging American Society," *Social Policy* 15, no. 1 (1984): 49–52.

44. Cockcroft, *Outlaws in the Promised Land*, 135.

45. *La Chicana: Building for the Future: An Action Plan for the 1980s* (Oakland, Calif.: National Hispanic Center, 1981).

46. De la Torre and Pesquera, *Building with Our Hands*, 4.

47. *Chicana Voices: Intersections of Class, Race, and Gender*, ed. Teresa Córdova et al. (Austin, Texas: Center for Mexican American Studies, 1986), is the publication of some of the best papers presented at this conference.

48. De la Torre and Pesquera, *Building with Our Hands*, 4–5.

49. Cristina Portillo, *Bibliography of Writings: La Mujer* (Berkeley, California: Chicano Studies Library Publications Unit, 1976).

50. *Chicana Studies Index* (Berkeley: Chicano Studies Library Publications Unit, 1993).

51. Gloria Anzaldúa, *Borderlands/La Frontera: The New Mestiza* (San Francisco: Spinsters/Ante Lute Book Company, 1987), 77–81.

52. Irene I. Blea, *La Chicana and the Intersection of Race, Class, and Gender* (New York, London, and Westport, Conn.: Praeger, 1992).

53. Ibid., 146.

54. For an analysis of the cultural and musical tradition for *La Bamba* as well as an analysis of the popularity of the movie, see Louis M. Holscher, Celestino Fernández, and Laura L. Cummings, "From Local Tradition to International

Phenomenon: *La Bamba,*" *Renato Rosaldo Lecture Series Monograph* (Tucson: Mexican American Studies and Research Center, 1991), 1–28.

55. "A Surging New Spirit," *Time,* 11 July 1988, 46–76.

56. Loza, *Barrio Rhythms,* 115, 280.

57. Shirley and Shirley, *Understanding Chicano Literature,* 88.

58. Ibid., 41–48. This book has a fine bibliography of surveys and original works on Chicano literature.

59. *New York Times,* 15 December 1992, 1; Rodolfo O. de la Garza, Luis De Sipio, F. Chris García, John García, and Angelo Falcón, *Latino Voices: Mexican, Puerto Rican, and Cuban Perspectives on American Politics* (Boulder, Colo., San Francisco, and Oxford: Westview Press, 1992).

60. Shirley and Shirley, *Understanding Chicano Literature.* Peter Skerry in *Mexican Americans: The Ambivalent Minority* offers a conservative critique of this view. His argument is that Mexican-American elites have succeeded in uniting constituents by playing on race consciousness and historical resentments to achieve power within a post-civil rights era where racial minority groups have been given benefit packages under affirmative action and the Voting Rights Act. He charges the Mexican-American elite with practicing anti-politics by using the immigrant masses to consolidate their position as arbiters of an oppressed minority even while hundreds of thousands of Mexican Americans have left the barrio for the suburbs.

ten

1. For a discussion of the biological consequences of the European "encounter" with the New World, see Alfred W. Crosby, *Ecological Imperialism: The Biological Expansion of Europe, 900–1900* (Cambridge and New York: Cambridge University Press, 1986), and *The Colombian Exchange: The Biological and Cultural Consequences of 1492* (Englewood Cliffs, N.J.: Prentice-Hall, 1972).

2. For an analysis of the way in which Latin Americans are changing the definition of culture see Jean Franco, "Remapping Culture," *Americas: New Interpretive Essays*, ed. Alfred Stepan (New York and Oxford: Oxford University Press, 1992), 172–88.

3. Ronald Takaki, *A Different Mirror: A History of Multicultural America* (Boston, Toronto, London: Little, Brown, 1993), 17.

4. Rubén G. Rumbaut, "The Americans: Latin American and Caribbean Peoples in the United States," in *Americas: New Interpretive Essays,* 303.

Bibliographic Essay

The richest sources for writing the history of Mexican Americans are cited in the Notes and References. These publications are the most useful guides for categorizing the literature into chronological eras. This essay, which arranges the literature into fields of study, includes publications not listed in the Notes and References, as well as many prominent works that inform the status of Chicano history.

Reference Guides

The more useful bibliographies for studying Mexican-American history are Matt S. Meier and Feliciano Rivera, *Bibliography of Mexican American History* (Westport, Conn.: Greenwood Press, 1984); Albert Camarillo, *Latinos in the United States: A Historical Bibliography* (Santa Barbara, Calif.: ABC-CLIO, 1986); Lillian Castillo-Speed, "Chicana Studies: A Selected List of Materials since 1980," *Frontiers: A Journal of Women's Studies* 11 (1990); John R. García, "Selected Bibliography on Mexicans and Mexican Americans in the Midwest," *Perspectives in Mexican American Studies*, vol. 2 (Tucson: Mexican American Studies Center, University of Arizona, 1989); John García et al., *Latinos and Politics: A Selected Research Bibliography* (Austin: University of Texas Press, 1991); and Jacqueline J. Etulain, *Mexican Americans in the Twentieth-Century West: A Bibliography*, Occasional Papers, No. 3 (Albuquerque: Center for the American West, 1990).

Students wishing to learn about how scholars have interpreted Chicano history over time should begin with Juan Gómez-Quiñones and Luis Leobardo Arroyo, "On the State of Chicano History: Observations on Its Development, Interpretations, and Theory, 1970–1974," *Western Historical Quarterly* 7 (1976). Good essays that update this historiography include Alex Saragoza, "The Significance of Recent Chicano-Related Historical Writings: An Apraisal," *Ethnic Affairs* 1 (1987); Arnoldo De León, "Texas Mexicans: Twentieth Century Interpretations," in *Texas through Time: Evolving Interpretations*, ed. Walter L. Buenger and Robert A. Calvert (College Station: Texas A & M University Press, 1990); and Richard Griswold del Castillo, "Chicano Historical Discourse: An Overview and Evaluation of the 1980s," in *Perspectives in Mexican American Studies*, vol. 4 (Tucson: Mexican American Studies Research Center, University of Arizona, 1993)

General Histories

The introduction to the study of Mexican-American history should begin with the now classic work of Carey McWilliams (updated by Matt S. Meier), *North from Mexico: The Spanish-Speaking People of the United States* (New York: Greenwood Press, 1990). Other excellent survey textbooks included Rodolfo Acuña, *Occupied America: A History of Chicanos,* 3d ed. (New York: Harper & Row, 1988); Matt S. Meier and Feliciana Ribera, *Mexican Americans, American Mexicans: From Conquistadores to Chicanos,* 2d ed. (New York: Hill & Wang, 1993); and Julian Samora and Patricia Vandel Simon, *A History of the Mexican American People,* 2d ed. (Notre Dame, Ind.: University of Notre Dame Press, 1993). Useful state histories include Arnoldo De León, *Mexican Americans in Texas: A Brief History* (Arlington Heights, Ill.: Harlan Davidson, 1993); Albert Camarillo, *Chicanos in California History: A History of Mexican Americans in California* (San Francisco: Boyd & Fraser Publishing Co., 1984); and Nancy L. Gonzales, *The Spanish Americans of New Mexico: A Historical Perspective* (Albuquerque: University of New Mexico Press, 1969). Briefer works on Mexican Americans outside the Southwest include Vicente V. Mayer, *Utah: A Hispanic History* (Salt Lake City: American West Center, University of Utah, 1975); and Michael Smith, *The Mexicans of Oklahoma* (Norman: University of Oklahoma Press, 1980). Examples of regional histories include Erasmo Gamboa, "Chicanos in the Northwest: A Historical Perspective," *El Grito* 6 (1973); Carlos Gil, "Washington's Hispano American Communities," in *Peoples of Washington: Perspectives on Cultural Diversity,* ed. Sid White and S. E. Solbert (Pullman: Washington State University Press, 1989); Richard W. Slatta, "Chicanos in the Pacific Northwest: A Demographic and Socioeconomic Portrait," *Pacific Northwest Quarterly* 70 (1979); and Richard W. Slatta, "Chicanos in the Pacific Northwest: An Historical Overview of Oregon's Chicanos," *Aztlán* 6 (1975).

Two essential anthologies that represent early Chicano historical writing are Manuel P. Servín, ed., *The Mexican Americans: An Awakening Minority* (Beverly Hills, Calif.: Glencoe Press, 1970); and Manuel P. Servín, ed., *An Awakened Minority: The Mexican Americans,* 2d ed. (Beverley Hills, Calif.: Glencoe Press, 1974).

Some of the more significant anthologies address the contributions of women. Among these are Adelaida R. del Castillo, ed., *Between Borders: Essays on Mexicana/Chicana History* (Encino, Calif.: Floricanto Press, 1990); Teresa Cordova et al., eds., *Chicana Voices: Intersections of Class, Race, and Gender* (Austin: NACS, Center for Mexican American Studies, 1986); and Adela de la Torre, *Building with Our Hands: New Directions in Chicana History* (Berkeley: University of California Press, 1993).

We have integrated works on women into the relevant categories below, but other specific studies deserve being listed separately. Overview texts on "herstory" are Marta P. Cotera, *Diosa y Hembra: The History and Heritage of Chicanas in the United States* (Austin: Information Systems Development, 1976), and Alfredo Mirandé and Evangelina Enríquez, *La Chicana: The Mexican American Woman* (Chicago: University of Chicago Press, 1979). Works that make a connection between women and community include Antonia I. Castañeda, *"Presidarias y Pobladoras*: Spanish-Mexican Women in Frontier Monterey, Alta California, 1770–1821,"* Ph.D. diss., Stanford University, 1990; Deena González, "The Spanish-Mexican Women of Santa Fe: Patterns of Their Resistance and Accommodation, 1820–1880," Ph.D. diss., University of California at Berkeley, 1986; Jane Dysart, "Mexican Women in San Antonio, 1830–1860: The Assimilation Process," *Western Historical Quarterly* 7 (1976); and David J. Langum, "Californio Women and the Image of Virtue," *Southern California Quarterly* 59 (1977).

Scholarly journals have seen fit to publish special issues on Mexican Americans; examples include *Frontiers: A Journal of Women Studies* 11 (1990); *The Great Plains Quarterly* 10 (1990); and *Journal of the West* 24 (1985). Also, the University of Arizona publishes two excellent series devoted to the field: *Renato Rosaldo Lecture Series Mongraphs* and *Perspectives on Mexican American Studies*. Additionally, the National Association for Chicano Studies publishes some of the papers presented at its yearly conference.

Art and Literature

The once-distorted picture of an illiterate Mexican-American community has been dispelled by a spate of works from scholars specializing in Chicano creative literature. Cordelia Candelaria, *Chicano Poetry: A Critical Introduction* (Westport, Conn.: Greenwood Press, 1986), gives a good overview of Mexican-American poetic expression during the last three decades. Original collections of short stories by women include Tey Diana Rebolledo et al., eds., *Las Mujeres Hablan: An Anthology of Nuevo Mexicana Writers* (Albuquerque: El Norte Publications, 1988). Interpretations of the Chicano literary past are provided in Ramón Gutiérrez and Genaro Padilla, eds., *Recovering the U.S. Hispanic Literary Heritage* (Houston: Arte Público Press, 1993); María Herrera-Sobek, *Reconstructing a Chicano Literary Heritage* (Tucson: University of Arizona Press, 1993); and Tey Diana Rebolledo, *Infinite Divisions: An Anthology of Chicana Literature* (Tucson: Univerity of Arizona Press, 1993). Analyses of personal recollections are given in the seminal work of Genaro Padilla, *My History, Not Yours: The Formation of Mexican American Autobiography* (Madison: University of Wisconsin Press, 1993).

Much attention has been given to New Mexican folklore, and informative studies include Stanely L. Robe, *Hispanic Folktales from New Mexico* (Berkeley: University of California Press, 1977); Lorin W. Brown et al., *Hispano Folktales of New Mexico* (Albuquerque: University of New Mexico Press, 1978); Fray Angelico Chávez, *My Penitente Land: Reflections on Spanish New Mexico* (Albuquerque: University of New Mexico Press, 1974); and Aurelio M. Espinoza, *The Folklore of Spain in the American Southwest: Traditional Spanish Folk Literature in Southern New Mexico and Southern Colorado* (Norman: University of Oklahoma Press, 1990). In Texas few studies excel that of Américo Paredes. They include *"With His Pistol in His Hand": A Border Ballad and Its Hero* (1958; Austin: University of Texas Press, 1971); and *Folklore and Culture on the Texas-Mexican Border* (Austin: Center for Mexican American Studies, University of Texas Press, 1993). Another good study is José E. Limón, *Dancing with the Devil: Society and Cultural Poetics in Mexican American South Texas* (Madison: University of Wisconsin, 1994). See also Richard

R. Flores, *"Los Pastores:* Performance, Poetics, and Politics in Folk Drama," Ph.D. diss., University of Texas at Austin, 1989.

Two studies that exemplify the directions currently being taken by students of Chicano journalism are Anabelle Oczón, "Bilingual and Spanish-Language Newspapers in Territorial New Mexico," *New Mexico Historical Review*, 54 (1979); and Roberto R. Treviño, *"Prensa y Patria:* The Spanish-Language Press and the Biculturation of the Tejano Middle Class, 1920–1940," *Western Historical Quarterly* 22 (1991).

Among the best bibliographies available to those wanting to acquaint themselves with the literature on painting and the arts is Tomas Ybarra Frausto and Shirfra Goldman, *Arte Chicano: A Comprehensive Annotated Bibliography of Chicano Art, 1965–1981* (Berkeley, Calif.: Chicano Studies Publications, 1985). More specific coverage of individual artists is contained in Jacinto Quirarte, "Mexican and Mexican American Artists in the United States, 1920–1970," in the Bronx Museum of the Arts, *The Latin American Spirit: Art and Artists in the United States, 1920–1970* (New York: Harry N. Abrams, 1989); Museum of Fine Arts, *Hispanic Art in the United States: Thirty Contemporary Painters and Sculptors* (New York: Abbeville Press, 1987); and Sid White et al., *Chicano and Latino Artists in the Pacific Northwest* (Olympia, Wash.: Evergreen State College, 1984). Lawrence P. Hurlburt, *The Mexican Muralists in the United States* (Albuquerque: University of New Mexico Press, 1989), brings to our attention the works done in the United States by such famous artists from Mexico as Diego Rivera, David Alfaro Siquieros, and José Clemente Orozco. William Wroth has devoted much time to studying the folk forms of New Mexico *santeros*, and some of his findings are provided in *Christian Images in Hispanic New Mexico* (Colorado Springs: Taylor Museum of Colorado Springs Fine Arts Center, 1982) and *Images of Penance, Images of Mercy: Southwestern Santos in the Late Nineteenth Century* (Norman: University of Oklahoma Press, 1991).

Immigration and Demography

Numerous older studies told the history of Spanish settlements in the Far North, but the literature is updated in David J. Weber's prize-winning monographs *The Mexican Frontier: The American Southwest under Mexico, 1821–1846* (Albuquerque: University of New Mexico Press, 1982) and *The Spanish Frontier in North America* (New Haven, Conn.: Yale University Press, 1992).

The study of modern migration into the United States remains the domain of sociologists and demographers, but several historical works significantly augment the data in those publications. The earliest work of importance is Manuel Gamio, *Mexican Immigration: The Life Story of the Mexican Immigrant to the United States* (New York: Arno Press, 1969). The political positions taken by American officials (often pressured by business interests) in importing (or deporting) Mexicans is explained in Gilberto Cárdenas, "U.S. Immigration Policy toward Mexico: A Historical Perspective," *Chicano Law Review* 2 (1976). Important works on immigration trends include Saúl Solache, "Urban Growth Patterns and Mexican Immigration to the United States, 1790 to 1970," Ph.D. diss., University of California at Los Angeles, 1981; Marilyn P. Davis, *Mexican Voices, American Dreams: An Oral History of Mexican Immigration to the United States* (New York: Henry Holt & Co., 1990). Christine Marie Sierra, "Latinos and the 'New

Immigration': Responses from the Mexican American Community," *Renato Rosaldo Lecture Monographs Series* 3 (1987); and David G. Gutiérrez, "Ethnicity, Ideology, and Political Developments: Mexican Immigration as a Political Issue in the Chicano Community," Ph.D. diss., Stanford University, 1988, provide discussions of Mexican Americans' views on migration from Mexico.

Works describing the interstate movements of Mexican Americans toward areas outside the borderlands include Michael Smith, "Beyond the Borderlands: Mexican Labor in the Central Plains, 1900–1930," *Great Plains Quarterly* 1 (1981); Robert Oppenheimer, "Acculturation and Assimilation: Mexican Immigrants in Kansas, 1900–World War II," *Western Historical Quarterly* 16 (1985); F. Arturo Rosales, "Mexican Immigration to the Urban Midwest during the 1920s," Ph.D. diss., Indiana University, 1978; and Erasmo Gamboa, "Mexican Migration into Washington State: A History, 1940–1950," *Pacific Northwest Quarterly* 72 (1981)

On the other hand, there have always been forced movements from the United States to Mexico. The repatriation of the 1930s is studied in Abraham Hoffman, *Unwanted Mexican Americans in the Great Depression: Repatriation Pressures, 1929–1939* (Tucson: University of Arizona Press, 1974); R. Reynolds McKay, "Texas Mexican Repatriation during the Great Depression," Ph.D. diss., University of Oklahoma at Norman, 1982; Marilyn Rhinehart and Thomas H. Kreneck, "'In the Shadow of Uncertainty': Texas Mexicans and Repatriation in Houston during the Great Depression," *Houston Review* 10 (1988); Camille Guerin-Gonzales, *Mexican Workers and American Dreams: Immigration, Repatriation, and California Farm Labor, 1900–1939* (New Brunswick: Rutgers University Press, 1994); and D. H. Dinwoodie, "Deportation: The Immigration Service and the Chicano Labor Movement in the 1930s," *New Mexico Historical Review* 52 (1977). Efforts to uproot Mexicans from the Midwest and repatriate them to Mexico are the focus of Neil Betten, "From Discrimination to Repatriation: Mexican Life in Gary, Indiana, during the Great Depression," *Pacific Historical Review* 42 (1973), and Daniel T. Simon, "Mexican Repatriation in East Chicago, Indiana," *Journal of Ethnic Studies* 2 (1974). Juan Ramón García, *Operation Wetback: The Mass Deportation of Mexican Undocumented Workers in 1954* (Westport, Conn.: Greenwood Press, 1980), treats McCarthy-era anti-immigrant nativism.

Life within Communities

The study of ethnicity, or ethnic identity, increasingly attracted the attention of scholars during the 1980s. How Mexican Americans perceived their region of settlement became the focus of such works as Rudolfo A. Anaya and Francisco Lomelí, *Aztlán: Essays on the Chicano Homeland* (Albuquerque: University of New Mexico Press, 1989). Studies that expanded on how Mexican Americans perceived themselves over the course of several generations include Carole E. Christian, "Joining the American Mainstream: Texas' Mexican Americans during World War I," *Southwestern Historical Quarterly* 93 (1989); Francisco Arturo Rosales, "Shifting Self-Perceptions and Ethnic Consciousness among Mexicans in Houston, 1908–1946," *Aztlán* 16 (1985); Douglas Monroy, "'Our Children Get So Different Here': Film, Fashion, Popular Culture, and the Process of Cultural Syncretization in Mexican Los Angeles, 1900–1935," *Aztlán* 19 (1988–90); Phillip Gonzales, "Political Construction of Latino Nomenclatures in Twentieth-Century New Mexico," *Journal of the Southwest* 35 (1993).

Gonzales takes his work further by noting the connection between identity and ethnic labels in Phillip Gonzales, "Spanish Heritage and Ethnic Protest in New Mexico, 1933," *New Mexico Historical Review* 61 (1986).

A great deal of the work done on Chicano history over the last 25 years has been in the area of social history, and we relied on it extensively in constructing this story of Mexican Americans. Miscellaneous studies of significance may be Mario Barrera, *Race and Class in the Southwest: A Theory of Racial Inequality* (Notre Dame, Ind.: Notre Dame University Press, 1979); Nicolás Kanellos, *Handbook of Hispanic Culture in the United States* (Houston: Arte Público Press, 1994); Arthur Campa, *Hispanic Culture in the Southwest* (Norman: University of Oklahoma Press, 1979); David Langum, *Law and Community on the Mexican California Frontier, 1821–1846* (Norman: University of Oklahoma Press, 1987); and Gerald E. Poyo and Gilberto M. Hinojosa, eds., *Tejano Origins in Eighteenth-Century San Antonio* (Austin: University of Texas Press, 1991). Books on the Mexican-American family include Robert R. Alvarez, Jr., *Familia: Migration and Adaptation in Baja and Alta California, 1800–1975* (Berkeley: University of California Press, 1987).

Contributions to the field of religion and Mexican Americans are in their embryonic states, but much is already known of Mexican American Christian beliefs, traditions, and practices. Among the most perceptive works are José Roberto Juárez, "La Iglesia Católica y el Chicano de Sud Tejas, 1836–1911," *Aztlán* 4 (1973); Roberto R. Treviño, *"La Fe:* Catholicism and Mexican Americans in Houston, 1911–1972," Ph.D. diss., Stanford University, 1993; Alberto Pulido, "Mexican American Catholicism in the Southwest: The Transformation of a Popular Religion," in *Perspectives in Mexican American Studies,* no. 4 (Tucson: Mexican American Studies and Research Center, 1993); and R. Douglas Brackenridge and Francisco O. García-Treto, *Iglesia Presbiteriana: A History of Presbyterians and Mexican Americans of the Southwest* (San Antonio: Trinity University Press, 1974). See also E. C. Orozco, *Republican Protestantism in Aztlán: The Encounter between Mexicanism and Anglo-Saxon Humanism in the United States Southwest* (Glendale, Ariz.: Petereins Press, 1980), and the essays on Mexican-American Catholics in California, and on missionaries in New Mexico, in Carl Guarneri et al., *Religion and Society in the American West: Historical Essays* (Lanham, Md.: University Press of America, 1987).

Aspects of popular religiosity have also interested scholars. Much insight is provided about the Penitentes of New Mexico by Lorayne Horka-Follick, *Los Hermanos Penitentes* (Los Angeles: Westernlore Press, 1969); Marta Weigle, *The Penitentes of the Southwest* (Santa Fe: Ancient City Press, 1970); and Marta Weigle, *Brothers of Light, Brothers of Blood* (Albuquerque: University of New Mexico Press, 1976). See further Janie Louise Aragón, "The Cofradías of New Mexico: A Proposal and a Periodization," *Aztlán* 9 (1978). On folk healing, instructive monographs include Robert T. Trotter II and Juan Antonio Chavira, *Curanderismo: Mexican American Folk Healing* (Athens: University of Georgia Press, 1981); E. Ferol Benavides, "The Saints among the Saints: A Study of Curanderismo in Utah," *Utah Historical Quarterly* 4 (1973); Carlos Larralde, "Santa Teresa: A Chicana Mystic," *Grito del Sol* 3 (1978); and Wilson M. Hudson, ed., *The Healer of Los Olmos and other Mexican Lore* (Dallas: Southern Methodist University Press, 1951). Marc Simmons, *Witchcraft in the Southwest: Spanish and Indian Supernaturalism on the Rio Grande* (Lincoln: University of Nebraska Press, 1980), treats a most neglected topic.

The list of studies of individuals who contributed to Mexican-American history keeps increasing, and only a sampling is provided here. On Nuevo Mexicanos, see the recent revisionist portrayal by Larry D. Ball, *Elfego Baca* (El Paso: Texas Western Press, 1992), as well as Fray Angelico Chávez, *But Time and Chance: The Story of Padre Martínez of Taos, 1793–1867* (Santa Fe: Sunstone Press, 1981); Joe Roy Luján, "Dennis Chávez and the Roosevelt Era, 1933–1945," Ph.D. diss., University of New Mexico, 1987; Charlotte Whaley, *Nina Otero-Warren of Santa Fe* (Albuquerque: University of New Mexico Press, 1994); and volume 67 (1992) of the *New Mexico Historical Review* on Miguel Antonio Otero. Works on Arizonenses include those by Manuel G. Gonzales, "Carlos I. Velasco," *Journal of Arizona History* 25 (1984); Manuel G. Gonzales, "Mariano G. Samaniego," *Journal of Arizona History* 31 (1990); and Matt S. Meier, "Estéban Ochoa: Enterpriser," *Journal of the West* 25 (1986). In Texas, the writing of biography has kept pace with that of other states, with the model set by Félix D. Alamaráz, whose first installment—"Carlos E. Castañeda, Mexican American Historian: The Formative Years, 1896–1927," *Pacific Historical Review* 42 (1973)—bodes well for the quality of his study on Carlos E. Castañeda, the great historian and civic activist. Other biographical works on Tejanos include Jesús F. de la Teja, ed., *A Revolution Remembered: The Memoirs and Selected Correspondence of Juan N. Seguín* (Austin: State House Press, 1991); Chris Strachuitz with James Nicolopulos, comps., *Lydia Mendoza: A Family Autobiography* (Houston: Arte Público Press, 1993); Jerry D. Thompson, ed., *Juan Cortina and the Texas-Mexico Frontier, 1859–1877* (El Paso: University of Texas at El Paso, 1994); John Denny Reilly, "Santos Benavides: His Influence on the Lower Rio Grande, 1823–1891," Ph.D. diss., Texas Christian University, 1976; and Gladys Ruth Leff, "George I. Sánchez: Don Quixote of the Southwest," M.A. thesis, North Texas State University, 1976. On California, see Mario T. García, ed., *Memories of Chicano History: The Life and Narrative of Bert Corona* (Berkeley: University of California Press, 1994).

Anglo-American perceptions (generally with a jaundiced eye) of Mexican-American communities attracted the interest of historians during the early stages of Chicano scholarship. Literature on the subject includes Burl Noggle, "Anglo Observers of the Southwest Borderlands, 1825–1890: The Rise of a Concept," *Arizona and the West* 1 (1959); Raymund Paredes, "The Mexican Image in American Travel Literature, 1831–1869," *New Mexico Historical Review* 52 (1977); Alvin P. Sensuri, *Seeds of Discord: New Mexico in the Aftermath of the American Conquest, 1846–1861* (Chicago: Nelson-Hall, 1979); Jesse de la Cruz, "Rejection Because of Race: Albert J. Beveridge and Nuevo Mexico's Struggle for Statehood, 1902–1903," *Aztlán* 7 (1976); Richard H. Peterson, "Anti-Mexican Nativism in California, 1848–1853," *Southern California Quarterly* 62 (1980). Attitudes toward women are investigated in David J. Langum, "Californio Women and the Image of Virtue," *Southern California Quarterly* 59 (1977), and Beverly Trulio, "Anglo American Attitudes toward New Mexico Women," *Journal of the West* 12 (1973).

The stereotypes portrayed in the film industry are the subject of Allen L. Woll, "Latin Images in American Films," *Journal of Mexican American History* 4 (1974); Bliane P. Lamb, "The Convenient Villain: Early Cinema Views of Mexican Americans," *Journal of the West* 14 (1975); Juan R. García, "Hollywood and the West: Mexican Images in American Films, 1894–1983," in *Old*

Southwest/New Southwest, ed. Judy N. Lensink (Tucson: Tucson Public Library, 1987); and, Arthur G. Pettit, *Images of the Mexican American in Fiction and Film* (College Station: Texas A & M University Press, 1980).

Labor

The scholarship on labor ranks among the most extensive in Mexican-American historiography, and the most important works are cited in the Notes and References. Historians have continued to find new topics to investigate, however, among which are women and the work force. Notable studies on this subject are Julia Kirk Blackwelder, *Women of the Depression: Caste and Culture in San Antonio, 1929–1939* (College Station: Texas A & M University Press, 1984); Richard Croxdale, "The 1938 San Antonio Pecan Shellers' Strike," in Richard Croxdale and Melissa Hield, *Women in the Texas Workforce: Yesterday and Today* (Austin: People's History in Texas, 1979); Laurie Coyle, Gail Hershatter, and Emily Honig, "Women at Farrah: An Unfinished Story," in Magdalena Mora and Adelaida R. del Castillo, eds., *Mexican Women in the United States: Struggles Past and Present* (Los Angeles: Chicano Studies Research Center, 1980); Susan González Baker, "Many Rivers to Cross: Mexican Immigrants, Women Workers, and the Structure of Labor Markets in the Urban Southwest," Ph.D. diss., University of Texas at Austin, 1989; Patricia Zavella, *Women's Work and Chicano Family Life: Cannery Workers in Santa Clara Valley* (Ithaca, N.Y.: Cornell University Press, 1987); Irene Ledesma, "Unlikely Strikers: Mexican-American Women in Strike Activity in Texas, 1919–1974," Ph.D. diss., Ohio State University, 1992; Barbara J. Rosek, "The Entry of Mexican Women into Urban-Based Industries: Experiences in Texas during the Twentieth Century," in *Women and Texas History: Selected Essays,* ed. Fane Downs and Nancy Baker Jones (Austin: Texas State Historical Association, 1993).

Studies that focus on the community of workers include Camilo Martínez, "The Mexican and Mexican American Labor Contributions to the Economic Development of the Lower Rio Grande Valley of Texas, 1870–1930," Ph.D. diss., Texas A & M University, 1987; and Gilbert González, "Labor and Community: Mexican Citrus Pickers in Southern California," *Western Historical Quarterly* 22 (1991).

Selected examples of writings that look at labor unionism and strike activity in the United States include Dick Meister and Anne Loftis, *A Long Time Coming: The Struggle to Unionize America's Farm Workers* (New York: Macmillian, 1977); Phil Mellinger, "'The Men Have Become Organizers': Labor Conflict and Union-ization in the Mexican Mining Communities of Arizona, 1900–1915," *Western Historical Quarterly* 23 (1992); Douglas Monroy, *"Anarquismo y Comunismo:* Mexican Radicalism and the Communist Party in Los Angeles during the 1930s," *Labor History* 24 (1983); Douglas Monroy, "Like Swallows at the Old Mission: Mexicans and the Radical Politics of Growth in Los Angeles during the Interwar Years," *Western Historical Quarterly* 14 (1983); Victor B. Nelson Cisneros, "La Clase Trabajadora en Tejas, 1920–1940," *Aztlán* 6 (Summer 1975); Charles Wollenberg, "Huelga 1928 Style: The Imperial Valley Cantaloupe Workers Strike," *Pacific Historical Review* 38 (1969); Abraham Hoffman, "The El Monte Berry Pickers Strike, 1933," *Journal of the West* 12 (1973); Francisco Rosales, "Chicano Steel Workers and Unionism in the Midwest," *Aztlán* 6 (1975); Devra

A. Weber, "The Organizing of Mexicano Agricultural Workers: Imperial Valley and Los Angeles, 1928–1934," *Aztlán* 3 (1972).

Politics

How the constabulary has been used to immobilize organizations within the Chicano community is the subject of various studies by Edward Joseph Escobar. His works on the Los Angeles Police Department and its treatment of barrio people include "Chicano Protest and the Law: Law Enforcment Responses to Chicano Activism in Los Angeles, 1850–1936," Ph.D. diss., University of California at Riverside, 1983; "The Dialectics of Repression: The Los Angeles Police Department and the Chicano Movement," *Journal of American History*, 79 (1993); "Mexican Revolutionaries and the Los Angeles Police: Harassment of the *Partido Liberal Mexicano*, 1907–1910," *Aztlán* 17 (1986); and "The Los Angeles Police Department and Mexican Workers: The Case of the 1913 Christmas Riot," in Juan R. García, *In Times of Challenge: Chicanos and Chicanas in American Society* (Houston: Mexican American Studies Program, 1988). An account that tells a similar story for Texas is Julian Samora et al., *Gunpowder Justice: A Reassessment of the Texas Rangers* (Notre Dame, Ind.: University of Notre Dame Press, 1979).

Examples of studies that explore episodes of white violence against Mexican Americans include William B. Secrest, *Juanita: The Only Woman Lynched during Gold Rush Days* (Fresno, Calif.: Saga-West Publishing Co., 1967); and Ellen Schneider and Paul H. Carlson, "Gunnysackers, *Carreteros*, and Teamsters: The South Texas Cart War of 1857," *Journal of South Texas* 1 (1988). The most intelligent study in this field of interest is Mauricio Mazón, *The Zoot-Suit Riots: The Psychology of Symbolic Annihilation* (Austin: University of Texas Press, 1984).

The literature that concentrates on Mexican Americans as politicians has continued to grow. A good starting point for studying this subject is Richard Griswold del Castillo, *The Treaty of Guadalupe Hidalgo: A Legacy of Conflict* (Norman: University of Oklahoma Press, 1990). Other works include F. Chris García, "Manitos and Chicanos in Nuevo Mexico Politics, *Aztlán* 5 (1975), and Christine Sierra, "Chicano Political Development: Historical Considerations," in Eugene E. García et al., *Chicano Studies: A Multidisciplinary Approach* (New York: Teachers College Press, 1984).

Among the best works that investigate the functions and goals of civic organizations based in Texas are Carl Allsup, *The American G.I. Forum: Origins and Evolution* (Austin: Center for Mexican American Studies, University of Texas Press, 1982); Benjamin Márquez, *LULAC: The Evolution of a Mexican American Political Organization* (Austin: University of Texas Press, 1993); and Cynthia E. Orozco, "The Origins of the League of United Latin American Citizens (LULAC) and the Mexican American Civil Rights Movement in Texas with an Analysis of Women's Political Participation in a Gendered Context, 1910–1929," Ph.D. diss., University of California at Los Angeles, 1992. On Arizona see Christine Marín, "Mexican Americans on the Home Front: Community Organizations in Arizona during World War II," in *Perspectives in Mexican American Studies*, vol. 4 (Tucson: Mexican American Studies and Research Center, 1993).

Scholarly works on urban politics are few, but they hold out the promise of more significant and better analytical investigations in the near future. Good works today are Richard Santillán, "Latino Politics in the Midwestern United States," in *Latinos and the Political System,* ed. F. Chris García (Notre Dame, Ind.: University of Notre Dame Press, 1988); Roberto R. Calderón, "Mexican Politics in the American Era, 1846–1900: Laredo, Texas," Ph.D. diss., University of California at Los Angeles, 1993; Rodolfo Rosales, "The Rise of Chicano Middle Class Politics in San Antonio, 1951–1985," Ph.D. diss., University of Michigan, 1991; and Guadalupe San Miguel, Jr., "'The Community is Beginning to Rumble': The Origins of Chicano Educational Protest in Houston, 1965–1970," *Houston Review* 13 (1991).

Self-help organizations that occasionally took part in urban politics have been the subject of many studies. A good introductory piece is Mario Barrera's "The Historical Evolution of Chicano Ethnic Goals: A Bibliographic Essay," *Sage Race Relations Abstracts* 10 (1985). Equally solid contributions include Julie Leininger Pycior, "La Raza Organizes: Mexican American Life in San Antonio, 1915–1930, as Reflected in *Mutualista* Activities," Ph.D. diss., University of Notre Dame, 1979; Nelson Pichardo, "Chicano Voluntary Organizations in California, 1910–1930," *Aztlán* 19 (1988–90); Olivia Arrieta, "The Alianza Hispano Americana in Arizona and New Mexico: The Development and Maintenance of a Multifunctional Ethnic Organization," in *Renato Rosaldo Lecture Series Monographs* 7 (1991); James McBride, "La Liga Protectora Latina: A Mexican American Benevolent Society in Arizona," *Journal of the West* 14 (1975); Nina L. Nixon "Mexican American Voluntary Associations in Omaha, Nebraska," *Journal of the West* 28 (1989). Other types of community organizations are studied in Christine Marín, *"La Asociación Hispano-Americana de Madres y Esposas:* Tucson's Mexican American Women in World War II," in *Renato Rosaldo Lecture Monographs Series* 1 (1985).

More contemporary politics, and specifically the Chicano movement, are treated in Ignacio García, *United We Win: The Rise and Fall of the Raza Unida Party* (Tucson: Mexican American Studies and Research Center, University of Arizona Press, 1989); Carlos Muñoz, *Youth, Identity, Power: The Chicano Movement* (New York: Verso, 1989); Douglas E. Foley et al., *From Peones to Politicos: Ethnic Relations in a South Texas Town, 1900–1977* (Austin: Center for Mexican American Studies, University of Texas Press, 1977); and John S. Shockley, *Chicano Revolt in a Texas Town* (Notre Dame, Ind.: University of Notre Dame Press, 1974).

There also exists a body of literature that describes the diverse ways in which Mexican American have resisted oppressive conditions. Works that look at New Mexico include Robert W. Larson, "The White Caps of New Mexico: A Study of Ethnic Militancy in the Southwest," *Pacific Historical Review* 44 (1975), and Andrew B. Schlesinger, *"Las Gorras Blancas,* 1889–1891," *Journal of Mexican American History* 1 (1971). Those works that have Texas as their setting include Mary Romero, "El Paso Salt War: Mob Action or Political Struggle," *Aztlán* 16 (1985), and Charles H. Harris and Louis R. Sadler, "The Plan of San Diego and the Mexican-United States Crisis of 1916: A Reexamation," *Hispanic American Historical Review* 58 (1978).

Urban and Rural History

A good introduction to patterns of Chicano urban settlement is Ricardo Romo, "The Urbanization of the Southwestern Chicanos in the Early Twentieth

Century," in *New Directions in Chicano Scholarship,* ed. Ricardo Romo and Raymund Paredes (La Jolla: University of California at San Diego, 1978). Works that elaborate on the California urban experience are George J. Sánchez, *Becoming Mexican American: Ethnicity, Culture, and Identity in Chicano Los Angeles, 1900–1945* (New York: Oxford University Press, 1993), and dissertations such as May L. Haas, "The *Barrios* of Santa Ana: Community, Class, and Urbanization, 1850–1947," Ph.D. diss., University of California at Irvine, 1985; Joseph A. Rodríguez, "The Making of a Multicentered Metropolis: Physical Communication and Urban Rivalry in the San Francisco Bay Area, 1850–1970," Ph.D. diss., University of California, Berkeley, 1990.

Studies adding considerable information on life in Texas towns and cities are Oscar J. Martínez, *The Chicanos of El Paso: An Assessment of Progress* (El Paso: Texas Western Press, 1980); Nina L. Nixon-Méndez, "*Los Fundadores Urbanos* (Urban Pioneers): The Hispanics of Dallas, 1850–1940," *Journal of the West* 32 (1993); and Francisco Arturo Rosales, "Mexicans in Houston: The Struggle to Survive, 1908–1975," *Houston Review* 3 (1981).

The *colonias* of the Midwest are studied in Dennis Nodín Valdes, *El Pueblo Mexicano en Detroit y Michigan: A Social History* (Detroit: Wayne State University Press, 1982); Judith Ann Fincher Laird, "Argentine, Kansas: The Evolution of a Mexican American Community, 1905–1940," Ph.D. diss., University of Kansas, 1975; Louise Año Nuevo Kerr, "The Chicano Experience in Chicago," Ph.D. diss., University of Illinois at Chicago Circle, 1976; and Arthur D. Martínez, "*Los de* Dodge City, Kansas: A Mexican American Community at the Heartland of the U.S.," *Journal of the West* 24 (1985).

The rich possibilities for capturing the Mexican-American urban experience through the camera lens are seen in Antonio Ríos-Bustamante, *An Illustrated History of Mexican Los Angeles, 1781–1985* (Los Angeles: Chicano Studies Research Center, 1986), and Thomas H. Kreneck, *Del Pueblo: A Pictorial History of Houston's Hispanic Community* (Houston: Houston International University, 1989).

Much less has been done on Mexican Americans in the rural sector than in the urban areas. Of course, the literature on Spanish ranching is vast, and it is updated and placed in historical perspective by Terry G. Jordan, *North American Cattle-Ranching Frontiers* (Albuquerque: University of New Mexico Press, 1993). See also Joe S. Graham, *El Rancho in South Texas: Continuity and Change from 1750* (Denton: University of North Texas Press, 1994), and other studies such as John O. Baxter, *Las Carneradas: Sheep Trade in New Mexico, 1700–1860* (Albuquerque: University of New Mexico Press, 1987).

Most studies on Mexican Americans and agriculture focus on union and strike activity in the farms, and some of those are listed under the category of "Labor" in this essay. An exciting new work that compares the lives of different ethnic groups as farm tenants is Neil Foley, "The New South in the Southwest: Anglos, Blacks, and Mexicans in Central Texas, 1880–1930," Ph.D. diss., University of Michigan, 1990.

The question of land grants has been addressed in many books and articles, and a recent example of great merit is Charles L. Briggs and John R. Van Ness, *Land, Water, and Culture: New Perspectives on Hispanic Land Grants* (Albuquerque: University of New Mexico Press, 1987). A personal story of land loss in Texas is told in Abel G. Rubio, *Stolen Heritage: A Mexican American's Rediscovery of His Family's Lost Land Grant* (Austin: Eakin Press, 1986).

The few books that investigate Mexican-American activity in the Southwestern mines include Roberto R. Calderón, comp. and ed., *South Texas Coal Mining: A Community History* (Eagle Pass, Texas: privately printed, 1984); Andrés E. Jiménez Montoya, *Political Domination in the Labor Market: Racial Division in the Arizona Copper Industry* (Berkeley: Institute for the Study of Social Change, 1977); and Olivia Arrieta, "The Mexicano Community of the Clifton-Morenci Mining District: Organizational Life in the Context of Change," in *Community Empowerment and Chicano Scholarship,* ed. Mary Romero and Cordelia Candelaria (National Association for Chicano Studies, 1992).

Contemporary Studies

There is a vast literature that can be used to understand contemporary developments among Mexican Americans and Latinas and Latinos. A general book that discusses Latino consciousness and culture is Earl Shorris, *Latinos: A Biography of the People* (New York and London: W. W. Norton, 1992). Alan Wolfe, ed., *America at Century's End: American Society in Transition* (Berkeley: University of California Press, 1991), has a number of essays comparing the Latino experience with that of other ethnic groups. A comprehensive comparative anthology of Latino culture is Denis Lynn Daly Heyck, ed., *Barrios and Borderlands: Cultures of Latinos and Latinas in the United States* (New York: Rutledge, 1994).

Political and economic comparisons between various Latino groups are increasingly of interest. Joan W. Moore and Raquel Pinderhughes, eds., *In the Barrios: Latinos and the Underclass Debate* (New York: Russell Sage Foundation, 1993), is a series of essays contrasting economic realities. Rodolfo O. de la Garza, Louis DeSipio, F. Chris García, John García, and Angelo Falcón, *Latino Voices: Mexican, Puerto Rican, and Cuban Perspectives on American Politics* (Boulder, Colo.: Westview Press, 1992), analyses the first comprehensive survey of Latino political opinion. Two studies focusing on the large Latino population in California and its implications for public policy are David Hayes-Bautista et al., *The Burden of Support: Young Latinos in an Aging Society* (Stanford, Calif.: Stanford University Press, 1988), and Hayes-Bautista, *No Longer a Minority: Latinos and Social Policy in California* (Los Angeles: Chicano Studies Research Center, 1992). A controversial book by Peter Skerry, *Mexican Americans: The Ambivalent Minority* (New York: Free Press, 1993), is based on an analysis of Chicano politics in San Antonio and Los Angeles.

Notable books treating the issue of immigration as affecting Chicanos are Thomas Muller and Thomas J. Sepenshade et al., *The Fourth Wave: California's Newest Immigrants* (Washington D.C.: Urban Institute, 1985), and David Reimers, *Still the Golden Door: The Third World Comes to America* (New York: Colombia University Press, 1985), along with James D. Cockcroft, *Outlaws in the Promised Land: Mexican Immigrant Workers and America's Future* (New York: Grove Press, 1986).

Important works dealing with the contemporary arts are Steven Loza, *Barrio Rhythm: Mexican American Music in Los Angeles* (Urbana and Chicago: University of Illinois Press, 1993). See also Eva Sperling Cockcroft and Holly Barnet Sánchez, eds., *Signs from the Heart: California Chicano Murals* (Albuquerque: Venice Socia and Political Arts Resource Center, 1993), and Richard Griswold del Castillo, Teresa McKenna, and Yvonne Yarbaro-Bejarano, eds., *CARA: Chicano Resistance and Affirmation* (Los Angeles: Wight Art Gallery, 1993). In film Rosalinda Fregoso, *The Bronze Screen: Chicano and Chicana Film Culture* (Minneapolis: University of Minnesota Press, 1993), and Chon Noriega, ed., *Chicanos and Film* (New York: Garland Publishers, 1992), have given us new interpretive approaches.

Latina and Latino writers of fiction and poetry continue to be tremendously productive so that any list is bound to leave out some emerging talents. Some very good writing can be found in the recent work of Richard Rodríguez, Sandra Cisneros, Alma Villanueva, Marta Sánchez, César Gonzales, Gloria Anzaldúa, Bernice Zamora, and Victor Villaseñor, to name just a few. Readers interested in Chicana poetry should first consult Marta Sánchez's excellent study, *Contemporary Chicana Poetry: Critical Approaches to an Emerging Literature* (Berkeley: University of California Press, 1985).

Finally, an admirable attempt has been made to synthesize Chicano history within a comparative historical frame by Ronald Takaki in *A Different Mirror: A History of Multicultural America* (Boston, Toronto, London: Little, Brown, 1993), and Takaki's edited anthology *From Different Shores: Perspectives on Race and Ethnicity in America* (New York: Oxford University Press, 1994). The anthology edited by Sucheng Chan, Douglas Henry Daniels, Mario T. García, and Terry P. Wilson, *Peoples of Color in the American West* (Lexington, Mass.: D. C. Heath, 1994), is the latest attempt to present a comparative historical view of the Chicano past.

Index

The Authors

Richard Griswold del Castillo received his Ph.D. in history from UCLA in 1974 and is professor of Mexican American Studies at San Diego State University. He has taught at the University of California at Berkeley, the University of California at San Diego, the Instituto Mora (Mexico City), and La Universidad de Monterrey. His books include *César Chávez: A Triumph of Spirit* (with Richard García; 1995), *Aztlán Reocupada: A Political and Cultural History since 1945* (1994), *The Treaty of Guadalupe Hidalgo: A Legacy of Conflict* (1990), *La Familia: Chicano Families in the Urban Southwest, 1848 to the Present* (1984), and *The Los Angeles Barrio, 1850–1890: A Social History* (1980).

Arnoldo De León earned his Ph.D. in history from Texas Christian University, Fort Worth, in 1974 and is the C. J. "Red" Davidson Professor of History at Angelo State University in San Angelo, Texas. He spent 1986 as a visiting scholar in the Mexican American Studies Program at the University of Houston. His books include *The History of Texas* (with Robert A. Calvert; 1996), *Mexican Americans in Texas: A Brief History* (1993), *Not Room Enough: Mexicans, Anglos, and Socio-Economic Change in Texas, 1850–1900* (with Kenneth L. Stewart; 1993), *Ethnicity in the Sunbelt: A History of Mexican Americans in Houston* (1989), *They Called Them Greasers: Anglo Attitudes toward Mexicans in Texas, 1836–1900* (1983), and *The Tejano Community, 1836–1900* (1982).

The Editor

Thomas J. Archdeacon is professor of history at the University of Wisconsin-Madison, where he has been a member of the faculty since 1972. A native of New York City, he earned his doctorate from Columbia University under the direction of Richard B. Morris. His first book, *New York City, 1664–1710: Conquest and Change* (1976), examines relations between Dutch and English residents of that community during the late seventeenth and early eighteenth centuries. Building on that work, he has increasingly concentrated his research and teaching on topics related to immigration and ethnic-group relations. In 1983 he published *Becoming American: An Ethnic History*.